Marketing Masters

Marketing Masters

250 S. Wacker Drive • Chicago, Illinois 60606 • (312) 648-0536

AMERICAN MARKETING ASSOCIATION

Copyright © 1991, 1999, American Marketing Association

Library of Congress Cataloging-in-Publication Data

Marketing masters.
  p.   cm.
ISBN: 0-87757-219-4
1. Marketing.   2. Marketing—Management.
I. American Marketing Association.
HF5415.M2997   1991
658.8—dc20   91-32691
CIP

Cover design by Frank Leone
Printed in the United States of America

FOREWORD

In 1936, *The American Marketing Journal,* published by the American Marketing Society, and *The National Marketing Review,* published by the National Association of Marketing Teachers, merged to form the *Journal of Marketing.* This event was followed six months later with the formation of the American Marketing Association by these same organizations.

Under the auspices of the American Marketing Association, the *Journal of Marketing* is enjoying its 55th year of providing thoughtful marketing practitioners and academics with insights into the complex and fascinating world of marketing theory and applications.

This volume pulls together many of the most interesting and most influential articles ever to appear in the *Journal of Marketing* over its fifty-five year history. Here you will find articles of historic importance by such renowned marketers as Leo Burnett, Wroe Alderson, Ernest Dichter, Reavis Cox, Alfred Politz, Peter Drucker, and Theodore Levitt. In addition, you will find modern classics by Philip Kotler, Edwards Deming, George Day, and Barton Weitz, to name just a few.

These thirty-four classic articles cover the marketing mix, with topics on advertising, personal selling, products and services, pricing, and distribution. In addition, the richness of marketing theory, macro marketing, and marketing research are presented in classic articles.

This compilation of readings is to be treasured and read with historic perspective, up-to-date interpretation, and great joy at the insightful ideas presented. Congratulations to the AMA on its fine choice out of all the great articles published in the *Journal of Marketing.*

Thomas C. Kinnear
University of Michigan
September 1991

TABLE OF CONTENTS

Advertising

Alfred Politz

The Dilemma of Creative Advertising

Why does so much of our contemporary advertising violate the rules of effective communication, the application of which could easily increase the power of advertising?

    This article explains why...by pointing out several factors which have been overlooked or misunderstood in advertising theory. It also tells how the advertiser can make his advertising operate much more effectively.

MARKETING people, as everyone else, have a sincere and understandable interest in observing the effects of their own activities. How else are they to know if their activities have real significance?

However, the vast majority of advertising men are denied this privilege. It is a pleasure reserved only for that small minority engaged in the preparation of advertisements which have some criterion of effectiveness built into them, such as mail-order ads.

Nevertheless, the experiences of this privileged minority have made possible the statement of certain principles which can be applied to advertising in general. Unfortunately, most of the advertising in our national media is witness to the fact that these principles are not very widely practiced.

On the other hand, advanced consumer research leads to conclusions almost identical to those which have been arrived at by advertising people who have been permitted to see directly the results of their own work. What are some of the conclusions about effective advertising which have emerged from consumer studies and experiments?

About the author. Alfred Politz is President of Alfred Politz Research, Inc., New York.

    Mr. Politz has received two awards for leadership in the development of scientific standards, and many plaudits for his unique contributions to marketing research. He pioneered in the application of probability sampling to marketing studies. He devised a statistical procedure to eliminate calling back on persons not at home for interviewing. He invented "duration sampling," a long-awaited solution to the problem of audience measurement for outdoor media. He has been continuously experimenting with various classifications of consumers in psychological dimensions relevant to their purchasing behavior.

Not Gimmicks for Advertising's Effectiveness

One conclusion is that intellectual gimmicks, cleverness, wittiness, or ingenious and tricky word combinations do not add to, but rather subtract from, the effectiveness of advertising. Even slogans are of doubtful value. In fact many of these so-called attention-getting devices actually operate as distractions.

Efficiency in advertising seems to depend on the use of simple language—simple direct presentation of sales arguments—and the avoidance of tricky attention-getting devices unrelated to the product itself. Here are a few examples.

An advertisement for phonograph records uses an illustration of a woman breaking a phonograph record by stepping on it. Presumably this illustration is intended to catch the consumer's attention and lead to the next revelation: that steel needles also ruin phonograph records. To be sure, the needles do not ruin them as thoroughly or as quickly as a woman stepping on them, but nevertheless they do serious harm. After this devious opening gambit, we are finally permitted to learn the moral of the story—the true sales point: diamond needles preserve records.

The creator of this copy apparently had convinced himself that the consumer would not be interested in the simple fact that phonograph records are ruined by steel needles but can be preserved by using diamond needles. Therefore, the copy writer felt compelled to try to catch the consumer's attention by the "more interesting" picture of a record being brutally broken by a woman's foot.

In another advertisement, traveler's checks were offered as the right way to carry money. But in the headline the word "right" was spelled "write." The copy writer seems to assume that the reader of the advertisement wants to be entertained, to be impressed by wittiness and by an unusual use of the English language. He assumes that the reader (presumed to be the common man with ordinary intelligence) will be pleasantly surprised to see this game of words. This pleasant feeling, he hopes, will generalize to the traveler's checks and will increase the reader's interest in using them instead of cash when he travels.

These examples are so extreme as to be almost unrealistic. However, in almost any copy of a national magazine we can find milder forms of the same disease: tomato catsup described as "what eggs scramble for," television picture-tube purchasers exhorted not to be "Vidiots," or a telephone instrument described as a "conversation piece." We can also find roses growing out of liquor bottles, dogs dressed as policemen, and women apparently walking on clouds. Are the products to be sold so pitifully drab and uninteresting that the consumer must be entertained or shocked before he will attend to them?

An even more innocent appearing example was brought to light several years ago. For many years the Socony Mobil Oil Company used the symbol of "the flying red horse" to identify its service station outlets. The argument in favor of using this symbol rather than the simple word "Mobil" was that the flying red horse gave pleasure to the motorists who viewed it, and suggested lightness, power, and speed, whereas the single word "Mobil" was drab and colorless. Considerable evidence had been accumulated that the horse was an inefficient communication.

As a final assault on this question, the following experiment was designed:

> "An automobile equipped with a movie camera was driven along roads where Mobilgas and other gas stations were located. As the camera moved along, it photographed every gasoline outlet on the way. After the film was developed, the number of Mobil stations and other brands was equalized. To avoid bias, the selection was random.
> "Various audiences were invited to see the movie thus prepared, and afterwards every member in each audience was requested to tell what brands of station signs were on the road, and approximately how many of each he thought there were. The frequency of the flying red horse sign was underestimated down to about one-half of that of its most efficient competitor."

The outcome of this experiment revealed that the station sign of Socony Mobil Oil Company was losing substantial parts of its competitive sales opportunities by clinging to a symbol which had associations which were pleasant but irrelevant to the problem of identifying Mobil stations.

These advertisements and signs communicate in a manner that deviates drastically from communication as it takes place in other phases of our daily life...in the editorials of newspapers and magazines, in teaching, in simple conversation, and in ordinary sales talk. Directness and simplicity have been replaced by carefully contrived detours, which can be very costly indeed.

A simple change in the wording of a headline may increase the efficiency of an advertisement by several hundred per cent. For example, in a split-run test the following two headlines were compared: "New Jobs Are Offered In Television Station" and "Television Courses for $11.60 per week." The first of these headlines returned six times as many orders as the second—six times the value for an identical investment in advertising space. If a change only in a headline can produce differences of this order of magnitude, imagine how these differences might be compounded by changes in the whole copy treatment.

It seems a modest hope that an increase in the knowledge of the principles of advertising will enable an advertiser to double, at least, the value he receives for each advertising dollar invested.

The Overlooked Familiarity Principle

The average "expert" in advertising must apply a substantial part of his ingenuity and inventiveness to tricks and gimmicks which *lower* the efficiency of advertising, rather than *raising* it. If it is true that a simple change in the wording of a headline can produce a six-fold change up or down in the efficiency of the ad, why do we not more often notice advertising campaigns leading to business disaster?

The reason is that at least two mechanisms operate in advertising. One of these, the "Persuasion Principle," has been widely discussed in writings on advertising. The second, which we may call the "Familiarity Principle," has been much neglected.

The familiarity mechanism in advertising is often overlooked in analytical discussions of advertising. However, it is possible for this mechanism to operate effectively even in an advertisement in which persuasion operates at an almost negligible level.

The Familiarity Principle is fairly easy to state and simple to understand: *Something that is known inspires more confidence than something that is unknown.*

Thus, a consumer confronted with two products, and having no knowledge of the physical characteristics of either of them, will almost certainly choose the one whose brand name is more familiar to him. Consequently, a piece of advertising which does nothing else but mention the name of the product will contribute something to the sales of that product, simply by creating an awareness of the brand name that generates this minimum amount of confidence.

Advertising can survive, and even give the appearance of some efficiency, by trading on this unavoidable, minimum effect of familiarity. Many advertisers, in fact, can afford to rest their whole case on it. Marketers of chewing gum, soft drinks, and cigarettes often have gained a powerful position through the deliberate use of advertising that concentrates on simply making the brand familiar by merely showing the brand name.

Copy and Flexibility

But advertising copy is intended to perform a function *beyond* the mere development of familiarity with the brand name. Copy is intended to shape motives and desires, to build believability, and to provide a reason for selecting a particular brand over all others. It is the most flexible part of the advertising message. (The word "copy," as is used here, refers to headlines, text, pictures, sound—everything intended to carry a message about the product, beyond its name, to the consumer.) In the development of advertising, it is the copy function which demands the greatest skill, creativeness, and intelligence.

Every advertising man wants to create "good" copy. And yet what criteria can the advertising man apply in deciding that one piece of copy is good and another bad? What are the criteria of efficiency in copy? The great problem is that we cannot relate a *specific* sales increase or decrease to a *specific* advertising act such as a copy treatment, a sound effect, a headline, or a sales point. Indeed, it is almost naive to imagine that any relationships can be established between specific advertising actions and sales.

The reasons are manifold. For one thing, even in the most favorable marketing situation which we can contrive, it is difficult to separate the *familiarity* effect from the *persuasive* copy effect of advertising. A piece of advertising with "depressing" copy can fall back upon the familiarity principle as long as a brand name is mentioned. Many advertising successes which are attributed to copy are in reality simply the unavoidable minimum success solidly secured by the Familiarity Principle.

Furthermore, when we attempt to relate specific advertising actions to specific sales effects, we must get rid of the cumulative effect of advertising over a period of years. For an old established product, the cumulative effect of previous advertising will greatly outweigh any specific contemporary advertising action. Therefore, old established products make the observation of causal relations between specific copy and specific sales impossible. Nor do we realize any advantage if we are dealing with an entirely new product. It is never possible to separate advertising's effect from the contributions of ingenuity in product design, packaging, or distribution. Thus, the copy writer must always be denied the advantage of being able to observe the effect of a specific copy action in a specific sales success.

In almost every other field of human endeavor, the development of proficiency and skill depends upon being able to observe the effects of our actions. Let us imagine that builders of pianos were forever forced to build their products in a vacuum where there is no sound and sell them to "clients" without ears. After forty years or so of working under such conditions, we should expect that the piano designers would be turning out very attractive pieces of furniture, but we should have no right to expect that this furniture could produce music. If we should happen to mention to the piano builder that his instruments do not sound good and that his activity is inefficient, he would probably not be surprised. Indeed, he would consider us unreasonable if we blamed him for his inefficiencies, so long as he is denied the privilege of hearing the results of his activity.

Today the copy writer creates his message in the vacuum of the modern distribution system without being able to see the effects of that message unfold. Then he sells his creations to a client who has no sensory organs to observe what a specific phrase does to a prospective consumer.

The creative advertising man is deprived of the natural rewards that any sincere individual wants. He wants to see the results of what he does; and yet our entire marketing system forces a blindfold over his eyes. The primary rewards of seeing the results of his actions are replaced by the secondary rewards of praise from his colleagues, bosses, and clients. And the people who confer these rewards are in no better position to see the results of the man's actions than is the copy writer himself.

Let us imagine that the copy writer proposes an entirely efficient piece of copy for his client. This copy consists of simple language and uncluttered, straight-forward sales presentations—without gimmicks, tricks, or intellectual surprises—copy equipped with the most ingenious and most invisible device of letting the product impress the listener or reader. The client reviews the copy and, before approving it, happens to think, "This copy writer does not seem to be using his imagination. He talks only about the product itself, and does not add anything of his own." So, the copy writer not only goes unrewarded for his efforts but is actually rebuked for failing to show "imagination."

It is quite natural, then, for the copy writer to resort to the use of tricks, gimmicks, and devices that will entertain, startle, or humor himself, his intellectual friends, and the client. The emphasis is shifted from ends to means— from *what* advertising should say, to *how* it should say it. It is unfortunate, but not surprising, that the creative man now diverts his efforts from making the *product* interesting to making the *advertising* interesting. Ultimately he is no longer selling the product to the consumer, but selling the advertising to his client.

The difficult and even unfair position in which the creative man finds himself may be illustrated by the following analogy. Imagine a room with a large window that looks out on a beautiful countryside. On the wall opposite the window are three mirrors. The first mirror is uneven, spotted, and dirty looking. The second mirror is clean and neat, and in addition is framed by a beautiful ornamental engraving. The third mirror has no frames or ornament, and is nothing but a plain, but perfectly flawless mirror. Now, an observer (critic or client) is taken into the room and his guide points to the first mirror and says, "What do you see?" The observer says, "I see a bad mirror." His guide points to the second mirror and asks again, "What do you see?" The observer says, "I see a beautiful mirror." Finally his guide points to the third mirror and says, "What do you see?" The observer says, "I see a beautiful scene out of an open window."

Obviously, the third mirror has done the most efficient job. It is the function of an efficient mirror to reveal with perfect clarity the object to be mirrored without interference—that is, without making the mirror itself visible!

It is likewise the function of perfect advertising to step behind its own means—its own tricks and gimmicks—and push the product so much into the foreground that the advertising itself, psychologically speaking, can be overlooked. It may be disappointing to the maker of mirrors to discover that his most efficient mirror is one of which the prospective customer is unaware. The very perfection of the mirror conceals itself from the observer. The advertising man, unless he takes pleasure in perfection, will also be disappointed to discover that the more perfect he makes his advertising, the less it becomes noticeable as "advertising."

The Advertiser's Opportunity

How can advertising rise above this situation in which only its inefficiencies are capable of producing rewards for its creator?

We cannot normally expect the copy writer to take the initiative. He is human, and must respond to the rewards and punishments which are offered to him. His client, the advertiser, on the other hand, is in a much better position because he controls the rewards and punishments meted out to the copy writer.

Let the client relieve the copy writer of the burden of having to prove his "imaginative" and "creative" powers by forcing him to resort to tricks and gimmicks. Let him trust the copy writer's professional competence to use correct grammar and an attractive style. Let him then concentrate on *what* the copy writer says, rather than *how* he says it. This would surely have the effect of restoring the sales point to its rightful position of importance in advertising.

The development of a sales point is one of the most challenging problems in advertising. Sometimes the best sales point is intimately related to the main function of the product. For example, the function of antihistamines is to relieve cold symptoms, and this turns out to be their best sales point. On the other hand, the main purpose of face soap is to clean the face. But the cleaning power of face soap is not an interesting sales point for face soap. It is not always easy to decide for a particular product what will be an efficient sales point. For hair tonic, for example, is it better to say that it prevents dandruff or that it keeps the hair in place? Is it better to say that a beer quenches thirst or that it has a distinctive flavor?

Advanced marketing research justifies its existence in terms of its ability to discover the most efficient sales points for a particular brand. This is the real core of advertising and its most challenging problem area. This is the center where creativeness can make its most fruitful contribution.

Only the advertiser has the opportunity to bring the sales points (and, therefore, the product) back into advertising...to make the advertising product-oriented rather than advertising-oriented.

Comfortable Illusion About Creativeness

Superficial reasoning easily sinks to the level of platitude where the following pseudo-logical argument sounds convincing. First of all, advertising has to get the attention of viewers, readers, and listeners. A given advertising message (not product!) competes within an inexhaustible number of other advertising messages (not products!). Therefore, a given piece of advertising, to meet this competition, must put something out of the ordinary before the eyes and ears of the potential consumers. Ideally, a given piece of advertising should look or sound different from any other piece of advertising.

This kind of reasoning bypasses the product and, therefore, the advertising function. The ideal statement should be formulated: "A given piece of advertising should make the product look different from all other products, without violating the truth."

That the easiest and least "creative" mental effort leads to the "attention-getting advertising" escapes superficial reasoning.

A printed ad under the headline "Your Father in the Cesspool" would get good attention. Not much useful imagination goes into the headline. However, it requires a surplus of intelligence, analytical power, and useful imagination (which together constitute "creativeness") to find an interesting headline which leads the reader to read the text in the anticipation of learning about a useful product.

In advertising discussions, the term "create" and its derivatives are partially misused and misunderstood. "Imagination" is confused with "creativeness." Imagination is a fundamental and elementary requirement. Creativeness denotes the *advanced* form of imagination where it is *purposively* used by abiding to rigid rules and by meeting practical conditions.

Children on a playground and many patients in mental hospitals display extraordinary imagination. But the imagination in these instances is usually without the discipline of organization, selection, and constructiveness. It is not, in other words, *creative*.

An advertising man who claims that the acceptance of rules and conditions interferes with his creativeness is probably unaware of the fact that he is seeking a license which the real creative geniuses in arts and sciences would consider embarrassing. Creativeness is the opposite of pure freedom of imagination. To create something means to *build* something along rules of usefulness or purposiveness...to build an intellectual or mechanical organism.

Leonardo da Vinci spent a lifetime seeking the rules within his visual imagination which could produce more powerful creations. To be creative in advertising means to have so much imagination that it does not "fizzle out" as soon as product orientation is imposed. If the advertising man believes that the product itself has no virtues worth the attention of the consumer, he should suggest taking it off the market. If he believes that the product has a right to be on the market, and yet believes that it has no property worth the attention of the public, he is obviously overlooking the most serious and most creative obligation of advertising—*to find an approach which makes a good product look good and thereby interesting.* If, in the advertising man's opinion a product is justified in being on the market, then the advertising man must consider it justifiable that consumers pay money for the product.

This, then, sums up to a fundamental principle in the world of consumers:

If a product has features worth paying money for, it must have features worth paying attention to.

Ernest Dichter

A Psychological View of Advertising Effectiveness

What is real advertising effectiveness?

MOST of the difficulties which have been encountered in attempting to appraise the effectiveness of advertising lie in a too literal interpretation of the problem.

A purchasing action is seldom a direct and immediate result of an advertisement. A number of intermediary processes take place in the mind of the potential buyer. Before the sales effectiveness of an advertisement can be measured, its psychological impact must be known. When an individual reads an advertisement or listens to a radio commercial a number of mental processes are stimulated. An appeal, a term so common to the vernacular of advertising, is really one of the most complex psychological devices. Since most of our actions are governed by our needs and desires, an effective appeal is a convincing promise of satisfaction of these needs.

The effectiveness of an advertisement depends, therefore, on the psychological results it produces in the mind of the reader. Even though an advertisement may be widely read, it is without value if it only serves to increase the reader's prejudice and dislike of the advertised product, or if it has no favorable effect.

How real advertising effectiveness can be measured

If we assume that all the people in whom an advertisement could arouse desirable associations and emotions to be represented by 100, then the number of people in whom this effect actually took place indicates one aspect of effectiveness. The first step in a psychological measurement of an advertising effectiveness is the establishment of a number of critical scales. Each one of these represents one specific observable psychological reaction. Thus we have an inventory of all possible reactions to an advertisement, such as identification, pity, agreement, hatred, argumentation, nostalgia, jealousy, fear, and so forth.

Each form of reaction produced by an advertisement is represented by a vertical rank-order line. The degree of reaction is indicated on the line. By connecting all points a psychological profile of the effect produced by the advertisement is derived.

In an analysis of the effectiveness of an advertisement, one chart might read, for instance: This advertisement produces a high degree of identification, a strong feeling of pity, and only weak mental images—indicating that very little mental rehearsal of the use of the product is taking place.

An analysis of such advertising profiles can show that in advertising copy simple basic words like "security" or "common sense" or even "sale" often call for translation into their emotional meanings. "Security" is only understood when it means "to stop worrying," "common sense" when it means "you and I," and "sale" when it means "you can feel like a smart buyer."

The psychological test of the impact of an advertisement and its graphic presentation in the form of a profile demonstrates what happens to the message in the mind of the prospective buyer. If we can show that it stirs no emotions, then its language and pictures must be translated into more provocative terms.

This method also makes it possible to determine what importance the atmosphere and mood of a publication have for each part of its contents. Analyzing all the charts, we will see for example, that advertisements read in one magazine tend to produce more vivid mental pictures, or more active thinking, or are more critically read than advertisements placed in another magazine.

Research techniques

In measuring whether an advertisement has produced the kind of effect it set out to achieve the actual research techniques which we apply are of a psychological nature. By investigating the immediate associations aroused as people look at each advertisement, we avoid the aesthetic judgments which are often completely irrelevant to the psychological and commercial effects of advertising.

In this way we arrive first at an inventory of the psychological mechanisms set in motion by a specific advertisement. From this information we are able to determine the general feeling created in the reader, and the extent to which a rehearsal of action leading to purchase has taken place.

We search the reader's mind to find out what memories were aroused, the extent to which he saw action in the illustration, whether it excited him, made him dream, made him feel good or bad, how he would change the advertisement, what associations and thoughts the product arouses, the extent to which these associations correspond with those stimulated by the advertisement and so forth.

Many of our questions resemble those asked in the so-called projective personality test. In these, dramatic pictures are shown to the subject, and his reactions to them—what he sees in the pictures and what they mean to him—offer clues to the effect of the pictures and to the personality being tested. In other words, the subject "projects" his own personality into the picture.

Regional, economic and sex differences, and other relevant factors are taken into consideration. However, it is just as important to watch for such controlling circumstances as are anchored in the personality of the readers themselves.

"Buckshot Advertising"

Many advertisements do not reach the degree of effectiveness which they should and could attain. The same space could be filled with a more active sales message, systematically directed toward a specific effect upon the reader.

Much of present advertising could be compared to the salesman, who, when the housewife opens her door to his ring, states simply: "I'm from the Woodhaven Company. Do you need any ashtrays today?" and then turns on his heel and goes. He may sell some ashtrays—but at what cost! By making use of real sales psychology in all its subtleties and refinements, he could easily double or triple his sales without increased physical effort.

There is much proof, unfortunately, that at present little scientific measurement of advertising effectiveness has been adopted. When we ask any typical manufacturer for what purpose he spent $375,000 on his advertising program last year, he will reply with some amazement, "Why, to sell my pipe tobacco and to establish good will towards my company, of course."

However, a brief experiment will often show how far he and his colleagues are from really working towards their intended goal. We may take current issues of any five national magazines and cut out all the advertisements for whiskey, soap, cosmetics, tires, refrigerators, etc., and group them together. Although every manufacturer will disclaim any similarity of quality and service between his and other products, we find that three out of four of the ad-

vertisements for each type of product read almost alike.

There is no toilet soap that will not give the user lovelier skin, no face cream that will not secure romance and eternal love for the purchaser, and no whiskey that is not milder, smoother, and longer aged than all others on the market. It is small wonder that the reader has great difficulty in distinguishing one brand from another.

This kind of advertising does sell merchandise. But at what price? Does it give the manufacturer the most he can get for his money? Does it make the best use of available space and effort?

Real advertising is not quite so simple. Else, why would millions of dollars and endless energy and ingenuity go into new advertising campaigns every year? It can only be proof of the intention to mold people's buying attitudes. And yet each new issue of *Life, The Saturday Evening Post, The New Yorker,* and each new radio commercial, and each new poster contain expensive and painful proof that wasteful "buckshot advertising" is the accepted method.

One would assume that an advertiser knows pretty well what he wants his advertising to do. He is often clear about his *commercial* purpose, but many times he does not realize the *psychological* requirements of his advertising.

Most current advertising states that "Soft Ride" car is safer, that "True Tone" radio has greater sound fidelity, or that "Tip Tap" typewriter takes less energy to operate than others. The main goal is always the same: to convince the potential customer that one's product outdoes the other's. Only the way in which this is expressed varies.

Most ice cream advertising, for example, strives to impress the public with the superior quality and flavor of one particular ice cream. These claims are augmented and illustrated with beautiful dishes of ice cream. To the advertiser the combination of copy and illustration adds up to good advertising. But is it enough—should not his goal be greater?

A psychological study showed the "voluptuous" nature of ice cream to be one of its main appeals. In talking about ice cream, people commented: "You feel you can drown yourself in it." and "You want to get your whole mouth into it." Nothing, however, in the advertising produced the effect which this psychological study showed that should have. The advertisements were not designed so as to satisfy people's desire for voluptuousness. Instead they created a feeling of neatness, an expectancy of sober enjoyment in eating X ice cream—all far removed from the emotionally loaded feelings most people have for ice cream.

In another study it was found that in the field of deodorants the appeal of social acceptance and safety is valid only for a small group of women. A much greater proportion considered such goals as much too far removed. What interested them more than anything else was to be able to like themselves, to feel clean, to consider themselves smart beauty technicians.

Very often in determining advertising campaigns, the advertiser makes the mistake of thinking that death, romance, fear or hope are valid and powerful appeals. This is a lay view of psychological facts. Actually the fear of being embarrassed or of having to consider oneself a failure far outweighs the power of such grandiose concepts as romance, love, death or happiness.

It can be shown again and again that the pure recital of technical claims about a product leaves the reader cold and does not arouse the emotions necessary to make him change to a new product. When buying cigarettes, the smoker is actually afraid to try a new brand. He does not want to give up the known security of his present brand, even though he may find fault with it, for the unknown, although possibly greater enjoyment of the new brand. Therefore to urge him to try brand X because it is different from anything he has ever tasted is a wrong and dangerous appeal.

Not every research method is capable of clarifying the real goals of an advertising campaign. In functional psychological research we distinguish between symptoms expressing the superficial rational explanations of an action, and the real, deeper reasons which form the emotional basis of such actions, and are connected with the functional role a product plays in the user's life.

For example, when interviewers told us that they consider the flavor the most important thing about ice cream, they were giving us only a symptom. The function played by ice cream in their lives stems from the whole emotional aura of voluptuousness, childhood experiences, and uninhibited over-indulgence. It is these functions which form the basis on which an advertiser can build an effective campaign.

There are few research assignments in which a similar way of thinking, a shift from symptoms to functions would not be effective in orienting advertising to do the precise job it should.

How can the desired effect be achieved in an advertisement?

When we know what effect an advertisement should produce, the next step is to investigate the best ways of achieving this effect. It is not sufficient to determine statistically that so many men read the whole shaving soap advertisement, while only so many women read it completely, or that the whiskey advertisement was read in toto by so many people, in part by so many more. While it is important to know how many people read an advertisement and how they do it, it is more important to know how they see it.

Every time a reader views an advertisement three successive steps are set in motion: a) an attempt to get into the advertisement, b) a registering of the psychological ef-

fects and c) a registering of the commercial effects of the advertisement.

a) Ways of getting into the advertisement. A reader viewing an advertisement for the first time tries to enter it by various means. Either he abandons the attempt after a few seconds of casual note, or he is caught by the advertisement.

Among the various processes which help him into an advertisement are these: identifying, being curious, arguing, accepting, rejecting, excluding, memorizing, dissecting, assembling, and emotionalizing—feeling pity, hatred, love, sympathy, and so forth.

The channels enabling the reader to enter the advertisement can be grouped into two large classifications: emotional and intellectual forms of immediate reactions.

An emotional entrance would be signified by: ''I'm glad they're not talking about me,'' or ''I hate that darn stuff.''

That an intellectual process has taken place would be indicated by the exclamation: ''Gee, that's an interesting story.'' or ''I'm curious to find out what this machine does.''

b) Ways of Registering the psychological effects of an advertisement. An advertisement may leave the reader with any of a number of possible gratifications: ''I feel relieved,'' ''I've learned something new,'' ''I feel sure of myself,'' ''My curiosity has been satisfied,'' or ''It makes me feel that I'm smart.''

These gratifications do not at all resemble the various ways of getting into the advertisement. An attempt should be made to keep the psychological effects clearly distinct from the first contact with the message.

What might be considered a well-planned advertisement can have negative psychological effects if one is not conscious of the mechanisms stimulated by it. This was the case in a study for a well-known reducing remedy. Although women accepted the desirability of slimness, they rejected the advertisement and the product. Investigation showed that the stout women featured in the ''before'' half of the ''before and after'' routine were too extreme to be accepted by the readers. Their reaction to the picture was ''That's not me'' and ''I don't look that bad.'' The effectiveness of the ad was lost because of this psychological blunder.

c) Ways of Registering the commercial effects of an advertisement. The real commercial effects of an advertisement are difficult to ascertain solely in terms of actual sales. It is a matter of dispute whether or not a valid conclusion about the commercial effects can be drawn from sales results alone. There are too many factors that may interfere between the immediate reaction and the final result in a sale.

If sales do not follow it is dangerous to say that the advertisement alone is at fault—it may be income tax time or everyone may be saving for vacations or the world news may be gloomy or the weather may be bad for shopping, and sales may suffer because of these factors.

The only real test of an advertisements effectiveness is a knowledge of the thoughts, associations and mental images produced in the reader. In concrete terms each purchasing act is really the result of a mental rehearsal for buying. A shoe advertisement for example, is successful if at some point the reader reacts with the thought. "I imagine myself trying on the shoes." Similarly, an airline advertisement produced a desirable commercial effect because it provoked such associations as "I'm daydreaming. I visualize myself sitting in a plane and I'm proud of myself," or "I see myself getting into a plane."

In other words, the closer any advertisement comes to producing thoughts which have the appearance of a purchasing act or which rehearse use of the product, the higher the commercial value of the effect of the advertisement.

Mobilization of Human Needs

Knowing and understanding the three steps in the mental process evoked by an advertisement enables the advertiser to avoid many pitfalls. The illustrations are many:

An advertiser of a nationally sold patent remedy for stomach distress was under the impression that his advertisements featuring a person suffering from indigestion were effective in making the reader identify, "When I have an upset stomach and feel like that, I'll take X too."

But psychological study showed that instead of identifying themselves with the sick person in the picture, most people wanted to help them.

Cartoon shoe advertisements appearing in children's comic magazines were rejected by the children as unreal because they introduced characters with magic, superhuman powers into a realistic framework.

Study of a constipation remedy advertisement showed that information on the nutritional value of the product, which the advertiser considered unimportant and had squeezed into one corner, was the only feature of a full page which satisfied the public's curiosity about the product.

An advertising program, brilliantly conceived and executed from a technical viewpoint, may miss completely if it neglects to control the psychological effects. The intangible implications of an advertisement often are more significant than its actual content. No item of merchandise is ever sold unless a psychological need exists which it satisfies. In other words, the actual merchandise is a secondary. Advertising's goal has to be the mobilization and manipulation of human needs as they exist in the customer.

Instead, most advertisers wallow lustily in an attempt to outdo each other in the employment of superlatives. Only when they learn to handle advertising as a scientific selling instrument so that it first becomes psychologically effective, will they have made real use of its potentialities.

Distribution

David L. Huff

Defining and Estimating a Trading Area

What are the conceptual properties of a trading area? What is the definition of the term? What testable propositions are currently available to validate its properties and thus give precision to the definition? This article gives answers to these questions.

MARKET analysts have long speculated about the nature and scope of trading areas. Such speculations have been based primarily upon conclusions drawn from empirical studies.

However, except for the "gravitationalists," few analysts, if any, have formulated their conclusions into propositions that are capable of being verified or refuted by empirical test. As a consequence, the conceptual properties of a trading area are extremely vague and perhaps in error. Furthermore, existing techniques for estimating trading areas are limited and subject to question.

The objectives of the present article are threefold: (1) to appraise the principal techniques used to delineate retail trading areas; (2) to enumerate significant conclusions derived from empirical studies using such techniques; and (3) to advance an alternative technique, believed to be better conceptually and superior predictively.

Estimating Techniques

The methods employed to delineate trading areas, particularly retail trading areas, generally involve surveys or the use of empirically derived mathematical formulations.

Survey Techniques

Typically, in the case of survey techniques, a sample of individuals representing either households or firms are interviewed at their places of origin or at the particular firm or

About the author. David L. Huff, is an Associate Professor of Business Administration at the University of California, Los Angeles. During 1963-64 Dr. Huff is on leave from UCLA to serve as a Fulbright Lecturer at the Universite d'Aix-Marseille.

The author is indebted to Professor William F. Brown, University of California, Los Angeles, for his constructive comments and suggestions about the present article.

center for which the trading area is being estimated.

Such interviews are designed primarily to determine the kind or kinds of products that are purchased by each respondent, the frequency of patronage, and the home-base location of each respondent. These data can then be used to prepare a map from which inferences can be drawn concerning the nature and scope of the trading area.

As a result of trading area studies using survey techniques, a number of important empirical regularities have been shown to exist:

1. The proportion of consumers patronizing a given shopping area varies with distance from the shopping area.
2. The proportion of consumers patronizing various shopping areas varies with the breadth and depth of merchandise offered by each shopping area.
3. The distances that consumers travel to various shopping areas vary for different types of product purchases.
4. The "pull" of any given shopping area is influenced by the proximity of competing shopping areas.

A number of market analysts have attempted to generalize about the nature and scope of trading areas by citing specific conclusions drawn from such empirical studies. For example, it is often maintained that the trading area for a certain size of retail facility offering a particular class of products will encompass a radial distance of some specified number of miles, of which the primary trading area will involve a certain proportion of the total area, etc., etc.

But generalizations of this kind may be subject to a great deal of error because of differences among regions with respect to transportation facilities, topographical features, population density, and the locations of competing firms.

Mathematical Techniques

A few analysts have attempted to formalize some of the general conclusions drawn from empirical studies. They have expressed their ideas in terms of mathematical propositions that are capable of being tested empirically. The work that has been done in this area is limited primarily to the so-called "retail gravitationalists."

Notable among these is William J. Reilly who made a significant contribution by formalizing a number of empirical observations concerning consumer shopping movements between cities.[1] The nature of his formal construct is shown below:

$$(1) \qquad \frac{B_a}{B_b} = \left(\frac{P_a}{P_b}\right)\left(\frac{D_b}{D_a}\right)^2$$

where B_a = the proportion of the retail business from an intermediate town attracted by city A;

B_b = The proportion of the retail business from an intermediate town attracted by city B;

P_a = the population of city A;

P_b = the population of city B;

D_a = the distance from the intermediate town to city A; and,

D_b = the distance from the intermediate town to city B.

The extensive empirical tests of Reilly's model that were made by P. D. Converse are also noteworthy.[2] In addition, Converse is to be credited for making a significant modification of Reilly's original formula.[3] This modification made it possible to calculate the approximate point between two competing cities where the trading influence of each was equal. As a consequence, a city's retail trading area could be delineated by simply calculating and connecting the breaking points between it and each of the competing cities in the region (see Figure 1). The breaking point formula derived by Converse is:[4]

$$(2) \qquad D_b = \frac{D_{ab}}{1 + \sqrt{\dfrac{P_a}{P_b}}}$$

where D_b = the breaking point between city A and city B in miles from B;

D_{ab} = the distance separating city A from city B;

P_b = the population of city B; and

P_a = the population of city A.

Limitations. The significance of the pioneering efforts of both Reilly and Converse to provide a systematic basis for estimating retail trading areas cannot be denied. The variables employed, the functional relationships advanced, and the estimated parameters provide precise and meaningful hypotheses that can be tested empirically.

However, there are several important conceptual an operational limitations associated with the use of the "Reilly-type" model.

First, the breaking point formula, as it now exists, is incapable of providing graduated estimates above or below the break-even position between two competing centers. See Figure 1. As a consequence, it is impossible to calculate objectively the *total* demand for the product(s) or service(s) of a particular distribution center.

Second, when the breaking point formula is used to delineate retail trading areas of several shopping areas within a given geographical area, the overlapping boundaries that result are inconsistent with the basic objective of the formula's use; to calculate the boundaries between competing shopping areas where the competitive position of each is equal. Furthermore, in the case of multi-trading area delineations derived from using the breaking point formula, there may be areas that are not even within the confines of any shopping area's trading area. Such a development is certainly not very realistic. A visual exemplification of these conditions is shown in Figure 2.

Finally, the parameter which was originally estimated empirically by Reilly should not be interpreted as a constant for all types of shopping trips as so many analysts have assumed. It seems quite logical to hypothesize that such an exponent will vary, depending on the type of shopping trip involved. As a result, a distribution center may

---

[1] William J. Reilly, *Methods for Study of Retail Relationships* (Austin: The University of Texas, Bureau of Business Research, Research Monograph, No. 4, 1929).

[2] P. D. Converse, *A Study of Retail Trade Areas in East Central Illinois* (Urbana: University of Illinois, Bureau of Economic and Business Research, Business Studies, No. 2, 1943); and *Consumer Buying Habits in Selected South Central Illinois Communities* (Urbana: University of Illinois, Bureau of Economic and Business Research, Business Studies, No. 6, 1948).

[3] This modification as well as other changes that Converse made of Reilly's original model is well summarized in P. D. Converse,"New Laws of Retail Gravitation," *Journal of Marketing,* Vol. 14 (January, 1949), pp. 379-384.

[4] Converse did not demonstrate how he derived the breaking point formula from Reilly's equation. However, the proof of such a derivation is simply:

(i) $\dfrac{B_a}{B_b} = 1$

(v) $\dfrac{D_b}{D_{ab} - D_b} = \sqrt{\dfrac{P_b}{P_a}}$

(ii) $\left(\dfrac{P_a}{P_b}\right)\left(\dfrac{D_b}{D_a}\right)^2 = 1$

(vi) $\dfrac{D_{ab}}{D_b} - 1 = \sqrt{\dfrac{P_a}{P_b}}$

(iii) $\dfrac{D_b}{D_a} = \sqrt{\dfrac{P_b}{P_a}}$

(vii) $\dfrac{D_{ab}}{1 + \sqrt{\dfrac{P_a}{P_b}}} = D_b$

(iv) $D_a = D_{ab} - D_b$

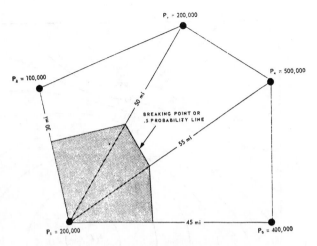

Calculation of Breaking Points:

$$D_2 = \frac{D_{12}}{1 + \sqrt{\dfrac{P_1}{P_2}}} = \frac{30}{1 + \sqrt{\dfrac{200,000}{100,000}}} = 12.4$$

$$D_3 = \frac{D_{13}}{1 + \sqrt{\dfrac{P_1}{P_3}}} = \frac{50}{1 + \sqrt{\dfrac{200,000}{200,000}}} = 25.0$$

$$D_4 = \frac{D_{14}}{1 + \sqrt{\dfrac{P_1}{P_4}}} = \frac{55}{1 + \sqrt{\dfrac{200,000}{500,000}}} = 33.0$$

$$D_5 = \frac{D_{15}}{1 + \sqrt{\dfrac{P_1}{P_5}}} = \frac{45}{1 + \sqrt{\dfrac{200,000}{400,000}}} = 26.3$$

FIGURE 1. Estimating a trading area with the breaking point formula.

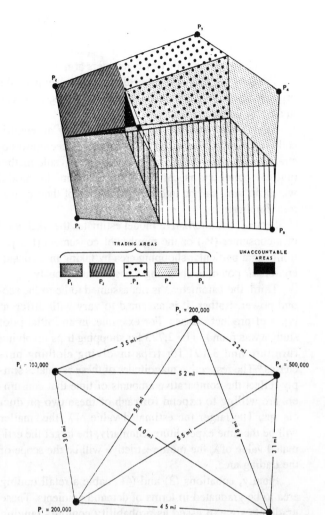

FIGURE 2. Estimating multiple trading areas with the breaking point formula.

have several different trading areas corresponding to the different classes of products that it sells.

An Alternative Model

An alternative model will now be presented which overcomes the limitations described above.

The principal focus of the model is on the consumer rather than on the firm. It is, after all, the consumer who is the primary agent affecting the trading area of the firm. The model describes the process by which consumers choose from among acceptable alternatives, a particular distribution center (a firm or group of firms) to obtain specific goods and services. A formal expression of the model is:

$$(3) \qquad P_{ij} = \frac{\dfrac{S_j}{T_{ij}^{\lambda}}}{\displaystyle\sum_{j=1}^{n} \dfrac{S_j}{T_{ij}^{\lambda}}}$$

where P_{ij} = the probability of a consumer at a given point of origin i traveling to a particular shopping center j;

S_j = the size of a shopping center j (measured in terms of the square footage of selling area devoted to the sale of a particular class of goods);

T_{ij} = the travel time involved in getting from a consumer's travel base i to a given shopping center j; and

λ = a parameter which is to be estimated empirically to reflect the effect of travel time on various kinds of shopping trips.

The *expected* number of consumers at a given place of origin i that shop at a particular shopping center j is equal to the number of consumers at i multiplied by the probability that a consumer at i will select j for shopping. That is,

$$(4) \qquad E_{ij} = P_{ij} \bullet C_i$$

where E_{ij} = the expected number of consumers at i that are likely to travel to shopping center j; and

C_i = the number of consumers at i.

In many respects the preceding model resembles the original model formulated by Reilly. It differs, however, in several important respects.

First, the alternative model is not merely an empirically contrived formulation. It represents a theoretical abstraction of consumer spatial behavior. As a result, mathematical conclusions can be deduced from the model which, in turn, can be interpreted in terms of their behavioral implications.[5]

Second, the alternative model estimates the likelihood of a consumer (P_{ij}) or the number of consumers (E_{ij}) patronizing a particular shopping area by taking into consideration *all* potential shopping areas simultaneously.

Third, the parameter λ is not assumed to be to the second power. Rather, it is assumed to vary with different types of product classes. For example, in an initial pilot study λ was found to be 2.723 for shopping trips involving furniture and 3.191 for trips involving clothing purchases.[6] The respective magnitudes of these estimates simply reflect the comparative amounts of time that consumers are willing to expend for each of these two product classes. The larger the estimated value of λ, the smaller will be the time expenditure. Similarly, the larger the estimated value of λ, the more restrictive will be the scope of the trading area.

Finally, equations (3) and (4) enable a retail trading area to be graduated in terms of demand gradients. These gradients are expressed as probability contours ranging from P<1 to P>0. An illustration of how these contours look when mapped is illustrated in Figure 3, in which a partial retail trading area has been calculated for shopping center J_1.

If the retail trading areas of shopping centers J_2 and J_{14} had also been calculated and superimposed over the trading area of J_1, it would be seen that parts of each shopping center's trading area envelop parts of the others. Furthermore, where these envelopments occur at intersections of contours having the same probability values, it would be possible to determine the breaking points between each of these competing centers.

General Conclusions

The following general conclusions can now be drawn concerning the nature and scope of a trading area:

1. A trading area represents a *demand surface* containing potential customers for a specific product(s) or service(s) of a particular distribution center.

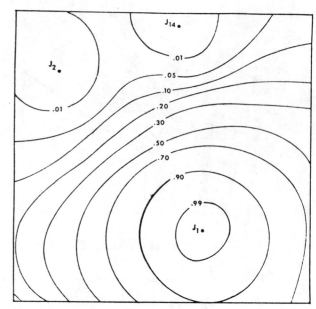

FIGURE 3. A retail trading area portrayed in terms of probability contours. Source: David L. Huff, *Determination of Intra-urban Retail Trade Areas* (Los Angeles: University of California, Real Estate Research Program, 1962).

2. A distribution center may be a *single firm or an agglomeration of firms*.

3. A demand surface consists of a series of *demand gradients* or zones, reflecting varying customer-sales potentials. An exception to the condition of demand gradients would be in the rare case in which only one distribution center existed in a unique geographical setting, thus representing an absolute monopoly in providing products and/or services that are of an absolute necessity. Under these conditions, no gradients would exist but rather a single homogeneous demand plane.

4. Demand gradients are of a *probabilistic* nature, ranging from a probability value of less than one to a value greater than zero (except in the complete monopoly situation in which the probability value equals one).

5. The total potential customers encompassed within a distribution center's demand surface (trading area) is *the sum of the expected number of consumers from each of the demand gradients.*

6. Demand gradients of competing firms overlap; and where gradients of like probability intersect, *a spatial competitive equilibrium —position is reached.*

Final Definition

Accordingly, a trading area can be defined as: *A geographically delineated region, containing potential customers for whom there exists a probability greater than zero of their purchasing a given class of products or services offered for sale by a particular firm or by a particular agglomeration of firms.*

[5] For a discussion of the theoretical aspects of the model, see David L. Huff, ''A Probabilistic Analysis of Consumer Spatial Behavior,'' in William S. Decker, Editor, *Emerging Concepts in Marketing* (Chicago: American Marketing Association, 1963), pp. 444-450.

[6] David L. Huff, *Determination of Intra-urban Retail Trade Areas* (Los Angeles: University of California, Real Estate Research Program, 1962).

This definition can be expressed symbolically as:

$$(5) \qquad T_j = \sum_{i=1}^{n} (P_{ij} \cdot C_i)$$

where T_j = the trading area of a particular firm or agglomeration of firms j, that is, the total expected number of consumers within a given region who are likely to patronize j for a specific class of products or services;

P_{ij} = the probability of an individual consumer residing within a given gradient i shopping a j; and

C_i = the number of consumers residing within a given gradient i.

By comparison, the currently accepted definition of the term "trading area," as expressed by the Committee on Definitions of the American Marketing Association, is: "A district whose size is usually determined by the boundaries within which it is economical in terms of volume and cost for a marketing unit to sell and/or deliver a good or service."[7] This definition provides little insight concerning the nature and scope of a trading area. Furthermore, this definition implies that a trading area does not encompass the entire region within which potential demand exists, but rather only that portion which a marketing unit finds it economical to sell and/or deliver a good or service.

It is obvious, however, that in order for a marketing unit to determine the specific region that it finds economical for distribution purposes, it first has to assess the demand in the entire potential trading area. In addition, no matter what cost variable is considered, for example, delivery or promotion, it is very likely that the cost of the service under consideration will not turn out to be a very satisfactory determinant of any precisely bounded trading area as suggested by the Committee's definition. Finally, this definition conveys the image that it is the marketing unit that determines the trading area rather than the consumer.

---

7 Committee on Definitions of the American Marketing Association, *Marketing Definitions: A Glossary of Marketing Terms* (Chicago: American Marketing Association, 1960).

Issues in Marketing Productivity and Quality

Wroe Alderson

A Formula for Measuring Productivity in Distribution*

Editor's Note: This article by the President of the American Marketing Association presents a device for measuring productivity in distribution.

O NE approach to the discussion of productivity in distribution is to describe the many facets of the problem and then to indicate the type of index which is required. The alternative approach which is followed here is to begin by proposing a specific formula for computing an index and then to consider the grounds on which it is based and its limitations in use.

The Formula

The formula which is set forth below rests on the assumption that an index of productivity is a ratio between input and output. Thus the basic problem is simply that of developing suitable expressions to represent input and output in distribution.

A practical index should of course be one which makes use of data which are readily available. At the present rather speculative state of consideration it is justifiable to conceive of an ideal index in relation to the objectives of measurement and leave the problem of collecting the necessary data for discussion at a later time. It is believed, however, that all of the data required could be readily obtained by various research and statistical methods.

The equation which is here adopted to represent the output of the distribution system is as follows:

$$\frac{\text{Number of retail unit sales}}{\text{Number of shopping hours}} = \frac{\text{Unit sales per}}{\text{shopping hour}}$$

The corresponding equation for input in distribution is as follows:

$$\frac{\text{Total expenses of distribution}}{\text{Average hourly wage rate}} = \frac{\text{Man hour}}{\text{equivalents}}$$

Unit sales per shopping hour and man hour equivalents should both be reduced to index form, adopting the same base period for the two indexes. The ratio expressed by the two indexes may also be regarded as an index. This final step in the calculation of the index may then be expressed as follows:

$$\frac{\text{Index of unit sales per shopping hour}}{\text{Index of man hour equivalents}} = \frac{\text{Productivity}}{\text{in distribution}}$$

Justification of Formula

The proposed formula will now be discussed from several angles, the first being the line of argument by which this formula is to be justified. The formula for the output of the distribution system starts from the consumer's point of view and tries to determine in the broadest terms what it is that the distribution system provides for the consumer.

Output Phase

If there were no distribution system at all, each consumer would have to visit the farm or factory or handicraft shop in which desired products were made; make their own selections; and arrange for transportation to their homes. What actually happens may be compared against this standard of zero distribution and the difference represents the output of the distribution system.

The job performed by distribution can be divided into two broad phases—one related to the number and variety of products offered to the consumer and the other to the amount of time which the consumer must spend in making selections and otherwise taking advantage of what the system offers. This is to say that since it is the business of the distribution system to transfer goods to the consumer, one consideration is the number of transfers effected and the other is the burden in time and effort which these transfers place upon the consumer. It would not be possible to

---

*This is a revision of a paper given before the Conference on Productivity sponsored by the Bureau of Labor Statistics in Washington in October 1947.

make a fair comparison of two systems or situations in distribution without taking account of both.

The number of retail unit sales is set up as the broadest single measure of the service the consumer gets from distribution. This figure has been going up steadily year after year for a number of reasons. The first reason is the greater and greater range of products which must be bought to sustain the standard of living for an average family. Secondly, there is the increasing rapidity of style changes or other forms of obsolescence. In the third place there is the greater frequency with which consumers wish to buy products to serve their immediate convenience, throwing the function of storage back into the distribution system.

A further consideration is the number of places in which the same consumer may want to buy a product. A simple example is the immediate demand for cigarettes that may be expressed by the same individual at home or at his place of work or at various places where he may be taken by travel or recreation such as train, boats, ballparks, etc.

In general, it seems likely that there is a simple, functional relationship between the growing complexity of the standard of living and the growing need for distribution services. The number of retail unit sales seems well adapted to express this relationship.

The cost to the consumer of making use of the distribution system can best be expressed by the number of shopping hours. Obviously different sorts of purchases are very different as to the amount of shopping time required. The purchase of an automobile or a major appliance may call for a good many hours from both husband and wife, spread over a period of several weeks. Shopping for a single item of clothing may cause the consumer to visit a number of stores or make several shopping trips before final selection. Staples such as standard foods, drugs and tobacco can be purchased in a much shorter time.

Many transactions are routine transactions since the consumer already has a clear idea of what is desired and may simply be re-ordering something which has been used many times before. Other transactions are fully negotiated with a full discussion of price and terms as well as the quality and special features of the product. Thus it would be very useful to establish a percentage of routine transactions among all consumer transactions.

The difficulty here is the lack of simple categories since there are many in-between situations which are not fully negotiated and yet are not wholly routine. It is clear, however, that the greater the percentage of routine transactions, the less would be the number of shopping hours, assuming the schedule of products to be purchased by the consumer is the same. Thus the number of shopping hours reflects the extent to which consumer transactions have been rendered routine, which is certainly one of the major ways in which the distribution system serves the consumer.

There are a number of detailed problems as to what is to be counted as shopping hours. The general solution proposed to is count only that time which the consumer spends on shopping trips outside the home. That would leave out time spent in talking to house-to-house salesmen or making selections from mail order catalogues. Both the difficulty of segregating such use of time and its relatively small place in the total lead to this conclusion. The same considerations apply to the time that is spent in reading or listening to advertising. All shopping time in retail stores would be included despite the fact that consumers may enjoy shopping. Some salesmen may enjoy selling but they are still paid for the time spent in selling since this time is preempted against any other use.

Input Phase

The formula for the input in distribution is relatively simple. In the numerator is the dollar cost of the whole distribution system over the year including retailing, wholesaling, and the sales costs of manufacturers. This figure for total distribution expense obviously covers the annual cost of amortizing buildings and equipment as well as the cost of labor. Investment and labor cost are to some extent interchangeable. Thus a self-service store reduces its labor costs by using more floor space and better fixtures in which to display the merchandise for consumer selection. Obviously the relative cost of space and equipment is correspondingly increased.

In the denominator of this expression is the average hourly wage rate in distribution. This rate is divided into the total cost of distribution and not merely into the cost of labor. Thus the labor part of the total cost is reduced to a man hour basis. The non-labor part of the total cost is considered as a substitute for labor and the price adjustment is made on the same basis. The resulting concept of manhour equivalents represents the total input for distribution, adjusted to allow for the changes in the cost of labor.

It is believed that the adjustment by wage rates is more appropriate than some other method of adjusting for price trends. The perennial problem of management in a distribution business is to balance the use of labor against the alternative use of space and equipment. Labor already represents the major share of the total cost and is coming to be a still larger portion year by year. The validity of the input equation perhaps becomes more apparent when it is broken down into two parts, namely, man hours of labor plus man hour equivalents for distribution costs other than labor.

The ratio between input and output as defined and measured should provide a fair reflection of productivity in distribution. The two quantities are not directly comparable and hence need to be reduced to an index basis before setting up the final ratio. That means that some base period has to be taken as 100 per cent in each case. No logical difficulty is involved in this step since the purpose of the final index is to measure changes of productivity in distribution rather than to make a critical comparison of output and input for any given date.

Applications of an Index of Productivity in Distribution

The formula presented attempts to measure the productivity of the distribution system rather than the productivity of distribution workers. It is well adapted, therefore, to several purposes for which such an index might be used. One purpose is to make a running comparison of the relative efficiency of manufacturing and distribution. Another is to provide a yardstick for evaluating changes in productivity within individual companies engaged in distribution. A third might be to compare the distribution systems of various countries such as Russia and the United States. All of these purposes are primary purposes of the marketing economist or distribution engineer whose function is to help bring about greater efficiency in specific companies or marketing situations.

The proposed formula is not *directly* adapted to problems of wage negotiation in the distribution field. It could not be used in itself to justify a percentage increase in wages in line with a percentage increase in productivity. Perhaps it is an illusion to suppose that a productivity index could ever be adequate to that purpose. Attempts were made to use the cost of living index in wage negotiations until labor and management both began to realize that wage increases must always outrun increases in the cost of living in an expanding economy. Similarly a productivity index would not provide the final answer in wage negotiation even if it were possible to define the specific contribution of the worker to productivity in distribution. After that calculation has been completed it might still be necessary to grant wage increases in excess of any increase in labor productivity both because of competitive necessity and public policy.

Other Applications of Index

There are at least two important uses for the index of productivity in distribution which the proposed index would serve less directly. One of these uses is in connection with wage negotiation and the other in evaluation of the efficiency of successive steps in the distribution process such as manufacturers' sales departments, wholesalers and retailers. In each case there are problems of imputation growing out of joint contribution to an end result.

Use in Wage Negotiation

Several indexes of productivity in both manufacturing and production use the number of workers in the field to represent input. This is equivalent logically to attributing all increases in productivity to labor. The validity of an index for use in wage negotiation is certainly affected if such an assumption is implicit in the index.

Actually productivity in distribution as in manufacturing is the joint product of management and labor. It is difficult to measure their separate contributions to productivity since this is a clear case of multiple causation like the contributions of the sun and the rain to a crop of wheat. Management can further an increase in productivity by providing better working tools and a better working environment. Labor can contribute by making more effective use of the tools provided. Either could be completely frustrated without the cooperation of the other.

Management is the coordinating factor which takes responsibility for combining the factors of production in the most favorable proportions. In distribution this means the coordination of store and warehouse facilities, advertising expenditures, and workers engaged in selling and other functions. The problem of coordination is constantly changing because of the changing values of capital investment and labor. Slow turnover was much more costly when the Department of Commerce was engaged in such studies as the Louisville Grocery Survey than it is today. As the author of many of those studies, I have watched the cost of labor over the last twenty years come to be the main concern of management in distribution as it is in manufacturing.

Among the phases of management which should be given special consideration with relation to productivity are planning, pricing, and promotion. Coordination of resources in distribution is largely in the form of planning since it takes time to provide stores, warehouses and trained personnel. Decisions about needs must be made well in advance of the event. Mistakes in judgment detract from the maximum productivity of the distribution system. The timing of improvements is also critical since low cost distribution depends on settled routines and yet routines must constantly be modified to meet changing conditions. A proper slogan for the distribution system as a whole is the sign that often appears in front of a store that is being remodelled, "No interruptions to business while alterations are in progress." An extremely important function of management is to establish effective prices. Regardless of all theories of monopolistic competition, administered prices, or maximization of net revenue, an effective price is one which causes goods to move. Without an effective price any other form of efficiency achieved in distribution is nullified. Thus correct judgments as to prices and price structures constitute a major contribution of management to productivity in distribution. In many cases the most effective price is the one which produces the greatest volume of sales. At this price there is the greatest revenue available to meet all claims on company earnings including workers, suppliers and owners.

Promotion is directed toward expanding the market for a product. It operates through the transmission of information and argument to those who may buy a product either as ultimate consumers or as intermediaries. Promotion becomes more necessary as products become more numerous and ways of living and working more complex. Many products could scarcely be produced and distributed at all without constant promotion since consumers must be stimulated to want them and taught how to use them. Thus the distribution system which starts out to offer simple services to the consumer ends by engaging in educational campaigns to persuade the consumer to utilize specific products and services. The concept of productivity in distribution must be broad enough to cover this function of modifying or stimulating consumer wants as well as the function of serving existing wants.

The contribution of labor in distribution depends to only a minor degree on physical effort or manual skills. The girl in the wrapping department may exhibit more dexterity and yet be less productive than the salesman on the floor. Knowledge of products is required almost universally, varying in degree from the rudimentary knowledge of the stock clerk to the style sense and judgment of current market values on the part of the expert buyer.

Many distribution workers are in contact with customers. Qualities of enthusiasm, initiative and adaptability are needed for effective contact work. The productivity of distribution workers may thus depend to a large extent on psychological factors such as loyalty toward the employer. A factory worker might perform his work effectively despite a hostile feeling toward the boss. Marked feelings of hostility would almost certainly diminish the effectiveness of a distribution worker. Many distribution workers are called upon to influence third parties, namely customers, in the interest of their employers. Mental attitudes are vitally important to productivity in such endeavors.

How then can an index of productivity be utilized in wage negotiation? Simply as one essential datum along with several others which both sides should take into account. Despite the strictures stated in an earlier paragraph, the cost of living index has some proper bearing on wage negotiation. If it be true that the trend in wages must outrun increases in the cost of living the index would at least provide the basis for defining minimum adjustments. That is to say that whenever the wage trend falls below the cost of living trend there may be a case for an adjustment at least sufficient to remedy this discrepancy.

In the same way a productivity index may be a convenient point of reference in negotiation even though it cannot be used alone to decide the issue. It may shed light on ability to pay since increased wage payments in any enterprise or industry must presumably come mainly out of increased productivity. But while indexes of productivity and of the cost of living may both be useful guideposts, the true target of negotiation lies in another direction. That is to approximate with the minimum error the equilibrium price for labor at the given time and place. The most objective yardstick, therefore, might be the forecast of the long-run trend in wages with the indexes that have been

mentioned being employed to define limits of tolerance around this trend line.

An accurate determination of the equilibrium price for labor will require a comprehensive view of the competitive forces in the labor market. From one viewpoint business concerns demand labor as they demand raw materials or equipment and compete for their share of the available labor supply. If the labor market was freely competitive in that sense, wages in each area would no doubt be determined by marginal productivity of labor in relation to the other factors of production.

A contrary and equally valid viewpoint would conceive of workers as demanding jobs rather than industry demanding labor. Big business, small business, government and the professions all lumped together are then seen as the institutional framework within which the competition between individuals takes place. There is keener competition for some types of positions than for others. Relatively there are more applications available for each position on the managerial side than on the labor side.

This conception of competition among individuals for ways of receiving income may be broadened to include persons who hope to draw income from savings or inheritance rather than from employment. Some of these individuals are widows, orphans, and persons with leisure class ideals who are not easily drawn into the labor market. The progressive decrease in bond yields and other interest rates tends to result in a constantly decreasing share of the national income available to this group as compared to those who participate in management and labor.

The net effect of this two-phase competition in the labor market is a generally upward trend in the share of national income going to labor. In fact the trend of wage increases may often outrun increases in labor productivity. The function of collective bargaining is to bring about these adjustments with the least possible disruption of economic processes. To the extent that negotiation succeeds in establishing the equilibrium price for labor with a minimum of error it will minimize monopoly gains or temporary bargaining gains for either management or labor.

Use in Measuring Productivity at Various Distribution Levels

Finally a word is in order with respect to the problem of measuring separately the trend in productivity at the various levels of distribution such as retailing, wholesaling, and manufacturers' sales. The method which has been proposed measures productivity of the entire distribution system by assuming that the output of distribution is the volume of services delivered to the ultimate consumer through retailers. In conformity with this general approach, other terminal points might be selected to measure the trend in services delivered at such points.

The most obvious extension of the general method would be to take the point of purchase by the nation's retailers as the next most important terminal point. For the number of unit retail sales would be substituted the number of unit retail purchases. Generally each unit purchase is represented by a line on the invoice which the retailer receives from the wholesaler.

It is somewhat more difficult to work out the parallel between consumer shopping hours and the cost to the retailer of using wholesale distribution services. The cost to the retailer of buying goods is only the beginning. A number of distribution functions can be shifted in greater or less degree from the wholesale to the retail level. These costs include storage and other expenses of carrying inventory not actually on sale in the display room. It would also include the cost of any advertising other than purely retail advertising which could be done either by the retailer or his suppliers.

Without taking account of the shifting of functions it would be quite impossible to get at the trend of productivity in wholesale distribution. The retailer can shift costs to the consumer in ways that show up in an increased number of shopping hours. The potentialities for shifting costs from the wholesale to the retail level are more varied and even more significant in reaching judgments about relative efficiency.

Given a separate index of productivity in wholesale distribution (defined to include distribution by manufacturers), it would be possible to isolate the separate contribution of retailing. This could be done by comparing the index for the whole distribution system with the index for wholesale distribution. They might even be combined to form a new index by putting the primary index in the numerator and the wholesale index in the denominator.

Another possibility for extending the usefulness of the indexes is to take certain types of retail stores as the terminal points and compute separate indexes of productivity for such fields as food distribution and drug distribution. This would, of course, involve identification of the wholesale distribution services lying behind each type of retailing. These separate indexed by trades might serve as a still more effective stimulus to the general drive for greater efficiency in distribution.

Macro Marketing

Peter F. Drucker

Marketing and Economic Development*

In the "underdeveloped" countries of the world, the more "glamorous" fields such as manufacturing or construction are generally high-lighted while marketing is treated with neglect, if not with contempt. Yet marketing holds a key position in these countries. It is generally the most backward of all areas of economic life.

Marketing is also the most effective engine of economic development, particularly in its ability rapidly to develop entrepreneurs and managers. And it contributes what is the greatest need of an "underdeveloped" country: a systematic discipline in a vital area of economic activity...a discipline which is based on generalized, theoretical concepts and which can, therefore, be both taught and learned.

Marketing as a Business Discipline

THE distinguished pioneer of marketing, whose memory we honor today, was largely instrumental in developing marketing as a systematic business discipline:

• In teaching us how to go about, in an orderly, purposeful and planned way to find and create customers;

• To identify and define markets; to create new ones and promote them;

• To integrate customers' needs, wants, and preferences, and the intellectual and creative capacity and skills of an industrial society, toward the design of new and better products and of new distributive concepts and processes.

On this contribution and similar ones of other Founding Fathers of marketing during the last half century rests the

rapid emergence of marketing as perhaps the most advanced, certainly the most "scientific" of all functional business disciplines.

But Charles Coolidge Parlin also contributed as a Founding Father toward the development of marketing as a *social discipline*. He helped give us the awareness, the concepts, and the tools that make us understand marketing as a dynamic process of society through which business enterprise is integrated productively with society's purposes and human values. It is in marketing, as we now understand it, that we satisfy individual and social values, needs, and wants—be it through producing goods, supplying services, fostering innovation, or creating satisfaction. Marketing, as we have come to understand it, has its focus on the customer, that is, on the individual making decisions within a social structure and within a personal and social value system. Marketing is thus the process through which economy is integrated into society to serve human needs.

I am not competent to speak about marketing in the

About the Author. Born in Vienna, and with basic education received in Austria, Mr. Drucker took his law degree from Frankfurt University in Germany. After four years of newspaper work, he was associated with an international banking house in London from 1933 to 1937. He then came to the United States and worked first as an American economist for British banks and insurance companies. For the past fifteen years he has been a consultant on business policy and management organization for some of the country's largest enterprises. He also served for a number of years as Professor of Politics at Bennington College and has been, since 1950, Professor of Management at the Graduate School of Business, New York University.

A steady contributor to *Harper's*, the *Harvard Business Review*, and *Nation's Business*, Mr. Drucker is the author of such well-known books as *The End of Economic Man* (1939), *The New Society* (1950), *Practice of Management* (1954), and *America's Next Twenty Years* (1957).

Editor's Note. This is the text of the Parlin Memorial Lecture, presented to the Philadelphia Chapter of the American Marketing Association on June 6, 1957. The annual lecture, given since 1945, is in memory of Charles Coolidge Parlin, for many years Director of Commercial Research at the Curtis Publishing Company, and frequently referred to as the founder of modern marketing research. The Parlin Memorial Award is presented each year to a lecturer chosen for his ability to make a distinguished contribution to the science of marketing and for outstanding achievement in the marketing field.

Although *The Journal of Marketing* ordinarily does not publish speeches as such, an exception is made in this case, because of the great significance of Mr. Drucker's remarks.

first sense, marketing as a functional discipline of business. I am indeed greatly concerned with marketing in this meaning. One could not be concerned, as I am, with the basic institutions of industrial society in general and with the management of business enterprise in particular, without a deep and direct concern with marketing. But in this field I am a consumer of marketing alone—albeit a heavy one. I am not capable of making a contribution. I would indeed be able to talk about the wants and needs I have which I, as a consumer of marketing, hope that you, the men of marketing, will soon supply:—a theory of pricing, for instance, that can serve, as true theories should, as the foundation for actual pricing decisions and for an understanding of price behavior; or a consumer-focused concept and theory of competition. But I could not produce any of these "new products" of marketing which we want. I cannot contribute myself. To use marketing language, I am not even "effective demand," in these fields as yet.

The Role of Marketing

I shall today in my remarks confine myself to the second meaning in which marketing has become a discipline: The role of marketing in economy and society. And I shall single out as my focus the role of marketing in the economic development, especially of under-developed "growth" countries.

My thesis is very briefly as follows. Marketing occupies a critical role in respect to the development of such "growth" areas. Indeed marketing is the most important "multiplier" of such development. It is in itself in every one of these areas the least developed, the most backward part of the economic system. Its development, above all others, makes possible economic integration and the fullest utilization of whatever assets and productive capacity an economy already possesses. It mobilizes latent economic energy. It contributes to the greatest needs: that for the rapid development of entrepreneurs and managers, and at the same time it may be the easiest area of managerial work to get going. The reason is that, thanks to men like Charles Coolidge Parlin, it is the most systematized and, therefore, the most learnable and the most teachable of all areas of business management and entrepreneurship.

International and Interracial Inequality

Looking at this world of ours, we see some essentially new facts.

For the first time in man's history the whole world is united and unified. This may seem a strange statement in view of the conflicts and threats of suicidal wars that scream at us from every headline. But conflict has always been with us. What is new is that today all of mankind shares the same vision, the same objective, the same goal, the same hope, and believes in the same tools. This vision

might, in gross over-simplification, be called "industrialization."

It is the belief that it is possible for man to improve his economic lot through systematic, purposeful, and directed effort— individually as well as for an entire society. It is the belief that we have the tools at our disposal— the technological, the conceptual, and the social tools—to enable man to raise himself, through his own efforts, at least to a level that we in this country would consider poverty, but which for most of our world would be almost unbelievable luxury.

And this is an irreversible new fact. It has been made so by these true agents of revolution in our times: the new tools of communication—the dirt road, the truck, and the radio, which have penetrated even the furthest, most isolated and most primitive community.

This is new, and cannot be emphasized too much and too often. It is both a tremendous vision and a tremendous danger in that catastrophe must result if it cannot be satisfied, at least to a modest degree.

But at the same time we have a new, unprecedented danger, that of international and interracial inequality. We on the North American continent are a mere tenth of the world population, including our Canadian friends and neighbors. But we have at least 75 per cent of the world income. And the 75 per cent of the world population whose income is below $100 per capita a year receive together perhaps no more than 10 per cent of the world's income. This is inequality of income, as great as anything the world has ever seen. It is accompanied by very high equality of income in the developed countries, especially in ours where we are in the process of proving that an industrial society does not have to live in extreme tension between the few very rich and the many very poor as lived all earlier societies of man. But what used to be national inequality and economic tension is now rapidly becoming international (and unfortunately also interracial) inequality and tension.

This is also brand new. In the past there were tremendous differences between societies and cultures: in their beliefs, their concepts, their ways of life, and their knowledge. The Frankish knight who went on Crusade was an ignorant and illiterate boor, according to the standards of the polished courtiers of Constantinople or of his Moslem enemies. But economically his society and theirs were exactly alike. They had the same sources of income, the same productivity of labor, the same forms and channels of investment, the same economic institutions, and the same distribution of income and wealth. Economically the Frankish knight, however much a barbarian he appeared, was at home in the societies of the East; and so was his serf. Both fitted in immediately and without any difficulty.

And this has been the case of all societies that went above the level of purely primitive tribe.

The inequality in our world today, however, between nations and races, is therefore a new—and a tremendously dangerous—phenomenon.

What we are engaged in today is essentially a race between the promise of economic development and the threat of international world-wide class war. The economic development is the opportunity of this age. The class war is the danger. Both are new. Both are indeed so new that most of us do not even see them as yet. But they are the essential economic realities of this industrial age of ours. And whether we shall realize the opportunity or succumb to danger will largely decide not only the economic future of this world—it may largely decide its spiritual, its intellectual, its political, and its social future.

Significance of Marketing

Marketing is central in this new situation. For marketing is one of our most potent levers to convert the danger into the opportunity.

To understand this we must ask: What do we mean by "under-developed?"

The first answer is, of course, that we mean areas of very low income. But income is, after all, a result. It is a result first of extreme agricultural over- population in which the great bulk of the people have to find a living on the land which, as a result, cannot even produce enough food to feed them, let alone produce a surplus. It is certainly a result of low productivity. And both, in a vicious circle, mean that there is not enough capital for investment, and very low productivity of what is being invested —owing largely to misdirection of investment into unessential and unproductive channels.

All this we know today and understand. Indeed we have learned during the last few years a very great deal both about the structure of an under-developed economy and about the theory and dynamics of economic development.

What we tend to forget, however, is that the essential aspect of an "under-developed" economy and the factor the absence of which keeps it "under-developed," is the inability to organize economic efforts and energies, to bring together resources, wants, and capacities, and so to convert a self-limiting static system into creative, self- generating organic growth.

And this is where marketing comes in.

Lack of Development in "Under-developed" Countries

(1) First, in every "under-developed" country I know of, marketing is the most under-developed—or the least developed—part of the economy, if only because of the strong, pervasive prejudice against the "middleman."

As a result, these countries are stunted by inability to make effective use of the little they have. Marketing might by itself go far toward changing the entire economic tone of the existing system—without any change in methods of production, distribution of population, or of income.

It would make the producers capable of producing marketable products by providing them with standards, with quality demands, and with specifications for their product. It would make the product capable of being brought to markets instead of perishing on the way. And it would make the consumer capable of discrimination, that is, of obtaining the greatest value for his very limited purchasing power.

In every one of these countries, marketing profits are characteristically low. Indeed the people engaged in marketing barely eke out a subsistence living. And "markups" are minute by our standards. But marketing costs are outrageously high. The waste in distribution and marketing, if only from spoilage or from the accumulation of unsalable inventories that clog the shelves for years, has to be seen to be believed. And marketing service is by and large all but non-existent.

What is needed in any "growth" country to make economic development realistic, and at the same time produce a vivid demonstration of what economic development can produce, is a marketing system:

- A system of physical distribution;
- A financial system to make possible the distribution of goods; and
- Finally actual marketing, that is, an actual system of integrating wants, needs, and purchasing power of the consumer with capacity and resources of production.

This need is largely masked today because marketing is so often confused with the traditional "trader and merchant" of which every one of these countries has more than enough. It would be one of our most important contributions to the development of "under-developed" countries to get across the fact that marketing is something quite different.

It would be basic to get across the triple function of marketing:

- The function of crystallizing and directing demand for maximum productive effectiveness and efficiency;
- The function of guiding production purposefully toward maximum consumer satisfaction and consumer value;
- The function of creating discrimination that then gives rewards to those who really contribute excellence, and that then also penalize the monopolist, the slothful, or those who only want to take but do not want to contribute or to risk.

Utilization by the Entrepreneur

(2) Marketing is also the most easily accessible "multiplier" of managers and entrepreneurs in an "under-developed" growth area. And managers and entrepreneurs are the foremost need of these countries. In the first place, "economic development" is not a force of nature. It is the result of the action, the purposeful, responsible, risk-taking

action, of men as entrepreneurs and managers.

Certainly it is the entrepreneur and manager who alone can convey to the people of these countries an understanding of what economic development means and how it can be achieved.

Marketing can convert latent demand into effective demand. It cannot, by itself, create purchasing power. But it can uncover and channel all purchasing power that exists. It can, therefore, create rapidly the conditions for a much higher level of economic activity than existed before, can create the opportunities for the entrepreneur.

It then can create the stimulus for the development of modern, responsible, professional management by creating opportunity for the producer who knows how to plan, how to organize, how to lead people, how to innovate.

In most of these countries markets are of necessity very small. They are too small to make it possible to organize distribution for a single-product line in any effective manner. As a result, without a marketing organization, many products for which there is an adequate demand at a reasonable price cannot be distributed; or worse, they can be produced and distributed only under monopoly conditions. A marketing system is needed which serves as the joint and common channel for many producers if any of them is to be able to come into existence and to stay in existence.

This means in effect that a marketing system in the "under-developed" countries is the creator of small business, is the only way in which a man of vision and daring can become a businessman and an entrepreneur himself. This is thereby also the only way in which a true middle class can develop in the countries in which the habit of investment in productive enterprise has still to be created.

Developer of Standards

(3) Marketing in an "under-developed" country is the developer of standards—of standards for product and service as well as of standards of conduct, of integrity, of reliability, of foresight, and of concern for the basic long-range impact of decisions on the customer, the supplier, the economy, and the society.

Rather than go on making theoretical statements let me point to one illustration: The impact Sears Roebuck has had on several countries of Latin America. To be sure, the countries of Latin America in which Sears operates— Mexico, Brazil, Cuba, V enezuela, Colombia, and Peru— are not "under-developed" in the same sense in which Indonesia or the Congo are "under-developed." Their average income, although very low by our standards, is at least two times, perhaps as much as four or five times, that of the truly "under-developed" countries in which the bulk of mankind still live. Still in every respect except income level these Latin American countries are at best "developing." And they have all the problems of economic development—perhaps even in more acute form than the countries of Asia and Africa, precisely because

their development has been so fast during the last ten years.

It is also true that Sears in these countries is not a "low-price" merchandiser. It caters to the middle class in the richer of these countries, and to the upper middle class in the poorest of these countries. Incidentally, the income level of these groups is still lower than that of the worker in the industrial sector of our economy.

Still Sears is a mass-marketer even in Colombia or Peru. What is perhaps even more important, it is applying in these "under-developed" countries exactly the same policies and principles it applies in this country, carries substantially the same merchandise (although most of it produced in the countries themselves), and applies the same concepts of marketing it uses in Indianapolis or Philadelphia. Its impact and experience are, therefore, a fair test of what marketing principles, marketing knowledge, and marketing techniques can achieve.

The impact of this one American business which does not have more than a mere handful of stores in these countries and handles no more than a small fraction of the total retail business of these countries is truly amazing. In the first place, Sears' latent purchasing power has fast become actual purchasing power. Or, to put it less theoretically, people have begun to organize their buying and to go out for value in what they do buy.

Secondly, by the very fact that it builds one store in one city, Sears forces a revolution in retailing throughout the whole surrounding area. It forces store modernization. It forces consumer credit. It forces a different attitude toward the customer, toward the store clerk, toward the supplier, and toward the merchandise itself. It forces other retailers to adopt modern methods of pricing, of inventory control, of training, of window display, and what have you.

The greatest impact Sears has had, however, is in the multiplication of new industrial business for which Sears creates a marketing channel. Because it has had to sell goods manufactured in these countries rather than import them (if only because of foreign exchange restrictions), Sears has been instrumental in getting established literally hundreds of new manufacturers making goods which, a few years ago, could not be made in the country, let alone be sold in adequate quantity. Simply to satisfy its own marketing needs, Sears has had to insist on standards of workmanship, quality, and delivery—that is, on standards of production management, of technical management, and above all of the management of people— which, in a few short years, have advanced the art and science of management in these countries by at least a generation.

I hardly need to add that Sears is not in Latin America for reasons of philanthropy, but because it is good and profitable business with extraordinary growth potential. In other words, Sears is in Latin America because marketing is the major opportunity in a "growth economy"—precisely because its absence is a major economic gap and the greatest need.

The Discipline of Marketing

(4) Finally, marketing is critical in economic development because marketing has become so largely systematized, so largely both learnable and teachable. It is the discipline among all our business disciplines that has advanced the furthest.

I do not forget for a moment how much we still have to learn in marketing. But we should also not forget that most of what we have learned so far we have learned in a form in which we can express it in general concepts, in valid principles and, to a substantial degree, in quantifiable measurements. This, above all others, was the achievement of that generation to whom Charles Coolidge Parlin was leader and inspiration.

A critical factor in this world of ours is the learnability and teachability of what it means to be an entrepreneur and manager. For it is the entrepreneur and the manager who alone can cause economic development to happen. The world needs them, therefore, in very large numbers; and it needs them fast.

Obviously this need cannot be supplied by our supplying entrepreneurs and managers, quite apart from the fact that we hardly have the surplus. Money we can supply. Technical assistance we can supply, and should supply more. But the supply of men we can offer to the people in the ''under-developed'' countries is of necessity a very small one.

The demand is also much too urgent for it to be supplied by slow evolution through experience, or through dependence on the emergence of ''naturals.'' The danger that lies in the inequality today between the few countries that have and the great many countries that have not is much too great to permit a wait of centuries. Yet it takes centuries if we depend on experience and slow evolution for the supply of entrepreneurs and managers adequate to the needs of a modern society.

There is only one way in which man has ever been able to short-cut experience, to telescope development, in other words, to *learn something*. That way is to have available the distillate of experience and skill in the form of knowledge, of concepts, of generalization, of measurement—in the form of *discipline*, in other words.

The Discipline of Entrepreneurship

Many of us today are working on the fashioning of such a discipline of entrepreneurship and management. Maybe we are further along than most of us realize.

Certainly in what has come to be called ''Operation Research and Synthesis'' we have the first beginnings of a systematic approach to the entrepreneurial task of purposeful risk- taking and innovation—so far only an approach, but a most promising one, unless indeed we become so enamored with the gadgets and techniques as to forget purpose and aim.

We are at the beginning perhaps also of an understanding of the basic problems of organizing people of diversified and highly advanced skill and judgment together in one effective organization, although again no one so far would, I am convinced, claim more for us than that we have begun at last to ask intelligent questions.

But marketing, although it only covers one functional area in the field, has something that can be called a discipline. It has developed general concepts, that is, theories that explain a multitude of phenomena in simple statements. It even has measurements that record ''facts'' rather than opinions. In marketing, therefore, we already possess a learnable and teachable approach to this basic and central problem not only of the ''under-developed'' countries but of all countries. All of us have today the same survival stake in economic development. The risk and danger of international and interracial inequality are simply too great.

Marketing is obviously not a cure-all, not a paradox. It is only one thing we need. But it answers a critical need. At the same time marketing is most highly developed.

Indeed without marketing as the hinge on which to turn, economic development will almost have to take the totalitarian form. A totalitarian system can be defined economically as one in which economic development is being attempted without marketing, indeed as one in which marketing is suppressed. Precisely because it first looks at the values and wants of the individual, and because it then develops people to act purposefully and responsibly—that is, because of its effectiveness in developing a free economy—marketing is suppressed in a totalitarian system. If we want economic development in freedom and responsibility, we have to build it on the development of marketing.

In the new and unprecedented world we live in, a world which knows both a new unity of vision and growth and a new and most dangerous cleavage, marketing has a special central role to play. This role goes:

- Beyond ''getting the stuff out the back door'';
- Beyond ''getting the most sales with the least cost'';
- Beyond ''the optimal integration of our values and wants as customers, citizens, and persons, with our productive resources and intellectual achievements''— the role marketing plays in a developed society.

In a developing economy, marketing is, of course, all of this. But in addition, in an economy that is striving to break the age-old bondage of man to misery, want, and destitution, marketing is also the catalyst for the transmutation of latent resources into actual resources, of desires into accomplishments, and the development of responsible economic leaders and informed economic citizens.

Wroe Alderson[1]

A Marketing View of Competition

MARKETING specialists are vitally affected by any legislation designed to regulate competition. So long as such legislation is pending or its outcome remains uncertain, marketing must be classed as one of the most hazardous of professions. For no other profession is faced with the possibility of such drastic revisions of the rules under which it must operate.

Perhaps we should also be judged as one of the most supine of professional groups if we do nothing about it. For surely no one is better qualified to play a leading part in the consideration of measures designed for the regulation of competition.

Since nothing less than the survival of the marketing profession is involved in this matter, it would appear worthy of the concentrated attention of the newly formed American Marketing Association. The association might very properly offer aggressive leadership in the formulation of a marketing view of competition.

The aim of this session is to precipitate discussion of these issues. The papers were chosen to illustrate the kind of materials bearing on competition which marketing studies can produce. We are not dealing with the Robinson-Patman Act or any specific piece of legislation as such. We are directing our attention instead to the notions concerning the nature of competition which are embodied in current attempts to regulate it.

What is Competition?

The Robinson-Patman Act is one aspect of the continuing movement for an ever broader regulation of competition. Eminent lawyers say that this act embodies an attitude toward competition which diverges sharply from that followed in the Clayton Act. But any attempt at detailed interpretation of its key provisions projects the question which was left hanging in the air with the passing of the N.R.A.—"What is competition?"

The two principal ideals which have been embodied in trade regulation are those of fair competition and free competition. In the Robinson-Patman Act the ideal of fairness seems to have definitely prevailed over the ideal of freedom.

The objective of fair competition is the prevailing one among business groups which are currently seeking trade regulation. Unfortunately the term is subject to as many interpretations as there are types of business concerns. But the ideal cannot be dismissed as the rationalization of special interests. There may be greater danger to the public welfare in the high cost of unfair competition than in the threat of high prices where competition is not wholly free.

Free competition, once the slogan of business interests, seems now to have been left largely in the hands of the economist. However useful the concept may be in price theory, it embodies a notion of economic freedom which is no longer popular. Business men are cold to the offer of freedom if it is freedom to face what they deem to be unfair competition. But insofar as the ideal of the economist involves keeping open the channels for change, for differentiation and for improvement in efficiency, it is the most fundamental objective from the public viewpoint.

The reconciliation of these viewpoints must come from the marketing profession. For the marketing profession, consisting of those who are active in marketing and those who function chiefly as observers is steadily engaged in watching markets at work. While economists assume a struggle for existence in a competitive jungle, only marketing men are prepared to write the natural history of the business jungle.

It is the responsibility of the marketing profession, therefore, to provide a marketing view of competition in order to guide efforts at regulation and to revitalize certain aspects of the science of economics.

Materials for a Theory of Competition

The thirteen numbered paragraphs below do not constitute a definitive statement of the marketing viewpoint of competition. The attempt is rather to list certain points which the marketing approach is likely to emphasize.

---

[1] Remarks at the Annual Convention of the American Marketing Society, Nov. 27, 1936.

The Journal of Marketing
Vol. 1 (January 1937), pp. 189-190

1. The question "What is competition?" may be answered tentatively with a very general definition derived from biological parallels. "Competition is the set of relations existing between organisms because of the fact that they are seeking interdependent objectives within the scarcity boundaries of a common environment."

2. On the business level the study of competition is the study of the adaptation of business enterprises to markets.

3. Markets, like natural environments, suffer sweeping changes. Qualitative changes in demand have even more crucial importance than quantitative changes in supply.

4. A market which is broadly homogeneous as to basic consumer need is divisible almost without limit in terms of minor variations in the character of the goods and services demanded.

5. A fundamental aspect of competitive adaptation is the specialization of suppliers to meet variations in demand whether involving slight differences in product or in the time and place at which the buyer takes delivery.

6. Semi-permanent relations grow up between each segment of the market and certain specialized suppliers. However, random pairing of buyer and seller, as under free competition, is always potentially present.

7. Semi-permanent pairings have been called quasi-monopoly or monopolistic competition, terms which are misnomers since entrenchment of specialized suppliers in separate segments of the market is a great obstacle to the growth of true monopoly.

8. The specialized supplier in the segmented market does not behave like a monopolist.[2] He seeks profits of adaptation, which are profits of efficiency but broader in scope, involving not only the idea of doing a given job well but also that of picking the right job to do.

9. The firm which seeks profits of adaptation is obliged to serve general economic welfare more directly and less wastefully than under orthodox analysis of over-investment, diminishing returns and mobility of capital.

10. Market research, cost analysis and consumer advertising receive proper recognition under such a view as important tools of business adaptation.

11. Price adjustments are also a basic aspect of business adaptation. Qualitative changes in demand and segmentation of markets give rise to price policy which is a prevalent aspect of price as it actually operates in the market.

12. Equally important with the concept of competitive equilibrium, is that of competitive balance in merchandise distribution. This balance is a vital aspect of the ideal of orderly marketing.

13. Competition includes strategic factors involving the survival or decline of whole broad types of business enterprise as well as individual concerns.

---

2 "Product Differentiation and the Integrating Price"—Wroe Alderson, *American Marketing Journal*—May 1936.

Wroe Alderson and Reavis Cox

Towards a Theory of Marketing

Editor's Note: The authors explain the need for the development of marketing theory and indicate some of the sources from which such a body of knowledge will come as well as some of the directions that further work along these lines might take. The editors invite comments and papers concerning the views expressed by the authors, gaps in existing theory not mentioned by them, possible additional areas upon which theory may draw and the proper organization of marketing theory into an integrated whole.

I. The Lively Interest in Marketing Theory

CONSPICUOUS in the professional study of marketing in recent years has been a lively and growing interest in the theory of marketing, i.e., the general or abstract principles underlying the body of facts which comprise this field. Perhaps the best overt evidence of this interest lies in the enthusiasm with which members of the American Marketing Association and its chapters respond to invitations that they attend meetings or prepare papers concerned with theoretical topics. This interest in theory seems to have arisen spontaneously and independently in a number of places at the same time.

Courses in marketing theory are now being given in several universities. Theory is assuming increasing prominence in books and articles written by men whose primary background is in marketing. Theory of marketing was emphasized initially in the establishment of the Parlin Memorial Lecture. Sections on theory have been regularly scheduled at the national conferences of the association beginning with the Pittsburgh meeting in 1946. The Philadelphia chapter of the American Marketing Association has held monthly luncheon meetings on this subject for the past two years. The Board of Directors of the association has approved the idea that the association establish an annual award in the theory of marketing. A symposium on the theory of marketing is now in preparation which is to be published as a special supplement to the *Journal of Marketing.*

The interest in theory expressed at one place or another and in one way or another by both the academic men and the practitioners of commercial research is real and substantial enough to merit careful attention. The time seems ripe to evaluate its significance—i.e., to determine as precisely as possible the nature of the interest, to survey the reasons for its appearance, and to consider the sort of intellectual discipline into which it is likely to mould the study of marketing if, as seems probable, it continues to grow in depth and scope during the years immediately ahead.

II. The Nature of the Interest in Marketing Theory

Data do not exist upon which to base a detailed description of the nature of this interest in theory among marketing men. Some part of it no doubt represents simple curiosity at a relatively high intellectual level. Part of it is a variety of follow-the-leader. When some people become avidly and outspokenly interested in anything, others will take a look to see what is going on. A few will act interested because they think they ought to be.

The central core of the foundation that underlies the interest in a new theoretical approach to marketing is, however, much more substantial than this. Apparently it consists of two principal parts. One is a very widespread and generally justified conviction that students of marketing thus far have reaped from their efforts remarkably small harvests of accurate, comprehensive and significant generalizations. Marketing literature offers its readers very few true and important "principles" or "theories." The other part is an evident belief among some observers that students of marketing have achieved too little even in setting fundamental and significant problems for themselves, to say nothing of working out procedures for solving such problems once they have been formulated.

At first glance the lively interest of marketing men in the theoretical aspects of their subject may seem to spring chiefly from the first source—dissatisfaction with the numbers and kinds of generalization thus far achieved through sedulous accumulation of innumerable facts. A second look suggests that what marketing men really seek is not an immediate statement of the generalizations to which effective study will in due course lead them, but a better statement of the problems to be solved and more ingenious methods to be applied in solving them. The multitude of facts thus far assembled seems to add up to very little. One must conclude that something has gone wrong with the method of attack—that a new and creative analysis is required.

Northrop, in his stimulating study of the logic of research,[1] holds that the most difficult part of an inquiry usually is its initiation. As he sees matters, inquiry begins with a problem circumstances have called to someone's attention. Ordinarily the problem arises because newly discovered facts upset accepted explanations.

The first step is to analyze the problem imaginatively, since its nature will dictate the methods that must be used to solve it. From the analysis of the problem springs an understanding of the sorts of fact that must be assembled to answer it and of the methods by which they can be assembled. After this come the actual assembly of the facts required, description and classification of these facts, derivation from them of fruitful and relevant hypotheses, and verification of the hypotheses thus deductively derived by inductive appeal to further facts.

Apparently what marketing men now seek in their appeal to theory is imaginative guidance into such a creative analysis of the problems of marketing. This can be put another way. Events in recent years have forced students of marketing to put a heavy emphasis upon problems of private management and public policy. One result has been to reveal the inadequacy of the earlier years of study in the field, which proceeded by almost haphazard accumulation of facts. It has become evident that if the difficulties raised by events in the areas of public and private policy as applied to marketing are to be solved, they must be put into a framework that provides a much better perspective than is now given by the literature. Only a sound theory of marketing can raise the analysis of such problems above the level of an empirical art and establish truly scientific criteria for setting up hypotheses and selecting the facts by means of which to test them.

III. Specific Reasons for the Interest in Marketing Theory

The nature of the demand students of marketing are making upon their would-be theorists can be clarified further by considering some of the specific problems they feel to be treated inadequately in the existing literature. Northrop, as we have seen, suggests that a problem calling for the initiation of some systematic inquiry usually makes its appearance when existing theories fail to satisfy students because they do not account for or take into consideration all of the relevant observed facts. In essence, this is today's situation in the study of marketing.

Conclusions as to policy and procedure in the field of marketing, and particularly those derived from the so-called principles stated in manuals of management or in the great body of general economic theory, often seem not to jibe with the observable facts. Furthermore, a good many such problems are thrown at marketing men where the facts have not been collected or, even more important, where no one has a clear understanding of the sorts of fact that must be assembled and analyzed. A few illustrations will serve to make clear the present less-than-satisfactory position of marketing theory.

(1) Problems of Price Discrimination

Difference in the prices competing buyers pay for goods bought from a common supplier or in the prices they receive from a common buyer raise critical problems of managerial and public policy. Here, as in other aspects of economic life, we come up against the twentieth century's version of an ancient problem—that of the just or fair price. Laws have been enacted and the courts have rendered judgments under these laws that alter profoundly prevailing views as to what is socially desirable in pricing and what is not.

Among marketing men there exists an uneasy feeling that at least some of the policies thus being established would be substantially different if the facts of marketing as they ought to be known to marketing men were included in the supporting theories. In particular, it seems to be felt that the policy decisions rest upon a careless acceptance of mere conventions as objective facts. Thus the conventional definition of price in narrow terms as a ratio between quantities of money and quantities of goods, rather than in terms of completely negotiated sales transactions, is taken to denominate price in connotations where only the broader definition can be valid.[2] Yet marketing men have done virtually nothing to correct the situation by defining a completely negotiated sales transaction and proceeding to work out theories based upon it.

(2) Spatial Aspects of Marketing

Students of the economics of land utilization have given much attention to problems raised by the location of various kinds of economic activity. Students of marketing have made very little contribution to that discussion. This is true despite the fact that repeatedly they must give attention to related managerial problems. For example, they often help business men determine how large a trading area is served by a particular store or by a particular cluster of stores. They advise operators as to where within a

---

[1] F. S. C. Northrop, *The Logic of the Sciences and the Humanities*, Macmillan Co., New York, 1947.

[2] Some aspects of this problem were considered in an earlier article by one of the present authors: Reavis Cox, "Non-Price Competition and the Measurement of Prices," *Journal of Marketing*, Vol. X, No. 4, April, 1946, pp. 370-383.

particular trading area a retail or wholesale enterprise should locate its physical facilities.

Neither the marketing man nor the analyst of land utilization has received much help from the general economist, with his theories of pure rent and his tendency simply to assume rather than to explain the existence of a spatial distribution of marketing activities such that forces of supply and demand can in some significant sense be brought to a focus in price. Hence, it appears that marketing men should assume the task of working out concepts that have true significance in analyzing the nature of the distributive space through which goods and services are marketed and the nature of the forces that have brought the existing distributive pattern into existence.

(3) Temporal Aspects of Marketing

Economic theory has sometimes evaded problems raised by time through analyzing instantaneous relationships instead of utilizing period analysis. This procedure in effect reduces the economy to a timeless universe in which other problems become more amenable to analysis. A market becomes an organization existing in full maturity at a given instant of time, rather than an organism growing and changing through time. Price becomes a unit of behavior taken at a particular instant and resulting from the interplay of forces that work themselves out instantaneously, rather than a structure or pattern extending over time. Consumption becomes an instantaneous process rather than one that requires appreciable periods of time.

Under some circumstances these distortions of fact do no harm and may be very helpful; but they also lead to erroneous results when the economist forgets to drop his rigid assumptions as he works with problems for which the passage of time is critically important, such as the negotiation of transactions, trading in futures, and the consumption of consumers' durables.

Unfortunately, many marketing people have themselves accepted uncritically conclusions resting upon such misleading assumptions. Only now are they coming to realize that theories built upon this kind of foundation fail to conform to what they know concerning the facts of price structures and price policies, of commodity exchanges, and of the use of consumer credit to finance the purchase of durables. It is clear the new concepts and new analyses based on new and more realistic assumptions are required if the nature and significance of market phenomena involving the passage of appreciable periods are to be explored thoroughly.

(4) Economic Entities

For purposes of economic analysis it is conventional to work with entities that are not always readily observable or measurable in the flesh. They are arbitrarily assumed to exist as identifiable units that make decisions and engage in economic behavior. They consequently are extremely important in analyses of the ways in which economic de-

cisions are reached. The firm, the market, and the economy are excellent illustrations.

Exposure to day-to-day problems and processes in marketing has suggested to some students that there are purposes for which other entities may be more meaningful. Thus in working with the problems raised by marketing functions and the costs of performing them, perhaps the marketing channel is a more meaningful concept than any of these others. Again, the dispersion market may be singled out for meaningful analyses. Yet again, marketing men know that for some purpose the most meaningful analysis emerges when, contrary to the most usual custom among economists, emphasis is put upon cooperative rather than upon competitive behavior. Economics as a pattern of mutually interacting and supporting activities consciously directed toward accomplishing a common, overall task, is a concept as valid as the one that emphasizes rivalry and competition in efforts to gain individual advantage. For an understanding of marketing as a social instrument, it may be the essential concept.

Despite the need, marketing men have made little progress toward setting up new fruitful concepts of economic entities derived from their experiences of economic activity or toward working out theoretical formulations based upon such concepts. In particular, they have done little toward working out a theory of cooperation in the broad sense, although they have given much attention to formally organized enterprises that describe themselves as cooperatives rather than as competitive businesses.

(5) Limitations upon the Alternatives Open to Economic Entities

Much of the prevailing economic theory and many of the public policies based upon it proceed upon the assumption that business management and the management of consumption both operate by making decisions intended to maximize results under a continuous function. Little or no weight is given to the fact that decisions are really discontinuous (made in "lumps" or "bundles," as it were) and that real choices must be made from specific alternatives of quite limited number and scope. Marketing men know these facts, yet they have done very little toward setting up alternative formulations based upon what they know concerning the limitations within which managers and consumers operate.

(6) Attitudes and Motivations of Buyers and Sellers

Every theory of management as well as every theory of economic behavior must rest upon some concept of human motivations and attitudes. The concepts, implicit or explicit, that underlie much of economic theory, clearly fall far short of conforming to the facts of human behavior. Although one turns first to psychologists for correctives, students of marketing themselves have a better opportunity than anyone else to observe human beings in action as buyers and sellers. With the aid of psychologists, sociologists and statisticians, they are developing increasingly effective ways to observe and measure. They cannot expect to reap the full harvest of their efforts, however, until they have worked out more meaningful concepts, problems, hypotheses and, eventually, theories into which they can fit their stores of fact concerning what people do.

(7) The Development of Market Organization

Characteristic of much economic analysis is the underlying assumption that the complex of human behavior required to set up, operate and continuously remodel a going market has already done its work. The going market simply exists. Little thought (perhaps none) is given to the fact that this assumption is not tenable—that someone has to exert great effort continuously if there is to be the intricate organization required to inform potential buyers and sellers, to bring them together in the actual negotiation of a transaction, and to make it possible for them to carry out all transactions negotiated.

Much of the criticism of marketing as wasteful stems fundamentally from taking this assumption as a statement of observed fact. It is self-evident that if we assume an effective market organization to be in existence and operating, any further effort to organize and operate it is by definition unnecessary. Students of marketing need to work out a theory built upon the assumption that the development, continuous adjustment, improvement, and steady operation of the machinery of marketing is an economic function as real and as important as any of the more familiar economic functions that can be performed only when the market organization as we know it, or some acceptable substitute for it, has been devised and set up and is kept in operation.

IV. Sources for a Theory of Marketing[3]

It would be a mistake to assume that the interest in marketing theory springs solely from a growing realization that the study of marketing must remain fragmentary, superficial and inaccurate in the absence of valid and profound theoretical formulations. Equally important, perhaps, is the dawning of a realization that here and there in the literature of several intellectual disciplines are appearing the elements from which an adequate theory of marketing will be constructed. Many of these elements are little more than vague ideas and suggestions. Only the barest start has been made toward refining them into really meaningful concepts and procedures that will serve as guides to hypothesis making and fact gathering. They are nevertheless numerous enough and suggestive enough to support a belief that a theory of marketing is becoming feasible as well as desirable. The appearance of feasibility has played a part in arousing interest no less important than that played by the realization of need.

The accumulating elements for at least a rudimentary theory of marketing are scattered throughout the literature of the social sciences. Many of them are isolated ideas, often little more than flashes of inspiration to be found in longer discussions of entirely different matters. Some of them are indirect suggestions concerning concepts and methodology that can be derived from the efforts of workers in economic fields other than marketing. Some exist only in the unpublished and partially formulated notes of scholars who have shared their ideas with others in talks before technical meetings, discussions before classes, or private conversations and correspondence.

Under such circumstances it is not to be expected that anyone can present a definitive bibliography of possible sources for a theory of marketing. All that will be attempted here is to list some of the ideas the present writers have picked up in their own cogitations and investigations. Enriched by the analogous discoveries of others, they should provide inspiration, stimulation and cross-fertilization of concept and procedure. Out of these in due course will come a comprehensive and valid theory of marketing.

(1) Contributions from Economic Theory

An obvious possible source for contributions to a meaningful theory of marketing is general economic theory itself. Since a theory of marketing must be in part a revision and correction of economic theory, it would perhaps be fair to say that the principal contribution economic theorists can make to its development is to work out economic theories that stimulate a search by specialized students of marketing for something that explains the known facts more fully. In so far as economic theorists work out doctrines that meet the needs and conform to the experience of marketing specialists, they will, of course, render the development of a specialized theory of marketing unnecessary.

In practice, starting points for a theory of marketing may be found in the work of theorists who have developed concepts that are readily adaptable to this field. Some of these are ideas accepted by the great body of orthodox theorists; others represent offshoots that have achieved only limited acceptance.

Institutional economics, for example, provides marketing theorists with a particularly useful set of concepts and formulations. As we shall see shortly, one of the most promising possible approaches to a theory of marketing is through the study of what we shall call group behaviorism. The sociologist's concept of institutions as patterns or configurations of group behavior provides the basic approach that has been applied by the institutionalists (with only limited success so far, it must be admitted) to the study of economic problems. Marketing men, much of whose work consists of seeking out general patterns of

---

[3] Formal references to the sources cited in this section will be found in the bibliography at the end of the article.

group behavior, should find this approach particularly fruitful.

It should be remembered that marketing men call one of their traditional approaches to the study of marketing the institutional approach. As used by most marketing men (the recently published text by Edward A. Duddy and David A. Revzan being a conspicuous exception), the term has been restricted to efforts to describe what goes on in marketing by classifying, describing and analyzing the operations of the two million or so individual establishments that participate in marketing. This approach is not institutional in the sociologist's sense. It is nevertheless adaptable to a more fundamental and far-reaching approach that would treat retailers, wholesalers and other entities active in marketing as institutions in the true sociological usage of the term. In this view, the agencies of marketing would become patterns of human behavior and communication clustered about some physical facility, such as a store or warehouse, that can be identified and located for counting and measurement. Similarly the economic entities discussed above could be viewed as clusters or patterns of group behavior.

Individual economists of the institutional school also offer specific fruitful ideas for the development of marketing theory. Thus John R. Commons provides the basic inspiration for dividing transactions into routine and fully negotiated ones. Upon this idea can be built a meaningful analysis of changes in the ways buyers and sellers do business and of the significances of these changes for costs of marketing.

Von Neumann and Morgenstern have taken the fully negotiated transaction as their point of departure in a book that brings a new mathematical approach to the analysis of market behavior. This may turn out to be the genuine revolution in economic theory which has been presaged by such diverse developments as Keynes' challenge to Says Law of Markets and the recasting of competitive theory by Chamberlin and others. Starting from an exhaustive analysis of the negotiated transaction they offer hope of a fresh attack on such problems as efficiency in distribution and monopolistic restriction.

Clark's pioneer work on overhead costs provided a source from which stems directly or indirectly, much of the fruitful effort of marketing men to work out definitions of cost and of the relations between cost and price from which in time will almost certainly come significant contributions to the theory of marketing.

Marketing is of necessity involved with competition and price. Therefore the core of marketing theory might well be modern price theory with its stress on different types of competitive situations.

The work of E. H. Chamberlin, Joan Robinson, Robert Triffin as well as such men as Bain and others in analyses of non-perfect competition, offers an especially vital challenge to marketing theorists. Marketing men will certainly follow their lead in questioning the validity as statements of fact of the assumptions underlying much traditional economic theory. At the same time, marketing men have every opportunity to advance monopolistic competition theory in providing alternative assumptions and hypotheses drawn from experience in the market.

Certainly the last word has not been said on product differentiation as a factor in what Triffin calls heterogeneous competition—a term, incidentally, which well might replace "monopolistic competition" as being more descriptive and not so weighted with objectionable connotations. Economic discussions tend to assume that product differentiation always represents a departure from uniformity but the reverse may be true with respect to units produced by the firm which differentiates. Suppose there is a field in which each producer is making a great many varieties of the same article in accordance with the diverse specifications demanded by purchasers. Then one enterprising firm has an opportunity to steal a march on competition by manufacturing only identical units. By adopting a standard formula within its own business it may achieve substantial advantages in mass production economies and be obliged to use only a part of the savings in sales and advertising expenses to attract to itself the buyers who are willing to accept its standardized product.

More broadly it may be said that differentiation is a basic function of the market which is carried out primarily through the channels of distribution and which is intimately related to the problem of efficiency in marketing. Chamberlin recognizes time and place utility and all specialized services as aspects of product differentiation but does not treat the subject exhaustively. For marketing theory a crucial problem is the point in the flow at which differentiation does or should take place. As a general principle it seems clear that it should be avoided as long as possible to maximize the proportion of the distribution job which can enjoy the economies of minimum differentiation.

The relation of sales cost to competition has been touched upon by many writers but remains an item of unfinished business for marketing theory. The general assumption appears to be that the effect of competition in imperfect markets is to raise sales costs. This assumption needs to be tested against an analysis which starts from the negotiated sale transaction as the norm and recognizes that there may be many ways of achieving the relative economy of routine sales transactions. Advertising may help to perform for one class of products the simplification of transactions achieved through commodity exchanges in another. It is not likely that distribution can ever achieve the economies which arise from the use of power machinery in production. It is well to remember, however, that specialization and routinization provide the original basis for improving efficiency in both production and distribution.

One of the most profound questions with respect to the heterogeneous competition which prevails in our economy today is whether we can develop a theory of competition which has any real relevance for public policy on such matters as the regulation of marketing policy. The apparent willingness of many influential economists to throw over the benefits of mass production in order to achieve a closer approach to atomistic competition is surely unrealistic. Following J. M. Clark and Robert Triffin, a radical revision of competitive theory may revolve around overhead costs and differentiated market position in a heterogeneous economy. Empirical studies of competition indicate that these two factors can provide the basis for dynamic equilibrium.

The direction for advance which is indicated here is an analysis of the process of price negotiation and the conditions for a balance of economic forces achieved through bargaining. Ordinarily there are limits observed by either side and principles by which their bargaining activities are guided which may result in a long- run outcome with respect to prices which is not too different from the long-run outcome under the supposition of pure competition. In a mass production economy the central consideration in negotiation may generally be expected to be the endeavor to balance access to markets through diversified channels against the need for enough volume to reach the breaking point in production costs.

The development of the so-called macroeconomics in recent years largely under the influence of Keynes has concentrated the attention of economists on national aggregates such as total consumer income, the level of employment, consumer expenditures, and capital formation. The results which may be hoped for in more reliable estimates and predictions of these aggregates have great practical significance for marketing research, which is quite generally concerned with evaluating the outlook for individual concerns or products. The theoretical significance of Keynes for marketing lies in other directions, as for example in underscoring the importance of market organization by advancing the thesis that the automatic functioning of the market mechanism cannot be taken for granted.

Work such as that exemplified in Bertil Ohlin's analysis of inter-regional trade has already provided the conceptual basis for one course in the theory of marketing.[4] It has also provided foundations for more meaningful analyses than have been widely attempted as yet of the economics of trading areas, economic regions within a na-

tional economy, and the various sections of a metropolitan community. Beginnings have been made toward these sorts of analyses; but they offer fruitful opportunities for more penetrating studies than have yet been made.

(2) Contributions from Systematic Studies of Group Behavior

A second possible source for contributions to the evolving theory of marketing will be found in studies of group behavior made by social scientists in fields other than economics, and notably in the work of anthropologists, sociologists and social psychologists. George Lundberg's application to marketing in his Parlin lecture of his concepts of measurable patterns and clusters of communication, is an example of what can be done with ideas borrowed directly from sociology. It offers a promising device to be used in analyzing the economic significance of such entities as cities, towns, trading centers, trading areas and individual retailers with their customers and their sources of supply; of advertising media and those they reach; and of the multitude of other patterns of communication through which human wants are converted into economic demand, information is distributed among sellers and buyers, and transactions are negotiated and carried into effect.

Kenneth Boulding speculates in a recent article on the limitations of the principle of maximization of returns as the foundation of the theory of the individual business enterprise. He suggests that the principle of organizational preservation may turn out to be more fruitful. One of the authors of this article has pointed out that organizations act is if they had a will to survive and that this drive arises from the individual's struggle for socio-economic status.[5]

Among psychologists, the topological concepts developed by the late Kurt Lewin and expounded in somewhat simpler form by his former student Robert W. Leeper, offer some promise of setting up procedures that may lead to a more effective understanding of human motivation that has thus far been achieved. In the field of industrial relations, Elton Mayo at Harvard and E. W. Bakke at Yale have developed promising concepts and procedures for inquiries into the factors that determine how human beings behave in the relations of employer to employee and in the development of trade unions. Such concepts and procedures give some evidence of being applicable to problems of marketing with good effect.

Students of public opinion and consumer attitudes, among whom Hadley Cantril may be mentioned, are virtually within the field of marketing; but they have drawn heavily upon other disciplines in their work.

---

4 This is a course in the theory of domestic commerce organized by E. T. Grether at the University of California. So far as the present writers have been able to discover, only three courses are currently given in the colleges of the country that specifically undertake a systematic presentation of a theory of marketing. In addition to Dean Grether's course, there is one give by E. D. McGarry at the University of Buffalo that builds upon an analysis of the functions of marketing. The third, give by Reavis Cox at the University of Pennsylvania, is built around analyses of the meaning and measurement of location in and flow through distributive space and time, problems of human behavior, patterns of social communication, prices and price structure, and problems of efficiency, waste and productivity.

5 Wroe Alderson, "Conditions For a Balanced World Economy," *World Economics*, Vol. II, No. 7, October, 1944, pp. 3-25.

(3) Contributions from Ecological Studies

Research by a wide variety of students into problems of human geography, population, traffic and city planning has offered many opportunities for enriching the theory of marketing. R. M. Haig's early essay on the economic functions of the metropolis and Harold Mayer's classification and analysis of the patterns of growth exhibited by secondary shopping centers in Chicago, are examples of useful analyses derived from the work of city planners.

W. J. Reilly's law of retail gravitation probably fits best into the ecological classification, although it could also be placed in the next section among the examples of work done in marketing research that is leading to a more fundamental understanding of the nature and function of marketing. Long neglected, Reilly's law has again begun to attract notice. After some revisions, it has provided the basic procedure used by Paul D. Converse to determine the directions and distances people go to shop for certain types of goods in Illinois. Still further revised, it has provided a system worked out in detail by the Curtis Publishing Company for dividing the entire country into trading areas for shopping goods. Although the immediate application has thus made been to the problems faced by individual merchants and individual communities in building their trade, this law as revised provides one starting point for a theory of the relationships of individual retailers or clusters and their customers.

Even more significant have been the efforts of John Q. Stewart to apply to the distribution of the population, and to the influences individual people and clusters of people exert upon each other at a distance, concepts much like those he has used in his work as a physicist and astronomer. His method, which he has summed up under the term social physics, may well lead to the clearest understanding yet attained and the most precise measurement thus far made of the forces that determine how people assemble themselves into markets and the ways in which they exert influence upon each other. It may thus provide a procedure for reducing to quantitative measurement the concept of patterns of social communication or influence devised by the sociologists.

(4) Contributions in Marketing Literature Itself

Tentative beginnings toward a meaningful theory of marketing may also be found scattered through the literature of marketing itself. It is impossible to make a complete listing here of the many significant contributions; but a few names may be mentioned so as to indicate the nature of these beginnings:

Melvin T. Copeland's early work in the classification of commodities on the basis of shopping methods used by the consumers who acquire them.

The work done in defining and describing the functions of marketing by such men as A. W. Shaw, Paul T. Cherington, Fred E. Clark and, more recently, E. D. McGarry.

E. T. Grether's use, noted above, of the concept of interregional trade as a frame upon which to build a theory of marketing, and his work with price discrimination and price structures.

The effort by Charles F. Phillips, since widely copied, to work the ideas and principles of value developed by neoclassical and monopolistic-competition economists into the body of marketing principles.

Robert W. Bartels' attempt to cull out of the literature of marketing all the principles or theories it contains.

Ralph W. Breyer's pioneer effort to struggle with the problems of space and time in marketing, with the concept of marketing as a social institution, and with the influence of changes in costs imposed at one level of the channel upon cost incurred at other levels.

The work done by John Paver, Victor H. Pelz, and others in using traffic flows and pedestrian movements as indicators of the structure of markets and trading areas.

Ralph Cassady's analyses of price discrimination and its legal significance, and the work done by Cassady and others with problems of decentralization in the retail trade of large cities.

The work of Roland S. Vaile and, more recently, Neil H. Borden in the study of the economic effects of advertising. This is supplemented by William B. Ricketts' work with procedures for evaluating the business effects of advertising.

Many other examples could be given; but these will suffice for present purposes. They make it clear that students who undertake to build a systematic theory of marketing will find stones at hand for the purpose. The stones must be dug out of the existing literature, reshaped, and supplemented by many others that remain to be discovered. They nevertheless provide material for a start.

V. A Possible Approach to an Integrated Theory of Marketing

Any comprehensive approach to the development of a marketing theory would need to meet several tests:

(1) It should give promise of serving the variety of needs that have created the current interest in marketing theory.

(2) It should be able to draw in a comprehensive way upon the starting points for theory already available in the literature, such as those listed above.

(3) It should provide a consistent theoretical perspective for the study of all the major classes of significant entities in marketing.

Such a viewpoint would appear to be available in what may be called group behaviorism as it has been developing in the social sciences. This view differs from the narrower use of the term behaviorism by Pavlov and Watson in that it gives a sociological rather than a physiological emphasis to the analysis. The basic concept of group behaviorism is the organized behavior system.

Marketing theory may be said to consist of making clear what we mean by behavior, what we mean by system, and what we mean by organization, all as applied to marketing. Application to marketing implies that principles pertaining to these basic concepts should be given specific form and content in relation to all of the types of organized behavior systems that are significantly involved in the marketing process. These types of behavior system include, as we have seen, the firms engaged in buying or selling, the family as an earning and consuming unit, the local dispersion market, the channel of distribution, the industry supplying a phase of consumer or industrial need, and the economic system as a whole.

Group behaviorism differs from institutionalism in that it is basically concerned with the concrete entities that interact within a behavior system. It differs from the approach to systems that has generally been followed in mathematical economics in that it takes account of the patterns of group behavior developed within specific systems as qualifying their operation. Thus, while it may make use of equilibrium concepts, it does not depend primarily on analogies drawn from the equilibrium systems discussed in physics.

Group behaviorism has the further distinction that it emphasizes those aspects of individual behavior that tend to perpetuate organized behavior systems and thus to render them at least semiconservative in the technical sense. Economic theory tends to assume that the systems under consideration do not obey the laws of conservation.

The approach through group behaviorism is most closely allied to what is usually called the functional approach in marketing. It would undertake to analyze marketing processes by taking primary account of the objectives they are designed to serve. Thus it retains the emphasis of the general economists on the forces of supply and demand but must go further in order to throw light on specific problems and situations in marketing. Eventually it should enable the market analyst to formulate the way in which market forces interact at any point in the system he has under investigation.

Marketing is still in what Northrop described as the first stage of scientific study, namely that of the gathering of vast compilations of fact. It was Francis Bacon, at the very beginning of modern scientific awakening, who felt that all problems would be solved if only enough facts were accumulated. Economic theory in the main has remained one step further back in a prescientific or metaphysical stage. It has occupied itself with the effort toward logical deductions from assumptions.

Neither economics nor marketing can lay much claim to being scientific until they attain the stage of continuous interaction between theory and research. The assumptions on which theory rests must more and more spring from careful empirical generalization. The facts which research gathers must more and more be relevant to hypotheses adopted on theoretical grounds.

VI. An Application of Group Behaviorism to Marketing Research

The feasibility and significance of approaching a theory of marketing through group behaviorism will be tested in an exploratory survey of the productivity of marketing in Philadelphia being organized this summer (1948). For purposes of this survey, the economic entity chosen is the Philadelphia dispersion market. Tentatively this has been defined as an organized behavior system embracing a group of people to whom goods and services flow through points of entry located within the Philadelphia area in so far as they do not originate within the area itself; the formal organizations, agencies or entities that do the work required to effectuate the flow in so far as the consumers do not do it for themselves; and the patterns of social communication, physical flow and movement through time by means of which the work is arranged and effectuated. For purposes of quantitative analysis, some arbitrary departures from the details of this definition doubtless must be made because of limitations upon the sorts of data to be had within limits of feasible financial expenditure. These concessions to practical difficulties will be held to the narrowest possible limits.

The specific objective of the project is to test the feasibility and significance of a long list of tentative formulas devised by one of the authors. These formulas are intended to serve as indicators of degrees of efficiency in dispersion marketing. The project will also give some indications, however, as to whether the basic theoretical approach being made is valid. In so doing it will, if it succeeds, meet the first of the tests suggested in the preceding section for the validity of approaches to the development of a marketing theory. That is, it will help satisfy the two basic needs underlying the demand for such a theory: First, it will provide a way of stating theoretical problems in marketing that, in the terms used by Northrop, permits the initiation of really meaningful inquiries. Second, it will make possible the drawing up of generalizations that have meaning and significance because they can be subjected to the test of relevant facts.

The project, if it succeeds, will also satisfy the test of making comprehensive drafts upon the literature for approaches, concepts and procedures. For example, the frame of reference that treats the dispersion market as the unit for observation comes from the developing realization already noted that new types of economic entities must be visualized.

The treatment of any such entity as an organized system of group behavior derives from the sociological concept of institutions as patterns of social communication. Emphasis will be placed upon the cooperative, as contrasted with the competitive aspects of the market, the objective being to determine what the market as a whole accomplishes for the people who compose it.

In setting up the formulas, which are essentially ratios between units of input and units of output, heavy reliance has been placed upon the functional approach to a study of marketing. "Functions" have been redefined for the purposes of analysis at this particular level; but the survey will hold closely to the basic concept of measuring the output or product of marketing in units of work defined by reference to the functions the dispersion market is supposed to perform.[6] A kind of equilibrium analysis will be achieved through establishing a concept of unit or optimum efficiency for each task the market performs. Against this unit efficiency, taken as a goal, the actual performance of the market in each particular can be evaluated. Instead of being looked upon as a device to introduce imperfections into an otherwise perfect market, the behavior system under analysis will be taken as designed to reduce the degree of imperfection already present.

The specific measures to be used derive in the last analysis from the numerous studies of which a few examples were given above under the headings "Ecological Studies" and "Marketing Literature Itself." Present indications are that the ecological studies will be particularly useful. In order to measure some aspects of effort expended and work done, reliance can best be put upon concepts of movement or flow through some one or more varieties of space and time against the resistance of some one or more varieties of obstacle. To use these concepts effectively, clear definitions will be required of distributive space and time, location or position, and flow or movement. The definitions will have to be so set up that the terms lend themselves to quantitative measurement. For these purposes, studies of the sort illustrated above by reference to Lundberg, Paver, Pelz, Reilly, Converse and Stewart will be particularly helpful. For the analysis of other aspects of effort expended and work done, reliance can perhaps best be made on other sources illustrated by Commons' suggestion of the contrast between fully negotiated and routine transactions, various studies of retail mortality, and struggles by many economists with problems of price differentiation and price structure.

There is every likelihood that this sort of comprehensive analysis of any entity such as the dispersion market will lead to significant formulations of theory, as this term has been defined above; that is, this sort of study should provide clear, detailed and specific statements of what is meant by behavior in marketing, what is meant by a system or pattern of behavior, and what is meant by organized or group patterns. It should be particularly useful in so far as it provides a procedure for reducing these various matters to quantitative measurement.

Furthermore, there are good prospects that what is worked out in this sort of survey will provide a theoretical perspective applicable to the study of other identifiable and significant entities in marketing. Thus it gives promise of meeting the third test suggested above. It bids fair to be not merely an isolated empirical study but a unit in something much larger. Should it prove successful, it will contribute substantially to creating the general theory so earnestly wanted by students of marketing.

VII. Marketing Theory and Economic Theory

An issue requiring the most careful consideration is whether the marketing field can satisfy its needs for a marketing theory until reformulation of economic theory has progressed further. Any market analyst who sees his role as that of facilitating adjustments of private and public policy in a world of change must grow impatient with the faltering attempts of economic theorists to deal with the dynamic aspects of an enterprise economy. The most acute marketing problems are precipitated by the facts of technological change. The market analyst is bound to wonder how the economists can expect to cope with change so long as he is so generally inclined to consider technology outside his proper field of interest.

The market analyst does not have the luxury of choice as to whether he will adopt a dynamic view. At the very least he must take account of technological change in marketing. Progressive changes in the technology of distribution, in the methods and channels of marketing, are surely significant for economic theory. They are of the essence of any perspective which might be distinguished as marketing theory. Thus the marketing theorist is obliged to break the economist's taboo on the discussion of technology at least as it applies to the techniques of marketing.

There is another aspect of the dynamics of market organization which is fundamental for marketing theory and eventually inescapable, it would appear, for economic theory. That is the fact that an organized behavior system is not a neutral framework or container for the actions and evaluations which take place within it. That is to say that a market changes day by day through the very fact that goods are bought and sold. While evaluation is taking place within a marketing structure, the structure itself is being rendered weaker or stronger and the changes in organization which follow will have an impact on tomorrow's evaluations. Marketing theory will not provide an adequate approach if it ignores this interaction between the system and the processes which take place within it. Whether economic theory can dispense with such considerations is another question.

---

6 For a statement of some views held by the present writers concerning ways of measuring productivity in marketing, see Reavis Cox, "The Meaning and Measurement of Productivity in Marketing," and Wroe Alderson, "A Formula for Measuring Productivity in Distribution," *Journal of Marketing*, Vol. XII, April, 1948, pp. 433-448.

REFERENCES

The ideas credited to the various authors mentioned in Section IV may be found in the following sources:

(1) Joe S. Bain, "Market Classifications in Modern Price Theory," *The Quarterly Journal of Economics*, LVI, No. 4, August, 1942, pp. 560-574.

(2) E. W. Bakke, *Mutual Survival: The Goal of Unions and Management* (New Haven: Yale University Labor and Management Center, 1946).

(3) E. W. Bakke, *Principles of Adaptive Human Behaviour*. (A mimeographed preliminary draft privately circulated.)

(4) Robert W. Bartels, "Marketing Principles," *Journal of Marketing*, Vol. IX, No. 2, October, 1944, pp. 151-157.

(5) Neil H. Borden, *The Economic Effects of Advertising* (Chicago: Richard D. Irwin, Inc., 1942).

(6) Kenneth E. Boulding, "Samuelson's *Foundations:* The Role of Mathematics in Economics," *Journal of Political Economy*, Vol. LVI, No. 3, June, 1948, pp. 187-199.

(7) William K. Bowden and Ralph Cassady, Jr., "Decentralization of Retail Trade in Metropolitan Market Area," *Journal of Marketing*, Vol. V, No. 3, January, 1941, pp. 270-275.

(8) Ralph F. Breyer, *Bulk and Package Handling Costs* (New York: American Management Association, 1944).

(9) Ralph F. Breyer, *The Marketing Institution* (New York: McGraw-Hill Co., 1934).

(10) Hadley Cantril and others, *Gauging Public Opinion* (Princeton: Princeton University Press, 1944).

(11) Ralph Cassady, Jr., "Some Economic Aspects of Price Discrimination Under Non-Perfect Market Conditions" and "Techniques and Purposes of Price Discrimination," *Journal of Marketing*, Vol. XI, No. 1, July, 1946, pp. 7-20, and No. 2, October, 1946, pp. 135-150.

(12) Ralph Cassady, Jr., and William K. Bowden, "Shifting Retail Trade Within the Los Angeles Metropolitan Market," *Journal of Marketing*, Vol. VIII, No. 4, April, 1944, pp. 398-404.

(13) Edward H. Chamberlin, The Theory of Monopolistic Competition: A Re-orientation of the Theory of Value (Cambridge: Harvard University Press, 1st ed., 1933, frequently revised since then).

(14) Paul T. Cherington, *The Elements of Marketing* (New York: Macmillan Co., 1920).

(15) Fred E. Clark, *Principles of Marketing* (New York: Macmillan Co., 1st ed., 1922, revised at intervals since).

(16) J. M. Clark, *Studies in the Economics of Overhead Costs* (Chicago: University of Chicago Press, 1923).

(17) John R. Commons, *Institutional Economics* (New York: Macmillan Co., 1934).

(18) Paul D. Converse, *Retail Trade Areas in Illinois* (Urbana: University of Illinois, 1946).

(19) *Melvin T. Copeland, "Relation of Consumers' Buying Habits to Marketing Methods," Harvard Business Review*, April, 1923, pp. 282-289.

(20) Richard P. Doherty, "The Movement and Concentration of Retail Trade in Metropolitan Areas" and "Decentralization of Retail Trade in Boston," *Journal of Marketing*, Vol. V, No. 4, April, 1941, pp. 395-401, and Vol. VI, No. 3, January, 1942, pp. 281-286.

(21) Edward A. Duddy and David A. Revzan, *Marketing: An Institutional Approach* (New York: McGraw-Hill Book Co., 1947).

(22) E. T. Grether, "Geographical Price Policies in the Grocery Trade, 1941," *Journal of Marketing*, Vol. VIII, No. 4, April, 1944, pp. 417-422.

(23) E. T. Grether, *Price Control Under Fair Trade Legislation* (New York: Oxford University Press, 1939).

(24) Robert Murray Haig, "Toward an Understanding of the Metropolis," *Quarterly Journal of Economics*, Vol. XL, February and May, 1926, pp. 179-208 and 402-434.

(25) J. M. Keynes, *The General Theory of Employment, Interest and Money* (New York: Harcourt, Brace & Co., 1936).

(26) Robert W. Leeper, *Lewin's Topological and Vector Psychology: A Digest and a Critique* (Eugene: University of Oregon, 1943).

(27) Kurt Lewin, *Principles of Topological Psychology* (New York: McGraw-Hill Book Co., 1936).

(28) Kurt Lewin, "The Conceptual Representation and the Measurement of Psychological Forces," *Contributions to Psychological Theory*, Vol. I, No. 5 (Durham: Duke University Press, 1938).

(29) George Lundberg, *Marketing and Social Organization* (Philadelphia: Curtis Publishing Co., 1945).

(30) George Lundberg and Mary Steele, "Social Attraction Patterns in a Village," *Sociometry*, Vol. I, January-April, 1938, pp. 375-419.

(31) Harold M. Mayer, "Patterns and Recent Trends of Chicago's Outlying Business Centers," iJournal of Land and Public Utility Economics, Vol. XVIII, No. 1, February, 1942, pp. 4-16.

(32) Elton Mayo, *Human Problems of an Industrial Civilization* (Boston: Harvard University, Division of Research, 2nd ed., 1946).

(33) Edmund D. McGarry, *The Functions of Marketing*. (Manuscript).

(34) Bertil Ohlin, *Interregional and International Trade* (Cambridge: Harvard University Press, 1935).

(35) John Paver and Miller McClintock, *Traffic and Trade* (New York: McGraw-Hill Book Co., 1935).

(36) Charles F. Phillips, *Marketing* (Boston: Houghton Mifflin Co., 1938).

(37) William J. Reilly, *Methods for the Study of Retail Relationships* (Austin: University of Texas, 1929).

(38) William B. Ricketts, *Testing and Measuring Advertising Effectiveness*. (Manuscript).

(39) Joan Robinson, *The Economics of Imperfect Competition* (London: Macmillan Co., 1933).

(40) A. W. Shaw, "Some Problems in Market Distribution," *Quarterly Journal of Economics*, August, 1912, pp. 703-765.

(41) John Q. Stewart, "Concerning 'Social Physics'," *Scientific American*, May, 1948, pp. 20-23.

(42) John Q. Stewart, "Empirical Mathematical Rules Concerning the Distribution and Equilibrium of Population," *Geographical Review*, Vol. XXXVII, No. 3, July, 1947, pp. 461-485.

(43) Frank Strohkarck and Katherine Phelps, "The Mechanics of Constructing a Market Area Map," *Journal of Marketing*, Vol. XII, No. 4, April, 1948, pp. 493-496. (A description of the method used by the Curtis Publishing Company in constructing its map, "Market Areas for Shopping Lines.")

(44) Traffic Audit Bureau, *Methods for the Evaluation of Outdoor Advertising* (New York: Traffic Audit Bureau, 1946. This study was done under the direction of Victor H. Pelz.)

(45) Robert Triffin, *Monopolistic Competition and General Equilibrium Theory* (Cambridge: Harvard University Press, 1940).

(46) Roland S. Vaile, *Economics of Advertising* (New York: Ronald Press Co., 1927).

(47) John Von Neumann and Oskar Morgenstern, *Theory of Games and Economic Behavior* (Princeton: Princeton University Press, 1944).

(48) Chester I. Barnard, *Organization and Management* (Harvard University Press, 1948).

(49) J. M. Clark, *Alternative to Serfdom* (Alfred A. Knopf,1948).

(50) Oswald Knauth, *Managerial Enterprise* (W. W. Norton, 1948).

Marketing Management

Joseph T. Plummer

The Concept and Application of Life Style Segmentation

The combination of two useful concepts provides a unique and important view of the market.

A NEW dimension for segmenting markets has been developed in recent years. This new method, called life style segmentation, has been useful for marketing and advertising planning. The purpose of this article is to describe the theory behind life style segmentation and discuss how it has been and can be applied.

Life style segmentation is the marriage of two concepts into a single system. One of the concepts is life style patterns and the other is market segmentation. In order to discuss the uses of life style segmentation, it is important first to examine briefly each component of the system and then the uses of the total system.

Life Style Patterns

The concept of life style patterns and its relationship to marketing was introduced in 1963 by William Lazer. He defined life style patterns as: "a systems concept. It refers to a distinctive mode of living in its aggregate and broadest sense. . . . It embodies the patterns that develop and emerge from the dynamics of living in a society."[1]

Since 1963, methods of measuring life style patterns and their relationship to consumer behavior have been developed and refined. The most widely used approach to life style measurement has been AIO (Activities, Interests, and Opinions) rating statements.[2] Life style as used in life style segmentation research measures people's activities in terms of (1) how they spend their time; (2) their interests, what they place importance on in their immediate surroundings; (3) their opinions in terms of their view of themselves and the world around them; and (4) some basic characteristics such as their stage in life cycle, income, education, and where they live. Table 1 lists the elements included in each major dimension of life style.

About the author. Joseph T. Plummer is vice president, special task force, at Leo Burnett U.S.A., Chicago.

The basic premise of life style research is that the more you know and understand about your customers the more effectively you can communicate and market to them.

Over the years, a number of constructs have been useful in better understanding the customer. The most popular constructs have been demographics, social class, and psychological characteristics. Demographics have received broad acceptance and lend themselves easily to quantification and consumer classification. However, demographics lack richness and often need to be supplemented with other data. Social class adds more depth to demographics, but it, too, often needs to be supplemented in order to obtain meaningful insights into audiences. Lastly, psychological characteristics are often rich but may lack reliability when applied to mass audiences. In addition, the findings from psychological scales frequently are difficult to implement.

The new construct, life style patterns, combines the virtues of demographics with the richness and dimensionality of psychological characteristics and depth research. Life style deals with everyday, behaviorally oriented facets of people as well as their feelings, attitudes, and opinions. It tells us things about our customers that most researchers did not really attempt to quantify in the past, when the focus was on the product or on widely used measures of classification such as demographics.

---

1 William Lazer, "Life Style Concepts and Marketing," *Toward Scientific Marketing*, Stephen Greyser, ed. (Chicago: American Marketing Assn., 1963), pp. 140-151.

2 William Wells and Doug Tigert, "Activities, Interests and Opinions," *Journal of Advertising Research*, Vol. 11 (August 1971), pp. 27-35, Joseph T. Plummer, "Life Style Patterns: A New Construct for Mass Communications Research," Journal of Broadcasting, Vol. 16 (Fall-Winter 1972), pp. 79-89; and Joseph T. Plummer, "Life Style Patterns and Commercial Bank Credit Card Usage," *Journal of Marketing*, Vol. 35 (April 1971), pp. 35-42.

The Journal of Marketing
Vol. 38 (January 1974), pp. 33-37.

The Concept and Application of Life Style Segmentation / 51

TABLE 1

LIFE STYLE DIMENSIONS

ACTIVITIES	INTERESTS	OPINIONS	DEMOGRAPHICS
Work	Family	Themselves	Age
Hobbies	Home	Social issues	Education
Social events	Job	Politics	Income
Vacation	Community	Business	Occupation
Entertainment	Recreation	Economics	Family Size
Club membership	Fashion	Education	Dwelling
Community	Food	Products	Geography
Shopping	Media	Future	City size
Sports	Achievements	Culture	Stage in life cycle

Life style attempts to answer questions like: What do women think about the job of housekeeping? Are they interested in contemporary fashions? Do they participate in community activities? Are they optimistic about the future? Do they see themselves as homebodies or swingers? When the answers to questions like these correlate significantly with product usage, magazine readership, television program preferences, or other mass communication variables, a picture emerges that goes beyond flat demographic descriptions, program ratings, or product-specific measures. Life style patterns provide a broader, more three-dimensional view of customers, so that one can think about them more intelligently in terms of the most relevant product positioning, communication, media, and promotion.

Market Segmentation

As long as people have been selling products to one another there has been some form of market segmentation. In the early days of marketing, segmentation (i.e., selection of a group or groups with common characteristics out of the total) was based on rather general dimensions such as buyers vs. nonbuyers, men vs. women, and the like. Refinements have been made over the years to adjust to the increasing complexity in the marketplace and the rise of mass marketing. One of these segmented buyers in terms of light users, moderate users, and heavy users. This segmentation basis was adopted when sellers realized that in many product categories, the heavy user segment accounted for as much as two-thirds of the business.[3]

Whether sophisticated or simple, segmentation exists and has been used for a long time. Marketing management knows that no single population is homogeneous and that there is no "average man." People are different and do things for different reasons. Thus there is a need to identify the differences and group them in such a way that a better understanding of the population under consideration emerges. The focus in segmentation is on the differences between identified groups on certain criteria, such as brand purchasing, brand attitudes, media patterns, and so on.

Segmentation is useful because it moves beyond total scores or averages and reveals important differences that can be acted upon. If, for example, research indicated that a new concept received an overall rating of only 3.2 on a 5-point scale among a hundred people, the concept might be dropped. However, if the sample were segmented into light, medium, and heavy users, and the new ratings developed for the concept were 2.1 among light users, 3.3 among medium users, and 4.7 among heavy users, the evaluation of this concept would be different. In this way, segmentation can reveal important insights that averages often hide. Segmentation is particularly useful in developing marketing objectives because it identifies important subgroups in the population as more efficient marketing targets than others.[4]

All of this discussion leads to the question: "Segmentation of the market is useful, but what concepts are the most useful in segmenting the market?" In order to answer this question, we first need to examine what the various approaches to segmenting the market are and then discuss the criteria to be used in selecting among these approaches.

Historically, there have been two general approaches to market segmentation: "people" oriented and "product" oriented. The people-oriented segmentation approaches have utilized various dimensions along which to measure people and then relate the people segments to the product or service. Those people-oriented segmentation dimensions that have enjoyed widespread usage are demo-

---

[3] Clark Wilson, "Homemaker Living Patterns and Marketplace Behavior," in *New Ideas for Successful Marketing*, John Wright and Jac Goldstucker, eds. (Chicago: American Marketing Assn., 1966), pp. 305-332.

[4] Daniel Yankelovich, "New Criteria for Market Segmentation," *Harvard Business Review*, Vol. 42 (March-April 1964), p. 83; and William Cunningham and William Crissy, "Market Segmentation by Motivation and Attitudes," *Journal of Marketing Research*, Vol. 9 (February 1972), pp. 100-103.

graphics, social class, stage in life cycle, product usage, innovativeness, and psychological characteristics. The product-oriented segmentation approaches have been designed to measure product characteristics, either directly or indirectly through consumers, in order to better understand the structure of the market. Those product-oriented segmentation dimensions that have enjoyed broad usage include: product benefits, product usage occasions, value, ingredients or taste, perceived attributes, and advertising appeals.

The criteria that should be employed in selecting a useful segmentation approach to aid in marketing and advertising planning are three-fold:

1. Is the segmentation approach based on theory consistent with the objectives?

2. Does the segmentation reveal significant differences between the defined segments on a usage or purchasing measure?

3. Can these differences be understood and acted upon to improve business?

The most recent trend in market segmentation has been in the direction of more sophisticated procedures and product-oriented segmentations. So often, however, the segments developed from a study on one product category have little or no relevance to another product category. Product-benefit, or attribute, segmentation has been useful to marketers and advertisers and is often the basis for multibrand development. As Wells has pointed out, however, these measures are still inadequate in their description and analysis of the consumer as a person. It is in this area that life style data—activities, interests, and opinions—have proved their importance as a means of "duplicating" the consumer for the marketing researcher.[5]

Life Style Segmentation

Life style is used to segment the marketplace because it provides a broad, everyday view of consumers. When combined with the theory of typologies[6] and clustering methods,[7] life style segmentation can generate identifiable whole persons rather than isolated fragments. Life style segmentation begins with people instead of products and classifies them into different life style types, each characterized by a unique style of living based on a wide range of activities, interests, and opinions. The rationale for this approach is that consumers have hundreds of products in their world in an average week. Although the product is most important to the marketer; to the consumer, he is most important.

The analytical procedure of relating the life style segments to a particular market is a two-step process. In this two-step process, life style segmentation adds important new dimensions to available information on consumers and other market segmentation approaches.

Step 1

The usual first step in the analysis of life style segmentation information is to determine which of the life style segments are best from the standpoint of efficiently producing the greatest number of customers for a brand. The selection of the important segments is derived by examining several product dimensions: (1) usage of the category; (2) frequency of usage of the category, that is, who the heavy users, moderate users, and light users are; (3) brand usage and brand share (if available); and (4) product attitudes and usage patterns.

Ideally, the key segments selected would have high product penetration and would contain the highest proportions of heavy users, indicating greater volume potential, a healthy position for the brand or brands under consideration, and favorable brand attitudes. This type of ideal situation would make the selection of target segments quite easy. Unfortunately, this ideal situation seldom occurs in reality.

The author's experience with life style segmentation has shown that there tend to be three basic results in relationships between life style segments and the marketing data.

First, two or three life style segments account for 60% or more of the total business in that category. This means that these segments (types of people) are crucial to success or failure in the category. They are the ones who need to be appealed to, reached through the media, and concentrated on in marketing.

Second, a number of segments contain important levels of heavy users of the category, and a few segments are relatively unimportant. Here one needs to go beyond the consumption data to examine the relative positions of the brands. Where is a brand strong and where is it weak? If a brand profile matches the heavy-user profiles by segments, then the task becomes one of maintaining the current position and perhaps expanding it. It may be that the segments where a brand is weak are different people with different needs, which might suggest a second brand.

If, on the other hand, a brand profile does not match the heavier-using segments very well, there is a need to determine how to capture some business from those segments where competition is doing much better.

Third, there are no significant differences in consumption among the segments, but definite attitude, product function, and life style similarities exist between groups

5 William D. Wells, "Seven Questions about Life Style and Psychographics," (Paper presented at the 55th International Marketing Congress, New York City, April 1972), p. 4.

6 William Stephenson, *The Study of Behavior* (Chicago: The University of Chicago Press, 1953); Carl Rogers, On Becoming a Person (Boston: Houghton Mifflin Co., 1961); and Joseph T. Plummer, "Audience Research in TV Program Development," *Educational Broadcast Review*, Vol. 2 (June 1968), pp. 23-30.

7 Richard Johnson, "How Can You Tell if Things Are Really Clustered?" (Paper presented to the American Statistical Association, New York, February 15, 1972).

of segments. This type of outcome may be the result of two factors: no one brand has attempted to "segment itself," or the product is such that once a purchase is made the individual no longer contributes to the market. It is in this type of situation where creativity and intuition play an important role in selecting segments on which to focus advertising and marketing efforts just on the basis of attitude, usage pattern, or life style similarities. There are really no guidelines for target selection in this situation. In some instances, one must try another basis for segmenting the market and hope the alternative approach will show significant and more useful differences in consumption patterns.

Step 2

Once the target segments have been selected, one can begin to define and describe the target customer in more depth and with more understanding of "why." At this point, thinking can begin on how to reach and communicate more efficiently and relevantly to the target customers (who are usually a composite of several segments). The insights and knowledge of the key life style segments will aid in determining the product positioning, the advertising, the media strategy, and the promotion strategy.

Benefits of Life Style Segmentation

Definition of the Key Target

Invariably, life style segmentation provides a redefinition of the key target. Instead of defining the target in demographic terms (i.e., middle-aged housewives with a large family and average income) or in product usage terms (i.e., the frequent user, the price buyer, the vacation traveler, etc.), life style segmentation demonstrates the diversity of those definitions, helps tighten them up, and provides new definitions. In addition to middle-aged white collar or blue collar housewives, life style provides definitions like "housewife role haters," "old-fashioned homebodies," and "active affluent urbanites."

Also, since life style segmentation involves many factors simultaneously, it has shown that certain demographics go together to define targets which, considered independently (i.e., one at a time), might not merge. Life style segmentation provides a richer redefinition of the key target audiences.

Provides a New View of the Market

In the past, it was often difficult to determine the structure of the market in terms of usage patterns. Because life style segmentation provides an overview of the market in a multidimensional sense, one can often learn a good deal about

8 Joseph T. Plummer, "Application of Life Style Research to the Creation of Advertising Campaigns," in *Life Style and Psychographics*, William Wells, ed. (in press).

the structure of the market. One such learning experience occurred where there had been a running controversy for years on whether the target was parents or children. Life style segmentation demonstrated that the target was heavy using households where both parents and children consumed more than average.

In another situation with which the author is familiar, where a marketer was involved in three closely allied product categories, life style segmentation showed them to be really three different categories. Although the demographic profiles of the heavy users for each category were well known and not dramatically different, life style segmentation indicated how different in life style and product orientation the key segments for each category were. This finding has helped lead to a different product positioning and product improvements for each category.

Product Positioning

Life style information can be used to complement more commonly used information such as product benefits, unique ingredients, and competitive advantages in positioning a product to customers.

Life style information can be employed to position a product based on the inferences drawn from the portrait of the consumer both in terms of his basic needs and how the product fits into his life. If, for example, the person's life style indicates a strong need to be with other people in a variety of settings, it may be that the product can be positioned to help satisfy this social need. Or one might learn how a product fits into a person's life. It may be that the basic function of a product is convenience. But if it is found that the target consumer enjoys cooking and is not convenience oriented, it may be appropriate to position the product as a shortcut in creating more elegant dishes.

Communication

Although there are many ways in which life style can be useful in the creation of advertising,[8] there are four major concepts that one can use in applying the findings for the creation of advertising communication. The most obvious one is that, for the creative person, life style data provide a richer and more life-like picture of the target consumer than do demographics. This enables the writer or artist to have in his own mind a better idea of the type of person he is trying to communicate with about the product. This picture also gives the creative person clues about what may or may not be appropriate to the life style of the target consumer. This has implications for the setting of the advertising, the type and appearance of the characters, the nature of the music and artwork, whether or not fantasy can be used, and so on.

A second and similar concept that can be used in applying the life style data are the insights into the basic *tone of voice* for the advertising. The creative user can get a sense of whether the tone should be serious or humorous, authoritative or cooperative, contemporary or traditional, from the life style dimensions of the target user portrait.

The third major concept which is helpful in developing advertising from life style information is that of the rewards people seek in their activities and interests. Do the target consumers obtain *rewards* by doing something nice for others, or are their rewards derived from more self-centered activities and interests?. If the target consumer obtains rewards through others, then it might be more relevant to portray her as doing the right thing for her family by purchasing the product.

The final major concept which is useful in developing advertising from life style portraits of consumers is the notion of the number and types of *roles* in which the target consumer sees himself. If the female consumer sees her major role as a housekeeper rather than wife or mother or socialite, then it would seem most appropriate to utilize that role in communicating to her. She would have a difficult time identifying or, perhaps, even believing spokesmen not congruent with that role.

Helps Develop Sounder Overall Marketing and Media Strategies

In addition to providing input into the "who" of a marketing plan, life style segmentation often provides insights into the amount of concentration in a market: how difficult conversion of nonusers might be, the potential role of promotion, and the potential role of new products. For example, in one product category it was quite evident that every brand except one was targeted at the same life style segment. Although important, this segment comprised less than half of the users. Here was an instance where a marketing opportunity existed to target a new brand or reposition an older one at the other, less-concentrated segments.

The author is aware of one situation in which life style segmentation was particularly useful in basic media strategy, when an important segment appeared to be more print-oriented and a light daytime television viewer. Using the demographics of that life style segment, further analysis of other media data suggested that a move to print media for part of the budget would be a good one to reach these important consumers.[9]

Can Suggest New Product Opportunities

Because life style segmentation provides a great deal of information on the different needs of types of people and the potential size of those "types" in the population, one can examine existing products to see how well they are meeting the needs of consumer types. In one situation, several segments had a need for more and better alternatives for their children's "spur of the moment meals." Given these unmet needs, some sense of the potential, and a rich definition of the target segments, it was not too difficult to develop some new products which currently are being tested.

Helps Explain the "Why" of a Product or Brand Situation

Knowledge of each segment's life style, attitudes, and usage patterns enables the marketer in many situations to explain or generate hypotheses on why certain segments use or do not use a particular product or brand very heavily. It is often because of several factors interacting rather than a single factor. Without the holistic view of the segments, it would be difficult to observe these interactions and put them into perspective. These insights are helpful in deciding not to appeal to particular segments when there are several "barriers" to conversion or increased usage. On the more positive side, these insights often can help explain why two rather similar brands are both doing well. Frequently, it is because they are used equally for different sets of motivations and reason by different types of people. Life style segmentation often uncovers this type of situation.

Conclusion

Life style segmentation is useful because it provides a unique and important view of the market. It begins with the people—their life styles and motivations—and then determines how various marketing factors fit into their lives. This perspective often provides fresh insights into the market and gives a more three-dimensional view of the target consumers.

This article has described the theory underlying life style segmentation, a two-step analytic process, and uses which have been made of the data. This unique and detailed knowledge of consumers has been a useful input to marketing and advertising planning for many of the companies that have been involved in life style segmentation studies.

---

9 "How Nestle Uses Psychographics," *Media Decisions*, Vol. 8 (July 1973), pp. 68-71.

Russell I. Haley

Benefit Segmentation: A Decision-oriented Research Tool

According to this article, most techniques of market segmentation rely only on DESCRIPTIVE factors pertaining to purchasers and are not efficient predictors of future buyer behavior. The author proposes an approach whereby market segments are delineated first on the basis of factors with a CAUSAL relationship to future purchase behavior. The belief underlying this segmentation strategy is that the benefits which people are seeking in consuming a given product are the basic reasons for the existence of true market segments.

MARKET segmentation has been steadily moving toward center stage as a topic of discussion in marketing and research circles. Hardly a conference passes without at least one session devoted to it. Moreover, in March the American Management Association held a three-day conference entirely concerned with various aspects of the segmentation problem.

According to Wendell Smith, "Segmentation is based upon developments on the demand side of the market and represents a rational and more precise adjustment of product and marketing effort to consumer or user requirements."[1] The idea that all markets can be profitably segmented has now received almost as widespread acceptance as the marketing concept itself. However, problems remain. In the extreme, a marketer can divide up his market in as many ways as he can describe his prospects. If he wishes, he can define a left-handed segment, or a blue-eyed segment, or a German-speaking segment. Consequently, current discussion revolves largely around which

of the virtually limitless alternatives is likely to be most productive.

Segmentation Methods

Several varieties of market segmentation have been popular in the recent past. At least three kinds have achieved some degree of prominence. Historically, perhaps the first type to exist was geographic segmentation. Small manufacturers who wished to limit their investments, or whose distribution channels were not large enough to cover the entire country, segmented the U.S. market, in effect, by selling their products only in certain areas.

However, as more and more brands became national, the second major system of segmentation—demographic segmentation—became popular. Under this philosophy targets were defined as younger people, men, or families with children. Unfortunately, a number of recent studies have shown that demographic variables such as age, sex, income, occupation and race are, in general, poor predictors of behavior and, consequently, less than optimum bases for segmentation strategies.[2]

More recently, a third type of segmentation has come

About the author. Russell I. Haley is Vice President and Corporate Research Director of D'Arcy Advertising in New York City. Prior to his current position he was Vice President and Associate Director of the Marketing and Research Department at Grey Advertising. While there, he developed new methods for measuring attitudes, a unique way of segmenting markets by attitude patterns, and improved methods of conducting large-scale market tests. Mr. Haley received his M.B.A. from Columbia in marketing and statistics.

Mr. Haley is a past president of the Cleveland Chapter of the American Statistical Association. He is a member of the American Marketing Association, the American Association for Public Opinion Research, and the Executive Committee of the Copy Research Council. Mr. Haley is currently Chairman of an A.R.F. Committee dealing with attitude measurement and is teaching at Rutgers University.

1 Wendell R. Smith, "Product Differentiation and Market Segmentation as Alternative Product Strategies," *Journal of Marketing*, Vol. XXI (July, 1956), pp. 3-8.

2 Ronald E. Frank, "Correlates of Buying Behavior for Grocery Products," *Journal of Marketing*, Vol. 31 (October, 1967), pp. 48-53; Ronald E. Frank, William Massy, and Harper W. Boyd, Jr., "Correlates of Grocery Product Consumption Rates," *Journal of Marketing Research*, Vol. 4 (May, 1967), pp. 184-190; and Clark Wilson, "Homemaker Living Patterns and Marketplace Behavior—A Psychometric Approach," in John S. Wright and Jac L. Goldstucker, Editors, *New Ideas for Successful Marketing*, Proceedings of 1966 World Congress (Chicago: American Marketing Association, June, 1966), pp. 305-331.

into increasing favor—volume segmentation. The so-called "heavy half" theory, popularized by Dik Twedt of the Oscar Mayer Company,[3] points out that in most product categories one-half of the consumers account for around 80% of the consumption. If this is true, the argument goes, shouldn't knowledgeable marketers concentrate their efforts on these high-volume consumers? Certainly they are the most *valuable* consumers.

The trouble with this line of reasoning is that not all heavy consumers are usually available to the same brand—because they are not all seeking the same kinds of benefits from a product. For example, heavy coffee drinkers consist of two types of consumers—those who drink chain store brands and those who drink premium brands. The chain store customers feel that all coffees are basically alike and, because they drink so much coffee, they feel it is sensible to buy a relatively inexpensive brand. The premium brand buyers, on the other hand, feel that the few added pennies which coffees like Yuban, Martinson's, Chock Full O'Nuts, and Savarin cost are more than justified by their fuller taste. Obviously, these two groups of people, although they are both members of the "heavy half" segment, are not equally good prospects for any one brand, nor can they be expected to respond to the same advertising claims.

These three systems of segmentation have been used because they provide helpful guidance in the use of certain marketing tools. For example, geographic segmentation, because it describes the market in a discrete way, provides definite direction in media purchases. Spot TV, spot radio, and newspapers can be bought for the geographical segment selected for concentrated effort. Similarly, demographic segmentation allows media to be bought more efficiently since demographic data on readers, viewers, and listeners are readily available for most media vehicles. Also, in some product categories demographic variables are extremely helpful in differentiating users from non-users, although they are typically less helpful in distinguishing between the users of various brands. The heavy-half philosophy is especially effective in directing dollars toward the most important parts of the market.

However, each of these three systems of segmentation is handicapped by an underlying disadvantage inherent in its nature. All are based on an ex-post facto analysis of the kinds of people who make up various segments of a market. They rely on *descriptive* factors rather than *causal* factors. For this reason they are not efficient predictors of future buying behavior, and it is future buying behavior that is of central interest to marketers.

Benefit Segmentation

An approach to market segmentation whereby it is possible to identify market segments by causal factors rather than descriptive factors, might be called "benefit segmentation." The belief underlying this segmentation strategy is that the benefits which people are seeking in consuming a given product are the basic reasons for the existence of true market segments. Experience with this approach has shown that benefits sought by consumers determine their behavior much more accurately than do demographic characteristics or volume of consumption.

This does not mean that the kinds of data gathered in more traditional types of segmentation are not useful. Once people have been classified into segments in accordance with the benefits they are seeking, each segment is contrasted with all of the other segments in terms of its demography, its volume of consumption, its brand perceptions, its media habits, its personality and life-style, and so forth. In this way, a reasonably deep understanding of the people who make up each segment can be obtained. And by capitalizing on this understanding, it is possible to reach them, to talk to them in their own terms, and to present a product in the most favorable light possible.

The benefit segmentation approach is not new. It has been employed by a number of America's largest corporations since it was introduced in 1961.[4] However, case histories have been notably absent from the literature because most studies have been contracted for privately, and have been treated confidentially.

The benefit segmentation approach is based upon being able to measure consumer value systems in detail, together with what the consumer thinks about various brands in the product category of interest. While this concept seems simple enough, operationally it is very complex. There is no simple straightforward way of handling the volumes of data that have to be generated. Computers and sophisticated multivariate attitude measurement techniques are a necessity.

Several alternative statistical approaches can be employed, among them the so-called "Q" technique of factor analysis, multi-dimensional scaling, and other distance measures.[5] All of these methods relate the ratings of each respondent to those of every other respondent and then seek clusters of individuals with similar rating patterns. If the items rated are potential consumer benefits, the clusters that emerge will be groups of people who attach similar degrees of importance to the various benefits. Whatever the statistical approach selected, the end result of the analysis is likely to be between three and seven consumer segments, each representing a potentially productive focal point for marketing efforts.

Each segment is identified by the benefits it is seeking. However, it is the *total configuration* of the benefits

---

3 Dik Warren Twedt, "Some Practical Applications of the 'Heavy Half' Theory" (New York: Advertising Research Foundation 10th Annual Conference, October 6, 1964).

4 Russell I. Haley, "Experimental Research on Attitudes Toward Shampoos," an unpublished paper (February, 1961).

5 Ronald E. Frank and Paul E. Green, "Numerical Taxonomy in Marketing Analysis: A Review Article," *Journal of Marketing Research*, Vol. V (February, 1968), pp. 83-98.

TABLE 1

TOOTHPASTE MARKET SEGMENT DESCRIPTION

Segment Name:	The Sensory Segment	The Sociables	The Worriers	The Independent Segment
Principal benefit sought:	Flavor, product appearance	Brightness of teeth	Decay prevention	Price
Demographic strengths:	Children	Teens, young people	Large families	Men
Special behavioral characteristics:	Users of spearmint flavored toothpaste	Smokers	Heavy users	Heavy users
Brands disproportionately favored:	Colgate, Stripe	Macleans, Plus White, Ultra Brite	Crest	Brands on sale
Personality characteristics:	High self-involvement	High sociability	High hypochondriasis	High autonomy
Life-style characteristics:	Hedonistic	Active	Conservative	Value-oriented

sought which differentiates one segment from another, rather than the fact that one segment is seeking one particular benefit and another a quite different benefit. Individual benefits are likely to have appeal for several segments. In fact, the research that has been done thus far suggests that most people would like as many benefits as possible. However, the *relative* importance they attach to individual benefits can differ importantly and, accordingly, can be used as an effective lever in segmenting markets.

Of course, it is possible to determine benefit segments intuitively as well as with computers and sophisticated research methods. The kinds of brilliant insights which produced the Mustang and the first 100-millimeter cigarette have a good chance of succeeding whenever marketers are able to tap an existing benefit segment.

However, intuition can be very expensive when it is mistaken. Marketing history is replete with examples of products which someone felt could not miss. Over the longer term, systematic benefit segmentation research is likely to have a higher proportion of success.

But is benefit segmentation practical? And is it truly operational? The answer to both of these questions is "yes." In effect, the crux of the problem of choosing the best segmentation system is to determine which has the greatest number of practical marketing implications. An example should show that benefit segmentation has a much wider range of implications than alternative forms of segmentation.

An Example of Benefit Segmentation

While the material presented here is purely illustrative to protect the competitive edge of companies who have invested in studies of this kind, it is based on actual segmentation studies. Consequently, it is quite typical of the kinds of things which are normally learned in the course of a benefit segmentation study.

The toothpaste market has been chosen as an example because it is one with which everyone is familiar. Let us as-

sume that a benefit segmentation study has been done and four major segments have been identified—one particularly concerned with decay prevention, one with brightness of teeth, one with the flavor and appearance of the product, and one with price. A relatively large amount of supplementary information has also been gathered (Table 1) about the people in each of these segments.

The decay prevention segment, it has been found, contains a disproportionately large number of families with children. They are seriously concerned about the possibility of cavities and show a definite preference for fluoride toothpaste. This is reinforced by their personalities. They tend to be a little hypochondriacal and, in their life-styles, they are less socially-oriented than some of the other groups. This segment has been named The Worriers.

The second segment, comprised of people who show concern for the brightness of their teeth, is quite different. It includes a relatively large group of young marrieds. They smoke more than average. This is where the swingers are. They are strongly social and their life-style patterns are very active. This is probably the group to which toothpastes such as Macleans or Plus White or Ultra Brite would appeal. This segment has been named The Sociables.

In the third segment, the one which is particularly concerned with the flavor and appearance of the product, a large portion of the brand deciders are children. Their use of spearmint toothpaste is well above average. Stripe has done relatively well in this segment. They are more ego-centered than other segments, and their life-style is outgoing but not to the extent of the swingers. They will be called The Sensory Segment.

The fourth segment, the price-oriented segment, shows a predominance of men. It tends to be above average in terms of toothpaste usage. People in this segment see very few meaningful differences between brands. They switch more frequently than people in other segments and tend to buy a brand on sale. In terms of personality, they are cognitive and they are independent. They like to think for themselves and make brand choices on the basis of their judgment. They will be called The Independent Segment.

Marketing Implications of Benefit Segmentation Studies

Both copy directions and media choices will show sharp differences depending upon which of these segments is chosen as the target—The Worriers, The Sociables, The Sensory Segment, or The Independent Segment. For example, the tonality of the copy will be light if The Sociable Segment or The Sensory Segment is to be addressed. It will be more serious if the copy is aimed at The Worriers. And if The Independent Segment is selected, it will probably be desirable to use rational, two-sided arguments. Of course, to talk to this group at all it will be necessary to have either a price edge or some kind of demonstrable product superiority.

The depth-of-sell reflected by the copy will also vary, depending upon the segment which is of interest. It will be fairly intensive for The Worrier Segment and for The Independent Segment, but much more superficial and mood-oriented for The Sociable and Sensory Segments.

Likewise, the setting will vary. It will focus on the product for The Sensory Group, on socially-oriented situations for The Sociable Group, and perhaps on demonstration or on competitive comparisons for The Independent Group.

Media environments will also be tailored to the segments chosen as targets. Those with serious environments will be used for The Worrier and Independent Segments, and those with youthful, modern and active environments for The Sociable and The Sensory Groups. For example, it might be logical to use a larger proportion of television for The Sociable and Sensory Groups, while The Worriers and Independents might have heavier print schedules.

The depth-of-sell needed will also be reflected in the media choices. For The Worrier and Rational Segments longer commercials—perhaps 60-second commercials—would be indicated, while for the other two groups shorter commercials and higher frequency would be desirable.

Of course, in media selection the facts that have been gathered about the demographic characteristics of the segment chosen as the target would also be taken into consideration.

The information in Table 1 also has packaging implications. For example, it might be appropriate to have colorful packages for The Sensory Segment, perhaps aqua (to indicate fluoride) for The Worrier Group, and gleaming white for The Sociable Segment because of their interest in bright white teeth.

It should be readily apparent that the kinds of information normally obtained in the course of a benefit segmentation study have a wide range of marketing implications. Sometimes they are useful in suggesting physical changes in a product. For example, one manufacturer discovered that his product was well suited to the needs of his chosen target with a single exception in the area of flavor. He was able to make a relatively inexpensive modification in his product and thereby strengthen his market position.

The new product implications of benefit segmentation studies are equally apparent. Once a marketer understands the kinds of segments that exist in his market, he is often able to see new product opportunities or particularly effective ways of positioning the products emerging from his research and development operation.

Similarly, benefit segmentation information has been found helpful in providing direction in the choice of compatible point-of-purchase materials and in the selection of the kinds of sales promotions which are most likely to be effective for any given market target.

Generalizations from Benefit Segmentation Studies

A number of generalizations are possible on the basis of the major benefit segmentation studies which have been conducted thus far. For example, the following general rules of thumb have become apparent:

• It is easier to take advantage of market segments that already exist than to create new ones. Some time ago the strategy of product differentiation was heavily emphasized in marketing textbooks. Under this philosophy it was believed that a manufacturer was more or less able to create new market segments at will by making his product somewhat different from those of his competitors. Now it is generally recognized that fewer costly errors will be made if money is first invested in consumer research aimed at determining the present contours of the market. Once this knowledge is available, it is usually most efficient to tailor marketing strategies to existing consumer-need patterns.

• No brand can expect to appeal to all consumers. The very act of attracting one segment may automatically alienate others. A corollary to this principle is that any marketer who wishes to cover a market fully must offer consumers more than a single brand. The flood of new brands which have recently appeared on the market is concrete recognition of this principle.

• A company's brands can sometimes cannibalize each other but need not necessarily do so. It depends on whether or not they are positioned against the same segment of the market. Ivory Snow sharply reduced Ivory Flakes' share of market, and the Ford Falcon cut deeply into the sales of the standard size Ford because, in each case, the products were competing in the same segments. Later on, for the same companies, the Mustang was successfully introduced with comparatively little damage to Ford; and the success of Crest did not have a disproportionately adverse effect on Gleem's market position because, in these cases, the segments to which the products appealed were different.

- New and old products alike should be designed to fit *exactly* the needs of some segment of the market. In other words, they should be aimed at people seeking a specific combination of benefits. It is a marketing truism that you sell people one at a time—that you have to get *someone* to buy your product before you get *anyone* to buy it. A substantial group of people must be interested in your specific set of benefits before you can make progress in a market. Yet, many products attempt to aim at two or more segments simultaneously. As a result, they are not able to maximize their appeal to any segment of the market, and they run the risk of ending up with a dangerously fuzzy brand image.

- Marketers who adopt a benefit segmentation strategy have a distinct competitive edge. If a benefit segment can be located which is seeking exactly the kinds of satisfactions that one marketer's brand can offer better than any other brand, the marketer can almost certainly dominate the purchases of that segment. Furthermore, if his competitors are looking at the market in terms of traditional types of segments, they may not even be aware of the existence of the benefit segment which he has chosen as his market target. If they are ignorant in this sense, they will be at a loss to explain the success of his brand. And it naturally follows that if they do not understand the reasons for his success, the kinds of people buying his brand, and the benefits they are obtaining from it, his competitors will find it very difficult to successfully attack the marketer's position.

- An understanding of the benefit segments which exist within a market can be used to advantage when competitors introduce new products. Once the way in which consumers are positioning the new product has been determined, the likelihood that it will make major inroads into segments of interest can be assessed, and a decision can be made on whether or not counteractions of any kind are required. If the new product appears to be assuming an ambiguous position, no money need be invested in defensive measures. However, if it appears that the new product is ideally suited to the needs of an important segment of the market, the manufacturer in question can introduce a new competitive product of his own, modify the physical properties of existing brands, change his advertising strategy, or take whatever steps appear appropriate.

Types of Segments Uncovered Through Benefit Segmentation Studies

It is difficult to generalize about the types of segments which are apt to be discovered in the course of a benefit segmentation study. To a large extent, the segments which have been found have been unique to the product categories being analyzed. However, a few types of segments have appeared in two or more private studies. Among them are the following:

The Status Seeker	...a group which is very much concerned with the prestige of the brands purchased.
The Swinger	...a group which tries to be modern and up to date in all of its activities. Brand choices reflect this orientation.
The Conservative	...a group which prefers to stick to large successful companies, and popular brands.
The Rational Man	...a group which looks for benefits such as economy, value, durability, etc.
The Inner-directed Man	...a group which is especially concerned with self-concept. Members consider themselves to have a sense of humor, to be independent and/or honest.
The Hedonist	...a group which is concerned primarily with sensory benefits.

Some of these segments appear among the customers of almost all products and services. However, there is no guarantee that a majority of them or, for that matter, any of them exist in any given product category. Finding out whether they do and, if so, what should be done about them is the purpose of benefit segmentation research.

Conclusion

The benefit segmentation approach is of particular interest because it never fails to provide fresh insight into markets. As was indicated in the toothpaste example cited earlier, the marketing implications of this analytical research tool are limited only by the imagination of the person using the information a segmentation study provides. In effect, when segmentation studies are conducted, a number of smaller markets emerge instead of one large one. Moreover, each of these smaller markets can be subjected to the same kinds of thorough analyses to which total markets have been subjected in the past. The only difference—a crucial one- is that the total market was a heterogeneous conglomeration of sub-groups. The so-called average consumer existed only in the minds of some marketing people. When benefit segmentation is used, a number of relatively homogeneous segments are uncovered. And, because they are homogeneous, descriptions of them in terms of averages are much more appropriate and meaningful as marketing guides.

Philip Kotler

The Major Tasks of Marketing Management

Marketers engage in a variety of tasks which are not carefully distinguished in the literature but which are radically different in the problems they pose. Eight different marketing tasks can be distinguished, each arising out of a unique state of demand. Depending upon whether demand is negative, nonexistent, latent, irregular, faltering, full, overfull, or unwholesome, the marketer finds himself facing a unique challenge to his craft and his concepts.

THE popular image of the marketer is that he is a professional whose job is to *create* and *maintain* demand for something. Unfortunately, this is too limited a view of the range of marketing challenges he faces. In fact, it covers only two of eight important and distinct marketing tasks. Each task calls for a special type of problem-solving behavior and a specific blend of marketing concepts.

Marketing management may be viewed generically as the *problem of regulating the level, timing, and character of demand for one or more products of an organization.* The organization is assumed to form an idea of a desired level of demand based on profit maximization, sales maximization subject to a profit constraint, satisficing, the current or desired level of supply, or some other type of analysis. The *current demand level* may be below, equal to, or above the *desired demand level.* Four specific demand states make up *underdemand:* negative demand, no demand, latent demand, and faltering demand. Two specific demand states make up *adequate demand:* irregular demand and full demand. Finally, two demand states make up *overdemand:* overfull demand and unwholesome demand. These eight demand states are distinguished primarily with respect to the level of current demand in relation to desired demand; although two additional factors, the timing of demand (irregular demand) and the character of demand (unwholesome demand), are also important. The set of demand situations is fairly exhaustive and the order fairly continuous.

Each demand situation gives rise to the specific market-

ing task described in column 2 of Table 1. Negative demand results in attempts to disabuse it; no demand, in attempts to create demand; latent demand, in attempts to develop demand; and so on. Each of these tasks is given the more formal name shown in column 3.

All of these tasks require a managerial approach consisting of analysis, planning, implementation, organization, and control. Furthermore, they all utilize the two basic steps of marketing strategy development: defining the *target markets* and formulating a *marketing mix* out of the elements of product, price, promotion, and place. In these respects, all of marketing management has a unity, a core theory. At the same time, the eight tasks are not identical. They involve or emphasize different variables, different psychological theories, different managerial aptitudes. The eight tasks can give way to specialization. Some marketers may become especially skillful at developmental marketing, others at remarketing, others at maintenance marketing, and others at demarketing. Not all marketers are likely to be equally skilled at all tasks, which is one of the major points to be considered in assigning marketers to tasks.

A marketer in a given job may face all of these tasks as the product moves through its life cycle. At the beginning of the product' life, there may be only latent demand and the task is one of developmental marketing. In the stage of high growth, there may be overfull demand in relation to the firm's ability to produce, and some need for systematic demarketing. When facilities have been built up and demand reaches the maturity stage of the product life cycle, the task may be primarily one of maintenance marketing. When demand begins to decline or falter, it may be time to face some basic questions on reshaping it, or remarketing. Finally, the product may eventually fall

About the author. Philip Kotler is Harold T. Martin Professor of Marketing at the Graduate School of Management, Northwestern University, Evanston, Illinois.

The Journal of Marketing
Vol. 37 (October 1973), pp. 42-49.

The Major Tasks of Marketing Management / 63

TABLE 1

THE BASIC MARKETING TASKS

Demand State	Marketing Task	Formal Name
I. Negative demand	Disabuse demand	Conversional marketing
II. No demand	Create demand	Stimulational marketing
III. Latent demand	Develop demand	Developmental marketing
IV. Faltering demand	Revitalize demand	Remarketing
V. Irregular demand	Synchronize demand	Synchromarketing
VI. Full demand	Maintain demand	Maintenance marketing
VII. Overfull demand	Reduce demand	Demarketing
VIII. Unwholesome demand	Destroy demand	Countermarketing

into the category of being unwholesome either for the consumer or the company, and someone may undertake steps to destroy demand by countermarketing.

Thus the task of marketing management is not simply to build demand but rather to regulate the level, timing, and character of demand for the organization's products in terms of its objectives at the time. This view applies to all organizations. In the discussion that follows, each of the basic marketing tasks is developed and illustrated with examples drawn from profit and nonprofit organizations.

Negative Demand

Negative demand might be defined as *a state in which all or most of the important segments of the potential market dislike the product and in fact might conceivably pay a price to avoid it.* Negative demand is worse than no demand. In the case of no demand, the potential market has no particular feelings about the product one way or another. In the case of negative demand, they actively dislike the product and take steps to avoid it.

Negative demand, far from being a rare condition, applies to a rather large number of products and services. Vegetarians feel negative demand for meats of all kinds. Some Jews and Arabs feel negative demand for pork. Many Americans feel negative demand for kidneys and sweetbreads. People have a negative demand for vaccinations, dental work, vasectomies, and gall bladder operations. A large number of travelers have a negative demand for air travel, and many others have a negative demand for rail travel. Places such as the North Pole and desert wastelands are in negative demand by travelers. Atheism, ex-convicts, military service, and even work are in negative demand by various groups.

The challenge of negative demand to marketing management, especially in the face of a positive supply, is to develop a plan that will cause demand to rise from negative to positive and eventually equal the positive supply level. We call this marketing task that of *conversional marketing*. Conversional marketing is one of the two most difficult marketing tasks a marketer might face (the other is countermarketing). The marketer faces a market that dislikes the object. His chief task is to analyze the sources of the market's resistance; whether they lie largely in the area of *beliefs* about the object, in the *values* touched upon by the object, in the raw *feelings* engendered by the object, or in the *cost* of acquiring the object. If the beliefs are misfounded, they can be clarified through a communication program. If the person's values militate against the object, the object can be put in the framework of other possible values that are positive for the person. If negative feelings are aroused, they may be modifiable through group processes[1] or behavioral therapy.[2] If the costs of acquisition are too high, the marketer can take steps to bring down the real costs. The marketer will want to consider the cost of reducing resistance and whether some other marketing opportunity might be more attractive and less difficult.

No Demand

There is a whole range of objects and services for which there is no demand. Instead of people having negative or positive feelings about the object, they are indifferent or uninterested. *No demand is a state in which all or important segments of a potential market are uninterested or indifferent to a particular object.*

Three different categories of objects are characterized by no demand. First, there are those familiar objects that are perceived as having no value. Examples would be urban junk such as disposable coke bottles, old barbed wire, and political buttons right after an election. Second, there are those familiar objects that are recognized to have value but not in the particular market. Examples would include boats in areas not near any water, snowmobiles in areas where it never snows, and burglar alarms in areas where there is no crime. Third, there are those unfamiliar

---

1 A classic discussion of alternative methods of trying to modify people's feelings is found in Kurt Lewin, "Group Decision and Social Change," in *Readings in Social Psychology*, Theodore M. Newcomb and Eugene L. Hartley, eds. (New York: Holt, Rinehart and Winston, Inc., 1952).

2 New behavioral therapies such as implosive therapy and systematic desensitization are discussed in Perry London, *Behavior Control* (New York: Harper and Row, 1969).

objects which are innovated and face a situation of no demand because the relevant market has no knowledge of the object. Examples include trinkets of all kinds that people might buy if exposed to but do not normally think about or desire.

The task of converting no demand into positive demand is called *stimulational marketing*. Stimulational marketing is a tough task because the marketer does not even start with a semblance of latent demand for the object. He can proceed in three ways. One is to try to connect the object with some existing need in the marketplace. Thus antique dealers can attempt to stimulate interest in old barbed wire on the part of those who have a general need to collect things. The second is to alter the environment so that the object becomes valued in that environment. Thus sellers of motor boats can attempt to stimulate interest in boats in a lakeless community by building an artificial lake. The third is to distribute information or the object itself in more places in the hope that people's lack of demand is really only a lack of exposure.

Stimulational marketing has drawn considerable attack from social critics. Since the consumer had no demand (not even latent demand), the marketer has intruded into his life as a manipulator, a propagandist, an exploiter. The target group had no interest in the object until the marketer, using the whole apparatus of modern marketing, "seduced" or "bamboozled" the consumer into a purchase.

Two things, however, must be said in defense of stimulational marketing. The buyer does not buy because he is forced or coerced by the seller. He buys because he sees the transaction as creating more value for him than avoiding it. The object, while he did not conceive of it on his own, is now seen as related to some need which he does have. The basic need is not manufactured by the marketer. At most, it is stimulated, activated, given a direction and object for expression. Social critics would also have to hold that it is not right for organizations to attempt to activate people's needs.

This nonintervention thesis becomes more difficult in light of the positive benefits that stimulational marketing can confer. Stimulational marketing applies to efforts to get villagers in developing nations to take immunization shots to protect them from dreadful diseases; farmers to adopt better means of farming; mothers to improve their child-rearing practices; and teenagers to improve their nutritional habits. Stimulational marketing is also responsible for accelerating the adoption of many material inventions for which there was no initial market interest. Altogether, a blanket condemnation of stimulational marketing would consign many positive developments, along with the negative ones, to a state of limbo.

Latent Demand

A state of *latent demand exists when a substantial number of people share a strong need for something which does not exist in the form of an actual product.* The latent demand represents an opportunity for the marketing innovator to develop the product that people have been wanting.

Examples of products and services in latent demand abound. A great number of cigarette smokers would like a good-tasting cigarette that does not yield nicotine and tars damaging to health. Such a product breakthrough would be an instant success, just as the first filter-tip cigarette won a sizeable share of the market. Many people would like a car that promised substantially more safety and substantially less pollution than existing cars. There is a strong latent demand for fast city roads, efficient trains, uncrowded national parks, unpolluted major cities, safe streets, and good television programs. When such products are finally developed and properly marketed, their market is assured.

The latent demand situation might seem not so much a problem in demand management as one in supply management. Yet it is thoroughly a marketing problem because the latent need must be recognized, the right product developed, the right price chosen, the right channels of distribution put together, and adequate and convincing product information disseminated. Such products as electric dishwashers and air conditioners were adopted slowly at first because people were not convinced that these products could do the job or were worth the price.

The process for effectively converting latent demand into actual demand is that of *developmental marketing*. The marketer must be an expert in identifying the prospects for the product who have the strongest latent demand and in coordinating all the marketing functions so as to develop the market in an orderly way.

In contrast to the substantial social criticism directed at stimulational marketing, most observers feel that developmental marketing is not only natural but highly desirable from a social point of view. Latent demand is the situation for which "the marketing concept" is most appropriate. It is not a question of creating desire but rather of finding it and serving it. The buyers and sellers have complementary interests. There is, however, one important qualification that has come to the surface in recent years. The sheer existence of a personal need may not be sufficient to justify its being served and satisfied. There are *needs* that people have which, if satisfied, are harmful to others or themselves through the spillover effects of consumption. Satisfying those needs may hurt a lot of people's *interests*. Thus it is no longer sufficient for a developmental marketer to say that his new product is justified because there is a real need for it. He may have to show that the need is salutary and the product will not lead to more social harm than private good.

Faltering Demand

All kinds of products, services, places, organizations, and ideas eventually experience declining or *faltering demand. Faltering demand is a state in which the demand for a product is less than its former level and where fur-*

ther decline is expected in the absence of remedial efforts to revise the target market, product, and/or marketing effort.

For example, the natural fur industry is in deep trouble today as demand declines in the face of the trend toward more casual living, the emergence of artificial furs, and the attacks of ecologists who see the fur industry as preying on endangered species. Railway travel has been a service in steady decline for a number of years, and it is badly in need of imaginative *remarketing.* Many grand hotels have seen their clientele thin out in the face of competition from bright new hotels with the most modern, though somewhat aseptic, facilities. The downtown areas of many large cities are in need of remarketing. Many popular entertainers and political candidates lose their following and badly need remarketing.

The challenge of faltering demand is revitalization, and the marketing task involved is remarketing. Remarketing is based on the premise that it is possible in many cases to start a new life cycle for a declining product. Remarketing is the search for new marketing propositions for relating the product to its potential market.

Remarketing calls for a thorough reconsideration of the *target market, product features, and current marketing program. The question of the appropriate target market* is faced, for example, by a grand old hotel in Southern California whose clientele was formerly aristocratic and is now moving toward the comfortable middle class. Still, the hotel continues to try to attract its old clientele and to base its services and prices on this target market —an approach which neither attracts them back nor succeeds in building up the new clientele to its true potential.

The task of revising *product features* is faced by AMTRAK, the new semi-public corporation charged with the responsibility for revitalizing railway passenger travel. AMTRAK's initial temptation was to carry on a massive advertising campaign to get people to try the trains again. However, this would have been fatal because it would have shown people how really bad trains and train service have become. It is a marketing axiom that the fastest way to kill a bad product is to advertise it. This accelerates the rate of trial and the rate of negative word-of-mouth which finally puts the death knell on the product. AMTRAK wisely decided that mass advertising should come *after* product improvement. A sharp distinction must be drawn between *cosmetic marketing,* which tries to advertise a new image without revising the product, and *remarketing,* which calls for a thorough reconsideration and revision of all aspects of the product and market that may affect sales.

The task of overhauling the *marketing program* was faced by American Motors, whose auto sales sank to only three percent of the U.S. car market in 1967. A new management team undertook a major effort to overhaul the field marketing and sales organization and to prune out hundreds of low volume dealers. They also took a maverick approach to car warranties, product design, and advertising. These and other remarketing steps have reversed the decline in their sales.

Remarketing is similar to the physician's job of curing a sick patient. It calls for good diagnosis and a long-term plan to build up the patient's health. The marketing consultant who is good and experienced at remarketing is usually worth his fees because the organization has so much unshiftable capital tied up in the flagging business. In some ways, however, it might be charged that the skilled remarketer serves to slow down progress by trying to preserve the weaker species in the face of stronger competitors. There is some truth to this in that the product in faltering demand would probably disappear or stagnate in the absence of creative marketing respiration. In some situations, perhaps the organization simply should take steps to adjust the supply downward to match the demand. On the other hand, when the faltering demand is due to poor marketing premises and not to natural forces, able remarketing can make a major contribution to saving the organization's assets.

Irregular Demand

Very often an organization might be satisfied with the average level of demand but quite unsatisfied with its temporal pattern. Some seasons are marked by demand surging far beyond the supply capacity of the organization, and other seasons are marked by a wasteful underutilization of the organization's supply capacity. *Irregular demand* is defined as *a state in which the current timing pattern of demand is marked by seasonal or volatile fluctuations that depart from the timing pattern of supply.*

Many examples of irregular demand can be cited. In mass transit, much of the equipment is idle during the off-hours and in insufficient supply during the peak hours. Hotels in Miami Beach are insufficiently booked during the off-seasons and overbooked during the peak seasons. Museums are undervisited during the week days and terribly overcrowded during the weekends. Hospital operating facilities are overbooked at the beginning of the week and under-utilized toward the end of the week to meet physician preferences.

A less common version of the irregular demand situation is where supply is also variable and in fact fluctuates in a perverse way in relation to demand. Imagine a kind of fruit which ripened in winter but which people yearned for in summer; or an animal species in which the mating instinct of the male peaked when the mating instinct of the female was at its nadir. Legal aid is more available to the poor in the summer (because of law students on vacations) but more in demand in the winter. Where demand and supply are both variable and move in opposite directions, the marketer has the option to attempt to (1) alter the supply pattern to fit the demand pattern, (2) alter the demand pattern to fit the natural supply pattern, or (3) alter both to some degree.

The marketing task of trying to resolve irregular demand is called *synchromarketing* because the effort is to bring the movements of demand and supply into better synchronization. Many marketing steps can be taken to alter the pattern of demand. For example, the marketer may promote new uses and desires for the product in the off-season, as can be seen in Kodak's efforts to show camera users that picture taking is fun on many occasions besides Christmas time and summer vacation. Or the marketer can charge a higher price in the peak season and a lower price in the off-season. This strategy is used in the sale of seasonal items such as air conditioners, boats, and ski equipment. Or the marketer can advertise more heavily in the off-season than in the peak season, although this is still not a common practice. In some cases, the pattern of demand will be readily reshaped through simple switches in incentives or promotion; in other cases, the reshaping may be achieved only after years of patient effort to alter habits and desires, if at all.

Full Demand

The most desirable situation that a seller can face is that of full demand. *Full demand is a state in which the current level and timing of demand is equal to the desired level and timing of demand.* Various products and services achieve this condition from time to time. When this state is achieved, however, it is not a time for resting o one's laurels and doing simply automatic marketing. Market demand is subject to two erosive forces that might suddenly or gradually disrupt the equilibrium between demand and supply. One force is changing needs and tastes in the marketplace. The demand for barber services, engineering educations, and mass magazines have all undergone major declines because of changing market preferences. The other force is active competition. A condition of full demand is a signal inviting competitive attack. When a new product is doing well, new suppliers quickly move in and attempt to attract away some of the demand.

Thus the task of the marketer in the face of full demand is to maintain it. His job is *maintenance marketing.* This is essentially the task of the product manager whose product is highly successful. The task is not as challenging as other marketing tasks, such as conversional marketing or remarketing, in which creative new thinking must be given to the future of the product. However, maintenance marketing does call for maintaining efficiency in the carrying out of day-to-day marketing activities and eternal vigilance in monitoring possible new forces threatening demand erosion. The maintenance marketer is primarily concerned with tactical issues such as keeping the price right, keeping the sales force and dealers motivated, and keeping tight control over costs.

Overfull Demand

Sometimes the demand for a product substantially begins to outpace the supply. Known as *overfull demand,* it is defined as *a state in which demand exceeds the level at* *which the marketer feels able or motivated to supply it.* It is essentially the reverse of the situation described earlier as faltering demand.

The task of reducing overfull demand is called *demarketing.*[3] More formally, *demarketing deals with attempts to discourage customers in general or a certain class of customers in particular on either a temporary or permanent basis.*

There are two major types of demarketing situations; general demarketing and selective demarketing. *General demarketing* is undertaken by a seller when he wants to discourage overall demand for his product. This can arise for two quite different reasons. First, he may have a *temporary shortage* of goods and want to get buyers to reduce their orders. This situation was faced by Eastman Kodak when it introduced its Instamatic camera in the early 1960s and faced runaway demand; by Wilkinson sword in the early 1960s when dealers besieged it for the new stainless steel blade; and by Anheuser-Busch in the late 1960s when it could not produce enough beer to satisfy demand. Second, the seller's product may suffer from *chronic overpopularity,* and he may want to discourage permanently some demand rather than increase the size of his plant. This situation is faced by small restaurants that suddenly are "discovered" but the owners do not want to expand; by the John F. Kennedy Center of the Arts in Washington which draws larger crowds than it can handle resulting in vandalism, damage to the property, and high cleaning bills; by certain tourist places, such as Hawaii, where the number of tourists has become excessive in terms of the objective of achieving a restful vacation; and by the Golden Gate Bridge in San Francisco, where authorities are urging motorists to reduce their use of the bridge. The Chinese mainland is engaged today in demarketing pork, a meat product which is historically more popular than beef in China but is in chronically short supply. U.S. electric power companies are demarketing certain uses of electricity because of the growing shortage of power generation facilities. Several of the far Western states are actively demarketing themselves as places to live because they are becoming overcrowded.

Selective demarketing occurs when an organization does not wish to reduce everyone's demand but rather the demand coming from certain segments of the market. These segments or customer classes may be considered relatively unprofitable in themselves or undesirable in terms of their impact on other valued segments of the market. The seller may not be free to refuse sales outright, either as a matter of law or of public opinion, so he searches for other means to discourage demand from the unwanted customers.

Many examples could be cited. A luxury hotel which

---

3 See Philip Kotler and Sidney J. Levy, "Demarketing, Yes, Demarketing," *Harvard Business Review*, Vol. 49 (November-December 1971), pp. 74-80.

primarily caters to middle-aged, conservative tourists resorts to selective means to discourage young jet-setters. A renowned university wants to discourage marginal applicants because of all the paper work and the wish to avoid rejecting so many applicants and creating bad feelings. A prepaid medical group practice wants to discourage its hypochondriac patients from running to them with every minor ailment. A police department wants to discourage nuisance calls so that its limited resources can be devoted to major crime prevention.

Demarketing largely calls for marketing in reverse. Instead of encouraging customers, it calls for the art of discouraging them. Prices may be raised, and product quality, service, promotion, and convenience reduced. The demarketer must have a thick skin because he is not going to be popular with certain groups. Some of the steps will appear unfair ways to ration a product. Some of the groups who are discriminated against may have just cause for complaint. Demarketing may be highly justified in some situations and ethically dubious in others.

Unwholesome Demand

There are many products for which the demand may be judged unwholesome from the viewpoint of the consumer's welfare, the public's welfare, or the supplier's welfare. *Unwholesome demand is a state in which any positive level of demand is felt to be excessive because of undesirable qualities associated with the product.*

The task of trying to destroy the demand for something is called *countermarketing* or *unselling*. Whereas demarketing tries to reduce the demand without impugning the product itself, countermarketing is an attempt to designate the product as intrinsically unwholesome. The product in question may be the organization's own product which it wishes to phase out, a competitor's product, or a third party's product which is regarded as socially undesirable.

Classic examples of unselling efforts have revolved around the so-called ''vice'' products: alcohol, cigarettes, and hard drugs. Various temperance groups mounted such an intense campaign that they succeeded in gaining the passage of the 18th Amendment banning the manufacture of alcoholic beverages. Antismoking groups managed to put enough pressure on the Surgeon General's office to get a law passed requiring cigarette manufacturers to add to each package the statement: ''Warning: The Surgeon General Has Determined That Cigarette Smoking Is Dangerous To Your Health.'' They also sponsored many effective television commercials aimed at ''unselling'' the smoker. Later, they managed to get a law passed prohibiting cigarette advertising on television. Antidrug crusaders have sponsored advertising aimed at unselling the youth on the idea of drug usage.

Unselling appears in other contexts as well. Peace groups for years tried to unsell the Vietnam War. Population control groups have been trying to unsell the idea of large families. Nutrition groups have been trying to unsell the idea of eating pleasing but nutritionally poor foods. Environmental groups have been trying to unsell the idea of being careless with the environment as if it were inexhaustible. Many manufacturers engage in campaigns to unsell competitor products or brands, such as a natural gas company trying to unsell electric heating or a compact car manufacturer trying to unsell large, gas-eating automobiles.

Unselling is the effort to accomplish the opposite of innovation. Whereas innovation is largely the attempt to add new things to the cultural inventory, unselling is the attempt to eliminate cultural artifacts or habits. It is an attempt to bring about the discontinuance of something. Whereas innovation usually ends with the act of adoption, unselling seeks to produce the act of disadoption. In the perspective of innovation theory, unselling may be called the problem of *deinnovation*. Many of the concepts in innovation theory might be usable in reverse. The countermarketer attempts to identify the varying characteristics of the early, late, and laggard disadopters so that unselling effort can be aimed at them in this order. He also considers the characteristics of the product that will tend to facilitate unselling, such as relative disadvantage, incompatibility, complexity, indivisibility, and incommunicability.

At the same time, every effort to unsell something may also be viewed as an effort to sell something else. Those who attempt to unsell cigarette smoking are attempting to sell health; those who attempt to unsell large families are trying to sell small families; those who attempt to unsell the competitor's product are trying to increase the sales of their own product. In fact, it is usually easier to sell something else. For example, instead of trying to unsell young people on drugs, the marketer can try to sell them on another way of achieving whatever they are seeking through drugs.

Efforts to turn off the demand for something can profitably draw on certain concepts and theories in psychology. In general, the effort is largely one of deconditioning or habit extinction theory. Instead of trying to build up a taste for something, the marketer is trying to break down a taste for something. Learning and reinforcement theory are suggestive in this connection. The marketer is trying to associate disgust, fear, disagreeableness, or shame with the use of the unwholesome object. He is trying to arouse unpleasant feelings in the potential or actual users of the product.

In addition to these psychological steps, the marketer also attempts to load the other marketing variables against the use of the product. He tries to increase the real or perceived price. He tries to reduce the product's availability through reducing or destroying channels of distribution. He tries to find an alternative product which is wholesome and which can be substituted for the existing product.

Clearly unselling is one of the most difficult and challenging marketing tasks. Unselling is an attempt to intervene in the lives and tastes of others. Unselling campaigns often backfire, as witness the popularity of X-rated movies and drugs whose evils are publicized. In its defense, however, two things must be said. First, unselling relies on exchange and communication approaches to bring about legal and/or public opinion changes. It is an alternative to violent social action. Second, unselling has as much social justification in a democracy as does selling. To set up a double standard where selling —say of alcohol and cigarettes —is allowable but unselling by those who object is not allowable would compromise the rights of free speech and orderly legislative due process.

Summary

The marketer is a professional whose basic interest and skill lies in regulating the level, timing, and character of demand for a product, service, place, or idea. He faces up to eight different types of demand situations and plans accordingly. If demand is negative, it must be disabused (conversional marketing; if nonexistent, it must be created (stimulational marketing); if latent, it must be developed (developmental marketing); if faltering, it must be revitalized (remarketing); if irregular, it must be synchronized (synchromarketing); if full, it must be maintained (maintenance marketing); if overfull, it must be reduced (demarketing); and finally, if unwholesome, it must be destroyed (countermarketing). Each demand situation calls for a particular set of psychological concepts and marketing strategies and may give rise to task specialization. Managerial marketing, rather than a singular effort to build or maintain sales, is a complex game with many scripts.

The author wishes to thank the many people who responded to preliminary presentations of this paper, including Professor Sidney J. Levy (Northwestern University), who suggested discussing irregular demand, and Ralph Gallay (New York University), who suggested discussing negative demand.

Wendell R. Smith

Product Differentiation and Market Segmentation as Alternative Marketing Strategies

DURING the decade of the 1930's, the work of Robinson and Chamberlin resulted in a revitalization of economic theory. While classical and neoclassical theory provided a useful framework for economic analysis, the theories of perfect competition and pure monopoly had become inadequate as explanations of the contemporary business scene. The theory of perfect competition assumes homogeneity among the components of both the demand and supply sides of the market, but diversity or heterogeneity had come to be the rule rather than the exception. This analysis reviews major marketing strategy alternatives that are available to planners and merchandisers of products in an environment characterized by imperfect competition.

Diversity in Supply

That there is a lack of homogeneity or close similarity among the items offered to the market by individual manufacturers of various products is obvious in any variety store, department store, or shopping center. In many cases the impact of this diversity is amplified by advertising and promotional activities. Today's advertising and promotion tends to emphasize appeals to *selective* rather than *primary* buying motives and to point out the distinctive or differentiating features of the advertiser's product or service offer.

The presence of differences in the sales offers made by competing suppliers produces a diversity in supply that is inconsistent with the assumptions of earlier theory. The reasons for the presence of diversity in specific markets are many and include the following:

1. Variations in the production equipment and methods or processes used by different manufacturers of products designed for the same or similar uses.

2. Specialized or superior resources enjoyed by favorably situated manufacturers.
3. Unequal progress among competitors in design, development, and improvement of products.
4. The inability of manufacturers in some industries to eliminate product variations even through the application of quality control techniques.
5. Variations in producers' estimates of the nature of market demand with reference to such matters as price sensitivity, color, material, or package size.

Because of these and other factors, both planned and uncontrollable differences exist in the products of an industry. As a result, sellers make different appeals in support of their marketing efforts.

Diversity or Variations in Consumer Demand

Under present-day conditions of imperfect competition, marketing managers are generally responsible for selecting the over-all marketing strategy or combination of strategies best suited to a firm's requirements at any particular point in time. The strategy selected may consist of a program designed to bring about the *convergence* of individual market demands for a variety of products upon a single or limited offering to the market. This is often accomplishead by the achievement of product differentiation through advertising and promotion. In this way, variations in the demands of individual consumers are minimized or brought into line by means of effective use of appealing product claims designed to make a satisfactory volume of demand *converge* upon the product or product line being promoted. This strategy was once believed to be essential as the marketing counterpart to standardization and mass production in manufacturing because of the rigidities imposed by production cost considerations.

In some cases, however, the marketer may determine that it is better to accept *divergent* demand as a market characteristic and to adjust product lines and marketing strategy accordingly. This implies ability to merchandise to a heterogeneous market by emphasizing the precision with which a firm's products can satisfy the requirements of one or more distinguishable market segments. The strategy of product differentiation here gives way to marketing programs based upon measurement and definition of market differences.

Lack of homogeneity on the demand side may be based upon different customs, desire for variety, or desire for exclusiveness or may arise from basic differences in user needs. Some divergence in demand is the result of shopping errors in the market. Not all consumers have the desire or the ability to shop in a sufficiently efficient or rational manner as to bring about selection of the most needed or most wanted goods or services.

Diversity on the demand side of the market is nothing new to sales management. It has always been accepted as a fact to be dealt with in industrial markets where production to order rather than for the market is common. Here, however, the loss of precision in the satisfying of customer requirements that would be necessitated by attempts to bring about convergence of demand is often impractical and, in some cases, impossible. However, even in industrial marketing, the strategy of product differentiation should be considered in cases where products are applicable to several industries and may have horizontal markets of headstantial size.

Long-Term Implications

While contemporary economic theory deals with the nature of product differentiation and its effects upon the operation of the total economy, the alternative strategies of product differentiation and market segmentation have received less attention. Empirical analysis of contemporary marketing activity supports the hypothesis that, while product differentiation and market segmentation are closely related (perhaps even inseparable) concepts, attempts to distinguish between these approaches may be productive of clarity in theory as well as greater precision in the planning of marketing operations. Not only do strategies of differentiation and segmentation call for differing systems of action at any point in time, but the dynamics of markets and marketing underscore the importance of varying degrees of diversity *through time* and suggest that the rational selection of marketing strategies is a requirement for the achievement of maximum functional effectiveness in the economy as a whole.

If a rational selection of strategies is to be made, an integrated approach to the minimizing of total costs must take precedence over separate approaches to minimization of production costs on the one hand and marketing costs

on the other. Strategy determination must be regarded as an over-all management decision which will influence and require facilitating policies affecting both production and marketing activities.

Differences Between Strategies of Differentiation and Segmentation

Product differentiation and market segmentation are both consistent with the framework of imperfect competition.[1] In its simplest terms, *product differentiation* is concerned with the bending of demand to the will of supply. It is an attempt to shift or to change the slope of the demand curve for the market offering of an individual supplier. This strategy may also be employed by a group of suppliers such as a farm cooperative, the members of which have agreed to act together. It results from the desire to establish a kind of equilibrium in the market by bringing about adjustment of market demand to supply conditions favorable to the *seller*.

Segmentation is based upon developments on the demand side of the market and represents a rational and more precise adjustment of product and marketing effort to consumer or user requirements. In the language of the economist, segmentation is *disaggregative* in its effects and tends to bring about recognition of several demand scheadules where only one was recognized before.

Attention has been drawn to this area of analysis by the increasing number of cases in which business problems have become soluble by doing something about marketing programs and product policies that overgeneralize both markets and marketing effort. These are situations where intensive promotion designed to differentiate the company's products was not accomplishing its objective—cases where failure to recognize the reality of market segments was resulting in loss of market position.

While successful product differentiation will result in giving the marketer a horizontal share of a broad and generalized market, equally successful application of the strategy of market segmentation tends to produce depth of market position in the segments that are effectively defined and penetrated. The differentiator seeks to secure a layer of the market cake, whereas one who employs market segmentation strives to secure one or more wedge-shaped pieces.

Many examples of market segmentation can be cited; the cigarette and automobile industries are well-known illustrations. Similar developments exist in greater or lesser degree in almost all product areas. Recent introduction of a refrigerator with no storage compartment for frozen foods was in response to the distinguishable preferences of the segment of the refrigerator market made up of

---

1 Imperfect competition assumes lack of uniformity in the size and influence of the firms or individuals that comprise the demand or supply sides of a market.

home freezer owners whose frozen food storage needs had already been met.

Strategies of segmentation and differentiation may be employed simultaneously, but more commonly they are applied in sequence in response to changing market conditions. In one sense, segmentation is a momentary or short-term phenomenon in that effective use of this strategy may lead to more formal recognition of the reality of market segments through redefinition of the segments as individual markets. Redefinition may result in a swing back to differentiation.

The literature of both economics and marketing abounds in formal definitions of product differentiation. *From a strategy viewpoint,* product differentiation is securing a measure of control over the demand for a product by advertising or promoting differences between a product and the products of competing sellers. It is basically the result of sellers' desires to establish firm market positions and/or to insulate their businesses against price competition. Differentiation tends to be characterized by heavy use of advertising and promotion and to result in prices that are somewhat above the equilibrium levels associated with perfectly competitive market conditions. It may be classified as a *promotional* strategy or approach to marketing.

Market segmentation, on the other hand, consists of viewing a heterogeneous market (one characterized by divergent demand) as a number of smaller homogeneous markets in response to differing product preferences among important market segments. It is attributable to the desires of consumers or users for more precise satisfaction of their varying wants. Like differentiation, segmentation often involves headstantial use of advertising and promotion. This is to inform market segments of the availability of goods or services produced for or presented as meeting their needs with precision. Under these circumstances, prices tend to be somewhat closer to perfectly competitive equilibrium. Market segmentation is essentially a merchandising strategy, merchandising being used here in its technical sense as representing the adjustment of market offerings to consumer or user requirements.

The Emergence of the Segmentation Strategy

To a certain extent, market segmentation may be regarded as a force in the market that will not be denied. It may result from trial and error in the sense that generalized programs of product differentiation may turn out to be effective in some segments of the market and ineffective in others. Recognition of, and intelligent response to, such a situation necessarily involves a shift in emphasis. On the other hand, it may develop that products involved in marketing programs designed for particular market segments may achieve a broader acceptance than originally planned, thus revealing a basis for convergence of demand and a more generalized marketing approach. The challenge to planning arises from the importance of determining, preferably in advance, the level or degree of segmentation that can be exploited with profit.

There appear to be many reasons why formal recognition of market segmentation as a strategy is beginning to emerge. One of the most important of these is decrease in the size of the minimum efficient producing or manufacturing unit required in some product areas. American industry has also establishead the technical base for product diversity by gaining release from some of the rigidities imposed by earlier approaches to mass production. Hence, there is less need today for generalization of markets in response to the necessity for long production runs of identical items.

Present emphasis upon the minimizing of marketing costs through self-service and similar developments tends to impose a requirement for better adjustment of products to consumer demand. The retailing structure, in its efforts to achieve improved efficiency, is providing less and less sales push at point of sale. This increases the premium placed by retailers upon products that are presold by their producers and are readily recognized by consumers as meeting their requirements as measured by satisfactory rates of stock turnover.

It has been suggested that the present level of discretionary buying power is productive of sharper shopping comparisons, particularly for items that are above the need level. General prosperity also creates increased willingness ''to pay a little more'' to get ''just what I wanted.''

Attention to market segmentation has also been enhanced by the recent ascendancy of product competition to a position of great economic importance. An expanded array of goods and services is competing for the consumer's dollar. More specifically, advancing technology is creating competition between new and traditional materials with reference to metals, construction materials, textile products, and in many other areas. While such competition is confusing and difficult to analyze in its early stages, it tends to achieve a kind of balance as various competing materials find their markets of maximum potential as a result of recognition of differences in the requirements of market segments.

Many companies are reaching the stage in their development where attention to market segmentation may be regarded as a condition or cost of growth. Their core market have already been developed on a generalized basis to the point where additional advertising and selling expenditures are yielding diminishing returns. Attention to smaller or *fringe* market segments, which may have small potentials individually but are of crucial importance in the aggregate, may be indicated.

Finally, some business firms are beginning to regard an increasing share of their total costs of operation as being fixed in character. The higher costs of maintaining market position in the channels of distribution illustrate this change. Total reliance upon a strategy of product differentiation under such circumstances is undesirable, since market share available as a result of such a promotion-oriented approach tends to be variable over time. Much may hinge, for example, upon week-to-week audience ratings of the television shows of competitors who seek to outdifferentiate each other. Exploitation of market segments, which provides for greater maximization of consumer or user satisfactions, tends to build a more secure market position and to lead to greater over-all stability. While traditionally, high fixed costs (regarded primarily from the production viewpoint) have created pressures for expanded sale of standardized items through differentiation, the possible shifting of certain marketing costs into the fixed area of the total cost structure tends to minimize this pressure.

Conclusion

Success in planning marketing activities requires precise utilization of both product differentiation and market segmentation as components of marketing strategy. It is fortunate that available techniques of marketing research make unplanned market exploration largely unnecessary. It is the obligation of those responsible for sales and marketing administration to keep the strategy mix in adjustment with market structure at any point in time and to produce in marketing strategy at least as much dynamism as is present in the market. The ability of business to plan in this way is dependent upon the maintenance of a flow of market information that can be provided by marketing research as well as the full utilization of available techniques of cost accounting and cost analysis.

Cost information is critical because the upper limit to which market segmentation can be carried is largely defined by production cost consideration. There is a limit to which diversity in market offerings can be carried without driving production costs beyond practical limits. Similarly, the employment of product differentiation as a strategy tends to be restricted by the achievement of levels of marketing cost that are untenable. These cost factors tend to define the limits of the zone within which the employment of marketing strategies or a strategy mix dictated by the nature of the market is permissive.

It should be emphasized that while we have here been concerned with the differences between product differentiation and market segmentation as marketing strategies, they are closely related concepts in the setting of an imperfectly competitive market. The differences have been highlighted in the interest of enhancing clarity in theory and precision in practice. The emergence of market segmentation as a strategy once again provides evidence of the consumer's preeminence in the contemporary American economy and the richness of the rewards that can result from the application of science to marketing problems.

Leo Burnett

Marketing Snags and Fallacies

This article is based on an address by Leo Burnett, head of one of the largest advertising agencies, when he was named 1966 Marketing Man of the Year by the Chicago Chapter of the American Marketing Association.

Mr. Burnett feels that marketing men are handicapped by five major fallacies. But he points with pride as well as views with alarm—he has some constructive suggestions for the field of marketing.

BY 1970 the United States can have an $800-billion economy; and by 1975 our economy can rise to one trillion dollars! This figure is so large and unprecedented in any economy that it cannot readily be grasped.

But in order to achieve this incredible rise in the economy, there will need to be at least one-third to one-half increase in consumer expenditures.[1] This means thousands of new products.

Our ability to produce the goods for this exploding economy is not the problem. What is really of concern is our capacity to ensure the consumption of them.

Our technology has been accelerating with a seemingly irrepressible momentum:

• Hundreds of millions of dollars are being spent today in a great variety of business on Research and Development, compared with a mere trickle of funds before 1950.

• In a single year du Pont scientists file as many as 800 patent applications.[2]

• The interval between discovery and application has been narrowing rapidly: It took 65 years from the time it was invented for the electric motor to be applied...33 years for the vacuum tube...and 18 years for the x-ray tube. But it took only 10 years for the nuclear reactor...only 5 years for radar...and less than 3 years for the transistor and the solar battery.

Leo Burnett is Chairman of the Board and founder of the Leo Burnett Company advertising agency of Chicago.

He is well known for his public service work. He is a Director of The Advertising Council; a trustee and member of the executive committee of the American Heritage Foundation; a member of the executive board of the Committee for Economic and Cultural Development of Chicago; a Director of the Better Business Bureau of Metropolitan Chicago; and a member of The Commercial Club of Chicago.

In 1955 Mr. Burnett was awarded the PRINTERS' INK annual "Advertising Man of the Year" gold medal.

• The cost of atomic energy has been slashed—contrary to all forecasts—from 60 mills per kilowatt-hour in 1957 to less than 4 mills today. With energy soon to be available almost everywhere, the distinction between the haves and havenots could rapidly vanish, expanding the market to the optimum.[3]

The basic issue is whether we have the ability to develop the marketing power necessary to discover, shape, and particularly to *move* the goods that will best fulfill the consumer's needs within the framework of desirable social and moral goals.

For far too long have we continued to venerate mere productivity as a goal. Yet high productivity is meaningless if it outstrips consumption and is not matched by marketing power.

In this generation of accelerated marketing power, is our marketing perspective adequate? Are we plagued by "diseases of the marketing eye," tending to limit our vision of the future?

Here are two of the symptoms of this:

1. *Fear of the inexact*—the fear of playing the odds, and the rejection of imprecise data.

2. *Lack of real consumer orientation*—too much research on consumer preferences as compared with consumer *satisfactions*.[4]

Five Fallacies in Marketing

To be even more specific, we are suffering from at least five fallacies in the field of marketing.

1 Alvin Hansen, *Postwar American Economy* (New York: W.W. Norton & Co., Inc., 1964), pp. 34-35.

2 *The Industry of Discovery* (Wilmington, Delaware: E.I. du Pont de Nemours & Company, 1965), p. 21.

3 Mario G. Salvadori, "The Environment of Change" (Time, Inc., 1964), p. 18.

4 Theodore Levitt, "Marketing Myopia," *Harvard Business Review*, Vol. 38 (July-August, 1960), pp. 45-46.

Fallacy as to Marketing Foresight

The first fallacy is that people already in the marketing field are the ones who understand it best and know what the potential customer wants.

Yet in actuality the only person who *really* knows what he wants is the customer himself. For example, if television producers really knew what the public wanted in entertainment, the mortality rate in programs would not be so wastefully high each new season.

In this connection, consider how many developments in any field of knowledge so often originate *outside* the ken of those specialists supposedly with the greatest insights:

- Three of the greatest discoveries of surgery, without which modern surgery would be impossible, are anesthesia, asepsis, and X-rays —and none of them was discovered by a surgeon!
- Of four important railroad devices, not one was invented by a railroad man. These were the air-brake, automatic coupling, the refrigerator car, and the streamlined train.
- It was not a physicist, but an anatomist, Galvani, who discovered current electricity.
- The development of tetraethyl lead came from outside the petroleum industry.
- The most successful innovation in inn-keeping, the motel, was not devised or developed by the traditional hotel-keepers, who looked with scorn upon this interloper until the success of motels forced the hotel corporations to enter the field.[5]
- The great movie-chains did not pioneer in that singular success, the drive-in movie, until long after newcomers had proved its viability. Everyone in the movie business "knew" that automobiles were to drive around in, not to watch a movie in.
- The break with traditional art and the rise of modern art forms was not encouraged by the museums and curators.
- Jazz was not developed within the halls of classical music.
- And the paperback books—one of the most successful revolutions in selling in our time—were not initiated by the giants of the book publishing business, who entered the field later and only when it was already thriving.

We continue to see some new products succeed and others fall by the wayside for the obvious reason that, although there seemed to be great need and promise for them and although they were heavily promoted, the consumer was less than enchanted. After all, the American purchaser is a "tough little baby" and does not have to be wrapped in cotton.

Given access to honest information, the consumer himself is the best judge of what he needs and wants, the form and the package it comes in, and the price he will pay.

---

5 John W. Gardner, *Self-Renewal* (New York: Harper & Row, 1963), p. 46.

Moreover, he is most likely to get what he wants under a system in which thousands of business enterprises are competing fiercely but fairly for his favor.

Often he does not even know he wants a purple cow until he sees one.

David Belasco said that the secret of good showmanship is giving people what they want just before they know what they want. This also is one of the major challenges of marketing, whether achieved through better research, or more openmindedness to fresh ideas from any source, or a combination of both.

Fallacy as to New Markets

The second fallacy is a limited definition of "competition," under which the chief marketing strategy is to attain the largest possible share of the existing market, rather than to create new markets and add to total consumption.

A few years ago the Brookings Institution completed a comprehensive study of successful and unsuccessful industries. The difference between success and failure hinged on a really simple thing—product leadership. Industries that failed to innovate and that failed to keep ahead of the market also failed to grow with the economy, and perished or were absorbed.

In the area of recent new product categories, consider the new "convenience" foods, which have had ten times the growth of foods in general over the last decade. Consider in this connection the "hi-fi" market of the last dozen years, bringing superbly recorded music to new and broader audiences. Consider also the record clubs by direct mail, which revitalized the whole record field—and which also flew in the face of conventional wisdom that "a person will not buy a record before he listens to it in a store."

We have had the recent boom in modified sports cars, with Ford's "Mustang" a tremendous success. And industry leaders invested some $200 million in developing color television without being sure whether people really wanted it or would demand it in large enough numbers to justify the investment.

It is true, of course, that many great companies are indeed bringing about innovation; and the overriding marketing strategy is to proliferate and diversify. Obviously, however, there is a tremendous need to *organize for change*—after all, the mere fact of corporate organization tends to conspire against it.

One way to lose money is to try to sell everyone on a given product. Many companies have learned this lesson just in time, and are now proliferating their marketing efforts to give the consumer what he wants rather than what the manufacturer thinks he ought to have.

Fallacy as to Competition

The third fallacy in the marketing world is that competition is a closed system, and that our competitors are those making substantially the same products, or offering the same services, that we are.

In studying Nielsen share-of-market reports, do we sometimes know *too much* about our competitors? By putting such high priority on "me-too" products and competitive counter-moves, are there not serious dangers of standardization of products rather than market expansion?

Many an entrepreneur has made almost "seat-of-the-pants" decisions, then has plunged adventurously ahead—sometimes with failure, but often with brilliant success.

By no means does this imply any minimization of the value of the information available today. It does imply anxiety about our interpretations of it, and often our dogmatic reliance upon it.

It is a mistake to feel that the competition for a Cadillac is either a medium-priced car or another quality car such as a Lincoln or Imperial. The Cadillac is a prestige item. The true competitor of the luxury car is the swimming pool, or the summer place, or the private plane, or the winter vacation, and all the other prestige items dangled before people with large discretionary incomes.[6]

Likewise, the makers of bowling or billiard equipment are not competing so much with other makers of similar equipment as they are with other providers of "leisure-time" satisfactions—whether skiing, or photography, or record-players, or ping-pong tables, or even adult-education courses.

All are competing for "disposable time" as much as for disposable income.

Fallacy as to Income Brackets

A fourth fallacy is the marketing theory of appealing mainly to present income brackets.

In the past, it was commonly believed, and it was generally true, that people bought "according to income." But today people increasingly are buying according to *expectations of future income.* Individual purchases have come to be more and more like company purchases—based on a projection into the next few years, and not necessarily on current income alone.[7]

The vast increase in credit purchases during the last dozen or so years, therefore, should not be viewed as mass imprudence (although undoubtedly in some cases families *are* imprudent), but as an expression of self-confidence and as a projection of a continuing upward curve in income.

People no longer buy solely what they "need," or even what they "want" for the present. They are anticipating new and future needs; and the industries that have grown most have been the ones catering to this sense of expectation.

Take, for example, the present booming "knowledge market." One of the important things about the expansion in knowledge is that its main appeal is not to the *affluent and educated,* but to the *aspiring and under-educated.* The encyclopedia field is a classic example: many families which buy encyclopedias perhaps cannot really "afford" them, in a practical dollars-and-sense way. Yet the growth of sales has been enormous precisely in this economic bracket, *because* these families have higher expectations for themselves, and most of all for their children.

All the demographic facts add up to a tremendous new market that is not based on the traditional concepts of "income" and "status" and "education" that have been our benchmarks in the past.

In addition, our cultural habits have changed enormously and are continuing to do so, and at a rapid rate. This also should make for a radical revision of our marketing concepts.

As one obvious example in the area of recreation alone, the game of golf used to be restricted very much to the so-called upper classes. Today it is an immensely popular recreation for all groups except the lowest economic fifth. Again, not so many years ago, skiing was considered a "class" sport. Each year, however, there are tens of thousands of new skiers drawn from a segment of the population which never would have been in the market a dozen years ago. They are taking up skiing as a part of their expectations, and not on the basis of present income.

In all this we have a dramatic example of *upward mobility.* The more prosperous we become, the higher do our expectations grow, and the more do new people become potential customers for markets that once seemed restricted.

Perhaps the most important marketing challenge of the decade ahead is properly to assess and satisfy the expectations and aspirations of this large group, rather than mapping out strategies on the basis of current income.

Fallacy as to Decision-making

The fifth fallacy is that because we are living in the age of the specialist, only qualified experts with specialized skills will be competent in the future to make basic decisions.

Actually, quite the reverse is happening. Our greatest need today is for the synthesizer, much more than for the specialist. He is not necessarily a computer programer; but he understands how computers work, and what they can do and cannot do.

In the field of advertising, he is not necessarily an accomplished copywriter or artist; but he has gone out of his way to understand what writing and artistry are about, as such acts are experienced by writers and artists.

He is not necessarily a laboratory technician; but he has absorbed enough science to understand and appreciate the scientific method.

After all the facts are in from the computers, research,

---

6 Peter F. Drucker, *Managing for Results* (New York: Harper & Row, 1964), p. 95.

7 Peter F. Drucker, *Managing for Results* (New York: Harper & Row, 1964), p. 95.

and elsewhere, the "gut" decision finally must be made by a man, or by a very small group of men. And these men cannot afford not to know how their field relates to other fields, and how all of them interlock. The basic decisions in today's economy have much broader and deeper ramifications than ever before.

Information keeps on spewing from the computers; but there comes a time when somebody has to put his own value system on the block and to say go or no go. Computers merely print out numbers and letters on paper when fed an appropriate signal. This is not a decision.

In the search for a new breed of synthesizer or "generalist," business and industrial leaders are beginning to call for a different kind of graduate from the nation's schools of business; and the schools are responding rapidly.

The wheel has almost turned full circle. The industrialization that made men specialize has now given us automation as its final flower. And automation is going to drive many specialists into other fields.

What we need most in the immediate future are more truly educated men and women, that is, people who know one thing well, but many related things fairly well. And to be educated, in any useful sense of the word, means that you can differentiate between what you know and what you do not know, that you know where to go to find out what you need to know, and that you know how to use the information once you get it.[8]

So What?

What does all this mean to us as marketers?

It means that change and the rate of change have been so rapid, and that the need for new marketing power is so great, that many a marketing man has been caught with his rusty calculus showing. He has not yet learned how to use the amazing new tools of cybernetics, electronic-data processing, and game theory, and is in fact scared silly by them, as he is by taking any kind of calculated risk.

Too many of us, I fear, who talk about "marketing" and the "Total Marketing Concept" still see it as a scientific, objective, statistical thing, which will be perfected as a mechanism, once we get sufficient information and data of a quantitative sort. Rather than regarding it as a *social* science, we are still trying desperately to emulate the physical sciences in precision, in calibration, in subtlety of analysis.[9]

We have research which describes the consumer in embarrassing detail—where she lives, what she wears, how many children she has borne, how much her husband earns, and how much education she has had. She stands before us, seemingly stripped of her every secret, clothed

only in the mantle of our statistics; but in a majority of cases we still do not know exactly what gives her the urge to buy or to prefer one product over another.

New research insights now tell us clearly that people are not all of a piece. They are rational and cautious in some areas and at some times, but enjoy adventures in buying in other areas and at other times. Also there are some products which are best defined psychologically rather than demographically, such as jewelry, alcoholic beverages, small appliances, and automobiles.

The successful marketing man has developed strong points of view (as he should) about the ingredients of success in the marketplace. These points of view have evolved from his pragmatic interpretations of experience. He has done something, and it has seemed to work. Frequently he has worked with a mix—a marketing mix—that has produced desired results. He has not always known which factors in the mix were working and which were not, but nonetheless he has had to adopt points of view. Parts of these points of view undoubtedly are valid, and others possibly are pure mythology.

We are becoming more perceptive about marketing and the various factors that together make up marketing. But also we are now beginning to witness *the clash of the new insights and the old mythologies.*

Yes, it is healthy for a marketing man to demand that research establish the legitimacy of its new insights. But is vital that he be receptive to these insights and seek to understand them, even those phenomena known as "inspiration" and "intuition."

The man who can assimilate the new, who can refurbish his arsenal of marketing weapons, and who can put them to use is the one most likely to "survive" and to contribute most to the new marketing power so urgently needed.

The real fight now is to preserve, foster, and encourage a climate wherein marketing creativity can soar and leap and grow. The marketing process is a fascinating adventure. But we shall have failed the future if we have not set up within our own business firms a climate where individual imagination can flower.

Nestled in the bosom of every person in the whole marketing chain are one or more great marketing ideas. Yet many of these will never see the light of day because nobody has had the sense or the patience to listen.

Obviously the things to be admired most in a marketing man are:

- an unwillingness to settle for the tried and true;
- a desire to seek the inherent promise in every product or service;
- a constant effort to put himself realistically into the shoes of the consumer;
- a belief that quality and thoroughness are significant in every detail of every job;

---

8 Alfred N. Whitehead, *The Aims of Education* (New York: Mentor Books, 1956), pp. 16-17.

9 John Madge, *Tools of Social Science* (New York: Anchor Books, Doubleday & Co., Inc., 1965), pp. 4-5.

- a conviction that what is worth doing is worth doing as creatively as possible; and

- a dedication to providing the right climate for individual growth as the best climate for meeting the new challenges confidently.

Marketing Research

W. Edwards Deming

Some Criteria for Judging the Quality of Surveys*

Editor's note: This is a critical analysis of certain aspects of sampling by a leading authority in the field

I. Probability Samples and Judgment Samples

Definitions

IN my own work it has seemed useful to recognize two general types of samples. These two types will be distinguished here by the adjectives *probability* and *judgment*, not that these are highly appropriate but because I have not found better ones. Fortunately the particular adjectives chosen are not important to the thesis. The two types of samples are described as follows:

> *Probability-samples,* wherein the sampling plan calls for virtual elimination of the biases of selection, nonresponse, and estimation, and for which a formula exists for calculating the sampling tolerances.

> *Judgment-samples,* wherein the biases and sampling errors cannot be calculated from the samples, but instead must be settled upon by judgment.

A probability-survey is carried out according to a statistical plan embodying automatic selection, of which more will be said later. In contrast, a judgment-survey depends on (a) a selection of "typical" or "representative" counties, cities, road-segments, blocks, households, firms, or farms; or (b) the interviewer's or someone else's judgment-selection of households or establishments within specified areas or classes of the population however selected; or (c) the tabulation of incomplete responses (as from a mailed questionnaire); or (d) the tabulation of responses, complete or incomplete, from a mailing list of "representative" households, selected on a judgment basis.

The important questions in sample-design are: How

large are these biases? And how large are the sampling errors?

The reliability of a probability-type survey is objective, being furnished and guaranteed by the plan itself. The reliability of a judgment-survey, on the other hand, is subjective, being decided by judgment. In case the experts disagree, the reliability of a judgment-type survey is undecided, and until resolved must be considered in doubt.

Mixtures of probability and judgment samples are possible, but a mixture is still a judgment-sample. One example would be a high-grade probability-selection of sample areas, such as urban blocks, followed by a judgment-selection of households within these areas. Bias in the selection of areas would have been removed, and the variances proper to the method of selecting them would be calculable. Moreover, the variance of selecting households by a judgment method within the specified areas, although not calculable, is nevertheless measurable; at least the procedure could easily be set up to make it so. But the biases in the quotas and in the judgment-selection of the sample households would remain unknown, hence the survey is still a judgment-sample. Of course the biases could be measured by comparison with an unbiased selection of households in these same areas, but there would be no need of two surveys except for experimental purposes.

Mathematical researches can increase the efficiency of judgment-samples as well as probability-samples. For example as my colleague Morris Hansen has pointed out repeatedly, the correct amount of stratification and the proper allocation of the sample to the various strata are mathematical problems, as important to judgement-samples as to probability-samples, but practically no attention seems to be given to such problems in the planning of judgment-surveys; usually far more stratification is carried out than is useable. (Further remarks on stratification will be made in Part III, *infra*.)

---

*Based on an address delivered at a meeting on the Measurement of Consumer Interest, sponsored by the University of Pennsylvania.

Similarities and differences

It is important in market research to recognize the similarities and differences between the two types of surveys, and to be aware of the advantages, disadvantages, and limitations of each.

There are circumstances in which a judgment-sample is entirely sufficient, as where the number of units (counties, cities, households) is necessarily very small, as a consequence of which it may be wiser to accept the biases of a judgment-selection in order to diminish the sampling errors, even though there is no objective measure of either one. Thus, in trying out a questionnaire or set of instructions, or for getting a rough idea of how much a certain operation is going to cost, or what the refusal-rate is likely to be, it may not be necessary to carry out a probability-survey; it will often be sufficient to conduct a trial in a particular county or city or even in a few blocks, chosen by judgment. Examples abound. The first drafts of the instructions and questionnaire for the decennial population census of 1940 were put to a test in St. Joseph and Marshall Counties in Indiana in August 1939. These counties were not selected as a probability-sample, but because they contained an abundance of "typical" situations. They served the purpose well.

Some recent results reported by Alfred Politz indicate that a judgment-survey may be adequate for ascertaining the degree of interest in receiving a magazine, yet inadequate to determine circulation figures, either total or by population classes.[1] There are many other circumstances in which a judgment-survey is suitable, but this is a subject on which much more study is needed.

The merit of a judgment-survey is not enhanced by dressing it up with probabilities—standard errors, fiducial limits, randomness, or any other adjectives borrowed from the literature of probabilities. A judgment-survey is entitled to merit in its own right.

As for comparison of costs, this is quite impossible. If in a particular problem the elimination of the biases of selection, nonresponse, and estimation is demanded, along with control of the sampling error, a probability-survey is required: a judgment-survey cannot substitute. The cost of a probability-survey is expressed as so many dollars for information possessing a certain band of sampling error, whereas the cost of a judgment-survey is ordinarily expressed as so much for so many interviews. Sampling tolerances and number of interview are two different things; the sampling tolerance cannot be computed purely from the number of interviews. (This remark is extended in Part IV.)

II. Validity and Reliability

Validity

The problem of validity is one of the proper approach to the problem, to discover what information is wanted and to find out how to draw it out if it can be had. Validity involves deep and thorough knowledge of the subject-matter, interviewing techniques, the construction of the questionnaire, and instructions to the field and office workers. In short, it is the problem of eliciting the right answers to the right questions.

The problems of validity are the same whether a complete count or a sample is to be taken.

Reliability

Figures are reliable if they are representative within known and controllable limits of error. The problem of reliability is thus the problem of covering a big enough sample of respondents by methods that eliminate or control the biases of selection and nonresponse, and permit calculation of the sampling tolerances. Proper planning demands that the sample should also be as small and inexpensive as possible in consideration of the uses that are to be made of the data. Reliability is meaningless unless assessable.

Developments in validity and reliability have given ascendancy to two important angles of specialization in the statistical profession—(a) the construction of questionnaires and technique of interviewing, and (b) the design of samples.

The construction of questionnaires and the technique of interviewing are special provinces of overlap between the statistician, psychologist, and expert in the subject-matter involved (population, agriculture, irrigation, retailer of clothing, public health, or some other subject) the aim of their endeavors being to elicit valid answers. In other words, their aim is to avoid the fifth and sixth biases in the list given in Part III, and thus to elicit answers that will be correctly interpreted.

The design of samples, on the other hand, is basically mathematical, requiring cooperation between the mathematical statistician and an expert in the subject-matter, with the aim of improving reliability and decreasing costs. Of course, the same man may serve in all these capacities, and frequently does, but it is convenient and enlightening to separate his functions.

Honesty and good intentions are not enough in sample-design. It is necessary to be aware of the weaknesses, limitations, advantages and disadvantages of different methods, thus not to get lulled into false confidence. Intuition, like the conscience, must be trained.

The problems of validity exist whether the survey is of the probability-type or the judgment-type; in fact they exist as well for a complete census as for a sample. The two types of survey are similar so far as the questionnaire and instructions are concerned; their differences lie purely in the sampling procedures. The question of reliability— what size sample to use and how to take it—does not

---

1 *Evaluation Study, MCCALL Qualitative Study of 1946.* (McCall Corporation, 230 Park Ave., New York 17).

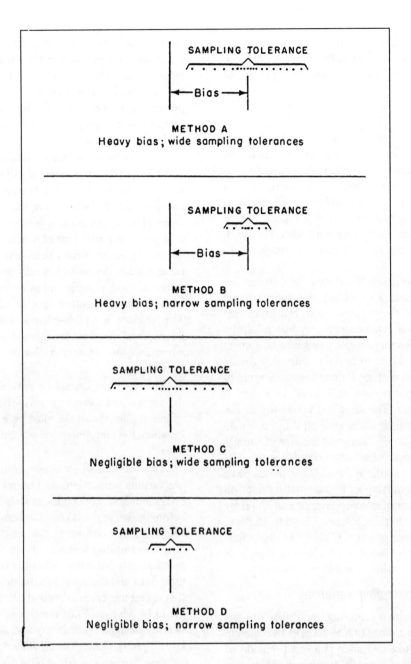

SAMPLING TOLERANCE

←—Bias—→

METHOD A
Heavy bias; wide sampling tolerances

SAMPLING TOLERANCE

←—Bias—→

METHOD B
Heavy bias; narrow sampling tolerances

SAMPLING TOLERANCE

METHOD C
Negligible bias; wide sampling tolerances

SAMPLING TOLERANCE

METHOD D
Negligible bias; narrow sampling tolerances

come up until the problems of validity have been met and successfully conquered—the questionnaire, instructions, and the proposed tabulation plans. Many a proposed survey never gets as far as the sampling stage.

Bias and sampling variability

This paper is mainly concerned with the distinctions between judgment and probability samples, hence it will deal particularly with questions of reliability rather than validity. The first step in the concept of reliability is the recognition of two kinds of errors—biases and sampling variability. Too much of either one can invalidate a survey, and thus lead to wrong decisions. Bias and sampling variability are different in nature, as shown by the chart further on. The insidious thing about biases is their constancy and the consequent difficulty of detecting them.

Tests conducted to demonstrate the absence of bias are oftentimes only experimental determinations of sampling error. To be specific, if the results of a large survey are divided into 10 piles at random, or are divided up according to geographic location of the regions whence they originate, inter-comparisons are incapable of detecting a bias in the over-all procedure, because the results in each pile may *all be wrong by the same amount.* Similarly, agreement year after year does not demonstrate the absence of a bias. Rather, such differences are manifestations of sampling variability. It should be remarked also that most biases are not removed or diminished simply by increasing the size of sample.

Contrasting with the constancy of biases, sampling variability is disclosed by a visible scattering of results about a centre of gravity as a survey is repeated. Sampling variability arises from accidental variations in the selection of the counties, blocks, road-segments, households, etc. Sampling variability exists whether the biases are appreciable or negligible.

Illustration

One of the simplest illustrations of bias and sampling variability is found in shots aimed at a target. The target might be the vertical line seen in the accompanying chart. If the centre of gravity of the shots falls to the right, as in the two top panels, there is a bias which can be corrected by changing the setting of the sights. But repeated shots do not all fall at the same spot; there is a scatter, even with a fixed setting of the sights. This scatter corresponds to sampling variability.

In the chart are four panels illustrating the different degrees of bias and sampling variability that are produced by different types of sample design. In the top panel heavy biases are present. One contributory bias might be the bias of selection—as for example exists when the interviewer's judgment is allowed to come into play (mentioned earlier), or when nothing is done to elicit responses from people who are not at home at first call, or who mislay their questionnaires. The sampling variability in the top panel is wide but this is under control; it can be made narrower (as in Panel B) by increasing the size of sample or changing the procedure of selection or using more efficient methods of estimation. In Panel C the biases have practically all been removed, as by automatic selection and energetic follow-up of nonresponse, or correction by other devices, but the sampling tolerance is wide. In Panel D the sampling tolerance of Panel C above has been narrowed, again possible by increasing the size of sample or making other suitable modifications in procedure.

Characteristics of sampling variability

It is important to note that sampling variability has the property of possessing a range or tolerance, as indicated in the chart. The sampling tolerance is a band outside of which practically no shots ever fall. *It is impossible to predict a hit* other than to say that it will fall *inside the sampling tolerance.* However, it is possible to control the width of the sampling tolerance. In shooting, the scatter (tolerance) is controlled by the quality, design, and uniformity of the ammunition, length of barrel, and in other ways. In surveys, the sampling tolerance can be made large or small by regulating the size of the sample (i.e., the number of households in it) and the way in which it is drawn and the way the estimates are calculated. By making the sample 100 per cent, i.e., by covering all the households in the country, the sampling variability would be reduced to zero.

However, in most surveys the expense of a complete coverage is far too great, and the job would become so enormous that the results, by the time they could be prepared, would be nigh useless, and be only a historical record. What is more, the bigger the job, the more liable it is to biases of various kinds that creep in and become troublesome. The bigger the job the more difficult it is to control, and the less selective one may be in the choice of the personnel required, and the less effective becomes any sort of training program. Many a small sample has been preferable to an attempted complete coverage.

In every proposed survey of the probability type there will be a permissible range of sampling variability within which no further precision is useful, but only represents wasted funds and effort. For example, in the population count of a city, or zone, a precision of better than from 1 to 3 per cent coefficient of variation is ordinarily not required; figures of greater precision would be no more useful in making decisions in problems of public health, allocation of food, planning a farm program, size and number of retail outlets required, type of advertising, and the like. The problem in a probability sample is therefore to meet the required sampling tolerance, but *only to meet it and no more, and thus to accomplish the purpose at the lowest possible cost.*

This problem cannot be solved quantitatively unless the biases and sampling variability are under control, which implies that there must be a mathematical formula by which the sampling tolerance can be aimed at and computed.

This formula will contain certain constants, representing various proportions and correlations in the universe; and often these constants are only approximately known before the survey is taken. The sampling tolerance obtainable at a given cost (or conversely, the cost of obtaining a desired sampling tolerance) can therefore not be computed exactly beforehand, but the point is that the formula must exist and that an approximate calculation is possible. It is in fact this calculation that determines the size of sample to be advised. Thus the risk of sampling, in a professionally designed probability sample, is under control and known pretty closely *in advance.*[2]

One further remark should be made concerning the chart. Like most illustrations it is over-simplified. Almost every sample actually consists of several samples—as many as there are questions to be tabulated, whereas the

---

[2] Some examples may be worth citing: Morris H. Hansen, Wm. N. Hurwitz, and W. Edwards Deming, *A Chapter in Population Sampling*, Bureau of the Census 1947; Deming and Simmons, "On the Design of a Sample for Dealers' Inventories," *Journal Amer. Stat. Assoc.* Vol. 41, PP. 16-33. In this last example the desired precision was a standard error of 1.5 per cent, which was agreed upon in view of the administrative uses of the data. Partly through coincidence, too close for illustrative purposes, the precision attained, as calculated from the returns, was exactly the precision aimed at. The other examples are not so close. All of them illustrate how an aimed-at precision can be attained within fairly close limits if a genuine effort is put forth.

It should be noted that the final evaluation of the precision attained is independent of any assumptions or misinformation used in the planning; see page 31 in the article just cited in the *Journal of the American Statistical Association.*

chart applies to any one question, but to only one at a time. In sample-design it is necessary to plan the sample so that the required reliability is obtained in whichever question is most difficult to attain with the desired precision. Thus, in a sample that is intended to produce a population count as well as population characteristics, the design would ordinarily be laid out along lines that will produce the required reliability in the population count (such as a standard error of 1 per cent), because a sample that will do this will yield more reliability than is usually required for characteristics such as age-distribution in 5-year age classes, the sex ratio, school attendance, classes of employment and unemployment, marital status, and other characteristics for which ordinarily only proportions in broad classes are desired.

III. BIASES

Partial list of biases

Biases can and do arise from many sources, some of which are listed below:[3]

(1) Bias arising from the method of selecting the respondents (the main topic of this discourse)[4]
(2) Bias of an unrepresentative date for the survey (not essentially different from the bias just mentioned)
(3) Bias of the estimating procedure
(4) Bias of nonresponse

The people that do not respond to a mailed questionnaire deserve representation. A professional job of sampling contains provision for a face-to-face interview of a subsample of the people who do not return their questionnaires. Similarly, in a survey carried out by interviews, some provision must be made for calling on a proper sample of people not at home at first call, or who refused to respond.

(5) Bias of the questionnaire
(6) Bias arising from errors in response

Bias rejected by the type of enquiry (mail, interview, invitational questionnaire)
Bias injected by the interviewer
Bias injected by the auspices (protection of self-interest)
Mistakes in response, intentional and unintentional
Under-stating age, or rounding to the nearest 5; up-grading the rent-level, or the husband's occupation or education; failure of memory.

The last two biases are definitely not peculiar to sampling. They present precisely the same problems in a complete coverage as in a small sample. They present problems of validity, not reliability (vide supra). The fourth (the bias of nonresponse) exists in both samples and attempted complete coverages and requires the same treatment in both

(vide infra). The first and third are definitely sampling biases, and the second one, in my opinion, ought to be classed likewise. Just a word or two now about each of the biases that are peculiar to sampling

The bias of selection

As is well recognized, information obtained from one segment of the population may not be valid for another segment. For example, ascription of the characteristics of telephone homes to nontelephone homes may lead to serious mistakes in marketing and other practice. Likewise, ascription of the characteristics and opinions of the people interviewed to the people not interviewed is dangerous if the selection of the sample is influenced by willingness to respond, convenience of the interviewer, expert judgment, or the fulfillment of quotas. In the hope of minimizing biases in selection arising from such sources, and at the same time to narrow the sampling tolerances, careful and elaborate controls are sometimes introduced.

Such devices may or may not have much effect. Considerable bias will often still remain, and the decrease in sampling error is sometimes provokingly small, as mathematical calculations can demonstrate. The fact is that no amount of stratification can take the place of automatic selection of areas, road-segments, blocks, households, firms, or farms from strata.

Automatic selection

Three of the main biases (viz., the bias of the method of selecting the respondents, the bias of nonresponse, and the bias of the estimating procedure) are under control *provided* certain procedures are carried out. These procedures require that *all elements* of the universe (as of households, firms, or farms or other areas) must have a chance of getting into the sample. Moreover, *these chances must be known* because they figure in the estimating techniques by which the final tables are computed, and also because they are needed for the computation of the sampling tolerance.

Now the chance of any particular household getting into the sample is meaningless unless certain rules of selection are followed faithfully. These rules require, among other things, *automatic selection* of the respondents, by which the final act of selecting the counties, cities, road-segments, blocks, households, firms, or farms from the various strata is carried out by rules that operate through the vagaries of chance. In a probability sample the selection

---

3 A more detailed list of the different kinds of errors that afflict surveys is contained in an article by W. Edwards Deming entitled "On Errors in Surveys" in the *American Sociological Review*, Vol. IX, 1944, pp. 359-369.
4 If the quota method is used, the bias arising from the method of selecting the respondents would be divided into two parts, both of which disappear when random sampling is used: (a) Wrong assignment of totals, owing to lack of recent information; (b) Misclassification and selectivity on the part of the interviewers.

does not depend on expert judgment concerning the representativeness of any county or road-segment or household, nor on the interviewer's judgment or convenience, nor the desire of any particular people to be in or out of the sample or to respond. Once in the sample, no substitutions.

Control of nonresponse

A probability sampling-plan must contain provision for eliciting information from all segments of the universe that do not yield information in the regular way (as through the mail or in response to the initial call made by the interviewer). Without such provision the not-at-homes, refusals, and nonresponses have no chance of getting into the sample. The cost of following up can be cut to its proper proportion by returning to only a subsample (perhaps 1 in 3 or 1 in 4) of the homes from which no answer was obtained at first call, and then weighting the results (by 3 or 4). An experienced interviewer assigned to revisit a subsample of 1 in 4 of the refusals may possibly but not always report 50 to 80 per cent success, thus decreasing the refusal rate to a half or a fifth of its initial value and enhancing the quality of the survey to a point where it can be used with confidence.[5]

It is to be noted that a probability survey is an impossibility if the refusal rate cannot be reduced to a safe figure, say 5 to 10 per cent.

Bias of the estimating procedure

The formula for the sampling error will depend not only on the number and method of selecting the households, but also on the procedure by which the estimates are prepared. The estimating procedure is laid out in advance as part of the sampling plan, and a biased procedure is never used unless the bias is negligible.

It is important not to confuse the estimating procedure of a probability-sample with manipulation such as weighting biased results by adjusting the segments of the sample to known totals or proportions (*cf.* the next section).

---

5 My colleague William N. Hurwitz has found a simple but important mathematical solution to the problem of what percentage of the nonrespondents of a questionnaire or initial call should be followed up by further interviews, in order to obtain the greatest possible amount of information for a given total expenditure. The important desideratum is the ratio of the cost of a mailed questionnaire to a personal call, or the ratio of the initial call to the average cost of the additional calls necessary to reduce the nonresponses to the required level. Mr. Hurwitz's solution was expounded 15 March 1943 at one of the Seminars in Sampling and Statistical Inference at the Graduate School of the Department of Agriculture. The results are being put to use in government surveys, with consequent savings and increase in reliability.

6 This is Eq. 3 in Morris H. Hansen and Wm. N. Hurwitz's article, "On the Theory of Sampling from Finite Populations," *Annals of Mathematical Statistics*, Vol. XIV, Dec. 1943, pp. 333-362. See also the book by Hansen, Hurwitz, and Deming, cited in footnote 2.

IV. Some Common Misconceptions Regarding Control of Bias and the Computation of Sampling Errors

What has just been said regarding the control of biases and sampling tolerance leads to some conclusions that are not always obvious and are often overlooked.

First, because the sampling tolerance is computable and controllable only when the selection of the households is automatic and removed from judgment, it follows that formulas and charts intended for the calculation of sampling tolerance are invalid and misleading unless automatic rules of selection have been followed.

Second, even then, each sample-design or plan of procedure has its own mathematical formula. A formula or chart applicable to one design does not apply to another. For example, the formula for the variance of samples of households selected at random from blocks which have themselves been selected at random from strata each composed of blocks of an equal number of households is very different from the formula that would be used for selecting households at random directly from the entire city.[6] If the blocks are drawn with probabilities proportional to size, one block per stratum, the formula is something else again.[7] No further evidence should be required as a protest against the sadly overworked npq formula and charts based thereon, appearing in certain textbooks as general-purpose guides. Unfortunately no single formula exists, even for random sampling, and still less for the quota method or any biased procedure of selection.

As stated earlier, although no formula exists for the sampling error of a quota selection, such a survey could be laid out with provision for measuring the sampling error empirically, at little extra cost.

If there is any truth in the foregoing statements, it follows that the important specification in a sample survey is *not how many interviews* but *how these interviews were selected,* and what was the final ratio of nonresponse.

Third, the development and even the use of formulas and charts for quantitative measures of sampling tolerance are professional problems in the province of mathematical statistics. Misinterpretations and mistakes may be expected when the underlying developments are not understood.

Fourth, a sampling procedure can not be credited (though it can be discredited) by comparing its results with data from other sources. A procedure must be judged by its design, not by its coincidences.

The statistician engaged in sampling is coolly unimpressed by comparisons. The reason is that he must know *in advance* to what degree the biases of selection and non-

---

7 Cf. Eqs. 9 and 13 in the Hansen-Hurwitz article cited in the preceding footnote. Incidentally, in further support of the point made here, the formulas cited apply only when one sampling unit is drawn per stratum. The formulas proper for two or more sampling units have not yet been derived as of this writing.

response are to be controlled, and he must know pretty closely in advance the width of his sampling tolerance (*vide supra*). He expects occasional good agreements and he expects some occasional errors. Too many good judgments would discredit his sampling theory. He thinks in terms of a distribution of results, with a sampling tolerance.

Even though a particular judgment procedure has been used over a period of years and has apparently always given good results, if no good reasons can be assigned for such performance, it does not and never has satisfied the requirements of a probability-sample, in the sense that there never has been an objective prediction of what to expect in a future survey. The science of sampling has been set back many years by too much faith in successful comparisons with complete counts.

Fifth, the practice of weighting results that have been elicited by biased methods is a dangerous practice.[8] This adjustment is often performed by forcing certain marginal totals or proportions in the sample to agree with corresponding totals or proportions as determined by censuses of population, agriculture, business, or manufacturing. Some of this forcing is carried out in the assignment of quotas. Unfortunately, unless the bias in a sample is extreme, one never knows whether by weighting or controlling in this manner he is removing the bias of selection or making it worse. Such procedures do not take the place of an unbiased method of selection. As a matter of fact, the assigned quotas or census totals used for the forcing may be and often are out of date, as is too well known. A probability-sample has the advantage of being unbiased even when the census data used in the design are out of date; the impairment of the sample is only an increase in the sampling error, usually slight or negligible.

V. Automatic Selection

Some methods of applying automatic selection

Automatic selection is carried out by some mechanical or systematic procedure by which convenience and judgment are not permitted to influence the final selection of the counties, cities, road-segments, blocks, households, firms, or farms that constitute the sample. This is the price of the elimination of bias and a guaranteed sampling tolerance.

One kind of automatic selection is called random within classes, and is equivalent to writing the addresses of all the households in a class on physically similar poker chips, one household to a chip, the chips thereupon being thoroughly shuffled and a sample of them (such as 100 of them, or 10 per cent of them) drawn blindfold. A variant is a random selection of clusters of households, by which several consecutive households are drawn as a unit. Another way is to arrange the chips in some sort of order, thereupon to decimate them by drawing out every tenth one for the sample, using a random start. This is a so-

called systematic selection. There are still other methods of drawing a sample by automatic selection, such as drawing elements with probability proportionate to size.[7]

It is not to be supposed that these methods are interchangeable. They all require different amounts and kinds of preparation, and they possess different efficiencies, as is evident from the fact they all have different formulas for the standard errors of various household characteristics. One method will require more or fewer households than another to meet a desired precision, and its cost will be more or less than the cost of another.

An interesting random procedure which eliminates the interviewers' bias of selection without detailed maps or lists has been developed and put to use by Alfred Politz, but there is no published reference to cite. In essence, the interviewer follows rules that lead him on a random walk, stopping at every nth dwelling, without selectivity.

Difficulties in applying automatic selection

Automatic selection is easy to talk about but not always easy to carry out. Some of the difficulties and dangers frequently met are contained in the following outline:

(a) Sample-design, with control of costs and reliability, requires the services of a sampling expert. When such services are not obtainable, or are thought not to be worth the cost, recourse may be had to a complete coverage. Frequently, however, a judgment sample is devised instead.

(b) Before automatic selection of households or areas is possible, it is necessary to acquire lists or maps showing the location and perhaps certain characteristics of the households or clusters of households that constitute the sampling units. These lists or maps may cost money and their preparation and use must be directed by a sampling expert.

(c) A household or area drawn into the sample by automatic selection may be difficult to reach, requiring an inconvenient trip across a city, or an uncomfortable and expensive journey into the country or over the mountains, perhaps in the cold and through mud.

(d) Automatic selection requires callbacks, although efficient sample-design will hold these to a minimum, as was mentioned. Substitution of one household for another is not permitted. It should be noted that no problem of callbacks is involved when, as in the quota method, an interviewer elicits information only from people who are at home.

Elimination of biases and control of sampling variability demands that difficulties of the kind just outlined be overcome in spite of their inconvenience. As for the ex-

---

8 One of the earliest warnings against this practice was given by Corrado Gini and Luigi Galvani in an article entitled, ''Di una Applicazione del Metodo Rappresentativo all'ultimo Censimento Italiano della Popolazione,'' *Annali di Statistica* (Rome), Serie VI, Vol. 4, 1929. This paper, well known to theoretical statisticians, should be brought into the open wherever statistical procedures are practiced.

pense, the net cost of the required reliability can be computed because the reliability is under control and is a known function of the cost.[9] If the desired reliability is deemed not worth the cost, two alternatives are open—abandon the survey, or accept wider sampling tolerances.

It should be added that by comparison, the difficulties and expense of carrying out a closely controlled quota selection are often greater and more nerve-racking than automatic selection.

Judgment indispensable

It would be decidedly incorrect to assume that in the use of automatic selection judgment is thrown to the wind and blind chance substituted. As a matter of fact, in modern sampling, judgment and all possible knowledge of the subject-matter under study are put to the best possible use. Knowledge and judgment come into play in many ways; for instance, in defining the kind and size of sampling units, in delineating homogeneous or heterogeneous areas and in classifying the households into strata in ways that will be contributory toward reduction of sampling error. There is no limitation to the amount of judgment or knowledge of the subject that can be used, but this kind of knowledge is not allowed to influence the final selection of the particular cities, counties, blocks, roads, households, or business establishments that are to be in the sample; this final selection must be automatic, for it is only then that the bias of selection is eliminated and the sampling tolerance is measurable and controllable.

Every effort should be put forth to learn how to use all kinds of cheap procedures of collection, such as the mailed questionnaire. One way is to provide, *as an integral part of the plan,* a proper sample of that segment of the universe of households or business establishments not represented in the biased response. In this way the biases are evaluated and subtracted out and the reliability of the

total is ensured. Soliciting responses from only a proper subsample of people initially not at home or refusing to give information is a special case of a more general approach which could be fruitfully exploited on a larger scale.[10]

VI. Considerations of Cost and Reliability in Government and Other Statistics

There are certain aspects of sampling that are important from the standpoint of cost, particularly when the cost comes out of public funds. If the survey is one in which the data are to be used in arriving at some critical decision involving the health, security, or property of some segment of the population, it may be very important that the reliability be measurable. The ability to compute objectively the reliability of results is therefore, in most government surveys, held to be of vital importance. One of the most important developments in modern sampling procedures is that the plan of procedure furnishes a measure of the sampling tolerance (such as 3 per cent, 5 per cent, 10 or 25 per cent), and also assures control of the biases of selection, estimation, and nonresponse. Thus, through proper planning, statistics can be bought on a quality-for-cost basis—so much quality (sampling tolerance) at a certain cost.

There is an important aspect of costs that needs to be expressly stated and emphasized, namely this: *it is impossible to compare the costs of two proposed methods of conducting a survey unless the reliability of each of them is known and controllable in the plans.* It is not sufficient that a procedure *might* give good results. A survey producing results of doubtful quality may not be a wise purchase, particularly if public funds are involved.

---

9 Of course, a relatively small preliminary survey on a judgment basis may be required to determine some of the variances and cost-factors involved.

10 Another example occurs in Morris H. Hansen's testimony before the Federal Communications Commission on 15 April 1946, transcripts of which are obtainable from Ward and Paul, 1760 Pennsylvania Avenue, Washington 6. Docket 6741. Still another example is furnished by *The Enumerative-Check Census* by Calvert L. Dedrick and Morris H. Hansen, BEING VOl. IV of the Census of Partial Employment, Unemployment, and Occupations: 1937.

Spyros Makridakis and Steven C. Wheelwright

Forecasting: Issues & Challenges for Marketing Management

A framework for relating the available techniques to specific situations.

FORECASTING plays an important role in every major functional area of business management. In the area of marketing however, forecasting is doubly important; not only does it have a central role in marketing itself, but marketing-developed forecasts play a key role in the planning of production, finance, and other areas of corporate activity. The importance of forecasting has become more widely acknowledged in the recent past due to substantial changes in the economic environment. The shortages and the increased inflation of the early 1970's, followed by a major recession, have focused renewed attention on forecasting and the benefits it can provide.

At the same time, there still exists a substantial gap between applications and what is both desirable and attainable. [16, 49, 95] An examination of the forecasting and marketing literature suggests that one of the things that is needed, if the full potential of forecasting is to be realized, is a structure for dealing with the issues that the practitioner must address. The purpose of this article is to bring together much of what is already known and to supply a framework that will provide guidance for the marketer in applying this knowledge to each situation and in focusing on what additional knowledge is needed.

Toward this end, the article is divided into four sections:

1. The first deals with the range of forecasting methodologies available and their characteristics. The framework used for this is somewhat different from those frequently suggested, and is one that the authors have found to be particularly useful for dealing with market-

ing forecasting problems.

2. The second section then builds upon that methodological classification in examining those issues that relate to the selection of a forecasting methodology for a particular situation. Since any marketing application of forecasting requires some explicit decision as to the methodology to be used, this is one of the key areas where the marketing manager can exert leverage on the potential effectiveness that forecasting can have in his own situation.

3. The third section deals with major issues and challenges that are more broadly based than methodological selection questions. These relate to the organizational, behavioral and technical characteristics of the environment within which forecasting for marketing must take place.

4. Building on these key issues and challenges, the fourth section outlines areas of research that are central to continued improvement in forecasting for marketing.

Available Methodologies

There are several dimensions that can be used in grouping existing forecasting methodologies. Many of these are technical in their orientation. For example, the distinction between statistical methods and non-statistical methods might be considered, or that between time series methods and causal methods. Still another technical distinction can be made between those methods that are quantitative in their orientation and those that are qualitative.

A somewhat different framework is that suggested by Chambers, et al[10] which is based more on the functional use of forecasting than on the mathematical characteristics of the techniques. This framework uses the marketing concept of the product life-cycle to identify the important characteristics of forecasting situations at different stages in a product's development. Those characteristics are then

About the authors. Spyros Makridakis is Professor of Management Science at INSEAD, Fontainebleu, France.

Steven C. Wheelwright is Associate Professor of Business Administration, Graduate School of Business Administration, Harvard University, Boston.

matched with the characteristics of different methodologies to determine the methodologies most appropriate for each different stage. While such a structure provides some insight into the range of situations where marketers can take advantage of forecasting and many of the techniques available, the overlap among methodologies makes it difficult to progress very far in selecting those most appropriate for various stages in a product's development.

Structure for Categorizing

Based on our own experience in marketing and other functional areas, we have found a more technical structure, like that shown in Exhibit 1, to be particularly useful in categorizing forecasting methodologies.

As can be seen from the left-hand side of the exhibit, a number of levels can be used in distinguishing such techniques. The most general distinction is between informal forecasting approaches and formal forecasting methods. The former are based largely on intuitive feel and lack systematic procedures that would make them easily transferable for application by others. The formal forecasting methodologies seek to overcome this weakness by systematically outlining the steps to be followed so that they can be repeatedly applied to obtain suitable forecasts in a range of situations.

At second level, formal methodologies can be divided into those that are qualitative in nature and those that are quantitative. The quantitative methods, in turn, can be subdivided into the categories of time series techniques and causal or regression techniques. The qualitative segment also includes two categories:

- Techniques based on subjective assessment (the judgment of managers).
- Techniques based on the forecasting of technological developments.

To understand the range of forecasting methodologies available, several aids are at hand. Three of these are summarized as part of Exhibit 1:

1. First is some understanding of the historical development of different methodologies. Generally, those techniques developed by statisticians are quite different in their properties and in the situations for which they are best suited, from those developed by economists or operations researchers. Exhibit 1 indicates the major field of development for each of the various forecasting methodologies and provides references from the literature that illustrates the development of each.

2. A second item of value in understanding available forecasting methodologies is empirical research on their frequency and range of application. Exhibit 1 summarizes the results given in four separate studies. These studies suggest that there are substantial differences among organizations as to their knowledge and application of various methodologies, as well as a wide range in the applicability of those methodologies generally.

3. A third item of benefit to the practitioner seeking to further develop his own ability at forecasting is available literature that provides an overview of existing methodologies and their characteristics. Exhibit 1 includes several references that have been chosen because of their emphasis on the significance of methodological characteristics for the forecasting practitioner. These are to be distinguished from more technical literature that concentrates on describing the mathematical characteristics of available methodologies.

Matching Situation & Methodology

A key reason for seeking to understand a range of methodologies is that the effective utilization of forecasting requires matching the characteristics of the marketing situation with the characteristics of an appropriate methodology. A number of different criteria have been suggested as a basis for making such a selection decision. These include accuracy, the time horizon of forecasting, the value of forecasting, the availability of data, the type of data pattern, and the experience of the practitioner at forecasting.

One of the key characteristics of a forecasting situation that can often be captured in the time horizon dimension is the type of data pattern. Forecasters have found it useful to distinguish four main types of pattern: *trend, seasonal, cyclical* and *randomness*. In the very short-term randomness is usually the most important of these four. As the time horizon is lengthened, *seasonality* takes on increasing importance, followed by trend. For the very long-term time horizon, seasonality becomes less important, and *trend* and *cyclical* patterns play a primary role.

We have found that the time horizon for which forecasts are being prepared can often serve as a surrogate for many of these criteria including the type of data pattern. A summary of available methodologies and their appropriateness for various time horizons appears in Exhibit 1. These time horizons reflect such correlated characteristics as the value of accuracy in forecasting, the cost of various methodologies, the timeliness of their results, and the types of data patterns involved in the forecasting situation. As a first cut in selecting a forecasting methodology for a marketing situation, Exhibit 1 has proven most useful in practice.[54, 55, 96]

Selecting a Methodology

Every application of forecasting requires an explicit selection of a methodology to be used, and there are a number of major issues that recur repeatedly when making this selection decision for marketing situations. These issues cannot be handled with the simple framework provided in Exhibit 1. They require a much more detailed analysis of the situation and a statement of forecasting objectives in that situation. Three of the most important of these issues and relevant research on them will be considered in this section:

EXHIBIT 1
Approaches to Forecasting

Approaches			Short Description	Statistics	Engineering
Informal Forecasting			Ad hoc, judgmental or intuitive methods.		
FORMAL FORECASTING METHODOLOGIES	Quantitative Methods — Causal or Regressive	Single and Multiple Regression	Variations in dependent variables are explained by variations in the independent one(s).		
		Econometric Models	Simultaneous systems of multiple regression equations.		
	Quantitative Methods — Time Series	Naive	Simple rules such as: forecast equals most recent actual value or equals last year's same month + 5%.		
		Trend Extrapolation	Linear, exponential, S-curve, or other types of projections.		
		Exponential Smoothing	Forecasts are obtained by smoothing, averaging, past actual values in a linear or exponential manner.		
		Decomposition	A time series is "broken" down into trend, seasonability, cyclicality and randomness.		
		Filters	Forecasts are expressed as a linear combination of past actual values. Parameters or model can "adapt" to changes in data.		38, 39
		Autoregressive/Moving Averages (ARMA), (Box-Jenkins Methodology)	Forecasts are expressed as a linear combination of past actual values and/or past errors.	6, 98	
	Qualitative Methods — Subjective Assessment	Decision Trees	Subjective probabilities are assigned to each event and the approach of Bayesian Statistics is used.	74, 80	
		Salesforce estimates	A bottom-up approach aggregating salesmen's forecasts.		
		Juries of Executive Opinion	Marketing, production and finance executives jointly prepare forecasts.		
		Surveys Anticipatory Research	Learning about intentions of potential customers or planes of businesses.		
	Qualitative Methods — Technological	Exploration	Uses today's assured basis of knowledge to broadly assess conditions of the future.		
		Normative	Starts with assessing future goals, needs, desires, objectives, etc. and works backwards to determine necessary developments to achieve goals, etc.		

* **A** Immediate (less than one month) **B** Short (one to three months) **C** Medium (three months to less than 2 years) **D** Long (two years or more)

Major Field of Development				% Usage in Different Surveys				Further Readings see [Bibliography]	Time Horizons of Forecasing			
Operations Research	Economics	Long Range Planning	Practice of Forecasting	15	95	88	23		A	B	C	D
	18, 36			17%	76%			73, 55, 18, 36				
	36, 42				65%			73, 55, 89, 36, 42, 43, 19				
			54, 62			50%		62, 64, 54, 55, 96, 8				
8, 33				36%		40%						
8, 97, 33				37%	75%	42%						
		81, 82, 51, 59						81, 82, 62, 59, 55				
								1, 55, 96, 63, 31, 32				
						40%	4%	49, 67, 66, 54, 6				
								76, 80, 96				
			88, 99, 93	48%	74%			48, 88, 99				
			88, 48, 37	52%	82%							
			16, 79, 83	37%								
		34, 48, 26					50%	4, 9, 23, 37, 74				
		34, 84, 101					50%					

Boldface numerals refer to Bibliography.

Legend: ■ Extensive ▨ Medium use ☐ Limited use

An Overview of Frequently Used Quantitative Forecasting Methods

The most frequently used time series methods of forecasting are based on the notion of assigning weights to recent observations of the item to be forecast (e.g., sales or shipments) and then using the weighted sum of those observed (actual) values as the forecast. Much of the variety in available time series methods is simply due to the number of different approaches for determining the set of weights that will be applied.

Naive Methods

One of the simplest time series methods is Naive I. This method uses the most recently observed value as a forecast. Thus, if product demand for the coming week were to be predicted, the observed value of demand for the most recent week would be used as that forecast. This is equivalent to giving a weight of 1.0 to the most recent observed value and a weight of 0.0 to all other observations.

Since the data series for many items that are forecast exhibit a seasonal pattern, a somewhat more sophisticated method, Naive II, might be applied. This method uses the most recently observed value as the basis for the forecast, but adjusts it for seasonality. This is done by deseasonalizing the most recent observation and then reseasonalizing for the period that is to be forecast.

An important application of such Naive methods is to use their forecasting accuracy as a basis for comparing alternative approaches. It is not uncommon to find that one of these Naive methods may provide adequate accuracy for certain situations. It may also be the case that more sophisticated methods (which are usually much more costly) do not give sufficient improvement in accuracy over these methods to justify their use.

Moving Average

When the time horizon for forecasting is fairly short, it is usually the randomness element that is major concern. One way to minimize the impact of randomness on individual forecasts is to average several of the past values rather than using only a single value (as we did with the Naive methods). The Moving Average approach is one of the simplest ways to reduce the impact of randomness. This method consists of weighting N of the recently observed values by 1/N. (Note that the N most recent terms are thereby included in the average.)

For example, if a regional sales manager were forecasting monthly shipments to a certain geographical region, it might be appropriate to use a moving average involving 12 terms. In forecasting the expected shipments for the next month, each of the values for the past 12 months would be given a weight of 1/12th and that weighted sum would be the forecast.

As new observations become available, they can be used in the average, making it a "moving" one through time. It should be noted that when a Moving Average is chosen that has the same number of terms as a complete seasonal pattern (for example, 12 terms if the data are monthly and there is an annual seasonal pattern), the seasonality is effectively removed in the forecast since an observation for each period in the season is included in the average.

Exponential Smoothing

This approach to time series forecasting is very similar to the Moving Average approach but does not use a constant set of weights for the N most recent observations. Rather, an exponentially decreasing set of weights is used so that the more recent values receive more weight than older values. This notion of giving greater weight to more recent information is one that has strong intuitive appeal for managers and makes sense based on studies of the accuracy of exponential smoothing methods. Additionally, the computational characteristics of this method make it unnecessary to store all of the past values of the data series being forecast. The only data required are the weight that will be applied to the most recent value (often called ALPHA), the most recent forecast and the most recent actual value.

There are actually several different approaches to Exponential Smoothing that have been described in the literature. Building on the most basic approach of simply applying decreasing weights to previous values, these variations seek to make adjustments for such things as trend and seasonal patterns. When such adjustments are made, they are often referred to as higher forms of Exponential Smoothing.

Auto-Regressive/Moving Average (ARMA)

The most sophisticated of the single time series approaches to forecasting are known as ARMA methods. These follow the same philosophy as the methods mentioned above, but use a different procedure for determining how many of the past observations should be included in preparing the forecast, and in determining the appropriate weight values to be applied to those observations.

The most commonly used of this class of methods is the procedure developed by Box and Jenkins. This procedure consists of a set of rules for identifying the most appropriate ARMA model (that is, determining the number of observations to be included in the model) and specifying the weights (the parameter values) to be used in that model. The basis on which the parameters are determined is sta-

tistical and is done in such a way that the error (the difference between the actual value and the forecast value for any time period) will be a minimum. This methodology also provides statistics about the forecast as well as an expected value for the forecast.

An alternative to the Box and Jenkins methodology that would also fall into the ARMA class of methodologies is that of Filtering. These methods are much like Box-Jenkins; only the means by which the appropriate model (that is, the terms to be included) and the weight values determined are different.

ARMA methodologies make a basic extension to the methods described above. In the simpler methods, only past values of the variable to be forecast are weighted in developing the forecast. For exam-

ple, if a company wanted to forecast its shipments on a quarterly basis, only the past values of quarterly shipments would be included in preparing the forecast. In the terminology of ARMA methodologies such a model would be referred to as autoregressive.

However, it may be possible to obtain more accurate forecasts if past values of the forecasting errors are weighted as well. When past values of the errors are weighted to obtain a forecast, the model is referred to as a moving average one (not to be confused with the method, Moving Average, as described above). Thus, an ARMA model is one that includes in its weighted terms both past values of the variable to be forecast and past values of the forecast errors.

Multiple Regression

In its simplest form this forecasting methodology can be thought of as a different way to determine the weights that will be applied to the past values of a variable. However, as normally used in marketing forecasts, the models are generally Multiple Regression forms that include more than a single variable. In Multiple Regression, the forecast is

based not only on past values of the item being forecast, but on other variables that are thought to have a causal relationship. For example, if a product manager wants to forecast monthly demand for his product line, he might use Multiple Regression so that his forecast would consider not only past observations of product demand but also

such things as his advertising budget, and perhaps the price differential between his own product and competitors' products. In this way, Multiple Regression allows one to determine the causal relationship between several variables and the item being forecast.

Econometrics

In strict technical terms, regression equations like that described above are part of econometrics. However, when most managers and practitioners talk about econometrics they are not talking about single regression equations (either simple or multiple) but are talking rather about sets of two or more regression equations. Thus, an Econometric Model that a company might develop of its industry would

include several equations to be solved simultaneously.

One of the advantages of Econometric Models is that the interrelationship among the independent variables in any single equation can be included in other equations and their values determined simultaneously. This tends to give a much better representation of reality since it begins to capture the complex interrelationships among factors. In

a single equation model, values for each independent variable must be specified by the forecaster.

The complexity of econometrics add greatly to the cost of such models and makes them generally attractive only for highly aggregated data (such as company, industry or national forecasts) or for long range projections.

- Time Series versus Causal methodologies.
- Continuation of a Historical Pattern versus Turning Point forecasting.
- The empirical performance of available methodologies as measured by their accuracy.

Causal vs. Time Series

The first of these issues might appear on the surface to be the most straightforward. The question is most often asked as to whether a causal method, such as regression analysis, will give better, more useful results than a time series method, such as exponential smoothing or Box-Jenkins. During the decade of the 1960's and moving into the early 1970's, causal or regression methods of forecasting became extremely popular, leading Naylor, et al,[63] to suggest that it might be appropriate to label the 1960's as "The Age of the Large-Scale Econometric Model."

The initial success of econometric models generated considerable optimism about their forecasting performance over the longer term. Unfortunately, however, the 1960's turned out to be a rather special period of economic activity. That period included 105 months of uninterrupted growth and prosperity, longer than any other similar period since 1850.[17] The fact that econometric models performed well during the 1960's turned out to be an incomplete indication of their level of accuracy when economic conditions were changing, as in the early and middle 1970's.

As would be expected, when structural changes are occurring in the economy, econometric models are not superior to time series approaches to forecasting.[11] Even a study conducted in the stable 1960's[87] found that econometric models were not entirely successful in improving accuracy in forecasting. In another study, Cooper[14] concluded that "econometric models are not, in general, superior to purely mechanical (time series) methods of forecasting." Naylor, et al,[66] made a more extensive and detailed comparison of alternative methods and examined the Box-Jenkins approach in contrast to the Wharton econometric model for the years 1963 through 1967. The results of this study, summarized in Exhibit 2, indicate that the accuracy of ARMA models of the Box-Jenkins type was considerably better than the accuracy of the Wharton econometric model for the time period examined.

A more recent study by Nelson[67] compared econometric (regression) and time series (ARMA) methods for an even longer time horizon. This comparison was made using the FRB-MIT-PENN econometric model. Nelson concluded that "the simple ARMA models are relatively more robust with respect to post-sample prediction than the complex FRB-MIT-PENN models...Thus if the mean squared error were an appropriate measure of loss, an unweighted assessment clearly indicates that a decision maker would have been best off relying simply on ARMA predictions in post-sample periods."

We are not aware of any studies that reach conclu-

EXHIBIT 2
Comparison of the Wharton Econometric Model with the Box-Jenkins Approach (1963–1967)

Items Compared	Average Absolute Error	
	Wharton	Box-Jenkins
I_p (investment in billions)	1.09	0.59
P (GNP price deflator in %)	0.22	0.11
Un (unemployment in %)	0.186	0.109
GNP (in billions)	2.51	2.01

Source: Naylor, et al. [66].

sions substantially different from those reported by Nelson, Naylor, Cooper, and others. However, the marketing manager faced with selecting a forecasting methodology in his own situation must still deal with the time series versus causal model. The real question is whether the additional information provided from causal models is worth the additional cost. Since the benefits of accuracy, often felt to justify the additional costs of such methods, do not appear to exist consistently, their benefit must lie in the knowledge they give management of the situation and the interaction of various factors.

Since much of what the marketing manager does involves decisions designed to affect sales, the value of a causal model is often justified because of the understanding it can provide the manager as to the causal effect of those decisions on sales performance. However, given a lack of extensive research to support such a claim, it is important that each situation be considered on its own merits when trying to decide between a time series technique and a causal or regression technique, rather than always going one way or the other.

Continuing Pattern vs. Turning Point

A second major issue in selection, that of determining whether the forecasting problem is one of predicting a continuing pattern as opposed to predicting a turning point in the pattern, is also related to the topic of selecting a methodology for a specific situation. The majority of work that has been done on forecasting uses accuracy measurements that are designed to evaluate a method's ability to identify and predict a continuing pattern in a data series, rather than to handle turning point in the series. As many first discovered during the recession of the mid-1970's, the prediction of turning points, while often difficult, can have a major impact on the firm's planning and ability to respond to its environment.

Often, what is required in a specific situation involves use of one methodology for on-going prediction of an existing pattern, than a separate methodology for tracking turning points. When a turning point is identified, a change is then made in the basic methodology being applied. Some of the research that has dealt with this subject includes that reported by McLaughlin and Boyle,[62] McLaughlin,[60] and Trigg.[91]

Most quantitative forecasting methods base their predictions on the assumption of constancy. Sudden changes in pattern violate this assumption and can cause significant deterioration in the accuracy of a forecasting method.

Patterns can also change in a less dramatic but still significant manner. When this happens, the great majority of forecasting techniques perform poorly. However, there are some promising exceptions where adaptation of the parameter values in the forecasting model and/or changes in the model itself are incorporated to allow the methodology to deal with changes in the basic pattern.[31, 35, 56, 92] However, the full implications of such approaches and their performance when patterns do not change is not well understood as yet.

An example of pattern change that is familiar to many marketers is that of a change in growth rate. For a product that has been growing at 10% a year, a decline in growth may have disastrous results for the company as a whole if the change in that pattern is not recognized quickly. If the product is one of 10,000 whose demand is forecast by some quantitative method, it will be particularly difficult to identify such changes in pattern at an early stage. What is needed is establishment of a tracking system as part of the formal forecasting procedure so that the build-up in error values can be automatically identified and brought to marketing management's attention. Some of these control procedures are straightforward and simply a matter of incorporating such measures as an integral part of the forecasting system.[71, 72, 91]

Another situation where predictions are not being made for continuance of an existing pattern is that which focuses on a single event. Subjective and/or informal methods have generally been most appropriate in such cases. However, some qualitative techniques are seeking to make such approaches more systematic and further improve the performance of forecasting.[30]

Qualitative vs. Quantitative

A third issue related to the selection of a methodology for a marketing situation is that of accuracy. A major question in the marketer's mind is which methodology will give the most accurate results. Although accuracy is not the only criterion for selecting a forecasting method,[96] it is usually given top priority and used as a measure that reflects several other criteria.

It is extremely difficult to assess the accuracy of informal and qualitative forecasting approaches in a way that allows meaningful comparison among techniques. This is due to the fact that these methods are not standardized in the type of forecasts that they provide; they rely heavily on the ability of experts; and they simply provide a general framework for channeling judgments into a forecast. A few studies have been reported that deal with informal

EXHIBIT 3
Sales Forecast Error Comparison
(Mean Absolute Deviation)

Year	Company Forecast	Exponential Smoothing	Harmonic Model	Box-Jenkins
1968	5749	5974	5408	4755
1969	3858	4470	4013	4403
1970	4013	2958	2998	3284
1971	6033	5657	5311	4785
1972	9782	8958	8384	8748
Average	5887	5603	5222	5195
MAPE*	15.9%	15.1%	14.1%	14.0%

Source: Mabert [49].   * Mean Absolute Percentage Error

and qualitative methods of forecasting and their accuracy. Most often these studies seek through comparison to bridge the gap between such methodologies and more quantitative approaches.

A comparison of qualitative and quantitative forecasting results has been reported by Mabert.[48] In this instance, the researcher selected a company where sales forecasts had been based historically on opinions of the sales force and corporate executives. The accuracy of those forecasts was compared with three different quantitative forecasting methods, both in terms of mean absolute deviation and mean absolute percentage error, as shown in Exhibit 3. All three of the quantitative methods gave more accurate results over the five-year time period covered by the study than did the company forecasts. In addition, Mabert found that in terms of timeliness and the cost of preparing forecasts, the quantitative techniques were more attractive than the qualitative approaches.

Anticipatory Surveys

A major form of marketing forecasts that has received considerable attention in the literature is that of anticipatory surveys. In one recent study, Rippe and Wilkinson[79] examined the forecasting accuracy of the McGraw-Hill Anticipatory Survey Data dealing with investment, sales and capacity. Those researchers concluded that the McGraw-Hill data were generally less accurate than the BEA-SEC Survey of anticipated investment for a one-year time horizon. However, the McGraw-Hill data were more timely and found to be more accurate than naive approaches and even than some sophisticated econometric models. In addition, the researchers report that anticipatory surveys done in the mid-1970's tend to be more accurate on average than older surveys.

One other study that considered the forecasting accuracy of technological methods was that reported by Kiernan.[40] That particular research examined the performance of airline industry forecasts of domestic revenue passenger-miles from 1959 through 1968. The results are summarized graphically in Exhibit 4. As is evident from the graph, the industry continually underestimated the growth in revenue passenger-miles throughout this entire period. Since the early 1970's, however, just the opposite has been true, with industry forecasts exceeding actual values.

In this particular instance, the major problem can be traced to a change from an exponential growth pattern to one best described by an S-curve. From the Exhibit, it appears that the forecasts being made throughout the 1960's by the airline industry assumed that the mature stage of product demand would be reached shortly. Then, in the early 1970's, when the industry finally decided that maturity was not imminent (when it appeared that in fact it was), forecasts exceeded actual values. These are some of the dangers of long-term forecasting with which the marketing manager must deal.

Comparing Individual Methodologies

Within the category of quantitative forecasting methods, several studies have been reported that compare the relative accuracy of individual methodologies. In the case of regression and econometric models, both Cooper[14] and Fromm and Klein[21] conclude that no single econometric model is overwhelmingly superior to all others. These researchers recognize that differences may exist in the forecasting performance for single items over a limited time horizon but, on the average, these differences and accuracies do not consistently favor one model over another.

A comparison of various time series methods in regard to their relative accuracy is more difficult than that done for econometric and regression models. The difficulties arise because there are many more methods to compare and because different studies have arrived at different and often conflicting conclusions, depending on the situations examined.

In a study reported by Kirby,[41] three different time series were compared: moving averages, exponential smoothing, and regression. Kirby found that in terms of month-to-month forecasting accuracy, the exponential smoothing methods performed best. Both moving averages and exponential smoothing had similar results when the forecasting horizon was increased to six months or longer. The regression model included in that study was the better method for longer term forecasts of one year or more. (These results support the use of the time horizon as a criterion for method selection as shown in Exhibit 1.)

In a study reported by Levine,[46] the same three forecasting methods examined by Kirby were compared. Levine concluded that while there was an advantage of simplicity associated with the moving average method, exponential smoothing offered the best potential accuracy for short-term forecasting. Other studies reported by Gross and Ray,[29] Raine,[76] and Krampf[44] have arrived at conclusions similar to those of Levine and Kirby. Essentially,

EXHIBIT 4
FAA Six-Year Forecasts & Actual, since 1961
(Billions of Domestic Revenue Passenger-Miles)

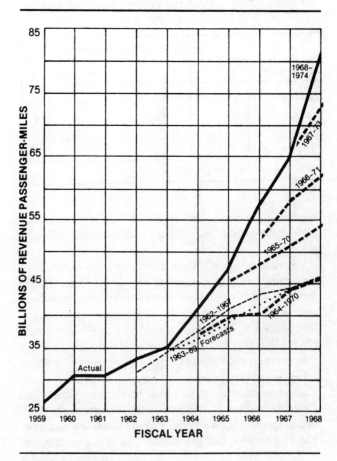

Source: Kiernan [40].

Legend: ——— Actual ----- Forecasts

these researchers have found that exponential smoothing models are generally superior in short-term forecasting situations, although among these researchers there was not much agreement as to the best specific exponential smoothing model.

Exponential Smoothing vs. Box-Jenkins

Unfortunately, comparisons among alternative decomposition methods and other techniques of forecasting have not been reported in the literature. However, studies have been published that compare exponential smoothing with Box-Jenkins models. Both Reid[78] and Newbold and Granger[69] conclude that the Box-Jenkins approach of ARMA models gives more accurate results than exponential smoothing or step-wise regression methods. When the comparison was made for a single period time horizon, the Box-Jenkins results were found to be the most accurate of the three in 73% of the cases. When the lead time for the forecasts was increased to six periods, Box-Jenkins

EXHIBIT 5
Comparison of Box-Jenkins (B-J), Holt-Winters (H-W) and Stepwise Autoregressive (S-A) Forecasts: Percentage of time first named method outperforms second for various lead times

Comparisons	Lead Times (in time periods)							
	1	2	3	4	5	6	7	8
B-J : H-W	73%	64%	60%	58%	58%	57%	58%	58%
B-J : S-A	68	70	67	62	62	61	63	63
H-W : S-A	48	50	58	57	55	56	58	59

Source: Newbold and Granger [69].

models still gave the best results of the three, but in only 57% of the cases (These results are summarized in Exhibit 5.)

Several studies[78] have concluded that exponential smoothing can give results that are almost as accurate as those of the Box-Jenkins methodology, and sometimes more so—a result that may be surprising to many marketing forecasters. In a study reported by Groff[28] it was concluded that the Box-Jenkins methodology gave results that were approximately equal in accuracy to those achieved using exponential smoothing, or slightly worse. That same conclusion was also reached by Geurts and Ibrahim,[24] although this latter study was somewhat limited in that it dealt with only a single marketing situation. The fact remains that exponential smoothing models, extremely simple as they are, compete in accuracy with ARMA models.

Consequently, knowing that the Box-Jenkins methodology does at least as well as large econometric models may lead one to wonder whether the use of econometric models is ever justified.

Challenges to Greater Effectiveness

As indicated previously, there are at least three major areas that represent significant challenges to the marketing manager if more effective forecasting is to become a reality. These supersede the question of selecting a methodology and deal with the practical problems of successful forecasting.

Technical Difficulties

The first of these challenges deals with what might be termed technical aspects of the available forecasting methods. Some of the challenges that the authors would include in this category are often viewed as lack of flexibility on the part of the manager. However, these are actually technical problems that need to be overcome in relation to the methodologies rather than expecting the manager to

adapt his own way of thinking and decision-making simply to accommodate inflexibility in existing techniques.

One such technical challenge is that when formalized forecasting is first introduced into a situation, it requires steps associated with obtaining a forecast through application of a methodology, but does not explicitly alter decision-making procedures to permit those forecasts to be used effectively. Thus, forecasting may not necessarily get the marketing manager to make better decisions. What it does is require the manager to adapt to the fixed form and limitations of the techniques themselves. Clearly, this presents special problems both in terms of adoption of such formalized methodologies and in terms of limiting the usefulness of their resultant forecasts.

Several researchers in the marketing area have recognized this particular problem and have responded to it by developing what might be termed comprehensive decision-making systems. For example, the NEWPROD approach suggested by Assmus,[3] as well as work by Massy,[57] Urban,[94] and Shoemaker and Staelin,[83] have sought to integrate the preparation of forecasts with the making of specific marketing decisions. Such an integrative approach to forecasting overcomes many of the problems that arise when a marketing manager is simply given forecasts and then left to personal subjective procedures for incorporating those into the decision-making process.

Another technical challenge in forecasting concerns the inadequacy of available methodologies for dealing with turning points in data patterns. Since marketing deals extensively with products that follow what is frequently referred to as the product life cycle, identification and prediction of such turning points is essential if formal forecasting methodologies are to meet the complete needs of the marketing manager.

Still another technical challenge facing the marketing manager is the fact that existing methodologies suffer from several fixed-form limitations. Formal forecasting methodologies require that data be available in a specific format (e.g., reported for each of several time periods of uniform length and consistent importance).

Generally it is difficult to acquire the data that are needed to initiate application of formalized forecasting. Even when they are obtained, the form that they require and the format of the forecasting information that they provide may be very restrictive to the marketing manager. Marketing managers who do not use systematic forecasting procedures generally have not defined, as part of their decision-making procedures, the collection of historical data for preparation of a forecast, and then the subsequent use of the forecast in the decision-making process. Rather, their procedure tends to be much more informal and intuitive, necessitating substantial changes before formalized methodologies can be successfully adopted.

Behavioral Problems

A second category of challenges confronting the marketing manager seeking to make more effective use of forecasting are behavioral in nature. Many behavioral problems associated with quantitative decision-making techniques have been studied in the general area of management science.[30, 75] These have only recently begun to attract attention from those focusing on forecasting and its application in marketing.

For the marketing manager, an important aspect of behavioral challenge involves the interface between preparers of forecasts (specialists) and the users of forecasts (marketing managers). Literature reporting empirical studies of such interactions suggests that what is required is better knowledge, respect, and understanding of the role and value that preparers have for users and vice versa. Based on this kind of understanding, there is then a need for a clear definition of tasks and priorities with regard to forecasting applications. A recognition of these disparities between the perceptions of preparers and users of the marketing forecast is important if the full benefits of forecasting are to be realized, and if the potential failures in such applications are to be avoided.[95]

An important form of the behavioral challenges are those caused by characteristics inherent in the techniques themselves and in the tasks for which the forecasting is intended. While these may appear trivial when stated in an article such as this, they often become the major roadblock to successful applications of forecasting.

One such roadblock is the failure to recognize that getting started in formalized forecasting, developing additional applications to complement existing forecasting, and transforming an occasional forecast into a routine application are all very different tasks. The role of the marketing manager is different; the role of the specialist is different; and the needs and requirements for support from others in the organization are different for each of these. Many failures in forecasting can be tied simply to a failure to recognize the type of situation involved and the most sensible procedure for handling it.

Organizational Roadblocks

A third category of challenges that must be overcome by the marketing manager in order to realize effective forecasting are organizational in nature. For example, a roadblock frequently overlooked by those wishing to increase the use of systematic forecasting is that the benefits of forecasting often accrue to organizational units other than the marketing group, and yet the bulk of the forecasting support must come from marketing. While everyone knows that, in theory, this may work to the good of the organization, in any given situation it may be extremely difficult for the marketing manager to give up some of his own scarce resources for such a ''worthy cause.''

Another organizational issue that frequently hinders forecasting is the fact that the results used to measure the performance of forecasting appear long after the expenditure of the effort for obtaining those forecasts. Even in short-run situations it might take several time periods to build up a history of performance that can be used to evaluate that application. Getting managers to adopt formalized procedures for forecasting on the promise of some often misunderstood and frequently unbelieved pledge of future good is not an easy task.

One of the major areas not understood by many marketing executives seeking to apply forecasting is that there are certain stages that organizations go through in the application of forecasting methodologies. In a study by Wheelwright and Clarke,[95] these were identified in terms of the methodologies actually applied. Exhibit 6 summarizes, for firms at three different stages in forecasting experience, the percentage using various methodologies. While this research is empirical in nature, more qualitative aspects of this study indicate that an evolutionary approach, as frequently suggested for the application of computer models, is particularly appropriate in the adoption of forecasting.

Understanding the importance of such phases can have a significant impact on the way in which forecasting support groups are organized and the type of forecasting resources that are sought. A better understanding of this aspect in forecasting can also aid in its integration with other marketing, planning, and budgeting procedures.

EXHIBIT 6
Use of Methodologies Given the Forecasting Status of the Company

Methodology	Preparers Placing Company:		
	Behind Industry	Average	Ahead of Industry
Time Series Smoothing	32.1% *	70.6%	65.9%
Box-Jenkins	10.7%	17.6%	31.7%
Regression Analysis	39.3%	70.6%	75.6%
Index Numbers	35.7%	41.2%	41.5%
Econometric Models	25.0%	52.9%	63.4%
Jury of Exec. Opinion	67.9%	84.3%	70.7%
Sales Force Composite	50.0%	64.7%	70.7%
Customer Expectations	28.6%	47.1%	51.2%
Other	17.9%	23.5%	31.7%

* **Read:** Of the companies placing themselves behind the industry in forecasting, 32.1% use Time Series Smoothing.

Source: Wheelwright and Clarke [95].

Directions for Future Research

While forecasting is always a risky business, those familiar with research on other management topics are aware that the groundwork for such research usually appears several years before the major impact of its results is felt. Based on existing work and the issues and challenges outlined in the literature, the need for research that can and should be conducted in the coming decade can be identified.

The first and perhaps easiest area to predict relates to the need for additional methodologies for time series analyses. The present state of development of time series techniques suggests that several methodologies will be further developed and applied to marketing problems in the coming decade. Particularly important are the techniques of filtering, such as those suggested over a decade ago by Kalman,[38] Kalman and Bucy,[39] and others. Also, while bivariate ARMA techniques are currently available, their extension to true multivariate time series analysis is likely in the next few years.[6,55] Finally, additional work is needed to improve existing time series methods, such as developing computer packages like that suggested by Makridakis and Wheelwright[54] and developing more automated decision rules for parameter specification within time series models as suggested by Trigg and Leach,[92] and McClain and Thomas.[58]

Development of several technological methods of forecasting would also be particularly useful to the marketing manager. From the range of qualitative methods currently available, it would seem that the surface of what is possible has only been scratched. Methods like the CATASTROPHE theory,[100] as well as other techniques, will undoubtedly be more fully developed in the coming decade and provide a much wider range of methodologies for use in marketing. A specific area where these would be especially useful would be in new product forecasting.

Another area in which research is likely to focus in the coming decade is the integration of qualitative and quantitative forecasts. This integration is required in order to more fully utilize the judgment of experts (particularly managers) and the results of systematic analyses of the environment. Some work has already been done in this area,[4, 5, 48] but more is needed.

Special Problems

There are a number of special problems in marketing requiring forecasts where existing methodologies seem to hold much promise but where little empirical work has been done. These include such things as forecasting cumulative demand (rather than demand for each of several sequential time periods), applying forecasting methods to data series where the periods are not of uniform length or where data values are missing, and mixing quantitative methodologies so that a different methodology is applied when the pattern is stable than when a turning point is occurring.[54]

As organizations build their base of experience, and the number of marketing managers and specialists with forecasting skill is further expanded, it is likely that administrative and procedural guidelines for effective forecasting also will be developed and tested. Much of this work will likely use techniques already available and will seek to develop more effective and efficient ways to utilize those in a wide range of marketing settings.

In conjunction with developments in the above areas, it is likely that the literature will begin to focus more on the problem-oriented or applications side of forecasting, such as sales forecasting, price forecasting, supply forecasting, etc., and less on the development of completely new methodologies. This will help to disperse forecasting knowledge and skills more broadly within marketing departments, and will undoubtedly lead to a stronger base on which marketing management can effectively use forecasting knowledge.

REFERENCES

1. B. D. O. Anderson, "A Qualitative Introduction to Wiener and Kalman-Bucy Filters," *Proceedings,* The Institute of Radio and Electricity Engineering of Australia, March 1971, pp. 93-103.

2. J. S. Armstrong and M. C. Grohman, "A Comparative Study of Methods for Long-Range Market Forecasting," *Management Science*, Vol. 19 No. 2 (October 1972), pp. 211-21.

3. Gert Assmus, "NEWPROD: The Design and Implementation of a New Product Model," *Journal of Marketing*, Vol. 39 No. 1 (January 1975), pp. 16-23.

4. R. U. Ayres, *Technological Forecasting and Long-Range Planning*, (New York: McGraw-Hill, 1969).

5. J. M. Bates and C. W. J. Granger, "Combination of Forecast," *Operational Research Quarterly*, Vol. 20 No. 4 (1969), pp. 451-68.

6. G. E. P. Box and G. M. Jenkins, *Time Series Analysis Forecasting and Control* (San Francisco: Holden-Day, revised 1976).

7. R. G. Brown, *Statistical Forecasting For Inventory Control* (New York: McGraw-Hill, 1959).

8. R. G. Brown, Smoothing, *Forecasting and Prediction* (Englewood Cliffs, NJ: Prentice-Hall, 1963).

9. M. Cetron, *Industrial Applications of Technological Forecasting* (New York: John Wiley & Sons, Inc., 1971).

10. J. C. Chambers, et. al., "How to Choose the Right Forecasting Technique," *Harvard Business Review*, July-August 1971.

11. C. F. Christ, "A Test of an Econometric Model of the United States, 1921-1974," in *Conference on Business Cycles* (New York: National Bureau of Economic Research, 1975).

12. C. F. Christ, "Judging the Performance of Econometric Models of the U.S. Economy," *International Economic Review*, Vol. 16 No. 1, (1975), pp. 57-81.

13. C. F. Christ, *Econometric Models and Methods* (New York: John Wiley & Sons, Inc., 1966).

14. R. L. Cooper, "The Predictive Performance of Quarterly Econometric Models of the United States," in B. G. Hickman, ed. *Econometric Models of Cyclical Behavior* (New York: National Bureau of Economic Research, 1972).

15. J. Cragg and B. Malkiel, "The Consensus and Accuracy of Some Predictions of the Growth in Corporate Earnings," *Journal of Finance* March 1968, pp. 67-84.

16. Douglas J. Dalrymple, "Sales Forecasting Methods and Accuracy," *Business Horizons*, December 1975, pp. 69-73.

17. C. A. Dauten and L. M. Valentine, *Business Cycles and Forecasting* (Cincinnati: South-Western Publishing, 1974).

18. N. R. Draper and H. Smith, *Applied Regression Analysis* (New York: John Wiley & Sons, 1966).

19. J. S. Duesenberry, et al., *The Brookings Quarterly Econometric Model of the United States* (Amsterdam: North Holland Publishing Company, 1965).

20. E. J. Elton and M. J. Gruber, "Earnings Estimates and the Accuracy of Expectational Data," *Management Science*, April 1972, pp. B

21. G. Fromm and L. R. Klein, "A Comparison of Eleven Econometric Models of the United States," *Proceedings of the American Economic Association*, May 1973, pp. 385-401.

22. A. Gelb, *Applied Optimal Estimation* (Cambridge, MA: The MIT Press, 1974).

23. A. Gerstenfeld, "Technological Forecasting," *Journal of Business*, Vol. 44 No. 1, (January 1971), pp. 10-18.

24. M. D. Geurts and I. B. Ibrahim, "Comparing the Box-Jenkins Approach with the Exponentially Smoothed Forecasting Model Application to Hawaii Tourists," *Journal of Marketing Research* Vol. XII, (May 1975), pp. 182-88.

25. A. S. Goldberger, *Econometric Theory* (New York: John Wiley & Sons, Inc., 1964).

26. T. J. Gordon and H. Hayward, "Initial Experiment with the Cross-Impact Matrix Method of Forecasting," *Futures*, Vol. 1 No. 1, (December, 1968).

27. D. Green and J. Segall, "The Predictive Power of First-Quarter Earnings Reports," *Journal of Business*, Vol. 40, (January, 1967), pp. 44-55.

28. G. K. Groff, "Empirical Comparison of Models for Short-Range Forecasting," *Management Science*, Vol. 20, (September 1973), pp. 22-31.

29. D. Gross and J. L. Ray, "A General Purpose Forecasting Simulator," *Management Science*, Vol. 11, (April 1965), pp. B119-35.

30. John S. Hammond, "The Roles of the Manager and Analyst in Successful Implementation," *Abstract*, XX Meeting of the Institute of Management Science, 1973.

31. P. J. Harrison and C. F. Stevens, "A Bayesian Approach to Short-Term Forecasting," *Operational Research Quarterly*, Vol. 22, (1971), pp. 341-62.

32. P. J. Harrison and C. F. Stevens, "Bayesian Forecasting in Action: Case Studies," University of Warwick, *Working Paper No. 14*, 1975.

33. C. C. Holt, "Forecasting Seasonal and Trends by Exponentially Weighted Moving Averages," Office of Naval Research, *Research Memorandum No. 52*, 1957.

34. E. Jantsch, *Technological Forecasting in Perspective* (Paris: O.E.C.D., 1969).

35. T. E. Johnson and T. G. Schmitt, "Effectiveness of Earnings per Share Forecasts," *Financial Management*, Summer 1974, pp. 64-72.

36. J. Johnston, *Econometric Methods* (Englewood Cliffs, NJ: Prentice-Hall, 1972).

37. Marvin A. Jolson and Gerald L. Rossow, "The Delphi Process in Marketing Decision-Making," *Journal of Marketing Research*, Vol. VIII (November 1971), pp. 443-48.

38. R. E. Kalman, "A New Approach to Linear Filtering and Prediction Problems," *Journal of Basic Engineering*, Vol. D82, (March 1960), pp. 35-44.

39. R. E. Kalman and R. S. Bucy, "New Results in Linear Filtering and Prediction Theory," *Journal of Basic Engineering*, Vol. D83 (March 1961), pp. 95-107.

40. J. D. Kiernan, "A Survey and Assessment of Air Travel Forecasting," *Urban Mass Transportation Project*, (Arlington, VA: U.S. Dept. of Commerce, April 1970).

41. R. M. Kirby, "A Comparison of Short and Medium Range Statistical Forecasting Methods," *Management Science*, Vol. 4, (1966), pp. B202-10.

42. L. R. Klein, *An Introduction to Econometrics* (Englewood Cliffs, NJ: Prentice-Hall, 1968).

43. L. R. Klein and A. S. Goldberger, *An Econometric Model of the United States* 1929-1952, (Amsterdam: North Holland Publishing Co., 1955).

44. R. F. Krampf, *The Turning Point Problem in Smoothing Models*, unpublished Ph.D. dissertation, University of Cincinnati, 1972.

45. C. E. V. Lesser, "A Survey of Econometrics," *The Journal of the Royal Statistical Society*, Series A, Vol. 131, (1968), pp. 530-66.

46. A. H. Levine, "Forecasting Techniques," *Management Accounting*, January 1967.

47. C. D. Lewis, *Demand Analysis and Inventory Control* (London: Heath and Lexington, 1975).

48. Harold A. Linstone and Murray Turoff, *The Delphi Method: Techniques and Applications* (Reading, MA: Addison-Wesley, 1975).

49. V. A. Mabert, *An Introduction to Short Term Forecasting Using the Box-Jenkins Methodology* (Atlanta: American Institute of Industrial Engineers, 1975).

50. A. Mabert, "Statistical Versus Sales Force—Executive Opinion Short Range Forecasts: A Time Series Analysis Case Study," Krannert Graduate School, *Working Paper*, Purdue University, 1975.

51. F. R. Macauley, *The Smoothing of Time Series* (National Bureau of Economic Research, 1930).

52. S. Makridakis, "A Survey of Time Series," *International Statistical Review*, Vol. 44 No. 1 (1976), pp. 29-70.

53. S. Makridakis, A. Hodson, and S. Wheelwright, "An Interactive Forecasting System," *American Statistician*, November 1974.

54. S. Makridakis and S. Wheelwright, *Interactive Forecasting: Univariate and Multivariate Methods*, 2nd Ed. (San Francisco: Holden-Day, 1976).

55. S. Makridakis and S. Wheelwright, *Forecasting : Methods and Applications* (Santa Barbara: Wiley-Hamilton, 1977).

56. S. Makridakis and S. Wheelwright, "Generalized Adaptive Filtering," *Operational Research Quarterly*, 1977.

57. William F. Massy, "Forecasting the Demand for New Convenience Products," *Journal of Marketing Research*, Vol. VI (November 1968), pp. 405-12.

58. J. D. McClain and L. J. Thomas, "Response-Variance Tradeoffs in Adaptive Forecasting," *Operations Research*, Vol. 21 No. 2 (March-April 1973), pp. 554-68.

59. R. L. McLaughlin, *Time Series Forecasting, Marketing Research Technique, Series No. 6* (Chicago: American Marketing Association, 1962).

60. R. L. McLaughlin, "A New Five-Phase Economic Forecasting System," *Business Economics*, September 1975, pp. 49-60.

61. R. L. McLaughlin, "The Real Record of the Econometric Forecasters," *Business Economics*, Vol. 10 No. 3 (1975), pp. 28-36.

62. R. L. McLaughlin and J. J. Boyle, *Short-Term Forecasting* (New York: American Marketing Association, 1968).

63. Roman Mehra, "Kalman Filters and Their Application to Forecasting," in S. Makridakis and S. Wheelwright, eds., *Forecasting* (Amsterdam, Netherlands: North-Holland Series in Management Science, forthcoming).

64. D. C. Montgomery and L. A. Johnson, *Forecasting and Time Series Analysis* (New York: McGraw-Hill, 1976).

65. T. H. Naylor and H. Schauland, "A Survey of Users of Corporate Planning Models," *Management Science* Vol. 22 No. 9, (May 1976), pp. 927-37.

66. T. H. Naylor, T. G. Seaks, and D. W. Wicherin, "Box-Jenkins Methods: An Alternative to Econometric Forecasting," *International Statistical Review* Vol. 40 No. 2, (1972), pp. 123-37.

67. C. R. Nelson, "The Prediction Performance of the FRB-MIT-PENN Model of the U.S. Economy," *The American Economic Review*, Vol. 62 (December 1972), pp. 902-17.

68. C. R. Nelson, *Applied Time Series Analysis for Managerial Forecasting* (San Francisco: Holden-Day, 1973).

69. P. Newbold and C. W. J. Granger, "Experience with Forecasting Univariate Time Series and the Combination of Forecasts," *The Journal of the Royal Statistical Society*, Series A, Vol. 137, Part 2 (1974), pp. 131-65.

70. V. Niederhoffer and D. Regan, *Barron's*, December 18, 1972, pg. 9.

71. E. S. Page, "On Problems in which a Change in Parameters Occurs at an Unknown Point," *Biometrica*, Vol. 4 (1957), pp. 249-60.

72. E. S. Page, "Cumulative Sum Charts," *Technometrics*, Vol. 3, (1961) pp. 1-10.

73. Robert S. Pindyk and D. L. Rubinfeld, *Econometric Models and Economic Forecasts* (New York: McGraw-Hill, 1976).

74. R. W. Prehoda, *Designing the Future* (Philadelphia: Chilton Book Company, 1967).

75. Michael Radnor and Rodney Neal, "The Progress of Management Science Activities in Large U.S. Industrial Corporations," *Operations Research*, Vol. 21 (1973), pp. 427-50.

76. H. Raiffa, *Decision Analysis* (Reading, MA: Addison-Wesley, 1968).

77. J. E. Raine, "Self-Adaptive Forecasting Considered," *Decision Sciences*, April 1971.

78. D. J. Reid, "Forecasting in Action: A Comparison of Forecasting Techniques in Economic Time Series," *Proceedings* of the Joint Conference of the Operations Research Society, Long-Range Planning and Forecasting, 1971.

79. R. D. Rippe and M. Wilkinson, "Forecasting Accuracy of the McGraw-Hill Anticipatory Data," *Journal of the American Statistical Association*, Vol. 69 No. 438 (December 1974), pp. 849-58.

80. Robert O. Schlaifer, *Analysis of Decisions Under Uncertainty* (New York: McGraw-Hill, 1968).

81. J. Shiskin, "Tests and Revisions of Bureau of the Census Methods of Seasonal Adjustments," *Technical Paper No. 5*, Bureau of the Census, 1961.

82. J. Shiskin, et al., "The X-11 Variant of the Census II Method Seasonal Adjustment Program," *Technical Paper No. 15*, Bureau of the Census.

83. Robert Shoemaker and Richard Staelin, "The Effects of Sampling Variation on Sales Forecasts for New Consumer Products," *Journal of Marketing Research*, Vol. XIII (May 1976), pp. 138-43.

84. J. V. Sigford and R. H. Parvin, "Project PATTERN: A Methodology for Determining Relevance in Complex Decision-Making," *LEEE Transactions on Engineering Management*, Vol. 12 No. 1 (March 1965).

85. W. A. Spurr and C. P. Bonini, *Statistical Analysis for Business Decisions* (Homewood, IL: Richard D. Irwin, 1973).

86. Thomas F. Ster, "Consumer Buying Intentions and Purchase Probability," *Journal of the American Statistical Association*, September 1966.

87. H. O. Steckler, "Forecasting with Econometric Models: An Evaluation," *Econometrica*, Vol. 36 (July-October 1968), pp. 437-63.

88. The Conference Board, *Sales Forecasting*, New York, 1970; also, *Forecasting Sales*, 1964.

89. Henri Theil, *Principles of Econometrics* (New York: John Wiley & Sons, 1971).

90. Henri Theil and R. F. Kosobud, "How Informative are Consumer Buying Intentions Surveys?" *Review of Economics and Statistics*, Vol. XLV (February 1968).

91. D. W. Trigg, "Monitoring a Forecasting System," *Operational Research Quarterly*, Vol. 15 (1964), pp. 271-74.

92. D. W. Trigg and D. H. Leach, "Exponential Smoothing with an Adaptive Response Rate," *Operational Research Quarterly*, Vol. 18, (1967), pp. 53-59.

93. R. E. Turner and R. Staelin, "Error in Judgmental Sales Forecasts: Theory and Results," *Journal of Marketing Research*, Vol. X (February 1973), pp. 10-16.

94. Glen L. Urban, "A New Product Analysis and Decision Model," *Management Science*, Vol. 14 (April 1968), pp. 490-517.

95. S. C. Wheelwright and D. G. Clarke, "Corporate Forecasting: Promise and Reality," *Harvard Business Review*, November-December 1976.

96. S. C. Wheelwright and S. Makridakis, *Forecasting Methods for Management*, 2nd. Ed. (New York: John Wiley & Sons, 1977).

97. P. R. Winters, "Forecasting Sales by Exponentially Weighted Moving Averages," *Management Science*, Vol. 6 (1960), pp. 324-42.

98. H. Wold, *A Study in the Analysis of Stationary Time Series* (Stockholm: Almquist and Wiksell, (first edition 1938), 1954).

99. Thomas R. Wotruba and Michael L. Thurlow, "Sales Force Participation in Quota Setting and Sales Forecasting," *Journal of Marketing*, Vol. 40 No. 2 (April 1976), pp. 11-16.

100. E. C. Zeeman, "CATASTROPHE Theory," *Scientific American*, April 1976, pp. 65-83.

101. F. Zwicky and G. Wilson, *New Methods of Thought and Procedure* (New York: Springer-Verlag, 1967).

Jagdish N. Sheth

The Multivariate Revolution in Marketing Research

Can the current multivariate methods revolution in marketing research be explained? What is the role of computer technology in the rapid diffusion of multivariate methods? This article defines multivariate analysis and discusses the reasons for the probable continuing increase in its use in marketing research.

MANY would agree with the statement that the computer has produced significant advances in the natural and social sciences. However, this general observation overlooks the fact that these two areas have applied computer technology in different ways.

The current diffusion of computer technology is occurring at a time when most of the natural sciences possess several well-developed and invariant laws based on deductive reasoning. Under these circumstances the computer has provided opportunities for model building and for programming a complex network of constructs which enables large-scale testing of physical laws. The most outstanding example of these applications has been provided by the successful exploration of outer space.

However, the social sciences, including marketing, have yet to develop invariant laws. The result is that most of the research in this area is empirical. Attempts are made to explore realities in order to understand the basic nature of the disciplines. Thus, since much of marketing research is empirical and exploratory, the computer has been primarily used to analyze, sort, process, and compact standard commercial data into manageable data banks.

Perhaps computer utilization for model building in the natural sciences and for data analysis in the social sciences provides the best indication of the anticipated rapid

adoption of multivariate methods in marketing research. In addition, two facilitating conditions have emerged which ensure large-scale diffusion of multivariate methods in the future.

The first condition refers to the fact that after three decades of systematic data-gathering, marketing research has learned the art of data collection. For example, procedures exist for drawing accurate samples from populations, training interviewers and respondents, receiving cooperation from respondents, designing structured questionnaires, and coding and tabulating collected data. In this respect, the marketing discipline may be more advanced than some of the other social sciences such as political science. In fact, the increasing accumulation and storage of market research reflects the validity and usefulness of the information collected. Today it is difficult to find a large-scale enterprise which has not been affected by the information explosion.

Second, the market place is a complex phenomenon. A multitude of factors intervene between the marketing activities of companies and market responses. A simple input-output approach does not seem to provide satisfactory answers to marketing problems. Therefore, attempts are constantly made to examine intervening factors and how they mediate between marketing activities and market responses. This has resulted in the collection of information which corresponds to the complexity of the phenomenon.

The capability of the computer to process these complex, large-scale data banks has resulted in the increased use of multivariate methods in marketing research. The extent of this "multivariate revolution" in marketing research is indicated by several factors. For example, a vast number of canned computer programs for these tech-

Jagdish N. Sheth is presently acting head and associate professor of business administration at the University of Illinois. He was formerly on the faculty of Columbia University and Sloan School of Management, M.I.T. In 1969, Professor Sheth was program chairman of the workshop in Multivariate Methods in Marketing sponsored by the American Marketing Association. His research and publications are primarily in consumer psychology, multivariate methods, and international marketing.

The Journal of Marketing
Vol. 35 (January 1971), pp. 13-19

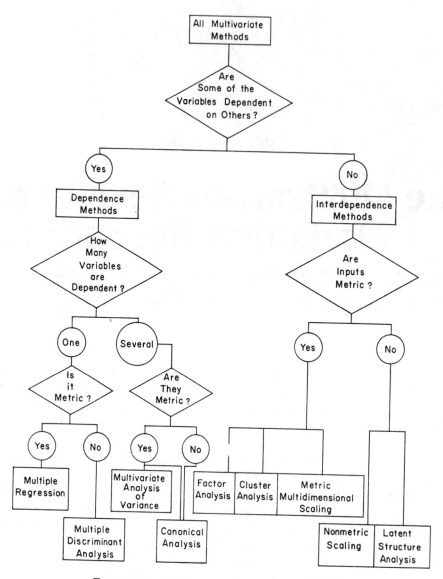

FIGURE 1. A classification of multivariate methods.

niques are already developed and available.[1] In addition, several reviews on the usages of multivariate methods in marketing have been written.[2] A third indication is provided by the increasing number of articles in such journals as the *Journal of Marketing, Journal of Marketing Research*, and *Journal of Advertising Research* which treat applications of multivariate methods to marketing problems.

Inevitably, some questions may be raised about this revolution: How long will it last? Is it not just another fad which will fade away as soon as a new one is introduced? What will be the consequences on future marketing research if multivariate methods are here to stay? Which techniques will be the most relevant and important? However, before these questions can be answered, existing multivariate methods should be understood and classified.

What is Multivariate Analysis?

Although Kendall gives a more technical definition,[3] it is possible to characterize multivariate analysis as all statistical methods which simultaneously analyze more than two variables on a sample of observations. As such these methods are extensions of univariate analysis (all known distributions including binomial, poisson, and normal distribution as well as probability system and Bayesian ap-

---

1 Kenneth M. Warwick, "Computerized Multivariate Methods," paper presented at AMA Workshop on Multivariate Methods in Marketing, Chicago, January 21-23, 1970.

2 Jagdish N. Sheth, "Multivariate Analysis in Marketing," *Journal of Advertising Research*, Vol. 10 (February, 1970), pp. 29-39; Ronald E. Frank and Paul E. Green, "Numerical Taxonomy in Marketing Analysis: A Review Article," *Journal of Marketing Research*, Vol. 5 (February, 1968), pp. 83-98; and Paul E. Green, Frank J. Carmone, and Patrick J. Robinson, "Nonmetric Scaling Methods: An Exposition and Overview," *Wharton Quarterly*, Vol. 2 (Winter-Spring, 1968), pp. 159-173.

3 Maurice G. Kendall, *A Course in Multivariate Analysis* (London: Charles Griffin & Company, 1957).

proaches to the analysis of one variable), and bivariate analysis (including cross-classification, correlation, and simple regression used to analyze two variables).

Figure 1 presents a classification of most of the multivariate methods. It is based on three judgments the marketing researcher must make about the nature and utilization of this data: (1) Are some of the variables dependent upon others, thereby requiring special treatment? (2) If yes, how many are to be treated as dependent in a single analysis? and (3) What are the presumed properties of the data? Specifically, are the data qualitative (nonmetric) in that the marketing reality is scaled on nominal or ordinal scales, or quantitative (metric) and scaled on interval or ratio scales? The technique to be utilized will depend upon the answers to these three questions.

Multiple regression, including several of its variants such as stepwise regression and simultaneous regression, is the appropriate method of analysis when the researcher has a single, metric dependent variable which is presumed to be a function of other independent variables. The objective of multiple regression is to predict the variability in the dependent variable based on its covariance with all the independent variables. This objective is then achieved by the statistical rule of least squares.

Whenever the researcher is interested in predicting the level of the dependent phenomenon, he would find multiple regression useful. For example, sales are predicted from the knowledge of their past relationship (covariance) with marketing efforts; market shares have been predicted based on consumer preference, retail structure, and point-of-purchase advertising and promotion; and consumer buying behavior is predicted from the knowledge of personality and socioeconomic profiles.

If the single dependent variable is dichotomous (e.g., male-female) or multichotomous (e.g., high-medium-low), and therefore nonmetric, the multivariate method of *multiple discriminant analysis* is appropriate. The primary objective of discriminant analysis is to *predict* an entity's likelihood of belonging to a particular class or group based on several predictor variables. For example, discriminant analysis has been widely used in marketing to predict whether (1) a person is a good or poor credit risk based on his socioeconomic and demographic profile, (2) innovators can be distinguished from noninnovators according to their psychological and socioeconomic profiles, and (3) private label buyers can be separated from national brand buyers based on socioeconomic and purchasing differences.[4]

The primary objective of multiple discriminant analysis is to correctly classify entities into mutually exclusive and exhaustive classes or groups. This objective is achieved by the statistical decision rule of maximizing the ratio of among-group to within-group variance-covariances on the profile of discriminating (predictor) variables. In addition to the prediction of class membership based on the profile, discriminant analysis reveals which specific variables in the profile account for the largest proportion of intergroup differences.

Multivariate analysis of variance (multi-ANOVA) is an extension of bivariate analysis of variance in which the ratio of among-groups variance to within- groups variance is calculated on a set of variables instead of a *single* variable. As such, multi-ANOVA is useful whenever the researcher is testing hypotheses concerning multivariate differences in group responses to experimental manipulations. For example, he may be interested in using one test market and one control market to examine the effect of an advertising campaign on sales as well as awareness, knowledge, and attitudes.

The objective in *canonical analysis* is to simultaneously predict a *set* of dependent variables from their joint covariance with a *set* of independent variables. Both metric and nonmetric data are acceptable in canonical analysis. The procedure followed is to obtain a set of weights for the dependent and independent variables which provides the maximum simple correlation between the composite dependent variable and the composite independent variable.

Canonical analysis appears very useful in marketing because the multitude of marketing and environmental factors tend to produce a variety of market responses. The writer, for example, is currently investigating the "heirarchy of effects" (awareness-interest-attitude-conviction-action) as multiple consequences of advertising and promotion.

Thus far the discussion has focused on multivariate methods applied to data which contain both dependent and independent variables. However, if the researcher is investigating the interrelations, and therefore the interdependence, among all the variables, several other multivariate methods are appropriate. These include factor analysis, cluster analysis, and metric multidimensional scaling if the variables are presumed to be metric, and nonmetric multidimensional scaling and latent structure analysis if they are presumed to be nonmetric.

Factor analysis is based on this proposition: If there is systematic interdependence among a set of observed (manifest) variables, it must be due to something more fundamental (latent) which creates this commonality. One can even consider all the manifest variables as simply *indicators* of this fundamental factor. What is this factor? Can it be extracted from the observed data and their relationships? Is it unidimensional or multidimensional? For example, can an individual's income, education, occupation, and dwelling area be considered as indicators of his social class? How can this factor be extracted? Conversely, factor analysis is also used as a data-reduction method which summarizes the commonality of all the manifest variables into a few factors.

The statistical approach utilized in factor analysis is to

---

4 Sheth, same reference as footnote 2.

maximally summarize all of the variance (information), including the covariance (interdependence), in as few factors as possible, while retaining the flexibility of reproducing the original relationship among the manifest variables.

Factor analysis has been widely used in marketing. It has been used to (1) extract latent dimensions of relative liquor preferences such as sweetness, price, and regional popularity; (2) cluster a series of night-time television programs or magazines based on their relative viewership and readership; and (3) systematically search for powerful predictors of a phenomenon under investigation.[5]

In *cluster analysis,* the objective is to classify a population of entities into a small number of mutually exclusive and exhaustive groups based on the similarities of profiles among entities. Unlike discriminant analysis, the groups are not predefined. In fact, two major objectives are to determine *how many* groups really exist in the population, and what is their composition.

Cluster analysis seems useful for market segmentation on personality, socioeconomic and demographic, psychological, and purchasing characteristics of the consumers. However, several other applications have been made in marketing. Examples include the clustering of test market cities in order that they may be selected and controlled for experimentation, and grouping a variety of computers based on their objective performance characteristics.[6] Most of the clustering methods are judgmental, however, and devoid of statistical inferences. In fact, judgment is needed in selecting and coding attributes, in obtaining indices of resemblance or similarity, in choosing among various clustering algorithms, and in naming and testing derived clusters.

Both *metric* and *nonmetric multidimensional scaling methods*, unlike all other multivariate methods, start with a single piece of information. This information relates to perceived relative similarities among a set of objects, such as products, from a sample of respondents. The basic assumption in both metric and nonmetric multidimensional scaling methods is that people perceive a set of objects as being more or less similar to one another on a number of dimensions (usually uncorrelated with one another) instead of only one. However, it may be impossible to directly obtain this multidimensional map from the respondents. One reason for this difficulty is that the respondent may not be consciously aware that he is judging similarities among objects based on these dimensions. A second reason is that he is unwilling to reveal factors (dimensions) that enter into his judgment on similarities. Given this impossibility of directly obtaining the dimensions, reliance is placed on statistical methods of multidimensional scaling to infer the number and types of dimensions that presumably underlie the expressed relative similarities among objects. Therefore, multidimensional scaling

methods are applicable in those areas of marketing research where *motivation research* is currently used.

In both metric and nonmetric multidimensional scaling, the judged similarities among a set of objects (e.g., products, suppliers) are statistically transformed into distances by placing those objects in a multidimensional space of some dimensionality. For example, if objects A and B are perceived by the respondent as being most similar compared to all other possible pairs of objects, these techniques will position objects A and B in such a way that the distance between them in multidimensional space is shorter than that between any two other objects.

Despite the similarities between metric and nonmetric multidimensional scaling, there are two important differences. First metric multidimensional scaling extracts the dimensionality of metric similarity data, whereas the input to nonmetric multidimensional scaling is nonmetric (ordinal) similarities. The metric similarities are often obtained on a bipolar similarity scale on which pairs of objects are rated one at a time. The nonmetric similarities are obtained by asking respondents to rank order (on the basis of similarity) all possible pairs then can be obtained from a set of objects. Various procedures such as dyadic or triadic combinations or rating scales can be used. Second, metric multidimensional scaling attempts to reduce the observed similarities to be represented in a space of minimum dimensions, from the trivial representation in n-1 dimensions, where n is the number of objects. In nonmetric multidimensional scaling, the objective is to metricize the nonmetric data by transforming nonmetric data into a metric space, and then by reducing the dimensionality. This is done by a decision rule of monotone transformation in which the observed rank orderings of pairs of objects are reproduced as closely as possible in an arbitrary metric space of some specified dimensions. This metric space is usually Euclidian, although non-Euclidian spaces can be created by the computer.

Although metric multidimensional scaling has not been applied to any large extent in marketing, nonmetric multidimensional scaling has become very popular in the last three years under the pioneering efforts of Paul Green. It has been applied to the dimensionality of similarities among automobiles, magazines, graduate schools, and several other sets of objects.[7]

Latent structure analysis shares both of the objectives of factor analysis: to extract latent factors and express relationship of manifest variables with these factors as their indicators, and to classify a population of respondents into pure types. Traditionally, nonmetric data have been the input to latent structure analysis, although recently metric data have also been used. In marketing, the only applica-

---

5 Sheth, same reference as footnote 2.
6 Frank and Green, same reference as footnote 2.

7 Green, Carmone, and Robinson, same reference as footnote 2.

tions of this method have been by Myers and Nicosia.[8] One of the main reasons for this has been the lack of computer programs to handle the tedious calculations inherent in this method.

Is Multivariate Revolution a Fad?

A number of compelling reasons suggest that the rapid use of multivariate methods in marketing is not a fad. Instead, these methods are so important that they will be used more frequently in the future.

First, let us examine the anatomy of several behavioral and operations research methods (e.g., pupil dilations, Markov chains) that degenerated into fads. This was due to three factors. First, some operations research methods clearly proved to be ahead of their time. They presumed (through model building) considerable knowledge about the response functions to marketing efforts at a time when no one actually understood how the marketing mix is related to market reactions. These research methods may prove useful once some laws of market behavior have been established. Second, other behavioral and operations research methods took a normative posture of how markets may or should behave at a time when the empirical inductive approach of descriptive research was considered more appropriate. Third, some methods, particularly in the behavioral area, proved to be genuine fads because they created the illusion that market complexity can be easily described by simple "buzz word" models.

None of these factors seems to be present in multivariate methods. Multivariate methods are largely empirical, deal with the market reality by working backward from reality to conceptualization, and easily handle the complexity presumed to be inherent in marketing research.

Second, multivariate methods as "innovative methods" seem to be consistent with modern marketing concepts of focusing on marketing research needs. And the most pressing need of marketing research is the ability to analyze complex data. This is clearly indicated by the following statement: "For the purposes of marketing research or any other applied field, most of our tools are, or should be, multivariate. One is pushed to a conclusion that unless a marketing problem is treated as a multivariate problem, it is treated superficially."[9]

As discussed earlier, this need for complex analysis is manifested today since data collection is a well-developed and standardized art, and computer capabilities are easily accessible.

Finally, a number of multivariate methods are simply extensions of univariate and bivariate analysis of data. Also, there exist a great variety of multivariate methods. Both of these factors contribute toward inhibiting their degeneration to fadism, because fads generally involve highly specialized research tools. However, some specific multivariate techniques may become fads due to overselling. In addition, we should expect the usual problems of co-

ordinating the man-machine interface which are inevitable in the use of multivariate methods.

However, none of these factors is likely to deter the progress of the multivariate revolution primarily because all the facilitating conditions are present today.

Role of the Computer in Multivariate Revolution

Perhaps the most important factor in the rapid diffusion of multivariate methods in marketing research is the availability of computer programs. In fact, we can assert that the lack of computer programs has been a major factor in the imbalance between the extensive data banks in existence today and their weak statistical analysis in most marketing research activities. It would seem that a union between multivariate methods and the computer will provide excellent opportunities for more scientific approaches to marketing problems.

What are the effects of this union on the development of marketing information systems? At present, marketing information systems in most companies basically consist of large data banks. However, a truly useful marketing information system requires an integrated approach between data banks and their retrieval and analysis in accordance with the needs of marketing management. Since most management decisions are complex, a truly multivariate analysis is needed that can be undertaken only if computer facilities are readily available. For example, a recurring decision in marketing management will involve budget allocation among several marketing forces, including advertising, direct mail, promotion, and personal selling. Ramond and Sheth have developed a marketing information system for budget allocation in which time-series audit data on market responses and marketing activities are analyzed by multivariate regression.[10] In essence, changes in shares of market responses such as sales are regressed on changes in shares of several marketing forces including advertising, direct mail, and promotion. Their relative weights and signs are then used by the marketing manager to choose one of the following alternatives given that his objective is to increase the profitability of marketing forces: (1) Maintain the present budget allocation policy. (2) Increase the total budget by a certain amount to reach the optimum level of profitability. (3) Reallocate the

8 John G. Myers and Francesco M. Nicosia, "New Empirical Directions in Market Segmentation: Latent Structure Models," in *Changing Marketing Systems: Consumer, Corporate and Governmental Interfaces*, Reed Moyer (ed.) (Chicago: American Marketing Association, 1967).

9 Ronald Gatty, "Multivariate Analysis for Marketing Research: An Evaluation," *Applied Statistics*, Vol. 15 (November, 1966), p. 158.

10 Charles Ramond and Jagdish Sheth, "Controlling Marketing Performance: Two Case Examples," paper presented to the Workshop on Marketing Information Systems, Association of National Advertisers, August 20, 1970.

budget among marketing forces proportionate to their relative weights. (4) Reduce the total budget by a certain amount to bring expenditures to the optimum level. (5) Phase out the product. This type of marketing information system could not be achieved without a complete interface between the computer and some multivariate method.

A second area benefiting from this interface is testing and estimating parameters of complex and comprehensive theories of the market place. Two specific examples may illuminate this point. First, in the area of advertising effectiveness, a number of researchers[11] have conceptualized a "heirarchy of effects" of advertising and promotion. This hierarchy usually begins with awareness and ends with purchase behavior; in between, several other effects such as interest, knowledge, preference, liking, and conviction are sequentially arranged. It is also presumed that advertising will have, in general, less impact as we move from awareness to action. It would seem that despite numerous empirical studies, no study has as yet attempted to validate the heirarchy by using an appropriate multivariate method.[12] Since the theory presumes a number of effects, canonical analysis appears most appropriate to test the theory and estimate parameters of relative relationships between the hierarchy of effects and a set of advertising variables such as media and copy. Unless such a complex multivariate analysis is done, it is not possible to either support or reject the theory of multiple advertising effectiveness. Much of the inconclusive support currently found in the research literature is perhaps due to this lack of multivariate analysis. Such multivariate analysis, however, was impossible without the appropriate computer capabilities.

Another example comes from an outstanding effort by Farley and Ring to fully test the Howard-Sheth theory of buyer behavior through the use of simultaneous linear equations and the computer.[13] Howard and Sheth have developed a comprehensive and complex theory of buyer behavior in which a large number of psychological constructs, such as attention, overt search, attitude, motives, and satisfaction, intervene between the marketing stimuli and the buyer's responses. In addition, a number of exogenous factors, such as social class, culture, and reference groups, also determine a buyer's responses via their influence on the psychological constructs. Finally, several of the constructs are dynamically interdependent on one another because of the theory's information processing framework. Farley and Ring operationally defined these interdependencies in terms of a set of eleven simultaneous equations; then, using the panel data collected as part of the Columbia Buyer Behavior Project on a sample of more than 900 respondents, they tested the theory. Although they were only moderately successful in validating the theory, their effort represents one of the best examples of how the union between the computer and multivariate methods facilitates the testing of complex theories.

There are several areas of marketing research in which only univariate data have been collected, although the phenomenon is recognized to be complex. In these areas, the combination of multivariate methods and the computer may be most beneficial in furthering systematic and scientific analysis to possibly generate some invariant laws. An example is the research on durable appliances, particularly related to purchasing plans of households. Despite the recognition that purchasing plans are determined by a composite of several important factors, most attempts at measuring them have remained univariate. A single scale is used on which the degree of certainty of buying intentions within a specified time period is obtained from the respondents. It is very probable that this univariate scale is used as a surrogate for more complex factors and has not represented the construct well enough to either predict or explain subsequent purchasing behavior. With the use of multivariate methods such as factor analysis, it is conceivable that buying intentions may indeed prove to be a multidimensional concept.

Conclusion

A number of facilitating factors suggest that multivariate methods may rapidly diffuse in marketing research, and may become a way of life in the statistical analysis of marketing data. These include (1) the empirical, inductive tendency in conducting marketing research due to lack of discovery of marketing laws; (2) collection of large-scale data on marketing problems; (3) confidence in data banks in terms of their reliability and validity; and (4) availability of computers and canned computer programs. The last factor is certainly the most important one in enhancing the diffusion of multivariate methods.

The role of the computer in furthering the maturity of the marketing discipline is thus immense. By diffusing multivariate methods, it is likely to enable marketing researchers to attempt large-scale marketing information systems in which an integrated marketing approach can be undertaken. It will enable researchers to test and estimate parameters of complex generalized theories and models. With the use of multivariate methods, the computer is likely to generate a sudden increase in in-depth scientific empirical research on well-known issues in marketing.

11 Robert C. Lavidge and Gary A. Steiner, "A Model for Predictive Measurement of Advertising Effectiveness," *Journal of Marketing*, Vol. 25 (October, 1961), pp. 59-62.

12 Kristian S. Palda, "The Hypothesis of a Hierarchy of Effects: A Partial Evaluation," *Journal of Marketing Research*, Vol. 3 (February, 1966), pp. 13-24.

13 John V. Farley and L. Winston Ring, "Deriving an Empirically Testable Version of the Howard-Sheth Theory of Buyer Behavior," paper presented at the Third Annual Buyer Behavior Conference, Columbia University, May, 1969.

Ernest Dichter

Seven Tenets of Creative Research

Research in its real sense means continuous searching. To be scientific, it has to submit to the same criteria whether applied in the marketing field or the atomic field. These standards involve the formulation of hypotheses and their validation.

In this provocative article, Dr. Dichter develops seven such tenets, which he sees as prerequisites for a sensitive and creative diagnosis of "why" questions in any field.

T HE world is faced with many problems, only a small portion of which are the specific concern of the advertiser and the groups working with him. Many of these problems have been and will continue to be solved without research...some by the application of industrious creativity, others by the application of industrious effort.

A problem may be so vast or so minute that to use research in its solution would be a waste and a fraud. Or a problem may be non-researchable by definition: research cannot prove that one publicist or one medium is better than another any more than it can prove that apples are better than pears.

However, when research is used for researchable problems, the techniques and the practitioners are subject to the same laws, whether the problem is "Why do people buy soap?" or "What causes cancer?"

Counting how many bars of soap are purchased or how many people have cancer in a year provides us with valuable information, but it is not research. It is census taking. But the word research has two important syllables which indicate its true meaning. *Re-search* is a continued

Ernest Dichter is President of the Institute for Motivational Research, Inc. He is author of a new book, "Strategy of Desire" (Doubleday), in which he discusses his personal and business philosophy concerning motivational research.

Dr. Dichter began as early as 1938, when he first arrived in the United States, to convince American businessmen and advertisers that psychological and social scientific techniques should be applied to the study of consumer buying habits. Since 1946, when he founded his own Institute, his organization has completed more than 1,500 psychological research assignments for leading firms in all parts of the world. In addition to the Research Center in Croton-on-Hudson, the Institute maintains a Los Angeles and a Miami branch office, as well as operations in Canada, Europe, England, Australia, and Latin America.

Dr. Dichter holds his doctorate in psychology from the University of Vienna, and his Licencie es lettres from the Sorbonne.

search, with the emphasis on the search.

The moment you attempt to understand a human action—whether you call it market research, copy research, media research, or motivation research—you practice one type of search, a search for an understanding of human phenomena—a purchase act, a racial prejudice, a voting choice. Your search is for an answer to the question, "Why?" Once you have determined the answer to that question, you have established the qualities you wish to count.

Percentages are not the criteria of good research, nor are large samples. Circulation of an incorrect explanation usually leads to compounding incorrect actions and to failure. In the field of applied research, the "Why?" must be answered before the "How many?" Research is no static matter. It is a sensitive and flexible instrument which must be applied with insight and creativity to the solution of many researchable problems.

Seven Tenets

Following are seven tenets as a credo for creative research in the years that lie ahead:

1. Diagnostic Principle

Diagnosis in the social sciences has to rely as much on the basic principle of scientific investigation as in other branches of science. No reputable medical researcher, physician, or physical scientist would ask his patient or, for that matter, his registering apparatus to tell him what he felt was the cause of pain. How can we, then, ask the respondent to form a judgment on the cause of his own actions without making sure that as diagnosticians we can check the veracity of his statement?

Yet the most frequent technique of marketing research is the questionnaire. In one form or another we try to get information by *asking* people for information. But, whenever it is possible for the respondent to distort answers either willfully or subconsciously, the results are potentially incorrect and unscientific.

2. Avoidance of Hidden Assumptions

Many so-called research studies, which pretend to be empirical and scientific, actually contain a number of hidden assumptions. For example, in trying to find out why people buy or do not buy evaporated milk, we may conduct research in which we compare users with non-users. Our assumption is that the differences we might find in age, income, marital status, etc. of users as compared with non-users will give the answers as to why people buy or do not buy evaporated milk. However, even if there are clear-cut differences, these differences may not be used as causative explanations.

"Let's get the facts," we say, as if this constitutes empirical research. But, in getting the facts in most instances, we are already biasing our results. The bias is caused by the kind of methods used when we say, "Let's ask 2,000 people." *Asking* segregates those people who can and will answer from those who cannot or do not wish to answer.

Another mistake is to test the potential success or failure of a new product among consumers who, because they have not had sufficient experience with the product, react to unfamiliarity rather than to the new product itself. It makes a lot a difference whether a person has smoked five packs of a new cigarette or is trying the first of a new brand. For a test of a new cigarette, the apparent advantages of its newness rapidly disappeared when we permitted the respondent to smoke five packages each of several new brands. It was found that the "new" brand becomes a familiar brand after five packs have been used. Most new brands were rejected on the first try, but it would have been wrong to assume that people were reacting to the product itself. By repeated testing, it was learned that they began by reacting to unfamiliarity and only after repeated trial were they able to react to the product.

Beware of the so-called fact finders. Instead, accept the need for continuous testing and observation. Intelligent and truly scientific research must admit that it introduces certain assumptions into its work. To state the existence of these assumptions, instead of pretending that they are not there, frees the researcher from naive empiricism.

3. Necessity of Hypotheses

The basic criterion for valid research is the quality and intelligence of the hypotheses formulated before the research is undertaken. The intelligence, depth, and originality of the hypotheses determine the worth of a study.

To state that a good researcher has to have pretty good guesses as to what the outcome of a study might be before he even starts is not blasphemy. Any reputable researcher, including particularly those in the field of atomic science, will tell you that real research is the validation or rejection of an intelligent hypothesis. We do not conduct 2,516 experiments in the hope that experiment 2,517 will give us the answer. We set up hypotheses, then determine what factors will have to be observed if these hypotheses are true, and we proceed to examine these pertinent facts.

4. Advertising as Communication

Much marketing research concerns itself with advertising. Advertising is communication, and communication is a two-way process. This means that any research based on the assumption that a respondent is the passive recipient of outside stimuli, must produce false results.

Retention, memory, impact—all these are terms describing passive registration. As such, they are misleading and useless. A viewer of a television commercial is no passive recipient. He talks back, restructures, identifies, and distorts the relationship between himself and the commercial.

The function of advanced research is to measure the dynamic inter-relationships between the viewer and the commercial. The terms and categories to be quantified and controlled have a different sound and connotation. They are empathy, identification, projection, mental rehearsal of purchase, ego-involvement.

Unless advertising research accepts this basic concept of the two-way dynamic relationship in communication, it is hopelessly outdated and incorrect; for modern psychology shows us that, in learning and memory retention, emotions are continuously involved. We forget to remember, because we identify ourselves with the message or because we hate or like a person. The learning process cannot be measured by mechanistic concepts fed into toy-like contraptions whose push buttons, registration apparatus, light-measuring devices, and other paraphernalia pass for research. Such devices bear no relationships to the human facts which explain the dynamics of communication.

5. Mass Marketing

The vast majority of marketing research studies still use age-old categories: marital status, sex, education, income group, occupation, age, etc. The origin of these categories is the census, where we seek additional knowledge concerning the universe; and it follows that we should use these categories to establish correct representative samples. The danger, however, lies in assuming a causative relationship—for instance, jumping to the conclusion that, when more people of a younger age group use a particular product, they do so because of their age.

We are conducting more and more studies in which we use motivational categories that cut across many of the more superficial categories customarily used. For instance, in studies concerned with car purchases, attitudes concerning new cars, dealers, and automobile advertising are colored by the question of whether a person has just purchased a new car or whether he has not bought one for a long time. Again, commercials for foods look entirely different on a full stomach than an empty stomach.

In a study for a group of home builders, it was found that the cost, physical layout, and materials used in the house were of minor importance, compared with the level of social aspiration of the female in the family, reflected in her image of the neighborhood.

In a study on eyedrops, the apparent correlation between usage and such dimensions as sex, age, and marital status turned out to be misleading when a much more meaningful classification was introduced: hypochondriacal tendencies. Such tendencies were far more prevalent among users than among non-users, and they cut across the categories previously established. With this knowledge, the manufacturer was able to develop a different and more accurate merchandising policy, and to select advertising media which allows it to reach the people who already used other proprietary drugs indicative of hypochondriacal tendencies.

6. Uniqueness Rather Than Superiority of Media

No amount of research can prove that the *Saturday Evening Post* reader is better, or richer, or poorer than the *Life* reader. In reality, all such research suffers from a basic misconception, namely, that a *Post* or a *Life* reader exists. If he does, he is the exception, for most people read five or six magazines, and read each because they feel they get something out of each that cannot be found in another publication. Correct media research, therefore, must concentrate on the uniqueness of each publication, each medium, each form of communication.

The very reason for the continued existence of a particular medium is that it offers something its competitor does not offer. While I am watching a Western on TV, I am physically the same person as when I read *Horizon*. I have the same character traits and the same intellectual capacity, but I temporarily lower my intelligence level when watching a Western because I want to relax; I raise it when I turn to *Horizon* or *Harper's* because my needs at that moment are different.

The real questions are: "What do I get out of watching a Western?" and "What satisfactions does *Horizon* give me?" Research directed to the answers to such questions can provide a real contribution to the understanding of the functions of communication in our modern world. Eventually it should also lead to advertising written for a particular psychological group of people who are in a particular mood while they read a particular publication.

7. The Myth of Public Opinion Polls

Attitude scales and questionnaires dealing with people's beliefs are interesting and valuable. They give us a measurement of people's prejudices and judgments. They do not tell us anything about people's actions, however.

We cannot assume that, because a person says he feels positively or negatively about an issue, a country, or a political candidate, he will act in the same way that he talks. Indeed, every child trained by television knows that the opposite often occurs: when a man and a woman hate each other long and strong, you may be certain that they will fall in love before the story ends. When we ask several thousand people to give us their opinion of a political candidate and to tell us whether or not they intend to vote for him, we cannot conclude that they will actually do as they say. What motivates their actions is much less logical, clear, and concise than their answers would indicate. Motivational research attempts to probe these nebulous areas; and much of the resentment against it comes from the fear of seeing ourselves as we really are. We just do not want it to be true that we really bought a house because it had nice red shutters and shrubs around it, while we rejected the more valuable and sturdier house next door because it looked bare.

Just as the good salesman recognizes the emotionality of his customers, so the competent researcher should also be aware that, when a person is asked his opinion concerning government spending or political issues, he gives an answer which may have little or nothing to do with facts. He has been asked to become an expert, and he does so even when he has nothing on which to base his expertness. This does not mean that people cannot be made aware of issues and of facts; it does mean that we have to take an honest look at the situation as it exists now if we expect to change it.

Basic Research

The principles stated are well known in the field of epistemology. They are the basic tenets of what can legitimately be called research.

Management, of course, does have the choice between pure intuitive procedures—hit-or-miss learning based on experience or the use of research. Once you have decided to spend money on research, however, you should be clear about what you are doing. Research in the sense described is tied to creativeness rather than opposed to it.

Unless we have the imagination to formulate original hypotheses, all consequent figures are meaningless. Research has to be validated and quantified. But quantification is only one of the many techniques of making certain that what you have stated is so. It is not, in itself, research.

William A. Marsteller

Marketing Notes

Putting the Marketing Research Department on the Executive Level

ROBERT ELDER and some others who have in their talks and writings traced a brief history of marketing research say that when the high-pressure salesmanship of the 20's proved inadequate in itself to move goods in the 30's, management turned to more calculated methods of market appraisal and sales stimulation. That is to say, marketing research began to be an accepted tool of business management.

Its growth was steady during the 1940's, but it was largely a growth of theory and fact, because in many companies marketing research was a pampered late child. Marketing research departments were born all over the American business scene during the 40's, but because of World War II and postwar prosperity which, incidentally, many marketing research departments misjudged, few marketing analysts were ever put to the test. That is to say, business was pretty generally good, and a great many marketing research departments have survived a decade without their efforts ever being measured against the scale of profit-making. As a matter of fact, many departments were the casual children of high corporate taxes.

We are, of course, in an extension of that period of the 40's. There is no immediate evidence that business management generally is going to ask a great deal more of marketing research during the next several years than it has in the past.

But the day will come when the marketing research manager will be expected to make day-to-day or hour-to-hour decisions just as is the production manager. American business history indicates that in periods of reduced sales, employment, and profits, management tends to look upon any function that fails to contribute to the day-to-day manufacturing or marketing of goods as a luxury. In the field of engineering and product research this lesson was learned in the 1930's. Almost without exception, company-operated laboratories turned their attention to problems having great immediacy, such as reduced material and manufacturing costs, product re-styling for increased sales appeal, etc. Even those companies which maintained

a successful long-range engineering research program, during that period kept short-range research in the front.

Such times will eventually come upon marketing research. The question, I think, is whether the business as a whole will have fallen into the muscle-atrophying habits of big-scale planning or whether it will accept the fact that it is purely a tool or mechanism of management to be used as frequently and almost as casually as a drafting board, a dictaphone, or an inter-office communication system.

Organizational Level of Marketing Research

A great deal has been said and written about whom the marketing research manager should report to. Most everyone in the business seems to agree that it is desirable for the marketing research manager to report to as high a corporate official as possible; for example, the president or the chairman of the board. I submit that many of the same people who cry that the marketing research department should be a wing of the president's office are guilty of operating a department which works in such a specialized realm that it can never truly be a function of the executive department.

As company size grows, the number of people reporting to the president or other chief executive tends to be reduced. The larger and more complex the corporation, the more necessary it becomes to classify skills, talents, and responsibilities into sub-groups so that on decisions of detail there is a buffer between operating heads and the executive office which must plan on a broader basis.

If the marketing research department is concerned solely with those six or eight major functions that the National Industrial Conference Board says it is in most cases, it automatically seeks a level somewhat below that of the sales manager in the corporate organization chart. Further, if the marketing research department has fallen into the habit, as so many have, of presenting reports that belabor the techniques used rather than the ends accomplished—that are, in effect, riddles instead of results—then too the marketing research department seeks its own level, for it must expect that between itself and top management there will be interposed an interpreter.

Suggestions for Improving Marketing Research

The following specific proposals are offered to guide the way toward greater versatility in marketing research and therefore, to greater prestige, service, financial rewards, and perhaps, if it is at all important, to eventual recognition as a profession.

No. 1. Report results and recommendations, not tables and techniques. How you arrived at a decision may be interesting to you, but it is detail to an executive. You are assumed to be technically competent to do your job, or you should not have the job. A chemical engineer who reports in detail what chemicals he put together in performing day to day research seldom gets the ear of the president. Top executives want guidance, suggestions, and results. They are seldom impressed with and often suspicious of an employee who dwells upon the special language and procedures of his own special field.

No. 2. Sell your entire line. A manufacturing plant is set up on the theory that production will be in balance as regards various items in the line. When production is out of balance, profits decline. The same thing is true of a marketing research department. To make money for the company, there should be a constant balance between the type of projects the department is performing at any given time. Emphasis should also be put on the ''sell.'' That is one of the places where defining marketing research as a profession, rather than a business, gets us into trouble. Most of our professions, rightly or wrongly, sit and wait for business. A marketing research department cannot afford to do that.

No. 3. Do not wait for management to suggest projects and areas of work; make suggestions to management on where marketing research can be used effectively. Top management can never be and should never be fully conversant with all the details of the operations of any of its departments. If marketing research is to be a wing of the executive department, it should translate its abilities into executive needs.

No. 4. Make sure there is agreement upon what the marketing research department is to do on a given assignment before it starts out. Be sure the question to be answered is defined. I have seen carefully prepared reports submitted by marketing research departments or marketing research agencies, which management received with surprise and disappointment because the report did not cover the problem. In such a case, it is usually assumed that the marketing research manager made the mistake. Whether he did

or did not is immaterial in such an argument because the work is wasted, and wasted overhead work is the purest waste and is invariably looked upon by management with a jaundiced eye.

No. 5. Get out of the office. Few well-run businesses are run from a desk. The most aggressive business managers today see customers, suppliers, stockholders, employees, politicians, and others in their native habitat. The marketing research manager and analyst, if they are to operate on an executive level, need to follow suit. All the monographs and census figures you can collect in your office are worthless unless applied to your company's problems, and to really understand their application, it is necessary to understand the business. A proper understanding of the whole business can be gained only by getting out.

No. 6. Report results on assignments in terms of cost-saving or profit-making. That is not easy, but it is important. Corporate suggestion systems really came of age only when somebody finally realized that it should be possible to put a dollar and cents value to the company on every suggestion. Likewise, advertising in recent years has been fighting the battle of financial results—reporting inquiries on the basis of cost per inquiry or sales on the basis of dollars of sales per dollar of advertising expenditure. The same thing can be done on marketing research although it is not easy and requires real ingenuity. Instead of recommending that salesman A's territory be reduced because of a summary of reasons that seem irrefutable, put in the added fillip of showing dollar savings to the company by reducing his territory. Instead of saying that it is apparent that your company should be able to capture 2 per cent more of the total asbestos market, show what those additional sales would do to the company's profit and loss statement. That is the key to adoption of the reports instead of filing for future reference.

No. 7. Do not be afraid to do another department's work. A number of marketing research departments have built a little fence around themselves, and as soon as their work moves toward the field of another department, they throw the responsibility upon that department. They avoid an accounting problem, or an engineering analysis, or any activity which is not strictly their own. That is an excellent way to shift blame, but it tends to create a bureaucracy which is wasteful to the company and eventually dangerous to you. I am not suggesting that marketing research department people should set themselves up as experts in all fields. That brings up point No. 8.

No. 8. To be fully effective the market research department should work with all other departments, not simply sales or engineering. If it is to be an executive department, it must work as the president's office does, with equal interest in and assistance to all departments.

No. 9. While maintaining a program of economic or marketing planning for the company, do not be afraid to take on projects which become actually an analysis of single units. Many marketing research operations seem to avoid any analysis which becomes a customer-by-customer study rather than a study of the whole field. They seem to feel that when a job becomes specific, it becomes the work of the sales department. However, it should be borne in mind that in many industrial companies the number of customers and prospects is extremely limited, and good market analysis is nothing more than a searching scrutiny of every single customer or prospect.

No. 10. You should know what is going on in the technical research departments at all times. Your best friend and closest ally should be the Director of Product Research. Your effectiveness will be greatly increased if the marketing research department is in at the start on new product planning rather than becoming a factor of market determination after product development is completed.

No. 11. Whether you are required to or not, make monthly summary reports to your management listing very briefly assignments completed during the past month, work in process, and that on the agenda. Operate your department on a business basis.

No. 12. Run your department on a budget whether your are required to or not. Make cost estimates before you start on all assignments, and keep costs showing the money expended to do individual jobs. In all cases, whether your management says you must or not, you should be prepared at any time to explain the operations of your department in terms of benefits to the company and costs as well.

Conclusion

All of that is a very pat pattern; the reaction of some people is "Well, that's all well and good if the marketing research department already reports to the president, but some of the things you suggest our company won't stand still for or isn't interested in." The question then is, "How does the marketing research department officially become a wing of the president's office?"

It does not do it because the president reads a speech by a marketing research manager saying that that is where the department belongs. It does not do it because the president becomes convinced that his marketing research manager is a whiz on the technicalities of market analysis.

It does do it when the president is convinced that the marketing research department looks, acts, talks, and thinks like a business manager. Organization charts are built around individuals, and management theories are rationalized to fit them. The reputation of individuals is, in turn, built upon the way they operate and the contributions they make.

In my opinion, the name marketing research is in itself too limiting a term. Basically a good marketing research department is a management research department. If it becomes highly specialized, it probably does not even deserve the term marketing research but instead should be called the business library department, or the economic analysis department, or the sales statistical department.

A versatile marketing research department is the seat of the greatest business opportunities. It is by all odds the most logical place for training young executives. It should be top management's feeding ground. If that conception is accepted, there is perhaps a different outlook on employment of new people for the marketing research department. A sound grounding in the principles of marketing research is desirable and in many cases essential, but it is not a substitute for hiring young men and women for the native abilities and personalities which must already be present if they are to some day grow into business managers.

Marketing Theory

Robert D. W. Bartels

Marketing Principles

Editor's Note: This article is based on the author's doctoral dissertation at the Ohio State University. It is hoped that it will arouse some discussion on this important topic. The author has taught at the University of Washington and at the University of California. At present he is in the United States Navy.

A CRITERION of the maturity of logical analysis is the extent to which principles of a subject are developed and stated. Measured by this standard, the study of marketing can be said to have made substantial progress, because during the past thirty years not only have many facts about marketing been collected, but many truths concerning it have been soundly generalized. Nevertheless, the relative absence of principles identified as such, suggests that something is yet to be desired in the statement of marketing theory.

It may be said at the outset that the existence of marketing principles has been widely presumed, for a long-standing objective of students of marketing has been to derive and to state them. Some writers have named their books *Principles of Marketing*, and others have set apart certain generalizations which they termed "principles."

Notwithstanding this long-expressed interest, there exists today neither a clearly identified body of marketing principles nor general agreement as to what a principle is. The absence of such a body of principles suggests one of two conclusions: either that the facts of the subject have not been sufficiently ascertained, or that the significance of methodological and theoretical problems is not fully appreciated. However, sufficient data describing the marketing process have been collected to suggest that the absence of principles is not due to ignorance of the subject. Their apparent absence must be attributable to another cause.

The Definition of "Principle"

One factor contributing to this lack of stated principles is the wide variety of meanings given the term, among which are the following: rule of action, general truth, fundamental assumption, and comprehensive or governing law.

It is generally agreed that a *principle* is an element of science falling between specific observation and theory.

Observation and experience are the prerequisites to thought which organizes itself as theory. Individual experiences repeated in one's own existence are habitual *rules of action*; repeated in the actions of others, they form *behavior patterns,* which are, more or less, summaries of individual experiences. Observed facts, consciously entertained, constitute the main postulate, elementary proposition, or fundamental assumption of deductive analysis.

Upon these premises are built theory and science. The statement of the relationships existing between seemingly causal and effectual phenomena, constitutes a *law, theory,* or *principle*. A body of such principles is a *doctrine*. *Science* is accumulated knowledge considered as a distinct field of study, and systematized with reference to the discovery of general laws.

In contrast to all of them, art is knowledge applied and made efficient by skill.

Because these terms have been employed interchangeably so that their exact meanings have been obscured, it is well to remember that a principle is a statement of causal relationship between two or more phenomena.

Principles in Economic and Marketing Literature

In both economic and marketing writings, a principle has properly been regarded as a statement of relationship between causes and effects. In theoretical economic writings, however, the attempt to demonstrate such relationships has resulted in lengthy explanations. The sets of relationships existing, for example, between various scales of operation and resultant costs of production cannot be set down in few words. The principles of valuation, specialization, exchange, et cetera, are also explained at length, but there rarely grows out of those explanations a concise statement which would serve as a basis for predicting the results likely to follow from given causal conditions. Nevertheless, although principles may not be explicitly formulated, they seem to be implicitly present in the discussions.

In marketing literature, on the other hand, the concept of principles has not been associated with such lengthy theoretical discourses. The subject has been neither so broadly generalized nor so penetratingly reduced to fundamental assumptions as theoretical economics. It has been more descriptive and practical, and, as a result, the principles derived have been of a simpler nature. For example, in studies of relationships existing between markets and the distributive means of reaching them, principles have tended to represent rules of action more than comprehensive and governing laws. As a matter of fact, the simpler type of principle, such as rules for choosing a particular channel under given circumstances, has been emphasized almost to the neglect of the broader factors governing channel choice in general.

That one or the other type of principle is necessarily the more suitable for either marketing or economics cannot be said. Each has its merits. And each field of study may benefit by employing to a greater extent the methodology characterizing the other.

There are a number of reasons for the failure to develop principles of the broader sort for the field of marketing. First, marketing was regarded more or less as an activity of institutions comparable to mechanisms performing a function. That type of study was thought most important which yielded improvements in operating techniques and developed rules of action. Second, the need for improved rules of action required the elaborate description of the marketing process. Consequently, emphasis was placed upon description, and such description did not at times exceed the bounds of summarization of the individual cases observed—it did not attain the status of generalization. Third, marketing writers have not always been conscious of the assumptions underlying their logic. They were, on the whole, generally concerned more with the practical than with the theoretical aspects of the subject.

In defense of the study of marketing, it may be said that inasmuch as the field is one commonly regarded as "applied economics," rules of action rather than generalized principles may be expected. Furthermore, it is perhaps fair to judge the study of marketing not by the maturity it has attained, but by the direction of its inclination. The youth of the study of marketing may preclude generalization, and, as in other more developed sciences, the broader principles may be derived only at a later stage. The character of the principles already stated may be peculiar to that elementary stage of a science in which facts are sought, concepts defined, and classifications delimited; in which the existence of law explaining relationships, effect, and change is assumed; and in which generalizations are made tentative pending fuller understanding. This stage precedes one in which more philosophical issues are taken up, and in which methodology, ideology, and rela-

tionships of various disciplines are investigated. The study of marketing may be ripe at present for scholars who will synthesize it and formulate the more general principles.

Principles in Marketing Literature

Perhaps the most convincing evidence of the type of principles thus far presented is found in the principles themselves. Below are listed some which have been found in a variety of marketing writings, and which are intended to be a sample rather than a comprehensive list of principles. Some have been taken verbatim from the writings; others have not been accredited to particular writers because the generalizations are so common in marketing thought that it would be unjust to attribute a statement of them to any one person. The categories into which they have been grouped are also merely suggestive rather than conclusive and final.

1. *Operational Principles*—those which pertain to business conduct, and which are accepted as laws or rules to be employed in the operation of a marketing institution.

The leasing of departments of a department store tends to be most desirable when skill, specialized knowledge, and extreme style risks are involved in handling the goods in question.

Good lighting is a requisite of successful merchandising, because it creates a pleasing atmosphere for trading, facilitates inspection of merchandise, enhances its appearance, and gives an impression of modernity and prosperity.[1]

The convenience of all concerned is the foremost consideration in store layout.[2]

For private brands to be successful, the demand for them must be consistent and steady.

The initial stock for a new store should consist approximately of the proportions of stocks in going stores. Subsequent stocking should reflect demand and supply peculiarities of the locality.

The pricing policy for a store cannot be based upon the gross margin of any one profitable item. When a number of items are handled, the general policy must be composite, reflecting the nature of demand for the goods, the availability of it to the seller, competition, cost, and ease of handling.

The combination of all possible resources for the creation of one distinct impression is the best means of attracting attention and putting across the selling idea.

In selling, greet customers promptly; remember names and facts; study your customer; know your goods; make things plain, tell the truth; do not argue, etc.[3]

---

1 H. C. Nolen, and H. H. Maynard, *Drug Store Management*, McGraw-Hill and Co., N.Y., 1941, p. 62.

2 *Ibid.*, p. 75.

3 *Ibid.*, pp. 260-261.

Every book on merchandising principles and practice will be found to abound in generalizations of this type. It has been the most common and abundant type of marketing principle presented.

2. *Principles Involving Institutional Relationships*—those pertaining to the combination of institutions into marketing channels and to the competitive relations of the establishments.

The outlets through which goods are distributed vary, depending upon the buying habits of customers with respect to the goods.

"In a seller's market the competition among middlemen to get the goods leads to specialization, but in a buyer's market the opposite tendency exists."[4]

"Retail price competition provides an impetus toward integration in the marketing process. The social aspects of retailing are evident in the constant tendency toward improvement in selling environment and extension of customer service. The basic economic aspect reasserts itself when competition begins to appear in pine-board stores or abandoned warehouses, but with lower prices."[5]

"When conditions demand modification in the existing marketing structure the change will be made either by modifying existing practices or by developing new institutions."[6]

"As independents are able to increase their efficiency and meet the chains on more even ground, the comparative advantages of the chains may be reduced to a point where tax burdens will be important limiting factors in further chain expansion."[7]

"When the number of potential users of a given product is large, the market scattered, the unit of sale low, the credit standing of consumers limited, demand irregular, prompt delivery of major importance, economies in shipment possible, little or no technical sales service required, repair service essential, and relatively little sales promotional effort produces satisfactory results; then the distributor channel is the most economical means, provided, of course, that the distributor operates with a reasonabe degree of efficiency."[8]

As changes occur in the retailing structure, changes will also occur in the wholesaling system.

3. *Principles Relating to the Marketing Task*—those which are drawn from the relationship of marketing to more general social and economic phenomena.

Because personal service and convenience usually mean more to consumers than mere mechanical efficiency, the use of mechanical and automatic labor-saving devices in distribution is more limited than in production

The enjoyment of the products of mass production depends upon the operation of a vast and complex system of distribution.

A simple economic organization is most conducive to direct selling.

As the income of a family increases, the percentage of income expended for food and housing decreases, and the

percentage expended for clothing and miscellaneous items increases.

The extent of the marketing task is dependent upon the character of production, even as the character of production is dependent upon the nature of the market and of the marketing facilities.

As peoples and nations advance in civilization, trade increases and the structure of marketing institutions becomes more complex.

"The demand for luxury goods tends to increase as wealth is concentrated in a minority of the population."[9]

The employment of women affects the market through both the character of demand and the volume of it.

4. *Hypothetical Principles*—those which, breaking away from observational and statistical bases, project generalizations into hypothetical situations from assumed bases.

So long as exchange is obstructed by a given condition, it will be a function of marketing to overcome that obstruction or difficulty.

"So long as tastes vary it will be impossible to standardize consumer goods in the same way as paving-bricks or steel rails can be standardized."[10]

So long as consumers demand and expect to obtain commodities immediately upon their decision to buy or their discovery of need, the cost of foresight and risk will be incurred by merchants and will be included in total distribution costs.

Continuous competition in marketing, expressed in experimentation in methods of distribution, types of enterprises, arrangement of functions, and new methods of performance, evolves new patterns of distribution.

Price in the market is determined in the long-run by general factors of demand and supply, and in the short-run by a variety of institutional pricing policies.

Because of their increasing overhead costs, department stores cannot expand their sales indefinitely without incurring proportionately higher costs of operation.

"With all the modifications of the system, the general level of retail prices depends on those of goods distributed through the channels which have earned the title of 'regular' because they are supposed to be made up of the types of concerns organized for the performance of the market-

4 P. W. Ivey, *Principles of Marketing*, Ronald Press Co., N.Y., 1921, p. 16.

5 Wm. Girdner, "Integranted Marketing Institutions," *The Annals of the American Academy of Political and Social Sciences*, May 1940, pp. 60-61.

6 H. H. Maynard, W. C. Weidler, T. N. Beckman, *Principles of Marketing*, The Ronald Press Co., N.Y., 1939, p. 18.

7 *Ibid.*, p. 154.

8 T. N. Beckman and N. H. Engle, *Wholesaling*, The Ronald Press Co., N. Y., 1937, p. 197.

9 Maynard Weidler, and Beckman, *op. cit.*, p. 18.

10 *Does Distribution Cost Too Much*, Twentieth Century Fund, 1940, p. 340.

ing functions in an orderly and economical fashion."[11]

"The seller under conditions of pure competition, will expand his output until his marginal cost is equal to his marginal revenue."[12]

5. *Truisms*—those principles the truth of which is so apparent as to be obvious, and the statement of which is worthwhile mainly for the attention it calls to the matter-of-fact.

Every middleman exists because of a demand for his service.

The growth of any marketing structure is evolutionary, not revolutionary.

The costs of direct selling increase with the addition of functions to be performed.

While marketing institutions can be eliminated, and functions shifted, the basic marketing functions cannot be eliminated.

"Demand for certain qualities of raw materials leads to the development of standards."[13]

"Whenever a farm crop reaches a tonnage which makes it of commercial importance, middlemen or buyers appear in the local market."[14]

In addition to falling into these classifications, the principles may also be identified as of long-run or short-run significance, of broad or narrow application, of inductive or deductive origin, etc. The number of such principles which may be stated and classified is limitless, both because innumerable ideas may be expressed concerning marketing and also because principles may be stated in different ways. The examples presented here merely begin the list of principles with which we are perhaps familiar, but many of which are not identified as principles. These examples do, however, present some of the sound generalizations reached, and indicate a few of the problems which are involved in deriving them.

Principles More Theoretical

If principles of marketing were developed in the manner of those found in economic writings, relationships would be drawn in a more general fashion, and the principles would be left more or less implicit in the theoretical discussion. Ideally, a study of principles would combine both broad investigation of related factors and concise statement of the more profound relationships.

If marketing principles were approached from this broader viewpoint, some of them may be developed as follows:

1. *Principle of Markets.* Whether or not there is a market for anything depends upon the existence of demand and supply. A market, however, is seldom an automatic, perfectly equilibrated transaction. On the contrary, numerous efforts are made to make commodities conform to expected demand, and demand is molded to make available commodities acceptable to it. The relationships of factors involved in the establishment or identification of the elements of exchange could be expressed as a wide variety of principles.

2. *Principle of Marketing Functions.* It is claimed that the functions of marketing are inherent in the marketing task, but disagreement among writers as to what the marketing functions are leaves no one to believe that there is only one list of such functions. Much needs yet to be written on the relationship between marketing task under different circumstances and the functions involved.

3. *Principle of Institutions.* Existing marketing institutions have come to be logically and popularly classified by types. The history of each is known. The relations between historical, economic, social, geographic, and other conditions and these institutions, however, have not been fully studied. It is known that with economic and social trends, changes have occurred in the structure of marketing institutions. A statement of principles involved in the development of institutional types would not only illuminate the understanding of the system, but would also be useful in shaping the progress of individual institutions faced with changing conditions.

4. *Principle of Distributive Channels.* The passage of various commodities through their channels has been traced, and the merits of different combinations of institutions as channels have been discussed at length. Nevertheless, there is still needed an organized presentation of the conditions and policies which result in the establishment of the diverse distributive channels.

5. *Principle of Operating Costs.* The economic principle of overhead costs has some special applications in the field of distribution, because the factors of production are combined in ways unexplained in traditional economic treatises. Although statistics present inconclusive evidence of trends and tendencies in distribution costs, the character of those costs is represented, and numerous relationships of costs and circumstances are discernible. Relationships between distribution costs and policies of market selectivity may also be more generally stated.

If it is believed that the principles suggested above have already been derived in the existing writings, it should be recalled that on the whole the treatment of the principles involved has been narrow compared to the scope which is possible. Both the names and the content suggested for principles of the more general type are offered in the hope that they may stimulate further consideration of the subject.

---

11 Paul T. Cherington, *The Elements of Marketing*, The Macmillan Co., N. Y., 1920, p. 37.

12 C. F. Phillips, *Marketing*, Houghton-Mifflin Co., Boston, 1938, p. 528.

13 Maynard, Weidler, and Beckman, op. cit., p. 293.

14 *Ibid.*, p.290.

Conclusion

The relative lack of stated principles points to a critical but hopeful condition in the study of marketing. On the one hand, it suggests that the deeper implications have not been drawn from the acknowledged facts; on the other hand, it offers one of the most fertile fields for marketing research.

As a knowledge of marketing principles is indispensable for the practice of marketing, so it is vital to the proper teaching of the subject. Courses may profitably be built around the study of principles, taking the principles either as a point of departure from which logic and illustration proceed, or as a destination toward which an investigation is directed. Being broad generalizations demanding interpretation, they form useful bases upon which students may be questioned and their perception and logic tested.

A knowledge of principles and of the place which they occupy at present in marketing literature serves also as a basis for evaluating additions to the available writings on marketing. Some books are primarily descriptive, others merely logical or interpretive, still others theoretical. Each has its advantages, and the character of each can be judged by its content of principles.

Finally, familiarity with principles serves as a basis upon which marketing doctrines or the science of marketing may be developed. The formulation of individual principles standing alone represents but one stage in marketing analysis. Another stage, and a significant one, includes the combination of principles in a manner by which a theory of marketing is formed. It is evident, therefore, that while the derivation of principles is of value in itself, its greater value lies in the promise of the broader study of marketing which it holds forth.

Philip Kotler and Sidney J. Levy

Broadening the Concept of Marketing

Marketing is a pervasive societal activity that goes considerably beyond the selling of toothpaste, soap, and steel. The authors interpret the meaning of marketing for nonbusiness organizations and the nature of marketing functions such as product improvement, pricing, distribution, and communication in such organizations. The question considered is whether traditional marketing principles are transferable to the marketing of organizations, persons, and ideas.

THE term "marketing" connotes to most people a function peculiar to business firms. Marketing is seen as the task of finding and stimulating buyers for the firm's output. It involves product development, pricing, distribution, and communication; and in the more progressive firms, continuous attention to the changing needs of customers and the development of new products, with product modifications and services to meet these needs. But whether marketing is viewed in the old sense of "pushing" products or in the new sense of "customer satisfaction engineering," it is almost always viewed and discussed as a business activity.

It is the authors' contention that marketing is a pervasive societal activity that goes considerably beyond the selling of toothpaste, soap, and steel. Political contests remind us that candidates are marketed as well as soap; student recruitment by colleges reminds us that higher education is marketed; and fund raising reminds us that "causes" are marketed. Yet these areas of marketing are typically ignored by the student of marketing. Or they are treated cursorily as public relations or publicity activities.

About the authors. Philip Kotler is Professor of Marketing at Northwestern University. He earned his PhD at M.I.T. He is the author of Marketing Management: Analysis, Planning and Control. Professor Kotler is Advisory Editor of the Holt, Rinehart and Winston Marketing Series and is an active consultant to many companies on marketing planning and information systems. Currently he is Chairman of the College on Marketing of The Institute of Management Sciences.

Sidney J. Levy is Professor of Marketing at Northwestern University and is Vice President of Social Research, Inc. He earned his PhD at the University of Chicago. Professor Levy is author of Promotion: A Behavioral View, co-author of Living with Television, and of many articles.

No attempt is made to incorporate these phenomena in the body proper of marketing thought and theory. No attempt is made to redefine the meaning of product development, pricing, distribution, and communication in these newer contexts to see if they have a useful meaning. No attempt is made to examine whether the principles of "good" marketing in traditional product areas are transferable to the marketing of services, persons, and ideas.

The authors see a great opportunity for marketing people to expand their thinking and to apply their skills to an increasingly interesting range of social activity. The challenge depends on the attention given to it; marketing will either take on a broader social meaning or remain a narrowly defined business activity.

The Rise of Organizational Marketing

One of the most striking trends in the United States is the increasing amount of society's work being performed by organizations other than business firms. As a society moves beyond the stage where shortages of food, clothing, and shelter are the major problems, it begins to organize to meet other social needs that formerly had been put aside. Business enterprises remain a dominant type of organization, but other types of organizations gain in conspicuousness and in influence. Many of these organizations become enormous and require the same rarefied management skills as traditional business organizations. Managing the United Auto Workers, Defense Department, Ford Foundation, World Bank, Catholic Church, and University of California has become every bit as challenging as managing Procter and Gamble, General Motors, and General Electric. These nonbusiness organizations have an increasing range of influence, affect as many livelihoods, and occupy as much media prominence as major business firms.

All of these organizations perform the classic business functions. Every organization must perform a financial function insofar as money must be raised, managed, and budgeted according to sound business principles. Every organization must perform a production function in that it must conceive of the best way of arranging inputs to produce the outputs of the organization. Every organization must perform a personnel function in that people must be hired, trained, assigned, and promoted in the course of the organization's work. Every organization must perform a purchasing function in that it must acquire materials in an efficient way through comparing and selecting sources of supply.

When we come to the marketing function, it is also clear that every organization performs marketing-like activities whether or not they are recognized as such. Several examples can be given.

The police department of a major U.S. city, concerned with the poor image it has among an important segment of its population, developed a campaign to "win friends and influence people." One highlight of this campaign is a "visit your police station" day in which tours are conducted to show citizens the daily operations of the police department, including the crime laboratories, police lineups, and cells. The police department also sends officers to speak at public schools and carries out a number of other activities to improve its community relations.

Most museum directors interpret their primary responsibility as "the proper preservation of an artistic heritage for posterity."[1] As a result, for many people museums are cold marble mausoleums that house miles of relics that soon give way to yawns and tired feet. Although museum attendance in the United States advances each year, a large number of citizens are uninterested in museums. Is this indifference due to failure in the manner of presenting what museums have to offer? This nagging question led the new director of the Metropolitan Museum of Art to broaden the museum's appeal through sponsoring contemporary art shows and "happenings." His marketing philosophy of museum management led to substantial increases in the Met's attendance.

The public school system in Oklahoma City sorely needed more public support and funds to prevent a deterioration of facilities and exodus of teachers. It recently resorted to television programming to dramatize the work the public schools were doing to fight the high school dropout problem, to develop new teaching techniques, and to enrich the children. Although an expensive medium, television quickly reached large numbers of parents whose response and interest were tremendous.

Nations also resort to international marketing campaigns to get across important points about themselves to the citizens of other countries. The junta of Greek colonels who seized power in Greece in 1967 found the international publicity surrounding their cause to be extremely unfavorable and potentially disruptive of international recognition. They hired a major New York public relations firm and soon full-page newspaper ads appeared carrying the headline "Greece Was Saved From Communism," detailing in small print why the takeover was necessary for the stability of Greece and the world.[2]

An anti-cigarette group in Canada is trying to press the Canadian legislature to ban cigarettes on the grounds that they are harmful to health. There is widespread support for this cause but the organization's funds are limited, particularly measured against the huge advertising resources of the cigarette industry. The group's problem is to find effective ways to make a little money go a long way in persuading influential legislators of the need for discouraging cigarette consumption. This group has come up with several ideas for marketing anti-smoking to Canadians, including television spots, a paperback book featuring pictures of cancer and heart disease patients, and legal research on company liability for the smoker's loss of health.

What concepts are common to these and many other possible illustrations of organizational marketing? All of these organizations are concerned about their "product" in the eyes of certain "consumers" and are seeking to find "tools" for furthering their acceptance. Let us consider each of these concepts in general organizational terms.

Products

Every organization produces a "product" of at least one of the following types:

Physical Products. "Product" first brings to mind everyday items like soap, clothes, and food, and extends to cover millions of *tangible* items that have a market value and are available for purchase.

Services. Services are *intangible* goods that are subject to market transaction such as tours, insurance, consultation, hairdos, and banking.

Persons. Personal marketing is an endemic *human* activity, from the employee trying to impress his boss to the statesman trying to win the support of the public. With the advent of mass communications, the marketing of persons has been turned over to professionals. Hollywood stars have their press agents, political candidates their advertising agencies, and so on.

Organizations. Many organizations spend a great deal of time marketing themselves. The Republi-

---

[1] This is the view of Sherman Lee, Director of the Cleveland Museum, quoted in *Newsweek*, Vol. 71 (April 1, 1968), p. 55.

[2] "PR for the Colonels," *Newsweek*, Vol. 71 (March, 18, 1968), p. 70.

can Party has invested considerable thought and resources in trying to develop a modern look. The American Medical Association decided recently that it needed to launch a campaign to improve the image of the American doctor.[3] Many charitable organizations and universities see selling their *organization* as their primary responsibility.

Ideas. Many organizations are mainly in the business of selling *ideas* to the larger society. Population organizations are trying to sell the idea of birth control, and the Women's Christian Temperance Union is still trying to sell the idea of prohibition.

Thus the "product" can take many forms, and this is the first crucial point in the case for broadening the concept of marketing.

Consumers

The second crucial point is that organizations must deal with many groups that are interested in their products and can make a difference in its success. It is vitally important to the organization's success that it be sensitive to, serve, and satisfy these groups. One set of groups can be called the *suppliers. Suppliers* are those who provide the management group with the inputs necessary to perform its work and develop its product effectively. Suppliers include employees, vendors of the materials, banks, advertising agencies, and consultants.

The other set of groups are the *consumers* of the organization's product, of which four sub-groups can be distinguished. The *clients* are those who are the immediate consumers of the organization's product. The clients of a business firm are its buyers and potential buyers; of a service organization those receiving the services, such as the needy (from the Salvation Army) or the sick (from County Hospital); and of a protective or a primary organization, the members themselves. The second group is the *trustees* or *directors,* those who are vested with the legal authority and responsibility for the organization, oversee the management, and enjoy a variety of benefits from the "product." The third group is the active *publics* that take a specific interest in the organization. For a business firm, the active publics include consumer rating groups, governmental agencies, and pressure groups of various kinds. For a university, the active publics include alumni and friends of the university, foundations, and city fathers. Finally, the fourth consumer group is the *general public.* These are all the people who might develop attitudes toward the organization that might affect its conduct in some way. Organizational marketing concerns the programs designed by management to create satisfactions and favorable attitudes in the organization's four consuming groups: clients, trustees, active publics, and general public.

Marketing Tools

Students of business firms spend much time studying the various tools under the firm's control that affect product acceptance: product improvement, pricing, distribution, and communication. All of these tools have counterpart applications to nonbusiness organizational activity.

Nonbusiness organizations to various degrees engage in product improvement, especially when they recognize the competition they face from other organizations. Thus, over the years churches have added a host of nonreligious activities to their basic religious activities to satisfy members seeking other bases of human fellowship. Universities keep updating their curricula and adding new student services in an attempt to make the educational experience relevant to the students. Where they have failed to do this, students have sometimes organized their own courses and publications, or have expressed their dissatisfaction in organized protest. Government agencies such as license bureaus, police forces, and taxing bodies are often not responsive to the public because of monopoly status; but even here citizens have shown an increasing readiness to protest mediocre services, and more alert bureaucracies have shown a growing interest in reading the user's needs and developing the required product services.

All organizations face the problem of pricing their products and services so that they cover costs. Churches charge dues, universities charge tuition, governmental agencies charge fees, fund-raising organizations send out bills. Very often specific product charges are not sufficient to meet the organization's budget, and it must rely on gifts and surcharges to make up the difference. Opinions vary as to how much the users should be charged for the individual services and how much should be made up through general collection. If the university increases its tuition, it will have to face losing some students and putting more students on scholarship. If the hospital raises its charges to cover rising costs and additional services, it may provoke a reaction from the community. All organizations face complex pricing issues although not all of them understand good pricing practice.

Distribution is a central concern to the manufacturer seeking to make his goods conveniently accessible to buyers. Distribution also can be an important marketing decision area for nonbusiness organizations. A city's public library has to consider the best means of making its books available to the public. Should it establish one large library with an extensive collection of books, or several neighborhood branch libraries with duplication of books? Should it use bookmobiles that bring the books to the customers instead of relying exclusively on the customers coming to the books? Should it distribute through school libraries? Similarly the police department of a city must

---

3 "Doctors Try an Image Transplant," *Business Week,* No. 2025 (June 22, 1968), pp. 64.

think through the problem of distributing its protective services efficiently through the community. It has to determine how much protective service to allocate to different neighborhoods; the respective merits of squad cars, motorcycles, and foot patrolmen; and the positioning of emergency phones.

Customer communication is an essential activity of all organizations although many nonmarketing organizations often fail to accord it the importance it deserves. Managements of many organizations think they have fully met their communication responsibilities by setting up advertising and/or public relations departments. They fail to realize that *everything about an organization talks.* Customers form impressions of an organization from its physical facilities, employees, officers, stationery, and a hundred other company surrogates. Only when this is appreciated do the members of the organization reorganize that they all are in marketing, whatever else they do. With this understanding they can assess realistically the impact of their activities on the consumers.

Concepts for Effective Marketing Management in Nonbusiness Organizations

Although all organizations have products, markets, and marketing tools, the art and science of effective marketing management have reached their highest state of development in the business type of organization. Business organizations depend on customer goodwill for survival and have generally learned how to sense and cater to their needs effectively. As other types of organizations recognize their marketing roles, they will turn increasingly to the body of marketing principles worked out by business organizations and adapt them to their own situations.

What are the main principles of effective marketing management as they appear in most forward-looking business organizations? Nine concepts stand out as crucial in guiding the marketing effort of a business organization.

Generic Product Definition

Business organizations have increasingly recognized the value of placing a broad definition on their products, one that emphasizes the basic customer need(s) being served. A modern soap company recognizes that its basic product is cleaning, not soap; a cosmetics company sees its basic product as beauty or hope, not lipsticks and makeup; a publishing company sees its basic product as information, not books.

The same need for a broader definition of its business is incumbent upon nonbusiness organizations if they are to survive and grow. Churches at one time tended to define their product narrowly as that of producing religious services for members. Recently, most churchmen have decided that their basic product is human fellowship. There

was a time when educators said that their product was the three R's. Now most of them define their product as education for the whole man. They try to serve the social, emotional, and political needs of young people in addition to intellectual needs.

Target Groups Definition

A generic product definition usually results in defining a very wide market, and it is then necessary for the organization, because of limited resources, to limit its product offering to certain clearly defined groups within the market. Although the generic product of an automobile company is transportation, the company typically sticks to cars, trucks, and buses, and stays away from bicycles, airplanes, and steamships. Furthermore, the manufacturer does not produce every size and shape of car but concentrates on producing a few major types to satisfy certain substantial and specific parts of the market.

In the same way, nonbusiness organizations have to define their target groups carefully. For example, in Chicago the YMCA defines its target groups as men, women and children who want recreational opportunities and are willing to pay $20 or more a year for them. The Chicago Boys Club, on the other hand, defines its target group as poorer boys within the city boundaries who are in want of recreational facilities and can pay $1 a year.

Differentiated Marketing

When a business organization sets out to serve more than one target group, it will be maximally effective by differentiating its product offerings and communications. This is also true for nonbusiness organizations. Fund-raising organizations have recognized the advantage of treating clients, trustees, and various publics in different ways. These groups require differentiated appeals and frequency of solicitation. Labor unions find that they must address different messages to different parties rather than one message to all parties. To the company they may seem unyielding, to the conciliator they may appear willing to compromise, and to the public they seek to appear economically exploited.

Customer Behavior Analysis

Business organizations are increasingly recognizing that customer needs and behavior are not obvious without formal research and analysis; they cannot rely on impressionistic evidence. Soap companies spend hundreds of thousands of dollars each year researching how Mrs. Housewife feels about her laundry, how, when, and where she does her laundry, and what she desires of a detergent.

Fund raising illustrates how an industry has benefited by replacing stereotypes of donors with studies of why people contribute to causes. Fund raisers have learned that people give because they are getting something. Many give to community chests to relieve a sense of guilt because of their elevated state compared to the needy. Many give to medical charities to relieve a sense of fear that they may be struck by a disease whose cure has not yet been found. Some give to feel pride. Fund raisers have stressed the importance of identifying the motives operating in the marketplace of givers as a basis for planning drives.

Differential Advantages

In considering different ways of reaching target groups, an organization is advised to think in terms of seeking a differential advantage. It should consider what elements in its reputation or resources can be exploited to create a special value in the minds of its potential customers. In the same way Zenith has built a reputation for quality and International Harvester a reputation for service, a nonbusiness organization should base its case on some dramatic value that competitive organizations lack. The small island of Nassau can compete against Miami for the tourist trade by advertising the greater dependability of its weather; the Heart Association can compete for funds against the Cancer Society by advertising the amazing strides made in heart research.

Multiple Marketing Tools

The modern business firm relies on a multitude of tools to sell its product, including product improvement, consumer and dealer advertising, salesman incentive programs, sales promotions, contests, multiple-size offerings, and so forth. Likewise nonbusiness organizations also can reach their audiences in a variety of ways. A church can sustain the interest of its members through discussion groups, newsletters, news releases, campaign drives, annual reports, and retreats. Its "salesmen" include the religious head, the board members, and the present members in terms of attracting potential members. Its advertising includes announcements of weddings, births and deaths, religious pronouncements, and newsworthy developments.

Integrated Marketing Planning

The multiplicity of available marketing tools suggests the desirability of overall coordination so that these tools do not work at cross purposes. Over time, business firms have placed under a marketing vice-president activities that were previously managed in a semi-autonomous fashion, such as sales, advertising, and marketing research. Nonbusiness organizations typically have not integrated their marketing activities. Thus, no single officer in the typical university is given total responsibility for studying the needs and attitudes of clients, trustees, and publics, and undertaking the necessary product development and communication programs to serve these groups. The university administration instead includes a variety of "marketing" positions such as dean of students, director of alumni affairs, director of public relations, and director of development; coordination is often poor.

Continuous Marketing Feedback

Business organizations gather continuous information about changes in the environment and about their own performance. They use their salesmen, research department, specialized research services, and other means to check on the movement of goods, actions of competitors, and feelings of customers to make sure they are progressing along satisfactory lines. Nonbusiness organizations typically are more casual about collecting vital information on how they are doing and what is happening in the marketplace. Universities have been caught off guard by underestimating the magnitude of student grievance and unrest, and so have major cities underestimated the degree to which they were failing to meet the needs of important minority constituencies.

Marketing Audit

Change is a fact of life, although it may proceed almost invisibly on a day-to-day basis. Over a long stretch of time it might be so fundamental as to threaten organizations that have not provided for periodic reexaminations of their purposes. Organizations can grow set in their ways and unresponsive to new opportunities or problems. Some great American companies are no longer with us because they did not change definitions of their businesses, and their products lost relevance in a changing world. Political parties become unresponsive after they enjoy power for a while and every so often experience a major upset. Many union leaders grow insensitive to new needs and problems until one day they find themselves out of office. For an organization to remain viable, its management must provide for periodic audits of its objectives, resources, and opportunities. It must reexamine its basic business, target groups, differential advantage, communication channels, and messages in the light of current trends and needs. It might recognize when change is needed and make it before it is too late.

Is Organizational Marketing a Socially Useful Activity?

Modern marketing has two different meanings in the minds of people who use the term. One meaning of marketing conjures up the terms selling, influencing, persuading. Marketing is seen as a huge and increasingly dangerous technology, making it possible to sell persons on buying things, propositions, and causes they either do no want or which are bad for them. This was the indictment in Vance Packard's *Hidden Persuaders* and numerous other social criticisms, with the net effect that a large number of persons think of marketing as immoral or entirely self-seeking in its fundamental premises. They can be counted on to resist the idea of organizational marketing as so much "Madison Avenue."

The other meaning of marketing unfortunately is

weaker in the public mind; it is the concept of sensitively *serving and satisfying human needs*. This was the great contribution of the marketing concept that was promulgated in the 1950s, and that concept now counts many business firms as its practitioners. The marketing concept holds that the problem of all business firms in an age of abundance is to develop customer loyalties and satisfaction, and the key to this problem is to focus on the customer's needs.[4] Perhaps the short-run problem of business firms is to sell people on buying the existing products, but the long-run problem is clearly to create the products that people need. By this recognition that effective marketing requires a consumer orientation instead of a product orientation, marketing has taken a new lease on life and tied its economic activity to a higher social purpose.

It is this second side of marketing that provides a useful concept for all organizations. All organizations are formed to serve the interest of particular groups: hospitals serve the sick, schools serve the students, governments serve the citizens, and labor unions serve the members. In the course of evolving, many organizations lose sight of their original mandate, grow hard, and become self-serving. The bureaucratic mentality begins to dominate the original service mentality. Hospitals may become perfunctory in their handling of patients, schools treat their students as nuisances, city bureaucrats behave like petty tyrants toward the citizens, and labor unions try to run instead of serve their members. All of these actions tend to build frustration in the consuming groups. As a result some withdraw meekly from these organizations, accept frustration as part of their condition, and find their satisfactions elsewhere. This used to be the common reaction of

ghetto Negroes and college students in the face of indifferent city and university bureaucracies. But new possibilities have arisen, and now the same consumers refuse to withdraw so readily. Organized dissent and protest are seen to be an answer, and many organizations thinking of themselves as responsible have been stunned into recognizing that they have lost touch with their constituencies. They had grown unresponsive.

Where does marketing fit into this picture? Marketing is that function of the organization that can keep in constant touch with the organization's consumers, read their needs, develop "products" that meet these needs, and build a program of communications to express the organization's purposes. Certainly selling and influencing will be large parts of organizational marketing; but, properly seen, selling follows rather than precedes the organization's drive to create products to satisfy its consumers.

Conclusion

It has been argued here that the modern marketing concept serves very naturally to describe an important facet of all organizational activity. All organizations must develop appropriate products to serve their sundry consuming groups and must use modern tools of communication to reach their consuming publics. The business heritage of marketing provides a useful set of concepts for guiding all organizations.

The choice facing those who manage nonbusiness organizations is not whether to market or not to market, for no organization can avoid marketing. The choice is whether to do it well or poorly, and on this necessity the case for organizational marketing is basically founded.

---

[4] Theodore Levitt, "Marketing Myopia," *Harvard Business Review*, Vol. 38 (July-August, 1960), pp. 45-56.

Richard P. Bagozzi

Marketing as Exchange

The exchange concept is a key factor in understanding the expanding role of marketing.

THE exchange paradigm has emerged as a framework useful for conceptualizing marketing behavior. Indeed, most contemporary definitions of marketing explicitly include exchange in their formulations.[1] Moreover, the current debate on "broadening" centers on the very notion of exchange: on its nature, scope, and efficacy in marketing.

This article analyzes a number of dimensions of exchange paradigm that have not been dealt with in the marketing literature. First, it attempts to show that what marketers have considered as exchange is a special case of exchange theory that focuses primarily on direct transfers of tangible entities between two parties. In reality, marketing exchanges often are indirect, they may involve intangible and symbolic aspects, and more than two parties may participate. Second, the media and meaning of exchange are discussed in order to provide a foundation for specifying underlying mechanisms in marketing exchanges. Finally, social marketing is analyzed in light of the broadened concept of exchange.

The following discussion proceeds from the assumptions embodied in the generic concept of marketing as formulated by Kotler, Levy, and others.[2] In particular, it is assumed that marketing theory is concerned with two questions: (1) Why do people and organizations engage in exchange relationships? and (2) How are exchanges created, resolved, or avoided? The domain for the subject matter of marketing is assumed to be quite broad, encompassing all activities involving "exchange" and the cause and ef-

fect phenomena associated with it. As in the social and natural sciences, marketing owes its definition to the outcome of debate and competition between divergent views in an evolutionary process that Kuhn terms a "scientific revolution."[3] Although the debate is far from settled, there appears to be a growing consensus that exchange forms the core phenomenon for study in marketing. Whether the specific instances of exchange are to be limited to economic institutions and consumers in the traditional sense or expanded to all organizations in the broadened sense deserves further attention by marketing scholars and practitioners. Significantly, the following principles apply to exchanges in both senses.

The Types of Exchange

In general, there are three types of exchange: restricted, generalized, and complex.[4] Each of these is described below.

Restricted Exchange

Restricted exchange refers to two-party reciprocal relationships which may be represented diagrammatically as A ↔ B, where "↔" signifies "gives to and receives from" and A and B represent social actors such as consumers, retailers, salesmen, organizations, or collectivities.[5] Most treatments of, and references to, exchange in the marketing literature have implicitly dealt with restricted exchanges; that is, they have dealt with customer-salesman, wholesaler-retailer, or other such dyadic exchanges.

1 See, for example, Marketing Staff of The Ohio State University, "A Statement of Marketing Philosophy," *Journal of Marketing*, Vol. 29 (January 1965), pp. 43-44; E. Jerome McCarthy, *Basic Marketing*, 5th ed. (Homewood, Ill.: Richard D. Irwin, 1975); Philip Kotler, *Marketing Management*, 2nd ed. (Englewood Cliffs, N. J.: Prentice-Hall, 1972), p. 12; and Ben M. Enis, *Marketing Principles* (Pacific Palisades, Calif.: Goodyear Publishing Co., 1974), p. 21.

2 Philip Kotler, "A Generic Concept of Marketing," *Journal of Marketing*, Vol. 36 (April 1972), pp. 46-54; and Philip Kotler and Sidney J. Levy, "Broadening the Concept of Marketing," *Journal of Marketing*, Vol. 33 (January 1969), pp. 10-15.

3 Thomas S. Kuhn, *The Structure of Scientific Revolutions*, 2nd ed. (Chicago: The University of Chicago Press, 1970).

4 The distinction between restricted and generalized exchange was first made by anthropologist Claude Levi-Strauss in *The Elementary Structures of Kinship* (Boston: Beacon Press, 1969). An extended critical analysis of restricted and generalized exchange may be found in Peter P. Ekeh, *Social Exchange Theory: The Two Traditions* (Cambridge, Mass.: Harvard University Press, 1974), Chap. 3.

5 Ekeh, same reference as footnote 4, p. 50.

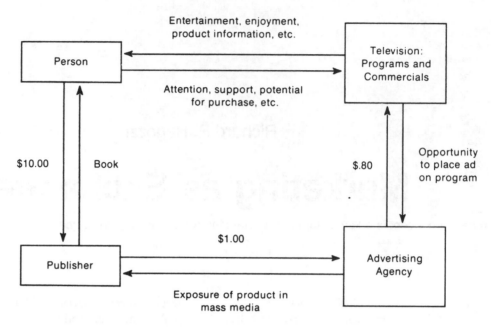

FIGURE 1. An example of complex circular exchange.

Restricted exchanges exhibit two characteristics:

First, there is a great deal of attempt to maintain equality. This is especially the case with repeatable social exchange acts. Attempts to gain advantage at the expense of the other is [*sic*] minimized. Negatively, the breach of the rule of equality quickly leads to emotional reactions. . . .Secondly, there is a *quid pro quo* mentality in restricted exchange activities. Time intervals in mutual reciprocities are cut short and there is an attempt to balance activities and exchange items as part of the mutual reciprocal relations.[6]

The "attempt to maintain equality" is quite evident in restricted marketing exchanges. Retailers, for example, know that they will not obtain repeat purchases if the consumer is taken advantage of and deceived. The "breach" in this rule of equality—which is a central tenet of the marketing concept—has led to picketing, boycotts, and even rioting. Finally, the fact that restricted marketing exchanges must involve a *quid pro quo notion* (something of value in exchange for something of value) has been at the heart of Luck's criticism of broadening the concept of marketing.[7] However, as will be developed below, there are important exceptions to the *quid pro quo* requirement in many marketing exchanges.

Generalized Exchange

Generalized exchange denotes univocal, reciprocal relationships among at least three actors in the exchange situation. Univocal reciprocity occurs "if the reciprocations involve at least three actors and if the actors do not benefit

each other directly but only indirectly."[8] Given three social actors, for instance, generalized exchange may be represented as A → B → C → A, where " → " signifies "gives to." In generalized exchange, the social actors form a system in which each actor gives to another but receives from someone other than to whom he gave. For example, suppose a public bus company (B) asks a local department store chain (A) to donate or give a number of benches to the bus company. Suppose further that, after the department store chain (A) gives the benches to the bus company (B), the company (B) then places the benches at bus stops for the convenience of its riders (C). Finally, suppose that a number of the riders (C) see the advertisements placed on the benches by the department store chain (A) and later patronize the store as a result of this exposure. This sequence of exchange, A → B → C → A, is known as generalized exchange; while it fails to conform to the usual notions of *quid pro quo,* it certainly constitutes a marketing exchange of interest.

Complex Exchange

Complex exchange refers to a system of mutual relationships between at least three parties. Each social actor is involved in a least one direct exchange, while the entire system is organized by an interconnecting web of relationships.

Perhaps the best example of complex exchange in marketing is the channel of distribution. Letting A represent a manufacturer, B a retailer, and C a consumer, it is possible to depict the channel as A ↔ B ↔ C. Such open-ended sequences of direct exchanges may be designated *complex chain exchanges.*

But many marketing exchanges involve relatively closed sequences of relationships. For example, consider

---

6 Ekeh, same reference as footnote 4, pp. 51-52.

7 David J. Luck, "Broadening the Concept of Marketing—Too Far," *Journal of Marketing*, Vol. 33 (January 1969), pp. 10-15; and Luck, "Social Marketing: Confusion Compounded," *Journal of Marketing*, Vol. 38 (October 1974), pp. 70-72.

8 Ekeh, same reference as footnote 4, pp. 48-50.

the claim made by Kotler that a "transaction takes place...when a person decides to watch a television program."[9] Recently, Carman and Luck have criticized this assertion, maintaining that it may not exhibit an exchange.[10] The differences stem from: (1) a disagreement on whether exchange must consist of transfers of tangible (as opposed to intangible) things of value, and (2) a neglect of the possibility of systems of exchange. Figure 1 illustrates the exchange between a person and a television program and how it may be viewed as a link in a system termed *complex circular exchange*.[11] In this system of exchange, the person experiences a direct transfer of intangibles between himself and the program. That is, he gives his attention, support (for example, as measured by the Nielsen ratings), potential for purchase, and so on, and receives entertainment, enjoyment, product information, and other intangible entities. The person also experiences an indirect exchange with the television program via a sequence of direct, tangible exchanges. Thus, after being informed of the availability of a book through an exchange with the television program and its advertising, a person may purchase it for, say, $10.00. The book's publisher, in turn, may purchase the services of an advertiser, paying what amounts to a percentage of each sale, say, $1.00. Finally, the advertiser receives the opportunity to place a commercial on the air from the television network in exchange for what again amounts to a percentage of each sale, say, $.80. In this particular example, the occurrence of the direct intangible exchange was a necessary prerequisite for the development of the series of indirect tangible exchanges. Thus, an exchange *can* occur between a person and a television program.

Complex chain and complex circular exchanges involve predominantly conscious systems of social and economic relationships. In this sense, there is an overt coordination of activities and expectations, which Alderson called an organized behavioral system and which he reserved for the household, the firm, and the channel of distribution.[12] However, it should be evident that the designation "organized" is a relative one and that other exchange systems, such as the one shown in Figure 1, also evidence aspects of overt coordination in an economic, social, and symbolic sense.

Generalized and complex exchanges are also present in relatively unconscious systems of social and economic

relationships. Thus, a modern economy may experience a covert coordination of activities through exchanges that occur when many individuals, groups, and firms pursue their own self-interest. This is what Adam Smith meant by his reference to an "invisible hand."[13] Similarly, in his analysis of primitive societies and marketing systems, Frazer has shown that exchange and the pursuit of self-interest can be the foundation for the web of kinship, economic, and social institutions.[14] The recent exchange theories of Homans and Blau are also based on this individualistic assumption of self-interest.[15] It should be stressed, however, that the exchange tradition developed by Levi-Strauss is not an individualistic one but rather is built on social, collectivistic assumptions associated with generalized exchange.[16] These differences will become more apparent when social marketing is analyzed below.

The Media and Meaning of Exchange

In order to satisfy human needs, people and organizations are compelled to engage in social and economic exchanges with other people and organizations. This is true for primitive as well as highly developed societies. Social actors obtain satisfaction of their needs by complying with, or influencing, the behavior of other actors. They do this by communicating and controlling the media of exchange which, in turn, comprise the links between one individual and another, between one organization and another. Significantly, marketing exchanges harbor meanings for individuals that go beyond the mere use of media for obtaining results in interactions.

The Media of Exchange

The media of exchange are the vehicles with which people communicate to, and influence, others in the satisfaction of their needs. These vehicles include money, persuasion, punishment, power (authority), inducement, and activation of normative or ethical commitments.[17] Products and services are also media of exchange. In consumer behavior research, marketers have extensively studied the

9 Kotler, same reference as footnote 2, p. 48.

10 James M. Carman, "On the Universality of Marketing," *Journal of Contemporary Business*, Vol. 2 (Autumn 1973), p. 5; and Luck, "Social Marketing," same reference as footnote 7, p. 72.

11 A form of circular exchange in primitive societies was first suggested by Bronislaw Malinowski in *Argonauts of the Western Pacific* (London: Routledge and Kegan Paul, 1922), p. 93; but in his concept the same physical items were transmitted to all parties, while in complex circular exchange as defined here different tangible or symbolic entities may be transferred.

12 Wroe Alderson, *Dynamic Marketing Behavior* (Homewood, Ill.: Richard D. Irwin, 1965), Chap. 1.

13 For a modern treatment of Adam Smith's contribution to exchange theory, see Walter Nord, "Adam Smith and Contemporary Social Exchange Theory," *The American Journal of Economics and Sociology*, Vol. 32 (October 1974), pp. 421-436.

14 Sir James G. Frazer, *Folklore in the Old Testament*, Vol. 2 (London: Macmillan & Co., 1919).

15 George C. Homans, *Social Behavior: Its Elementary Forms*, rev. ed. (New York: Harcourt Brace Jovanovich, 1974); and Peter M. Blau, *Exchange and Power in Social Life* (New York: John Wiley & Sons, 1964).

16 Levi-Strauss, same reference as footnote 4. See also, Ekeh, same reference as footnote 4, Chaps. 3 and 4.

17 Talcott Parsons, "On the Concept of Influence," *Public Opinion Quarterly*, Vol. 27 (Spring 1963), pp. 37-62; and Parsons, "On the Concept of Political Power," *Proceedings of the American Philosophical Society*, Vol. 107 (June 1963), pp. 232-262. See also, Richard Emerson, "Power Dependence Relations," *American Sociological Review*, Vol. 27 (February 1962), pp. 31-40.

effects of these vehicles on behavior. Moreover, it has been suggested that a number of these vehicles be used in conjunction with sociopsychological processes to explain the customer-salesman relationship.[18] It should be noted, however, that marketing is not solely concerned with influence processes, whether these involve manufacturers influencing consumers or consumers influencing manufacturers. Marketing is also concerned with meeting existing needs and anticipating future needs, and these activities do not necessarily entail attempts to influence or persuade.

To illustrate the multivariate nature of media in marketing exchanges, consider the example of the channel of distribution, a complex chain exchange. The firms in a channel of distribution are engaged in an intricate social system of behavioral relationships that go well beyond the visible exchange of products and money.[19] Typically, the traditional channel achieves its conscious coordination of effort through the mutual expectations of profit. In addition, each firm in the channel may influence the degree of cooperation and compliance of its partners by offering inducements in the form of services, deals, or other benefits or by persuading each link in the channel that it is in its own best interest to cooperate. A firm may also affect the behavior or decisions of another firm through the use of the power it may possess. Wilkinson has studied five bases of power in the channel of distribution—reward, coercive, legitimate, referent, and expert power—and has tested aspects of these relationships between firms.[20] Finally, a firm may remind a delinquent member in the channel of its contractual obligations or even threaten the member with legal action for a breach of agreement. This influence medium is known as the activation of commitments.

The Meaning of Exchange

Human behavior is more than the outward responses or reactions of people to stimuli. Man not only reacts to events or the actions of others but he self-generates his own acts.[21] His behavior is purposeful, intentional. It is motivated. Man is an information seeker and generator as well as an information processor. In short, human behavior is a conjunction of meaning with action and reaction.

Similarly, exchange is more than the mere transfer of a product or service for money. To be sure, most market-

ing exchanges are characterized by such a transfer. But the reasons behind the exchange—the explanation of its occurrence—lie in the social and psychological significance of the experiences, feelings, and meanings of the parties in the exchange. In general, marketing exchanges may exhibit one of three classes of meanings: utilitarian, symbolic, or mixed.

Utilitarian Exchange. A utilitarian exchange is an interaction whereby goods are given in return for money or other goods and the motivation behind the actions lies in the anticipated use or tangible characteristics commonly associated with the objects in the exchange. The utilitarian exchange is often referred to as an economic exchange, and most treatments of exchange in marketing implicitly rely on this usage. As Bartels notes with regard to the identity crisis in marketing:

> Marketing has initially and generally been associated exclusively with the distributive part of the *economic* institution and function. . . .
> The question, then, is whether marketing is identified by the *field* of economics in which the marketing techniques have been developed and generally applied, or by the so-called marketing *techniques,* wherever they may be applied.
> If marketing relates to the distributive function of the economy, providing goods and services, that *physical* function differentiates it from all other social institutions.[22]

Most marketers have traditionally conceptualized the subject matter of the discipline in these terms, and they have proceeded from the assumptions embodied in utilitarian exchange.

In general, utilitarian exchange theory is built on the foundation of *economic man.*[23] Thus, it is assumed that:

1. Men are rational in their behavior.
2. They attempt to maximize their satisfaction in exchanges.
3. They have complete information on alternatives available to them in exchanges.
4. These exchanges are relatively free from external influence.

Coleman has developed an elaborate mathematical framework for representing exchange behavior that assumes many of the features of economic man.[24] His model is based on the theory of purposive action, which posits that each "actor will choose that action which according to his estimate will lead to an expectation of the

18 Richard P. Bagozzi, "Marketing as an Organized Behavioral System of Exchange," *Journal of Marketing*, Vol. 38 (October 1974), pp. 77-81.

19 See, for example, Louis W. Stern, *Distribution Channels: Behavioral Dimensions* (New York: Houghton Mifflin Co., 1969).

20 Ian Wilkinson, "Power in Distribution Channels," *Cranfield Research Papers in Marketing and Logistics*, Session 1973-1974 (Cranfield School of Management, Cranfield, Bedfordshire, England); and Wilkinson, "Researching the Distribution Channels for Consumer and Industrial Goods: the Power Dimension," *Journal of the Market Research Society*, Vol. 16 (No. 1, 1974), pp. 12-32.

21 This dynamic, as opposed to mechanistic, image of human behavior is described nicely in R. Harre and P. F. Secord, *The Explanation of Social Behavior* (Totawa, N. J.: Littlefield, Adams & Co., 1973).

22 Robert Bartels, "The Identity Crisis in Marketing," *Journal of Marketing*, Vol. 38 (October 1974), p. 75. Emphasis added.

23 For a modern treatment of economic man, see Harold K. Schneider, *Economic Man* (New York: The Free Press, 1974).

24 James S. Coleman, "Systems of Social Exchange," *Journal of Mathematical Sociology*, Vol. 2 (December 1972).

most beneficial consequences.''[25] Among other things, the theory may be used to predict the outcomes and degree of control social actors have for a set of collective actions in an exchange system.

Symbolic Exchange. Symbolic exchange refers to the mutual transfer of psychological, social, or other intangible entities between two or more parties. Levy was one of the first marketers to recognize this aspect of behavior, which is common to many everyday marketing exchanges:

> . . . *symbol* is a general term for all instances where experience is mediated rather than direct; where an object, action, word, picture, or complex behavior is understood to mean not only itself but also some *other* ideas or feelings.
>
> The less concern there is with the concrete satisfactions of a survival level of existence, the more abstract human responses become.
>
> As behavior in the market place is increasingly elaborated, it also becomes increasingly symbolic. This idea needs some examination, because it means that sellers of goods are engaged, whether willfully or not, in selling *symbols,* as well as practical merchandise. It means that marketing managers must attend to more than the relatively superficial facts with which they usually concern themselves when they do not think of their goods as having symbolic significance...*People buy things not only for what they can do, but also for what they mean.*[26]

Mixed Exchange. Marketing exchanges involve both utilitarian and symbolic aspects and it is often very difficult to separate the two. Yet, the very creation and resolution of marketing exchanges depend on the nature of the symbolic and utilitarian mix. It has only been within the past decade or so that marketers have investigated this deeper side of marketing behavior in their studies of psychographics, motivation research, attitude and multi-attribute models, and other aspects of buyer and consumer behavior. Out of this research tradition has emerged a picture of man in his true complexity as striving for both economic and symbolic rewards. Thus, we see the emergence of *marketing man,* perhaps based on the following assumptions:

1. Man is sometimes rational, sometimes irrational.
2. He is motivated by tangible as well as intangible rewards, by internal as well as external forces.[27]
3. He engages in utilitarian as well as symbolic exchanges involving psychological and social aspects.
4. Although faced with incomplete information, he pro-

ceeds the best he can and makes at least rudimentary and sometimes unconscious calculations of the costs and benefits associated with social and economic exchanges.
5. Although occasionally striving to maximize his profits, marketing man often settles for less than optimum gains in his exchanges.
6. Finally, exchanges do not occur in isolation but are subject to a host of individual and social constraints: legal, ethical, normative, coercive, and the like.

The important research question to answer is: *What are the forces and conditions creating and resolving marketing exchange relationships?* The processes involved in the creation and resolution of exchange relationships constitute the subject matter of marketing, and these processes depend on, and cannot be separated from, the fundamental character of human and organizational needs.

Social Marketing

The marketing literature is replete with conflicting definitions of *social marketing.* Some have defined the term to signify the *use* of marketing skills in social causes,[28] while others have meant it to refer also to ''the *study* of markets and marketing activities within a total social system.''[29] Bartels recently muddied the waters with still a new definition that is vastly different from those previously suggested. For him, social marketing designates ''the *application* of marketing techniques to *nonmarketing* fields.''[30] Since these definitions cover virtually everything in marketing and even some things outside of marketing, it is no wonder that one author felt compelled to express his ''personal confusion'' and ''uncomfortable'' state of mind regarding the concept.[31]

But what is social marketing? Before answering this question, we must reject the previous definitions for a number of reasons. First, we must reject the notion that social marketing is merely the ''use'' or ''application'' of marketing techniques or skills to other areas. A science or discipline is something more than its technologies. ''Social Marketing'' connotes what is social and what is marketing, and to limit the definition to the tools of a discipline is to beg the question of the meaning of marketing. Second, social marketing is not solely the study of marketing within the frame of the total social system, and it is even more than the subject matter of the discipline. Rather, the meaning of social marketing—like that of marketing itself—is

25 James S. Coleman, *The Mathematics of Collective Action* (Chicago: Aldine-Atherton, 1973).

26 Sidney J. Levy, ''Symbols for Sale,'' *Harvard Business Review*, Vol. 37 (July-August 1959), pp. 117-119.

27 It should be stressed that man is motivated by the hope or anticipation of future rewards, and these may consist of classes of benefits not necessarily experienced in the past. See Homans's individualistic exchange theory, a learning perspective, same reference as footnote 15; Levi-Strauss's collectivistic, symbolic perspective, same reference as footnote 4; and Ekeh, same reference as footnote 4, pp. 118-124, 163.

28 Philip Kotler and Gerald Zaltman. ''Social Marketing: An Approach to Planned Social Change,'' *Journal of Marketing*, Vol. 35 (July 1971), p. 5.

29 William Lazer and Eugene J. Kelley, eds., *Social Marketing: Perspectives and Viewpoints* (Homewood, Ill.: Richard D. Irwin, 1973), p. 4. Emphasis added.

30 Same reference as footnote 22. Emphasis added.

31 Luck, ''Social Marketing,'' same reference as footnote 7, p. 70.

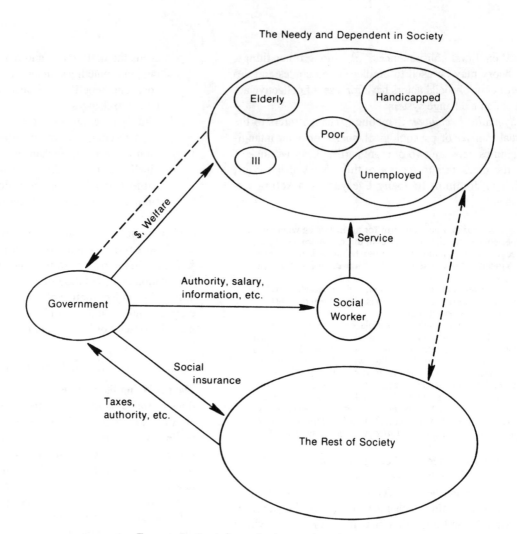

The Needy and Dependent in Society

Elderly

Handicapped

Poor

Ill

Unemployed

$, Welfare

Government

Authority, salary,
information, etc.

Service

Social
Worker

Social
insurance

Taxes,
authority, etc.

The Rest of Society

Figure 2. Social marketing and exchange.

to be found in the unique *problems* that confront the discipline. Thus, as the philosopher of science, Popper, notes:

> The belief that there is such a thing as physics, or biology, or archaeology, and that these "studies" or "disciplines" are distinguishable by the subject matter which they investigate, appears to me to be a residue from the time when one believed that a theory had to proceed from a definition of its own subject matter. But subject matter, or kinds of things, do not, I hold, constitute a basis for distinguishing disciplines. Disciplines are distinguished partly for historical reasons and reasons of administrative convenience (such as the organization of teaching and of appointments), and partly because the theories which we construct to solve our problems have a tendency to grow into unified systems. But all this classification and distinction is a comparatively unimportant and superficial affair. We are not students of some subject matter but students of problems. And problems may cut right across the borders of any subject matter or discipline.[32]

32 Karl R. Popper, *Conjectures and Refutations* (New York: Harper & Row, 1963), p. 67.

33 For a conceptual framework comparing marketing and other social relationships, see Richard P. Bagozzi, "What is a Marketing Relationship?" *Der Markt*, No. 51, 1974, pp. 64-69.

34 Luck, "Social Marketing," same reference as footnote 7, p. 71.

Social marketing, then, addresses a particular type of problem which, in turn, is a subset of the generic concept of marketing. That is, social marketing is the answer to a particular question: Why and how are exchanges created and resolved in social relationships? Social relationships (as opposed to economic relationships) are those such as family planning agent-client, welfare agent-indigent, social worker-poor person, and so on.[33] Social marketing attempts to determine the dynamics and nature of the exchange behavior in these relationships.

But is there an exchange in a social relationship? Luck, for example, feels that "a person who receives a free service is not a buyer and has conducted no exchange of values with the provider of the service."[34] It is the contention in this article that there is most definitely an exchange in social marketing relationships, but the exchange is not the simple *quid pro quo* notion characteristic of most economic exchanges. Rather, social marketing relationships exhibit what may be called generalized or complex exchanges. They involve the symbolic transfer of both tangible and intangible entities, and they invoke various media to influence such exchanges.

Figure 2 illustrates a typical social marketing exchange. In this system, society authorizes government—through its votes and tax payments—to provide needed social services such as welfare. In return, the members of society receive social insurance against common human maladies. Government, in turn, pays the salaries of social workers, gives them authority to provide social services, and so on. It also distributes welfare payments directly to the needy. These relatively contemporaneous transfers make this marketing system one of generalized exchange. In addition, a number of symbolic and delayed transfers occur that make the system also one of complex exchange. For example, as shown by dotted lines in the figure, in many cases the needy and dependent have given to the government in the past, since they may have paid taxes and voted. Moreover, members of society anticipate that they, or a number of their members, will become dependent and that social services represent an investment as well as an obligation. Hence, in one sense there is a mutual exchange between society and the needy separated, in part, by the passage of time. Finally, it should be noted that there are other tangential exchanges and forces occurring in this social marketing system that, depending on their balance, give it stability or promote change. The system achieves stability due, first, to the presence of the exchanges described above, which create mutual dependencies and univocal reciprocities; and, second, to symbolic exchanges, which reinforce the overt transfers. For example, the social worker gives to the needy but also receives back gratitude and feelings of accomplishment. The system undergoes change due to the dynamics of competing interests, as is exemplified in the efforts of lobbies and pressure groups to bring their needs to bear on the legislative process.

Thus, social marketing is really a subset of the generic concept of marketing in that it deals with the creation and resolution of exchanges in social relationships. Marketers can make contributions to other areas that contain social exchanges by providing theories and techniques for the understanding and control of such transactions. They do not usurp the authority of specialists in areas such as social work, but rather they aid and complement the efforts of these social scientists. It is not so much the fact that the subject matter of marketing overlaps with that of other disciplines as it is that the problems of marketing are universal. In answer to Bartels's query, "Is marketing a specific function with general applicability or a general function that is specifically applied?"[35]—one may state that it is nei-

ther. Rather, marketing is a general function of universal applicability. It is the discipline of exchange behavior, and it deals with problems related to this behavior.

Conclusions and Implications

A number of broad research questions may be posed:

1. Why do marketing exchanges emerge? How do people and organizations satisfy their needs through exchange?
2. Why do some marketing exchanges persist in ongoing relationships while others fall apart?
3. What are the processes leading to changes in marketing exchange relationships? How do the social actors or third parties influence or control an exchange?
4. What are the consequences of imbalances in power, resources, knowledge, and so on, in a marketing exchange? What is an equitable exchange?
5. What are the relationships between conflict, cooperation, competition, and exchange?
6. At what level may marketing exchanges be analyzed? What are the consequences of viewing exchanges as single dyads or complex systems of relationships? What are the consequences of employing the individualistic reductionism of Homans versus the collectivistic orientation of Levi-Strauss for understanding exchange behavior?
7. Is the exchange paradigm universal? Does it apply to the free-enterprise countries of the western world, the planned economies of the communist countries, and the primitive economies of the third world?
8. How well does the exchange paradigm meet the requirements for theory as specified by philosophy of science criteria?

Although marketing seems to defy simple definition and circumscription, it is essential that marketers locate the distinctive focus (or foci) of the discipline. Failure to do so impedes both the growth of the discipline and the character of its performance. Exchange is a central concept in marketing, and it may well serve as the foundation for that elusive "general theory of marketing." This article has attempted to explore some of the key concepts in the exchange paradigm. Future research and discussion must search for specific social and psychological processes that create and resolve marketing exchanges.

---

35 Same reference as footnote 22, p. 73.

The author wishes to acknowledge his gratitude to Professors Clewett, Kotler, and Levy and Associate Dean Westfall of Northwestern University, and to the reviewers, for the exchange of ideas that led to this article.

Paul F. Anderson

Marketing, Strategic Planning and the Theory of the Firm

The strategic planning process is inextricably linked with the issue of corporate goal formulation. It is argued that greater progress will be made in understanding marketing's participation in strategic planning if marketing's role in the goal formulation process can be explicated. Unfortunately, the extant theories of the firm are inadequate in varying degrees for this purpose. A new theory of the firm is proposed that attempts to specify the role of marketing and the other functional areas in the goal setting and strategic planning process.

> Would you tell me, please, which way I ought to go from here? asked Alice.
> That depends a good deal on where you want to get to, said the Cat.
> I don't much care where, said Alice.
> Then it doesn't matter which way you go, said the Cat.
> Lewis Carroll—*Alice's Adventures in Wonderland*

THE obvious wisdom of the Cheshire's statement reveals an important fact concerning strategic planning: without a clear set of objectives, the planning process is meaningless. Two authorities on the subject refer to strategy as "the major link between the goals and objectives the organization wants to achieve and the various functional area policies and operating plans it uses to guide its day-to-day activities" (Hofer and Schendel 1978, p. 13). Other strategy experts generally agree that the process of goal formulation must operate prior to, but also be interactive with, the process of strategy formulation (Ackoff 1970, Ansoff 1965, Glueck 1976, Newman and Logan 1971). Given the growing interest of marketers in the concept of strategic planning, it would appear fruitful to assess the current state of knowledge concerning goals and the goal formulation process.

Over the years, this general area of inquiry has fallen under the rubric of the "theory of the firm." One objective of this paper is to review some of the major theories of the firm to be found in the literature. The extant theories have emerged in the disciplines of economics, finance and management. To date, marketing has not developed its own comprehensive theory of the firm. Generally, marketers have been content to borrow their concepts of goals and goal formulation from these other disciplines. Indeed, marketing has shown a strange ambivalence toward the concept of corporate goals. The recent marketing literature pays scant attention to the actual content of corporate goal hierarchies. Even less attention is focused on the normative issue of what firm goals and objectives ought to be. Moreover, contemporary marketing texts devote little space to the subject. Typically, an author's perspective on corporate goals is revealed in his/her definition of the marketing concept, but one is hard pressed to find further development of the topic. There is rarely any discussion of how these goals come about or how marketing may participate in the goal formulation process.

This is not to say that received doctrine in marketing has been developed without regard for corporate objectives. The normative decision rules and procedures that have emerged always seek to attain one or more objectives. Thus it could be said that these marketing models implicitly assume a theory of the firm. However, the particular theory that serves as the underpinning of the model is rarely made explicit. More importantly, marketing theorists have devoted little attention to an exploration of the nature and implications of these theories. For example, the product portfolio (Boston Consulting Group 1970, Cardozo and Wind 1980), and PIMS (Buzzell, Gale and Sultan 1975) approaches that are so much in vogue today implicitly assume that the primary objective of the firm is the maximization of return on investment (ROI). This ob-

About the author. Paul F. Anderson is Associate Professor of Marketing, Virginia Polytechnic Institute and State University. The author wishes to thank George Day, Larry Lauden and two anonymous referees for their very helpful comments and suggestions. He also wishes to thank his colleagues at Virginia Tech's Center for the Study of Science in Society for their many helpful suggestions.

jective seems to have been accepted uncritically by many marketers despite its well-documented deficiencies (e.g., its inability to deal with timing, duration and risk differences among returns and its tendency to create behavioral problems when used as a control device; Hopwood 1976, Van Horne 1980). However, the concern expressed in this paper is not so much that marketers have adopted the wrong objectives, but that the discipline has failed to appreciate fully the nature and implications of the objectives that it has adopted.

As a result, in the last sections of the paper the outline of a new theory of the firm will be presented. It will be argued that the theories of the firm developed within economics, finance and management are inadequate in varying degrees as conceptual underpinnings for marketing. It is asserted that the primary role of a theory of the firm is to act as a kind of conceptual backdrop that functions heuristically to guide further theory development within a particular discipline. As such, the proposed model is less of a theory and more a Kuhnian-style paradigm (Kuhn 1970). Moreover, for a theory of the firm to be fruitful in this respect it must be congruent with the established research tradition of the field (Laudan 1977). It will be demonstrated, for example, that the theories emerging from economics and finance are inconsistent with the philosophical methodology and ontological framework of marketing. However, the proposed model is not only fully consonant with marketing research tradition, but, unlike existing theories, it explicitly considers marketing's role in corporate goal formulation and strategic planning. Thus it is hoped that the theory will be able to provide a structure to guide future research efforts in these areas.

Economic Theories of the Firm

In this section three theories of the firm are reviewed. The first, the neoclassical model, provides the basic foundation of contemporary microeconomic theory. The second, the market value model, performs a similar function within financial economics. Finally, the agency costs model represents a modification of the market value model to allow a divergence of interests between the owners and managers of the firm. In this sense, it operates as a transitional model between the economically oriented theories of this section and the behavioral theories of the section to follow. However, all three may be classified as economic models since they share the methodological orientation and conceptual framework of economic theory. Note that each postulates an economic objective for the firm and then derives the consequences for firm behavior under different assumption sets.

The Neoclassical Model

The neoclassical theory of the firm can be found in any standard textbook in economics. In its most basic form the theory posits a single product firm operating in a purely competitive environment. Decision making is vested in an owner-entrepreneur whose sole objective is to maximize the dollar amount of the firm's single period profits. Given the standard assumptions of diminishing returns in the short run and diseconomies of scale in the long run, the firm's average cost function will have its characteristic U-shape. The owner's unambiguous decision rule will be to set output at the point where marginal costs equal marginal revenues. The introduction of imperfections in the product market (such as those posited by the monopolistically competitive model) represent mere elaborations on the basic approach. The objective of the firm remains single period profit maximization.

The neoclassical model is well known to marketers. Indeed, it will be argued below that the profit maximization assumption of neoclassical economics underlies much of the normative literature in marketing management. It will be shown that this is true despite the fact that neoclassical theory is inconsistent with the basic research tradition of marketing. Moreover, the neoclassical model suffers from a number of limitations.

For example, the field of finance has challenged the profit maximization assumption because it fails to provide the business decision maker with an operationally feasible criterion for making investment decisions (Solomon 1963). In this regard, it suffers from an inability to consider risk differences among investment alternatives. When risk levels vary across projects, decision criteria that focus only on profitability will lead to suboptimal decisions (Copeland and Weston 1979, Fama and Miller 1972, Van Horne 1980). As a result of these and other problems, financial economists have generally abandoned the neoclassical model in favor of a more comprehensive theory of the firm known as the market value model.

The Market Value Model

Given the assumptions that human wants are insatiable and that capital markets are perfectly competitive, Fama and Miller (1972) show that the objective of the firm should be to maximize its present market value. For a corporation this is equivalent to maximizing the price of the firm's stock. In contrast to the profit maximization objective, the market value rule allows for the consideration of risk differences among alternative investment opportunities. Moreover, the model is applicable to owner-operated firms as well as corporations in which there is likely to be a separation of ownership and control.

The existence of a perfectly competitive capital market allows the firm's management to pursue a single unambiguous objective despite the fact that shareholders are likely to have heterogeneous preferences for current versus future income. If, for example, some stockholders with more income than the firm is currently paying in dividends, they can sell some of their shares to make up the difference. However, if other shareholders prefer less current income in favor of more future income, they can lend their dividends in the capital markets at interest. In either case shareholder utility will be maximized by a policy that maximizes the value of the firm's stock.

The value maximization objective is implemented within the firm by assessing all multiperiod decision alternatives on the basis of their risk-adjusted net present values (Copeland and Weston 1979, Fama and Miller 1972, Van Horne 1980):

$$NPV_j = \sum_{i=1}^{n} \frac{A^i}{(1 = k_j)^i} \qquad (1)$$

where NPV_j equals the net present value of alternative j, A_i equals the net after-tax cash flows in year i, n is the expected life of the project in years, and k_j is the risk-adjusted, after-tax required rate of return on j. In the absence of capital rationing, the firm should undertake all projects whose net present values are greater than or equal to zero. Assuming an accurate determination of k_j, this will ensure maximization of the firm's stock price. The discount rate k_j should represent the return required by the market to compensate for the risk of the project. This is usually estimated using a parameter preference model such as the capital asset pricing model or (potentially) the arbitrage model (Anderson 1981). However, it should be noted that there are serious theoretical and practical difficulties associated with the use of these approaches (Anderson 1981; Meyers and Turnbull 1977; Roll 1977; Ross 1976, 1978).

From a marketing perspective this approach requires that all major decisions be treated as investments. Thus the decision to introduce a new product, to expand into new territories, or to adopt a new channel of distribution should be evaluated on the basis of its risk-adjusted net present value. While similar approaches have been suggested in marketing (Cravens, Hills and Woodruff 1980; Dean 1966; Howard 1965; Kotler 1971; Pessemier 1966), it has generally not been recognized that this implies the adoption of shareholder wealth maximization as the goal of the firm. Moreover, these approaches are often offered in piecemeal fashion for the evaluation of selected decisions (e.g., new products), and are not integrated into a consistent and coherent theory of the firm.

Despite the deductive logic of the market value model, there are those who question whether corporate managers are motivated to pursue value maximization. An essential assumption of the market value theory is that stockholders can employ control, motivation and monitoring devices to ensure that managers maximize firm value. However, in the development of their agency theory of the firm, Jensen and Meckling (1976) note that such activities by shareholders are not without cost. As a result, it may not be possible to compel managers to maximize shareholder wealth.

The Agency Costs Model

The separation of ownership and control in modern corporations gives rise to an agency relationship between the stockholders and managers of the firm. An agency relationship may be defined as "a contract under which one or more persons (the principal(s)) engage another person (the agent) to perform some service on their behalf which involves delegating some decision making authority to the agent" (Jenson and Meckling 1976, p. 308). In any relationship of this sort, there is a potential for the agent to expend some of the principal's resources on private pursuits. As such, it will pay the principal to provide the agent with incentives and to incur monitoring costs to encourage a convergence of interests between the objectives of the principal and those of the agent. Despite expenditures of this type, it will generally be impossible to ensure that all of the agent's decisions will be designed to maximize the principal's welfare. The dollar value of the reduction in welfare experienced by the principal along with the expenditures on monitoring activities are costs of the agency relationship. For corporate stockholders these agency costs include the reduction in firm value resulting from management's consumption of nonpecuniary benefits (perquisites) and the costs of hiring outside auditing agents.

The tendency of managers of widely held corporations to behave in this fashion will require the stockholders to incur monitoring costs in an effort to enforce the value maximization objective. Unfortunately, perfect monitoring systems are very expensive. Thus the stockholders face a cost-benefit trade-off in deciding how much to spend on monitoring activities. Since it is unlikely that it will pay the shareholders to implement a "perfect" monitoring system, we will observe corporations suboptimizing on value maximization even in the presence of auditing activities. This leads to implications for managerial behavior that are quite different from those predicted by the market value model. For example, the Fama-Miller model predicts that managers will invest in all projects that will maximize the present value of the firm. However, the agency costs model suggests that management may actually invest in suboptimal projects and may even forego new profitable investments (Barnea, Haugen and Senbet 1981).

The recognition that a firm might not pursue maximization strategies is a relatively new concept to the literature of financial economics. However, in the middle 1950s and early 1960s, various economists and management specialists began to question the neoclassical assumption of single objective maximization on the basis of their observations of managerial behavior. This led directly to the development of the behavioral theory of the firm.

Behavioral Theories of the Firm

In this section two behaviorally oriented theories of the firm will be reviewed. While other approaches could also be included (Bower 1968, Mintzberg 1979), these models will lay the foundation for the development of a constituency-based theory in the last sections of the paper. The first approach is the behavioral model of the firm that emerged at the Carnegie Institute of Technology. The behavioral model can best be understood as a reaction against the neoclassical model of economic theory. The second approach is the resource dependence model of Pfeffer and Salancik (1978). The resource dependence perspective builds on a number of ideas contained in the behavioral model. For example, both approaches stress the coalitional nature of organizations. Moreover, both models emphasize the role of behavioral rather than economic factors in explaining the activities of firms.

The Behavioral Model

The behavioral theory of the firm can be found in the writings of Simon (1955, 1959, 1964), March and Simon (1958), and especially in Cyert and March (1963). The behavioral theory views the business firm as a coalition of individuals who are, in turn, members of subcoalitions. The coalition members include "managers, workers, stockholders, suppliers, customers, lawyers, tax collectors, regulatory agencies, etc." (Cyert and March 1963, p. 27).

The goals of the organization are determined by this coalition through a process of quasi-resolution of conflict. Different coalition members wish the organization to pursue different goals. The resultant goal conflict is not resolved by reducing all goals to a common dimension or by making them internally consistent. Rather, goals are viewed as "a series of independent aspiration-level constraints imposed on the organization by the members of the organizational coalition" (Cyert and March 1963, p. 117).

As Simon (1964) points out, in real world decision making situations acceptable alternatives must satisfy a whole range of requirements or constraints. In his view, singling out one constraint and referring to it as the goal of the activity is essentially arbitrary. This is because in many cases, the set of requirements selected as constraints will have much more to do with the decision outcome than the requirement selected as the goal. Thus he believes that it is more meaningful to refer to the entire set of constraints as the (complex) goal of the organization.

Moreover, these constraints are set at aspiration levels rather than maximization levels. Maximization is not possible in complex organizations because of the existence of imperfect information and because of the computational limitations faced by organizations in coordinating the various decisions made by decentralized departments and divisions. As a result, firm behavior concerning goals may be described as satisficing rather than maximizing (Simon 1959, 1964).

Cyert and March (1963) see decentralization of decision making leading to a kind of local rationality within subunits of the organization. Since these subunits deal only with a small set of problems and a limited number of goals, local optimization may be possible, but it is unlikely that this will lead to overall optimization. In this re-gard, the firm not only faces information processing and coordination problems but is also hampered by the fact that it must deal with problems in a sequential fashion. Thus organizational subunits typically attend to different problems at different times, and there is no guarantee that consistent objectives will be pursued in solving these problems. Indeed, Cyert and March argue that the time buffer between decision situations provides the firm with a convenient mechanism for avoiding the explicit resolution of goal conflict.

Thus in the behavioral theory of the firm, goals emerge as "independent constraints imposed on the organization through a process of bargaining among potential coalition members" (Cyert and March 1963, p. 43). These objectives are unlikely to be internally consistent and are subject to change over time as changes take place in the coalition structure. This coalitional perspective has had a significant impact on the development of management thought. Both Mintzberg (1979) and Pfeffer and Salancik (1978) have developed theories of the firm that take its coalitional nature as given. In the following section the resource dependence approach of Pfeffer and Salancik is outlined.

The Resource Dependence Model

Pfeffer and Salancik (1978) view organizations as coalitions of interests which alter their purposes and direction as changes take place in the coalitional structure. Like Mintzberg (1979) they draw a distinction between internal and external coalitions, although they do not use these terms. Internal coalitions may be viewed as groups functioning within the organization (e.g., departments and functional areas). External coalitions include such stakeholder groups as labor, stockholders, creditors, suppliers, government and various interested publics. Pfeffer and Salancik place their primary emphasis on the role of environmental (i.e., external) coalitions in affecting the behavior of organizations. They believe that "to describe adequately the behavior of organizations requires attending to the coalitional nature of organizations and the manner in which organizations respond to pressures from the environment" (Pfeffer and Salancik 1978, p. 24).

The reason for the environmental focus of the model is that the survival of the organization ultimately depends on its ability to obtain resources and support from its external coalitions. Pfeffer and Salancik implicitly assume that survival is the ultimate goal of the organization and that to achieve this objective, the organization must maintain a coalition of parties willing to "legitimize" its existence (Dowling and Pfeffer 1975, Parsons 1960). To do this, the organization offers various inducements in exchange for contributions of resources and support (Barnard 1938, March and Simon 1958, Simon 1964).

However, the contributions of the various interests are not equally valued by the organization. As such, coalitions that provide "behaviors, resources and capabilities that are most needed or desired by other organizational participants come to have more influence and control over the organization'' (Pfeffer and Salancik 1978, p. 27). Similarly, organizational subunits (departments, functional areas, etc.) which are best able to deal with critical contingencies related to coalitional contributions are able to enhance their influence in the organization.

A common problem in this regard is that the various coalitions make conflicting demands on the organization. Since the satisfaction of some demands limits the satisfaction of others, this leads to the possibility that the necessary coalition of support cannot be maintained. Thus organizational activities can be seen as a response to the constraints imposed by the competing demands of various coalitions.

In attempting to maintain the support of its external coalitions, the organization must negotiate exchanges that ensure the continued supply of critical resources. At the same time, however, it must remain flexible enough to respond to environmental contingencies. Often these objectives are in conflict, since the desire to ensure the stability and certainty of resource flows frequently leads to activities limiting flexibility and autonomy. For example, backward integration via merger or acquisition is one way of coping with the uncertainty of resource dependence. At the same time, however, this method of stabilizing resource exchanges limits the ability of the firm to adapt as readily to environmental contingencies. Pfeffer and Salancik suggest that many other activities of organizations can be explained by the desire for stable resource exchanges, on the one hand, and the need for flexibility and autonomy on the other. They present data to support their position that joint ventures, interlock directorates, organizational growth, political involvement and executive succession can all be interpreted in this light. Other activities such as secrecy, multiple sourcing and diversification can also be interpreted from a resource dependence perspective.

Thus the resource dependence model views organizations as ''structures of coordinated behaviors'' whose ultimate aim is to garner the necessary environmental support for survival (Pfeffer and Salancik 1978, p. 32). As in the behavioral model, it is recognized that goals and objectives will emerge as constraints imposed by the various coalitions of interests. However, the resource dependence model interprets these constraints as demands by the coalitions that must be met in order to maintain the existence of the organization.

Research Traditions and the Theory of the Firm

In reflecting on the various theories of the firm presented herein, it is important to recognize that one of their primary roles is to function as a part of what Laudan calls a

''research tradition'' (Laudan 1977). A research tradition consists of a set of assumptions shared by researchers in a particular domain. Its main purpose is to provide a set of guidelines for theory development. In so doing it provides the researcher with both an ontological framework and a philosophical methodology.

The ontological of the research tradition defines the kinds of entities that exist within the domain of inquiry. For example, in the neoclassical model such concepts as middle management, coalitions, bureaucracy and reward systems do not exist. They fall outside the ontology of neoclassical economics. Similarly, the concepts of the entrepreneur, diminishing returns and average cost curves do not exist (or at least are not used) in the resource dependence model. The ontology of the research tradition defines the basic conceptual building blocks of its constituent theories.

The philosophical methodology, on the other hand, specifies the procedure by which concepts will be used to construct a theory. Moreover, it determines the way in which the concepts will be viewed by the theorists working within the research tradition. For example, the neoclassical, market value and agency costs models have been developed in accordance with a methodology that could be characterized as deductive instrumentalism. The models are deductive in that each posits a set a assumptions or axioms (including assumptions about firm goals) from which implications for firm behavior are deduced as logical consequences (Hempel 1965, p. 336). The models are also instrumentalist in that their component concepts are not necessarily assumed to have real world referents. Instrumentalism views theories merely as calculating devices that generate useful predictions (Feyerabend 1964, Morgenbesser 1969, Popper 1963). The reality of a theory's assumptions or its concepts is irrelevant from an instrumentalist point of view.

It is essentially this aspect of economic instrumentalism that has drawn the most criticism from both economists and noneconomists. Over 30 years ago concerns for the validity of the theory among economists emerged as the famous ''marginalism controversy'' which raged in the pages of the American Economic Review (Lester 1946, 1947; Machlup 1946, 1947; Stigler 1946, 1947). More recently, much of the criticism has come from proponents of the behavioral theory of the firm (Cyert and March 1963, Cyert and Pottinger 1979). Perhaps the most commonly heard criticism of the neoclassical model is that the assumption of a rational, profit-maximizing decision maker who has access to perfect information is at considerable variance with the real world of business management (Cyert and March 1963, Simon 1955). Moreover, these critics fault the ''marginalists'' for concocting a firm with ''no complex organization, no problems of control, no standard operating procedures, no budget, no controller, [and] no aspiring middle management'' (Cyert and March 1963, p. 8). In short, the business firm assumed into existence by neoclassical theory bears little resemblance to the modern corporate structure.

Concerns with the realism of assumptions in neoclassical theory have been challenged by Friedman (1953) and Machlup (1967). In Friedman's classic statement of the "positivist" viewpoint, he takes the position that the ultimate test of a theory is the correspondence of its predictions with reality. From Friedman's perspective the lack of realism in a theory's assumptions is unrelated to the question of its validity.

Machlup, in a closely related argument, notes that much of the criticism of neoclassical theory arises because of a confusion concerning the purposes of the theory (1967). He points out that the "firm" in neoclassical analysis is nothing more than a theoretical construct that is useful in predicting the impact of changes in economic variables on the behavior of firms in the aggregate. For example, the neoclassical model performs well in predicting the direction of price changes in an industry that experiences an increase in wage rates or the imposition of a tax. It does less well, however, in explaining the complex process by which a particular firm decides to implement a price change. Of course, this is to be expected since the theory of the firm was never intended to predict the real world behavior of individual firms.

Thus the question of whether corporations really seek to maximize profits is of no concern to the economic instrumentalist. Following Friedman, the only consideration is whether such assumptions lead to "sufficiently accurate predictions" of real world phenomena (1953, p. 15). Similarly, the financial economist is unmoved by criticism related to the lack of reality in the market value and agency cost models. The ultimate justification of a theory from an instrumental viewpoint comes from the accuracy of its predictions.

In contrast to the instrumentalism of the first three theories of the firm, the behavioral and resource dependence models have been developed from the perspective of realism. The realist believes that theoretical constructs should have real world analogs and that theories should describe "what the world is really like" (Chalmers 1978, p. 114). Thus, it is not unexpected that these models are essentially inductive in nature. Indeed, in describing their methodological approach Cyert and March state that they "propose to make detailed observations of the procedures by which firms make decisions and to use these observations as a basis for a theory of decision making within business organizations" (1963, p. 1).

Thus it can be seen that the theories of the firm that have been developed in economics and financial economics emerged from a very different research tradition than the behaviorally oriented theories developed in management. This fact becomes particularly significant in considering their adequacy as a framework for marketing theory development. For example, the discipline of marketing appears to be committed to a research tradition dominated by the methodology of inductive realism, yet it frequently employs the profit maximization paradigm of neoclassical economic theory. Despite the recent trend toward the incorporation of social objectives in the firm's goal hierarchy, and the recognition by many authors that firms pursue multiple objectives, profit or profit maximization figures prominently as the major corporate objective in leading marketing texts (Boone and Kurtz 1980, p. 12; Markin 1979, p. 34; McCarthy 1978, p. 29; Stanton 1978, p. 13). More significantly perhaps, profit maximization is the implicit or explicit objective of much of the normative literature in marketing management. While the terms may vary from return on investment to contribution margin, cash flow or cumulative compounded profits, they are essentially profit maximization criteria. Thus such widely known and accepted approaches as product portfolio analysis (Boston Consulting Group 1970), segmental analysis (Mossman, Fischer and Crissy 1974), competitive bidding models (Simon and Freimer 1970), Bayesian pricing procedures (Green 1963), and many others all adhere to the profit maximization paradigm. It may seem curious that a discipline that drifted away from the research tradition of economics largely because of a concern for greater "realism" (Hutchinson 1952, Vaile 1950) should continue to employ one of its most "unrealistic" assumptions. In effect, marketing has rejected much of the philosophical methodology of economics while retaining a significant portion of its ontology.

It would seem that what is required is the development of a theory of the firm that is consistent with the existing research tradition of marketing. Such a theory should deal explicitly with the role of marketing in the firm and should attempt to explicate its relationship with the other functional areas (Wind 1981) and specify its contribution to the formation of corporate "goal structures" (Richards 1978). In this way it would provide a framework within which marketing theory development can proceed. This is particularly important for the development of theory within the area of strategic planning. It is likely that greater progress could be made in this area if research is conducted within the context of a theory of the firm whose methodological and ontological framework is consistent with that of marketing.

Toward a Constituency-Based Theory of the Firm

The theory of the firm to be outlined in this section focuses explicitly on the roles performed by the various functional areas found in the modern corporation. There are basically two reasons for this. First, theory development in business administration typically proceeds within the various academic disciplines corresponding (roughly) to the functional areas of the firm. It is felt that a theory explicating the role of the functional areas will be of greater heuristic value in providing a framework for research within these disciplines (and within marketing in particular).

Second, a theory of the firm that does not give explicit recognition to the activities of these functional subunits fails to appreciate their obvious importance in explaining firm behavior. As highly formalized internal coalitions operating at both the corporate and divisional levels, they often share a common frame of reference and a relatively consistent set of goals and objectives. These facts make the functional areas an obvious unit of analysis in attempting to explain the emergence of goals in corporations.

The proposed theory adopts the coalitional perspectives of the various behaviorally oriented theories of the firm and relies especially on the resource dependence model. As a matter of analytical convenience, the theory divides an organization into both internal and external coalitions. From a resource dependence perspective, the task of the organization is to maintain itself by negotiating resource exchanges with external interests. Over time the internal coalitions within corporate organizations have adapted themselves to enhance the efficiency and effectiveness with which they perform these negotiating functions. One approach that has been taken to accomplish this is specialization. Thus certain coalitions within the firm may be viewed as specialists in negotiating exchanges with certain external coalitions. By and large these internal coalitions correspond to the major functional areas of the modern corporate structure.

For example, industrial relations and personnel specialize in negotiating resource exchanges with labor coalitions; finance, and to a lesser extent, accounting specialize in negotiating with stockholder and creditor groups; materials management and purchasing specialize in supplier group exchanges; and, of course, marketing specialists in negotiating customer exchanges. In addition, public relations, legal, tax and accounting specialize to a greater or lesser extent in negotiating the continued support and sanction of both government and public coalitions. In most large corporations the production area no longer interacts directly with the environment. With the waning of the production orientation earlier in this century, production gradually lost its negotiating functions to specialists such as purchasing and industrial relations on the input side and sales or marketing on the output side.

The major resources that the firm requires for survival include cash, labor and materiel. The major sources of cash are customers, stockholders and lenders. It is, therefore, the responsibility of marketing and finance to ensure the required level of cash flow in the firm. Similarly, it is the primary responsibility of industrial relations to supply the labor, and materials management and purchasing to supply the materiel necessary for the maintenance, growth and survival of the organization.

As Pfeffer and Salancik point out, external coalitions that control vital resources have greater control and influence over organizational activities (1978, p. 27). By exten-sion, functional areas that negotiate vital resource exchanges will come to have greater power within the corporation as well. Thus the dominance of production and finance in the early decades of this century may be attributed to the fact that nearly all vital resource exchanges were negotiated by these areas. The ascendance, in turn, of such subunits as industrial relations and personnel (Meyer 1980), marketing (Keith 1960), purchasing and materials management (Business Week 1975) and public relations (Kotler and Mindak 1978) can be explained in part by environmental changes which increased the importance of effective and efficient resource exchanges with the relevant external coalitions. For example, the growth of unionism during the 1930s did much to enhance the role and influence of industrial relations departments in large corporations. Similarly, the improved status of sales and marketing departments during this same period may be linked to environmental changes including the depressed state of the economy, the rebirth of consumerism, and a shift in demand away from standardized "Model-T type products" (Ansoff 1979, p. 32). More recently, the OPEC oil embargo, the institutionalization of consumerism, and the expansion of government regulation into new areas (OSHA, Foreign Corrupt Practices Act, Affirmative Action, etc.) has had a similar impact on such areas as purchasing, public relations and legal.

Thus the constituency-based model views the major functional areas as specialists in providing particular resources for the firm. The primary objective of each area is to ensure an uninterrupted flow of resources from the appropriate external coalition. As functional areas tend to become specialized in dealing with particular coalitions, they tend to view these groups as constituencies both to be served and managed. From this perspective, the chief responsibility of the marketing area is to satisfy the long-term needs of its customer coalition. In short, it must strive to implement the marketing concept (Keith 1960, Levitt 1960, McKitterick 1957).

Of course, in seeking to achieve its own objectives, each functional area is constrained by the objectives of the other departments. In attempting to assure maximal consumer satisfaction as a means of maintaining the support of its customer coalition, marketing will be constrained by financial, technical and legal considerations imposed by the other functional areas. For example, expenditures on new product development, market research and advertising cut into the financial resources necessary to maintain the support of labor, supplier, creditor and investor coalitions. When these constraints are embodied in the formal performance measurement system, they exert a significant influence on the behavior of the functional areas.

In this model, firm objectives emerge as a series of Simonian constraints that are negotiated among the various functions. Those areas that specialize in the provision of crucial resources are likely to have greater power in the negotiation process. In this regard, the marketing area's desire to promote the marketing concept as a philosophy of the entire firm may be interpreted by the other functional areas as a means of gaining bargaining leverage by attempting to impress them with the survival value of customer support. The general failure of the other areas to embrace this philosophy may well reflect their belief in the importance of their own constituencies.

Recently, the marketing concept has also been called into question for contributing to the alleged malaise of American business. Hayes and Abernathy (1980) charge that excessive emphasis on marketing research and short-term financial control measures has led to the decline of U.S. firms in world markets. They argue that American businesses are losing more and more of their markets to European and Japanese firms because of a failure to remain technologically competitive. They believe that the reliance of American firms on consumer surveys and ROI control encourages a low-risk, short run investment philosophy, and point out that market research typically identifies consumers' current desires but is often incapable of determining their future wants and needs. Moreover, the short run focus of ROI measures and the analytical detachment inherent in product portfolio procedures tends to encourage investment in fast payback alternatives. Thus Hayes and Abernathy believe that American firms are reluctant to make the higher risk, longer-term investments in new technologies necessary for effective competition in world markets. They feel that the willingness for foreign firms to make such investments can be attributed to their need to look beyond their relatively small domestic markets for success. This has encouraged a reliance on technically superior products and a longer-term payoff perspective.

From a resource dependence viewpoint the Hayes and Abernathy argument seems to suggest that the external coalitions of U.S. firms are rather myopic. If the survival of the firm is truly dependent on the adoption of a longer-term perspective, one would expect this to be forced on the firm by its external coalitions. Indeed, there is ample evidence from stock market studies that investor coalitions react sharply to events affecting the longer run fortunes of firms (Lev 1974, Lorie and Hamilton 1973). Moreover, recent concessions by government, labor and supplier coalitions to Chrysler Corporation suggest a similar perspective among these groups.

However, the real problem is not a failure by internal and external coalitions in recognizing the importance of a long run investment perspective. The real difficulty lies in designing an internal performance measurement and reward system that balances the need for short run profitability against long-term survival. A number of factors combine to bias these reward and measurement systems in favor of the short run. These include:

- Requirements for quarterly and annual reports of financial performance.
- The need to appraise and reward managers on an annual basis.

- The practical difficulties of measuring and rewarding the long-term performance of highly mobile management personnel.
- Uncertainty as to the relative survival value of emphasis on short run versus long run payoffs.

As a result of these difficulties, we find that in many U.S. firms the reward system focuses on short run criteria (Ouchi 1981). This naturally leads to the use of short-term financial control measures and an emphasis on market surveys designed to measure consumer reaction to immediate (and often minor) product improvements. In some cases the marketing area has adopted this approach in the name of the marketing concept.

However, as Levitt (1960) noted more than two decades ago, the real lesson of the marketing concept is that successful firms are able to recognize the fundamental and enduring nature of the customer needs they are attempting to satisfy. As numerous case studies point out, it is the *technology* of want satisfaction that is transitory. The long run investment perspective demanded by Hayes and Abernathy is essential for a firm that focuses its attention on transportation rather than trains, entertainment rather than motion pictures, or energy rather than oil. The real marketing concept divorces strategic thinking from an emphasis on contemporary technology and encourages investments in research and development with long-term payoffs. Thus, the "market-driven" firms that are criticized by Hayes and Abernathy have not really embraced the marketing concept. These firms have simply deluded themselves into believing that consumer survey techniques and product portfolio procedures automatically confer a marketing orientation on their adopters. However, the fundamental insight of the marketing concept has little to do with the use of particular analytical techniques. The marketing concept is essentially a state of mind or world view that recognizes that firms survive to the extent that they meet the real needs of their customer coalitions. As argued below, one of the marketing area's chief functions in the strategic planning process is to communicate this perspective to top management and the other functional areas.

Implications For Strategic Planning

From a strategic planning perspective, the ultimate objective of the firm may be seen as an attempt to position itself for long run survival (Wind 1979). This, in turn, is accomplished as each functional area attempts to determine the position that will ensure a continuing supply of vital resources. Thus the domestic auto industry's belated downsizing of its product may be viewed as an attempt to ensure the support of its customer coalition in the 1980s and 1990s (just as its grudging acceptance of the UAW in the late 1930s and early 1940s reflected a need to ensure a continuing supply of labor).

Of course, a firm's functional areas may not be able to occupy all of the favored long run positions simultaneously. Strategic conflicts will arise as functional areas (acting as units at the corporate level or as subunits at the divisional level) vie for the financial resources necessary to occupy their optimal long-term positions. Corporate management as the final arbiter of these disputes may occasionally favor one area over another, with deleterious results. Thus, John De Lorean, former group executive at General Motors, believes that the firm's desire for the short run profits available from larger cars was a major factor in its reluctance to downsize in the 1970s (Wright 1979). He suggests that an overwhelming financial orientation among GM's top executives consistently led them to favor short run financial gain over longer-term marketing considerations. Similarly, Hayes and Abernathy (1980) believe that the growing dominance of financial and legal specialists within the top managements of large U.S. corporations has contributed to the slighting of technological considerations in product development.

Against this backdrop marketing must realize that its role in strategic planning is not preordained. Indeed, it is possible that marketing considerations may not have a significant impact on strategic plans unless marketers adopt a strong advocacy position within the firm (Mason and Mitroff 1981). On this view, strategic plans are seen as the outcome of a bargaining process among functional areas. Each area attempts to move the corporation toward what it views as the preferred position for long run survival, subject to the constraints imposed by the positioning strategies of the other functional units.

This is not to suggest, however, that formal-analytical procedures have no role to play in strategic planning. Indeed, as Quinn's (1981) research demonstrates, the actual process of strategy formulation in large firms is best described as a combination of the formal-analytical and power-behavioral approaches. He found that the formal planning system often provides a kind of infrastructure that assists in the strategy development and implementation process, although the formal system itself rarely generates new or innovative strategies. Moreover, the study shows that strategies tend to emerge incrementally over relatively long periods of time. One reason for this is the need for top management to obtain the support and commitment of the firm's various coalitions through constant negotiation and implied bargaining (Quinn 1981, p. 61).

Thus, from a constituency-based perspective, marketing's role in strategic planning reduces to three major activities. First, at both the corporate and divisional levels it must identify the optimal long-term position or positions that will assure customer satisfaction and support. An optimal position would reflect marketing's perception of what its customers' wants and needs are likely to be over the firm's strategic time horizon. Since this will necessarily involve long run considerations, positioning options must be couched in somewhat abstract terms. Thus the trend toward smaller cars by the domestic auto industry represents a very board response to changing environ-

mental, social and political forces and will likely affect the industry well into the 1990s. Other examples include the diversification into alternative energy sources by the petroleum industry, the movement toward ''narrowcasting'' by the major networks, and the downsizing of the single family home by the construction industry. The length of the time horizons involved suggests that optimal positions will be determined largely by fundamental changes in demographic, economic, social and political factors. Thus strategic positioning is more likely to be guided by long-term demographic and socioeconomic research (Lazer 1977) than by surveys of consumer attitudes.

Marketing's second major strategic planning activity involves the development of strategies designed to capture its preferred positions. This will necessarily involve attempts to gain a competitive advantage over firms pursuing similar positioning strategies. Moreover, the entire process is likely to operate incrementally. Specific strategies will focus on somewhat shorter time horizons and will be designed to move the firm toward a particular position without creating major dislocations within the firm or the marketplace (Quinn 1981). Research on consumers' current preferences must be combined with demographic and socioeconomic research to produce viable intermediate strategies. For example, Detroit's strategy of redesigning all of its subcompact lines has been combined with improved fuel efficiency in its larger cars (*Business Week* 1980).

Finally, marketing must negotiate with top management and the other functional areas to implement its strategies. The coalitional perspective suggests that marketing must take an active role in promoting its strategic options by demonstrating the survival value of a consumer orientation to the other internal coalitions.

Marketing's objective, therefore, remains long run customer support through consumer satisfaction. Paradoxically, perhaps, this approach requires marketers to have an even greater grasp of the technologies, perspectives and limitations of the other functional areas. Only in this way can marketing effectively negotiate the implementation of its strategies. As noted previously, the other functional areas are likely to view appeals to the marketing concept merely as a bargaining ploy. It is the responsibility of the marketing area to communicate the true long run focus and survival orientation of this concept to the other interests in the firm. However, this cannot be accomplished if the marketing function itself does not understand the unique orientations and decision methodologies employed by other departments.

For example, the long run investment perspective implicit in the marketing concept can be made more comprehensible to the financial coalition if it is couched in the familiar terms of capital budgeting analysis. Moreover, the marketing area becomes a more credible advocate for this position if it eschews the use of short-term ROI measures as its sole criterion for internal decision analysis. At the same time, an appreciation for the inherent limitations of contemporary capital investment procedures will give the marketing area substantial leverage in the negotiation process (Anderson 1981).

In the final analysis, the constituency model of the firm suggests that marketing's role in strategic planning must be that of a strong advocate for the marketing concept. Moreover, its advocacy will be enhanced to the extent that it effectively communicates the true meaning of the marketing concept in terms that are comprehensible to other coalitions in the firm. This requires an intimate knowledge of the interests, viewpoints and decision processes of these groups. At the same time, a better understanding of the true nature of the constraints imposed by these interests will allow the marketing organization to make the informed strategic compromises necessary for firm survival.

REFERENCES

Ackoff, Russell (1970), *A Concept of Corporate Planning*, New York: John Wiley & Sons.

Anderson, Paul F. (1981), "Marketing Investment Analysis," in *Research in Marketing*, 4, Jagdish N. Sheth, ed., Greenwich, CT: JAI Press, 1-37.

Ansoff, Igor H. (1965), *Corporate Strategy*, New York: McGraw-Hill.

____ (1979), "The Changing Shape of the Strategic Problem," in *Strategic Management: A View of Business Policy and Planning*, Dan E. Schendel and Charles W. Hofer, eds., Boston: Little Brown and Company, 30-44.

Barnard, Chester I. (1938), *The Functions of the Executive*, London: Oxford University Press.

Barnea, Amir, Robert A. Haugen and Lemma W. Senbet (1981), "Market Imperfections, Agency Problems and Capital Structure: A Review," *Financial Management*, 10 (Summer), 7-22.

Boone, Louis E. and David L. Kurtz (1980), *Foundations of Marketing*, 3rd ed., Hinsdale, IL: Dryden Press.

Boston Consulting Group (1970), *The Product Portfolio*, Boston: The Boston Consulting Group.

Bower, Joseph L. (1968), "Descriptive Decision Theory from the 'Administrative Viewpoint," in *The Study of Policy Formation*, Raymond A. Bauer and Kenneth J. Gergen, eds., New York: Collier-Macmillan, 103-148.

Business Week (1975), "The Purchasing Agent Gains More Clout," (January 13), 62-63.

____ (1980), "Detroit's New Sales Pitch," (September 22), 78-83.

Buzzell, Robert D., Bradley T. Gale and Ralph G. M. Sultan (1975), "Market Share: A Key to Profitability," *Harvard Business Review*, 53 (January-February), 97-106.

Cardozo, Richard and Yoram Wind (1980), "Portfolio Analysis for Strategic Product_Market Planning," working paper, The Wharton School, University of Pennsylvania.

Chalmers, A. F. (1978), *What is This Thing Called Science? St. Lucia*, Australia: University of Queensland Press.

Copeland, Thomas E. and J. Fred Weston (1979), *Financial Theory and Corporate Policy*, Reading, MA: Addison-Wesley Publishing Company.

Cravens, David W., Gerald E. Hills and Robert B. Woodruff (1980), *Marketing Decision Making*, rev. ed., Homewood, IL: Richard D. Irwin.

Cyert, Richard M. and James G. March (1963), *A Behavioral Theory of the Firm*, Englewood Cliffs, NJ: Prentice-Hall.

____ and Garrel Pottinger (1979), "Towards a Better Microeconomic Theory," *Philosophy of Science*, 46 (June), 204-222.

Dean, Joel (1966), "Does Advertising Belong in the Capital Budget?" *Journal of Marketing*, 30 (October), 15-21.

Dowling, John and Jeffrey Pfeffer (1975), "Organizational Legitimacy," *Pacific Sociological Review*, 18 (January), 122-36.

Fama, Eugene and Merton H. Miller (1972), *The Theory of Finance*, Hinsdale, IL: Dryden Press.

Feyerabend, Paul K. (1964), "Realism and Instrumentalism: Comments on the Logic of Factual Support," in *The Critical Approach to Science and Philosophy*, Mario Bunge, ed., London: The Free Press of Glencoe, 280-308.

Friedman, Milton (1953), "The Methodology of Positive Economics," in *Essays in Positive Economics*, Chicago: University of Chicago Press.

Glueck, William (1976), *Policy, Strategy Formation and Management Action*, New York: McGraw-Hill.

Green, Paul E. (1963), "Bayesian Decision Theory in Pricing Strategy," *Journal of Marketing*, 27 (January), 5-14.

Hayes, Robert H. and William J. Abernathy (1980), "Managing Our Way to Economic Decline," *Harvard Business Review*, 58 (July-August), 67-77.

Hempel, Carl G. (1965), *Aspects of Scientific Explanation*, New York: Macmillan Publishing Co.

Hofer, Charles W. and Dan Schendel (1978), *Strategy Formulation: Analytical Concepts*, St. Paul, MN: West Publishing Company.

Hopwood, Anthony (1976), *Accounting and Human Behavior*, Englewood Cliffs, NJ: Prentice-Hall.

Howard, John A. (1965), *Marketing Theory*, Boston: Allyn and Bacon.

Hutchinson, Kenneth D. (1952), "Marketing as a Science: An Appraisal," *Journal of Marketing*, 16 (January), 286-93.

Jensen, Michael C. and William H. Meckling (1976), "Theory of the Firm: Managerial Behavior, Agency Costs and Ownership Structure," *Journal of Financial Economics*, 3 (October), 305-60.

Keith, Robert J. (1960), "The Marketing Revolution," *Journal of Marketing*, 24 (January), 35-38.

Kotler, Philip (1971), *Marketing Decision Making*, New York: Holt, Rinehart and Winston.

____ and William Mindak (1978), "Marketing and Public Relations," *Journal of Marketing*, 42 (October), 13-20.

Kuhn, Thomas S. (1970), *The Structure of Scientific Revolutions*, 2nd ed., Chicago: University of Chicago Press.

Laudan, Larry (1977), *Progress and Its Problems*, Berkeley, CA: University of California Press.

Lazer, William (1977), "The 1980s and Beyond: A Perspective," *MSU Business Topics*, 25 (Spring), 21-35.

Lester, R. A. (1946), "Shortcomings of Marginal Analysis for Wage-Employment Problems," *American Economic Review*, 36 (March), 63-82.

____ (1947), "Marginalism, Minimum Wages, and Labor Markets," *American Economic Review*, 37 (March), 135-48.

Lev, Baruch (1974), *Financial Statement Analysis: A New Approach*, Englewood Cliffs, NJ: Prentice-Hall.

Levitt, Theodore (1960), "Marketing Myopia," *Harvard Business Review*, 38 (July-August), 24-47.

Lorie, James H. and Mary T. Hamilton (1973), *The Stock Market: Theories and Evidence*, Homewood, IL: Richard D. Irwin.

Machlup, Fritz (1946), "Marginal Analysis and Empirical Research," *American Economic Review*, 36 (September), 519-54.

____ (1947), "Rejoinder to an Antimarginalist," *American Economic Review*, 37 (March), 148-54.

____ (1967), "Theories of the Firm: Marginalist, Behavioral, Managerial," *American Economic Review*, 57 (March), 1-33.

March, James G. and Herbert A. Simon (1958), *Organizations*, New York: John Wiley & Sons.

Markin, Rom (1979), *Marketing*, New York: John Wiley & Sons.

Mason, Richard O. and Ian I. Mitroff (1981), "Policy Analysis as Argument," working paper, University of Southern California.

McCarthy, E. Jerome (1978), *Basic Marketing*, 6th ed., Homewood, IL: Richard D. Irwin.

McKitterick, J. B. (1957), "What is the Marketing Management Concept?" in *Readings in Marketing 75/76*, Guilford, CT: Dushkin Publishing Group, 23-26.

Meyer, Herbert E. (1980), "Personnel Directors Are the New Corporate Heros," in *Current Issues in Personnel Management*, Kendrith M. Rowland et al., eds., Boston: Allyn & Bacon, 2-8.

Meyers, Stewart C. and Stuart M. Turnbull (1977), "Capital Budgeting and the Capital Asset Pricing Model: Good News and Bad News," *Journal of Finance*, 32 (May), 321-336.

Mintzberg, Henry (1979), "Organizational Power and Goals: A Skeletal Theory," in *Strategic Management*, Dan E. Schendel and Charles W. Hofer, eds, Boston: Little, Brown and Company.

Morgenbesser, Sidney (1969), "The Realist-Instrumentalist Controversy," in *Philosophy*, Science and Method, New York: St. Martin's Press, 200-18.

Mossman, Frank H., Paul M. Fischer and W. J. E. Crissy (1974), "New Approaches to Analyzing Marketing Profitability," *Journal of Marketing*, 38 (April), 43-48.

Newman, William H. and James P. Logan (1971), *Strategy*, Policy and Central Management, Cincinnati: South-Western Publishing Company.

Ouchi, William G. (1981), *Theory Z*, Reading, MA: Addison-Wesley.

Parsons, Talcott (1960), *Structure and Process in Modern Societies*, New York: Free Press.

Pessemier, Edgar A. (1966), *New-Product Decisions: An Analytical Approach*, New York: McGraw Hill.

Pfeffer, Jeffrey and Gerald R. Salancik (1978), *The External Control of Organizations*, New York: Harper and Row.

Popper, Karl R. (1963), *Conjectures and Refutations*, New York: Harper & Row.

Quinn, James Brian (1981), "Formulating Strategy One Step at a Time," *Journal of Business Strategy*, 1 (Winter), 42-63.

Richards, Max D. (1978), *Organizational Goal Structures*, St. Paul: West Publishing Company.

Roll, Richard (1977), "A Critique of the Asset Pricing Theory's Tests: Part I," *Journal of Financial Economics*, 4 (March), 129-76.

Ross, Stephen A. (1976), "The Arbitrage Theory of Capital Asset Pricing," *Journal of Economic Theory*, 13 (December), 341-360.

____ (1978), "The Current Status of the Capital Asset Pricing Model (CAPM)," *Journal of Finance*, 33 (June), 885-901.

Simon, Herbert A. (1955), "A Behavioral Model of Rational Choice," Quarterly *Journal of Economics*, 69 (February), 99-118.

____ (1959), "Theories of Decision Making in Economics and Behavioral Science," *American Economic Review*, 49 (June), 253-83.

____ (1964), "On the Concept of Organizational Goal," *Administrative Science Quarterly*, 9 (June), 1-22.

Simon, Leonard S. and Marshall Freimer (1970), *Analytical Marketing*, New York: Harcourt, Brace & World.

Solomon, Ezra (1963), *The Theory of Financial Management*, New York: Columbia University Press.

Stanton, William J. (1978), *Fundamentals of Marketing*, 5th ed., New York: McGraw-Hill.

Stigler, G. J. (1946), "The Economics of Minimum Wage Legislation," *American Economic Review*, 36 (June), 358-65.

____ (1947), "Professor Lester and the Marginalists," *American Economic Review*, 37 (March), 154-57.

Vaile, Roland S. (1950), "Economic Theory and Marketing," in *Theory in Marketing*, Reavis Cox and Wroe Alderson, eds., Chicago: Richard D. Irwin.

Van Horne, James C. (1980), *Financial Management and Policy*, 5th ed., Englewood Cliffs, NJ: Prentice-Hall.

Wind, Yoram (1979), "Product Positioning and Market Segmentation: Marketing and Corporate Perspectives," working paper, The Wharton School, University of Pennsylvania.

____ (1981), "Marketing and the Other Business Functions," in *Research in Marketing*, 5, Jagdish N. Sheth, ed., Greenwich, CT: JAI Press, 237-64.

Wright, Patrick J. (1979), *On A Clear Day You Can See General Motors*, Grosse Pointe, MI: Wright Enterprises.

Personal Selling

Barton A. Weitz

Effectiveness In Sales Interactions: A Contingency Framework

A new approach for research on effectiveness in sales interactions is proposed. This approach is based on considering the moderating effect of the salesperson's resources, the customer's buying task, and the customer-salesperson relationship. A contingency framework is presented and research directions related to the framework are suggested.

IN 1978, the average expenditure for training each industrial salesperson was over $15,000 (*Sales and Marketing Management* 1979). Even though annual sales training expenses are well over one billion dollars, there is only limited knowledge about which selling behaviors are most effective in customer interactions. A conceptual framework for exploring this issue is presented in this paper.

To demonstrate the focus of this framework, a scheme for classifying variables related to salesperson performance is shown in Figure 1. The initial classification is based on whether the variable relates to the salesperson's macroenvironment or microenvironment. Macroenvironmental variables include territorial characteristics such as potential and workload and the level of effort expended by the salesperson in covering the territory. However, the objective of the framework presented in this paper is to delineate factors related to the effectiveness of salespeople in influencing customers during interpersonal interactions. Thus, the framework focuses on the effectiveness of sales behaviors in the microenvironment of the sales interaction.

Variables related to effectiveness in the microenvironment are further classified into those related to the sales situation and those related to the salesperson. Variables related to the salesperson's effort during customer interactions are not treated in the framework. Thus, the framework focuses on the shaded areas in Figure 1.

The fundamental idea behind the framework is that ef-

fectiveness in sales interactions can be understood best by examining the interactions between sales behaviors, resources of the salesperson, the nature of the customer's buying task, and characteristics of the salesperson-customer relationship. This framework provides a mechanism for integrating previous research and a direction for future research.

In the next section, the shortcomings of prior research on effectiveness in sales interactions are discussed. These shortcomings suggest the need for a contingency approach. After presenting the nature and applications of a contingency approach, the approach is expanded into a framework. The basic postulate of the framework is stated, constructs in the framework are defined, and a set of propositions is developed. These propositions are supported by research in leadership, bargaining, social psychology, and personal selling. Further research is needed to complete the framework; however, the portions of the framework presented in this paper suggest a potentially fruitful direction for studying effectiveness in sales interactions. The paper concludes with a discussion of a research program to explore this new direction.

Research on Effectiveness in Sales Interactions

Research concerning effectiveness in sales interactions has concentrated on uncovering salesperson behaviors, behavioral predispositions, and capabilities related to performance. Each of these research streams is reviewed below. (See Weitz 1979 for a more detailed review.)

Sales Behaviors and Behavioral Predispositions

The study of sales behaviors has been limited to experimental studies examining the effectiveness of different types

About the author. Barton A. Weitz is Assistant Professor, Graduate School of Management, University of California at Los Angeles. The author acknowledges theoretical contributions from Robert Saxe and comments on earlier manuscripts from James Bettman, Erin Anderson, and Scott MacKenzie.

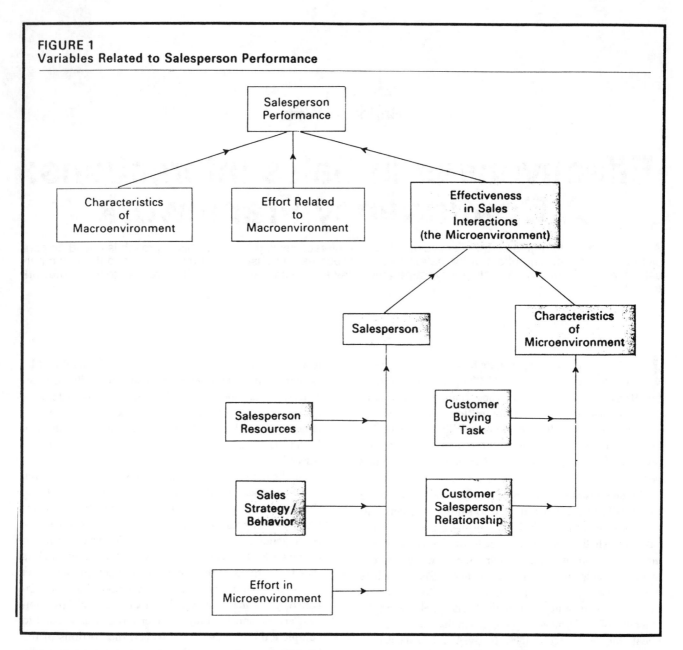

FIGURE 1
Variables Related to Salesperson Performance

of messages delivered by salespeople.[1] These studies have found little difference in effectiveness across message types. Levitt (1965) found that a "good presentation" was more effective than a "poor presentation." Jolson (1975) reported that a "canned" presentation generated

more purchase intention than an "extemporaneous" presentation but the universality of this finding has been questioned (Reed 1976). There were no significant differences in the effectiveness of a product oriented-versus a personal-oriented message (Farley & Swinth 1967); "hard sell," emotional appeals versus "soft-sell," rational appeals (Reizenstein 1971); and six different sales appeals based on Bales Interaction Process Analysis categories (Capon 1975). Thus, experimental studies have failed to uncover influence strategies consistently related to effectiveness in an interaction.

Correlational studies have attempted to uncover relationships between personality traits/behavioral predispositions and performance. The results of these studies are summarized in Table 1.[2] This summary demonstrates that the relationship between these personality traits and perform-

[1] Several descriptive studies (Olshavsky 1973; Pennington 1968; Taylor and Woodside 1968; Willett and Pennington 1966) have examined sales behavior but have not explicitly considered the effectiveness of sales behaviors.

[2] In this table, personality traits indicating a predisposition toward forceful behavior in interpersonal relations (such as dominance, ego drive, achievement motivation, and aggressiveness) have been combined under sociability. To facilitate comparisons across studies, the performance measure used to report the results shown in Tables 1 and 2 is the most objective measure considered in the study. Thus, relationships with sales and sales to quota are reported rather than relationships to sales manager's evaluations.

TABLE 1
Behavioral Predispositions and Performance

Significantly Related to Performance	Not Significantly Related to Performance
Forcefulness	
oil company (Harrell 1960)	oil company (Miner 1962)
life insurance (Merenda & Clarke 1959, Greenberg & Mayer 1964)	life insurance (Zdep & Weaver 1967)
retail/trade (Howells 1968)	retail (Howells 1968)
technical rep (Howells 1968)	stockbroker (Ghiselli 1973)
commodities (Howells 1968)	
mutual fund (Greenberg & Mayer 1964)	
automobile (Greenberg & Mayer 1964)	
trade (Dunnette & Kirchner 1960)	
stockbroker (Ghiselli 1973)	
food, appliance wholesaler (Mattheiss et al. 1977)	
Sociability	
life insurance (Merenda & Clarke 1959)	oil company (Miner 1962, Harrell 1960)
technical rep (Howells 1968)	industrial (Pruden & Peterson 1971)
retail (Howells 1968)	real estate (Scheibelhut & Albaum 1973)
retail/trade food (Howells 1968)	utility (Scheibelhut & Albaum 1973)
	industrial (Bagozzi 1978)
	food, appliance wholesaler (Mattheiss et al. 1977)

ance is equivocal. Characteristics associated with forcefulness were significantly related to performance in ten studies but were not significantly related to performance in four studies. Social orientation was significant in two studies and insignificant in six studies.

Capability and Resources of Salespeople

A second stream of research has examined relationships between performance and the salesperson's resources and capabilities. Several studies have examined the relationship between performance and specific abilities conceptually related to interpersonal persuasion. These studies indicate that effectiveness in sales interactions is related to the salesperson's ability to develop accurate impressions of customer beliefs about product performance (Weitz 1978); the salesperson's ability to use these impressions in selecting influence strategies (Weitz 1978), and the salesperson's ability to detect the impact of influence strategies and make adaptations (Grikscheit and Crissy 1973).

The results of studies that have examined more general measures of capabilities are summarized in Table 2. This summary indicates that the relationship between capabilities and performance, like the relationship between performance and behavioral predispositions, is quite *inconsistent,* and in some cases, even *contradictory.* In some cases these inconsistencies may be due to variations in methodology across studies. However, several studies have used the same methodology across different sales forces and reported inconsistent results (Dunnette and Kirchner 1960; Howells 1968; Mattheiss et al. 1977; Scheibelhut and Albaum 1973). Even variables that can be assessed with high accuracy and reliability, such as age, education, and

sales experience, are related to performance in some studies and unrelated in others.

Customer Characteristics—The Dyadic Approach

The disappointing results from prior research on sales behaviors, behavioral predispositions, and general salesperson capabilities have led to a growing interest in dyadic research approaches. While there are a wide variety of studies associated with the dyadic approach, the unifying theme of these studies is that characteristics of the customer as well as those of the salesperson are considered. This approach is consistent with a contingency approach because it suggests that effectiveness in sales interactions is moderated by or dependent upon characteristics of both the salesperson and the customer.

Dyadic similarity studies have not demonstrated a meaningful relationship between similarity and effectiveness. Several correlational studies have either not supported the relationship (Doreen, Emery, and Sweitzer 1979) or found similarity explains a low percentage of the variance (Churchill, Collins, and Strang 1975). In addition, the correlation studies (Churchill et al. 1975; Evans 1963; Riordan, Oliver and Donnelly 1977) have not controlled for the plausible rival hypothesis that customers who made purchases perceived that they were more similar to the salespeople than customers who did not make purchases (Davis and Silk 1972). While experimental studies found that similarity is a significant factor in determining sales performance, it has not been as important as expertise (Bambic 1978; Busch and Wilson 1976; Woodside and Davenport 1974).[3]

TABLE 2
Salesperson Capabilities and Performance

Significantly Related to Performance	Not Significantly Related to Performance
Age	
industrial (Kirchner et al. 1960)	household durable (Cotham 1969)
retail (Mosel 1952, Weaver 1969)	life insurance (Tanofsky et al. 1969; Meranda and Clarke, 1959)
	industrial (Lamont & Lundstrom 1977)
	retail (French 1960)
Education	
life insurance (Merenda & Clarke 1959)	speciality food manufacturer (Baehr & Williams 1968)
retail (Mosel 1952, Weaver 1969)	insurance (Tanofsky et al. 1969)
	industrial (Lamont & Lundstrom 1977)
	household durable (Cotham 1969)
	retail (French 1960)
Sales Related Knowledge, Sales Experience, Product Knowledge, Training	
Life insurance (Baier & Dugan 1957)	life insurance (Tanofsky et al. 1969, Meranda & Clarke 1959)
	speciality food manufacturer (Baehr & Williams 1968)
	household durable (Cotham 1969)
	retail (French 1960)
Intelligence	
stockbroker (Ghiselli 1973)	oil company (Harrell 1960)
oil company (Miner 1962, Harrell 1960)	trade (Dunnette & Kirchner 1960)
industrial (Bagozzi 1978)*	appliance wholesaler (Mattheiss et al. 1977)
Empathy	
new automobile (Tobolski & Kerr 1952)	used automobile (Tobolski & Kerr 1952)
automobile (Greenberg & Mayer 1964)	industrial (Lamont & Lundstrom 1977)
life insurance (Greenberg & Mayer 1964)	
mutual fund (Greenberg & Mayer 1964)	

*significant but negatively related.

Research exploring the effectiveness of dyadic similarity has not provided the new approach needed for studying effectiveness in sales interactions. These dyadic studies have focused on a single, static property and have not considered the interaction between sales behaviors and dyadic characteristics. The contingency framework presented in this paper expands upon the dyadic approach by describing the relationship between effectiveness, sales behaviors, and a variety of salesperson and customer characteristics.

Contingency Factors and Personal Selling Effectiveness

Past research efforts have attempted to uncover universal characteristics or behaviors that enable salespeople to perform successfully across a wide range of situations. Interactions between sales behaviors and aspects of the sales situation have not been considered. This research has ignored the unique advantage of personal selling in a company's marketing communication mix. Salespeople have the opportunity to match their behavior to the specific customer and situation they encounter. They can consider each interaction individually and present themselves and their product so as to be maximally effective in that interaction. In some interactions salespeople might find it more advantageous to present themselves as similar to their customers, while in other interactions salespeople might find it more advantageous to be perceived as an expert.

Prior Considerations of Contingency Factors

The impact and managerial significance of examining the interaction between sales behaviors and sales environment

---

[3] The expertise conditions explained more variance than the similarity conditions. These differences may be due to the weaker relationship between similarity and effectiveness, but they may also be due to differences in the strengths of the manipulations.

is not a novel idea. Thompson (1973, p. 8) states that "every contact a salesman has...involves different human problems or situations. In brief, *there is no one sales situation and no one way to sell.*" Gwinner (1968) proposed that four traditional approaches to selling have advantages and drawbacks that make each suitable in particular selling environments. In addition, it has been suggested that different approaches and salesperson characteristics are needed to be effective in selling new business versus selling to established customers (Kahn and Shuchman 1961), selling to purchase-oriented versus salesperson-oriented customers (Blake and Mouton 1970), and selling to customers who vary on the dimensions of dominance-submissive and hostile-warm (Buzzota, Lefton, and Sherberg 1972).[4]

Although little empirical research has explicitly considered interactions between environmental variables and sales behaviors, several researchers have demonstrated empirically that the relationship between performance and behavioral predispositions varies across sales circumstances. Differences in the relationship between personality traits and effectiveness have been found for industrial/trade salespeople and retail sales clerks (Ghiselli 1969), trade and industrial salespeople (Dunnette and Kirchner 1960; Howells 1968), real estate and private utility salespeople (Scheibelhut and Albaum 1973), and new and used car salespeople (Tobolski and Kerr 1952). Chapple and Donald (1947) found that the relationships between communication styles and performance differed across retail selling situations. For example, speech initiation behavior was related to the performance of salespeople operating in an open floor environment but not related to salespeople working behind a counter.

Contingency Factors in Leadership Research

The leadership research illustrates the benefits to be gained by considering interactions between behaviors and moderating variables. The analogy between personal selling and leadership is particularly appropriate due to the similarity in behaviors considered and the similarity in historical development. Personal selling can be defined as the process by which a salesperson attempts to influence a customer to purchase his/her product, while leadership is defined as the "process whereby one person exerts social influence over the members of a group" (Filley, House, and Kerr 1976, p. 211). Thus, the salesperson directs influence behaviors toward customers just as the leader directs influence behaviors toward group members.

Three approaches have been used to study leadership effectiveness (Filley et al. 1976). The first approach looked for personality traits that differentiate effective and ineffective leadership. These studies were followed by attempts to identify behavior patterns associated with effective leadership. The inability to find universally effective behaviors has led researchers over the past twenty years to direct their attention toward studying the interaction be-

tween leader characteristics, leader behaviors, and characteristics of the work situation (Filley et al. 1976). Theories based on these interactions are referred to as contingency theories since the relationship between performance and leader behavior is contingent upon or moderated by characteristics of the leader, the subordinates, and the work situation.

A contingency approach also provides a promising framework for studying the effectiveness of interpersonal influence behaviors in sales situations. Such a framework is developed in the next section. After stating a basic postulate, each construct is defined and propositions describing the relationship between the constructs are presented.

A Contingency Framework for Sales Effectiveness Across Interactions

A contingency framework for investigating the effectiveness of sales behaviors across interactions is shown in Figure 2. The basic elements of the framework are (a) the behavior of the salesperson in customer interactions, (b) the salesperson's resources, (c) the customer's buying task, and (d) the customer-salesperson relationship. The following basic postulate describes the interrelationship of these elements:

Basic Postulate   The effectiveness of sales behaviors across customer interactions is contingent upon or moderated by (a) the salesperson's resources, (b) the nature of the customer's buying task, (c) the customer-salesperson relationship and interactions among (a), (b), and (c).

This framework for personal selling specifies that effectiveness is related to the first-order interaction between behaviors and characteristics associated with the salesperson, the customer, and the dyad. Potential higher-order interactions are anticipated in the basic postulate. Based on this postulate it is not surprising that previous research on personal selling has failed to find consistent, main effect relationships between performance and individual elements such as behavioral tendencies (forceful or sociable personality traits), behaviors (hard sell versus soft sell or establishing referent versus expertise influence bases), salesperson resources (intelligence, empathy), and characteristics of customer-salesperson relationships (dyadic similarity).

Each of the constructs associated with the framework

---

4 While Blake and Mouton (1970) and Buzzota et al (1972) recognize that the effectiveness of sales behaviors varies across customers, their conceptualizations on personal selling are not contingency approaches of the type suggested in this paper. Both of these conceptualizations contend that one sales behavior, either warm-dominant (Q4 type in Buzzota et al.) or problem-solving oriented (9-9 type in Blake and Mouton), is most effective across all sales situations. A contingency approach is based on the notion that the most effective sales behavior varies across sales situations.

FIGURE 2
A Contingency Model of Salesperson Effectiveness

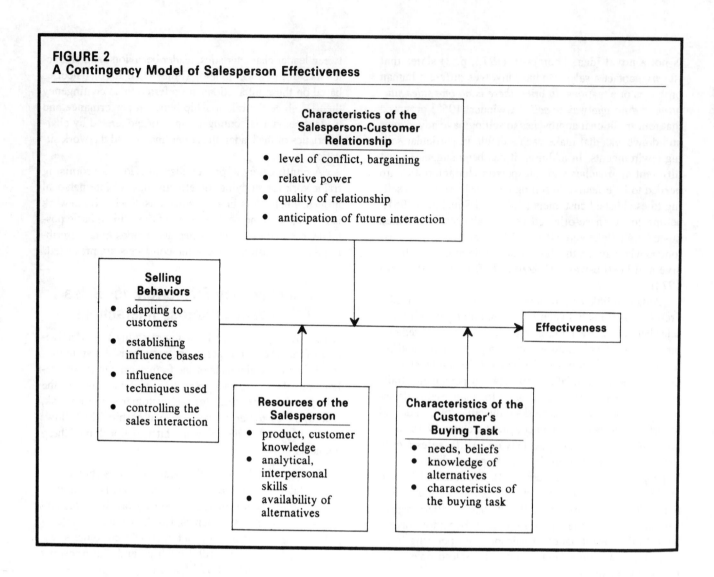

is discussed in the next section, followed by some propositions derived from past research. The elements and propositions discussed in this paper were selected on the basis of past research in personal selling and leadership. They are not intended to exploit completely the potential set of propositions that can be developed from the framework.

Constructs in a Contingency Framework

Salesperson Effectiveness

Effectiveness is defined from the perspective of the salesperson rather than the salesperson-customer dyad. This perspective differs from a conceptualization of the salesperson-customer interaction as a problem solving activity in which two parties attempt to reach a mutually beneficial solution (Willett and Pennington 1966). The problem solving perspective is not used because it does not consider the inherent advocacy nature of the salesperson's activities. While salespeople are somewhat interested in searching for a solution to the customer's problem that maximizes customer satisfaction, they and their managers

strongly prefer solutions that incorporate the purchase of the products or services they are selling.

Consistent with the salesperson and sales management perspective, effectiveness in sales interactions is defined by the degree in which the "preferred solutions" of salespeople are realized *across their customer interactions*.[5] This definition of effectiveness incorporates the fundamental interest of management in the performance of salespeople and selling behaviors across the entire set of interactions in which salespeople engage. The outcome of a specific interaction is of secondary interest.[6]

---

[5] An interaction is defined as beginning when a salesperson first contacts a customer in an attempt to make a sale. The interaction concludes when the salesperson makes the sale or decides to discontinue efforts in this direction. An interaction may be concluded during one face-to-face encounter or may continue over a sequence of encounters.

[6] This framework focuses on individual differences in effectiveness across interactions that are due to interpersonal influence behavior. However, traditional measures of performance across interactions such as sales or sales-to-quota incorporate other important sources of variance in effectiveness (see Figure 1). These factors must be controlled when testing propositions developed from this framework.

Even though this definition of effectiveness does not explicitly consider customer satisfaction, customer satisfaction is considered implicitly because effectiveness is defined across customer interactions. The following illustration demonstrates the implications associated with an effectiveness measure based on performance across interactions rather than during one interaction. Suppose a salesperson made a sale by using a deceptive influence strategy. From the salesperson's perspective, this influence strategy would have been effective in the interaction. However, the customer might not be satisfied with the product, and realizing the deception, would not buy products from the salesperson in the future. Thus, the use of deceptive influence strategies would not be effective for the salesperson across interactions with the customer, even though it was effective in one specific interaction.

Adopting a salesperson perspective does not mean that the customer's characteristics and needs are not considered. Customer characteristics and needs are considered in the framework, but only in terms of their moderating influence on the effectiveness of a salesperson's behavior.

Salesperson Behaviors

While marketers have described salesperson orientations (Blake and Mouton 1970) or general sales approaches (Gwinner 1968), most empirical research on salesperson behaviors have considered microbehaviors such as the effectiveness of specific sales messages. Little though has been directed toward identifying underlying dimensions in which a salesperson's behavior can be assessed. In the remaining portion of this section, some of these dimensions are discussed.

Adapting to the Customer. The behavior of salespeople can be characterized by the degree to which they adapt their behavior to the interaction. At one extreme, salespeople are nonadaptive when they deliver the same "canned" presentation (Jolson 1975) to all customers. In contrast to this nonadaptive behavior, salespeople can engage in a unique behavior pattern oriented to each customer.

Dimensions on which sales behavior can be adapted are discussed in following sections. It seems reasonable to assume that the effectiveness of influence bases, influence techniques, specific messages and formats, and the degree of control exerted varies across a salesperson's customers. Thus a salesperson could increase effectiveness in a specific interaction by altering behavior along the above mentioned dimensions (Weitz 1980).

Measures of adaptivity in sales behavior have not been developed; however, there are some personality measures that indicate a predisposition to engage in adaptive behaviors. For example, one would expect dogmatism and authoritarianism to be negatively related to adaptivity while tolerance for ambiguity would be positively related to adaptivity. A dispositional measure that appears to be closely

related to adaptive behavior is self-monitoring. Snyder (1974) has developed a scale to measure the degree to which people monitor their environment and use these environmental cues to alter their behavior. One would expect that high self-monitors would be more adaptive in sales situations.

Establishing a Base of Influence. Another dimension of salesperson behavior is attempting to establish a base of influence. Wilson (1975) suggests that salespeople need to develop source credibility and legitimacy during the initial stages of an interaction. Without such a base of influence, salespeople cannot effectively influence their customers.

In a review of the use of influence bases in organizational setting, McCall (1979) concluded that "the relevance of a given power base, the appropriateness of various tactics, and the likely impacts of power use are intimately linked with each other and with the situation at hand." (p. 205) Thus, given a set of possible influence bases (French and Raven 1959), salespeople need guidance as to which bases are most effective in specific circumstances. Propositions concerning variables that moderate the effectiveness of these influence bases are presented in the next section.

Influence Techniques Used. Salesperson behaviors can be classified in terms of the influence techniques used. Several studies have been directed toward defining and analyzing a wide variety of influence techniques (Capon and Swasy 1977; Falbo 1977; Spiro and Perreault 1979). These studies suggest that influence techniques can be classified using the following dimensions: (a) open/direct v. closed/indirect and (b) business/product-related v. emotional/person-related. When open/direct influence attempts are used, the purpose of the influence attempt is not hidden. Closed influence techniques involve the use of deception and hidden purposes. (See Yalch 1979 for a discussion of closed sales techniques used in finalizing a sale.)

Product-related influence techniques are defined as business or task oriented messages—information messages directed toward the product and the purchase decision. In contrast, emotional messages are directed toward the customer with the intent of appealing to psychological needs and improving customer-salesperson relations. Emotional messages attempt to reduce risks associated with the social consequences of the purchase decision, while product messages attempt to reduce risks associated with product performance (Newton 1967).

Influence techniques can also be classified by the target and format of the messages delivered. The target can be defined as the specific cognitive element, belief, or value toward which the message is directed. Message formats include comparative v. noncomparative messages and one-sided v. two-sided appeals.

Controlling the Interaction. The final dimension of sales behavior to be considered is the extent to which the salesperson controls the sales interaction. This behavioral dimension is closely related to the dominant-submissive dimension proposed by Buzzota, Lefton, and Sherberg (1972), the salesperson-oriented dimension proposed by Blake and Mouton (1970), and the traditional salesperson behavior of using high or low pressure. The use of control or pressure is a method of aggressively directing the flow of the interaction toward making a sale. Several researchers have attempted to assess the degree of control exercised by salespeople by analyzing recordings of sales interactions (Willett and Pennington 1966, Olshavsky 1973).

Some insights into control behaviors of salespeople can be gained by examining leader control behaviors. Autocratic and ''initiating structure'' leader behaviors are associated with a high degree of leader control. In the context of a sales interaction, autocratic behavior is related to the use of high pressure tactics. Initiating structure behavior is related to the salesperson aggressively structuring the customer's problem so that the solution involves purchasing the salesperson's product.

Moderating Variables

A wide variety of moderating variables are suggested by personal selling and leadership research. In the contingency framework shown in Figure 2 moderating variables are organized into the following three categories: (a) the customer's buying task, (b) the salesperson's resources, and (c) the customer-salesperson relationship. These categories parallel the following moderating variables used in Fiedler's leadership studies (Fiedler and Chemers 1974): the structure of the group's task, the leader's resources (position power), and the leader-member relations.

Customer's Buying Task. Several researchers have suggested that sales behaviors should vary depending on the buying task confronting the customer. Robinson, Farris, and Wind (1967) defined three types of buying tasks—new buy, modified rebuy, and straight rebuy. The new buy task begins as an ill-structured problem that the customer has not confronted in the past, while the straight rebuy is a highly structured, routinized decision. Since these tasks differ in amount of information needed and the level of uncertainty or risk associated with the purchase decision, one would expect that different sales behaviors would be appropriate for each situation. The different sales behaviors required in these situations have led Kahn and Shuchman (1961) to suggest that salespeople should specialize in either selling new customers (new buy or modified rebuy situations) or existing customers (straight rebuy situations).

Hakansson, Johanson, and Wootz (1977) and Newton (1967) have classified purchase decision in terms of the

risk associated with decision outcomes. They have defined specific types of risks and suggested appropriate sales behaviors for each risk type. While the Robinson et al (1967) classification scheme has received wide acceptance in the marketing literature, measures of the underlying dimensions have not been developed. In Fiedler's leadership research, task structure is also an important moderating variable. Task structure is operationalized by examining the following task characteristics: (a) goal clarity, (b) goal-path multiplicity, (c) decision verifiability, and (d) decision specificity. These characteristics in a buying task context represent the degree to which the product requirements are known by the customer, the degree to which a variety of products could satisfy the customer's needs, and the degree to which the customer is able to evaluate the performance of the product after the sale.

The Salesperson's Resources. The salesperson enters a customer interaction with a set of skills or abilities, a level of knowledge about the products and the customer, and a range of alternatives that can be offered to the customers. These factors can amplify the effectiveness and/or constrain the range of behaviors in which the salesperson can act effectively. The inclusion of salesperson resources as moderating variables is related to the notion that salespeople should ''lead from strength.'' It is reasonable to assume that salespeople are more effective when they engage in behaviors related to the skills, abilities, and personal characteristics they possess. For example, a highly trained salesperson would be more effective at establishing an expert base on influence and delivering highly informational communications.

In addition to personal resources, the company which the salesperson represents provides resources that can moderate the effectiveness of sales behaviors. Some of these company-provided resources are company reputation, the range of alternatives the salesperson can offer, and the degree to which the salesperson can alter characteristics of the extended product (price, delivery, terms, etc.) to satisfy customer needs. Levitt (1965) demonstrated that the effectiveness of the quality of a sales presentation is moderated by the reputation of the salesperson's company. Saxe (1979) found that the effectiveness of customer-oriented sales behaviors (assessing customer needs, offering products that will satisfy those needs, describing products accurately, avoiding high pressure, etc.) is moderated by the salesperson's ability to help the customer. Ability to help was operationalized as the match between the salesperson's products and the customers needs, the time available to the salesperson, and the support provided by the salesperson's company.

The Customer-Salesperson Relationship. As mentioned previously, dyadic similarity is the only variable associated with the customer-salesperson relationship that has been considered in sales effectiveness research. This research, reviewed above, indicates that the dyadic similarity is, at best, weakly related to effectiveness.[7]

Two characteristics of the customer-salesperson relationship that have not been considered in sales effectiveness research are the relative power and the level of conflict between the members of the dyad. Both power and conflict have received considerable attention in social psychology (Raven and Rubin 1976), organizational behavior (McCall 1979; Thomas 1976) and channels of distribution (Reve and Stern 1979).

Relative power can be defined in terms of dependency (Emerson 1962). The relative power of a salesperson over a customer is related to the degree to which the salesperson mediates the customer's achievement of a goal and the importance the customer places on achieving the goal. Thus, a salesperson possessing unique information concerning a solution to a customer's problem would have power over the customer. The more important the problem is to the customer, the more power the salesperson possesses. Conversely, if the salesperson's rewards (income) are dependent upon the customer's business, the customer has power over the salesperson. Thus, the relative power in an interaction could be measured in terms of the importance of each party's goals related to the purchase decision and the degree to which each party affects the other party's achievement of those goals.

Conflict, like relative power, has not been considered in personal selling research. Conflict includes a wide variety of phenomena such as:

> (1) *Antecedent conditions* (for example, scarcity of resources, policy differences) of conflict behavior, (2) *affective states* (e.g., stress, tension, hostility, anxiety) etc., (3) *cognitive states* of individuals (i.e., their perception of awareness of conflict situations), and (4) *conflictful behavior,* ranging from passive resistance to overt aggression (Pondy 1967, p. 268).

In a salesperson-customer relationship, the level of conflict is reflected in the quality of the relationship, the amount of negotiating or bargaining associated with making a sale, the level of competition the salesperson faces, and the degree to which the salesperson's offerings can satisfy the customer's needs.

In addition to relative power and conflict, *the nature of the present customer-salesperson relationship and the anticipation of future interactions* can moderate the effectiveness of sales behaviors. One important aspect of the salesperson-customer relationship is whether the salesperson represents an ''in'' or an ''out'' supplier. An ''in'' salesperson is presently selling the product to the customer, while an ''out'' salesperson is attempting to make an initial sale. Both Kahn and Shuchman (1961) and Robinson et al. (1967) have suggested that ''in'' and ''out'' salespeople need to perform different functions. Thus, one would expect that different sales behaviors would be appropriate in each situation.

A final characteristic of the customer-salesperson relationship is the anticipation of future interactions. Research

has shown that this characteristic influences the bargaining behavior undertaken by two parties (Rubin and Brown 1975) and presumably the effectiveness of sales behaviors. For example, one would expect that effective retail and industrial salespeople typically engage in different behaviors because industrial salespeople typically have continuing relationships with customers, while the retail salespeople do not.

Contingency Propositions

Some propositions incorporating the previously defined constructs are presented in this section. These propositions are stated so that testable hypotheses can be derived to direct future research efforts.

Propositions Concerning Adaptive Behavior

Proposition 1: Engaging in adaptive sales behaviors across interactions is positively related to effectiveness in the following circumstances:

Salesperson resources—the salesperson has the resources, both personal abilities and product alternatives, to engage in adaptive sales behaviors.

Customer buying tasks—the salesperson's customers typically are engaged in complex buying tasks that could result in large orders.

Customer-salesperson relationship—the salesperson has a good relationship with the customer characterized by a low level of conflict and the salesperson anticipates future relationships with the customer.

In general, the salesperson who adapts his/her behavior to the specific interaction situation will be better at presenting a product as a solution to the customer's problem. Thus, one would expect the degree of adaptive behavior to be positively related to effectiveness in a specific interaction.

However, a salesperson's effectiveness across a series of interactions may not be positively related to adaptiveness because there is a cost associated with adaptive sales behavior. The salesperson must spend time during the interaction to collect information from the customer. This information is used to adapt the sales presentation to the spe-

---

[7] The lack of a meaningful relationship may be due to the definition of similarity used in the studies. In an extensive review on source credibility, Simons et al. (1970) concluded that only relevant similarities between the communicator and the recipient of the communications have significant impact on attitude change. Relevancy is defined in terms of beliefs or experiences pertaining to the object of the attitude. Thus, one would expect that only similarity of beliefs and experiences with respect to the product and the buying decision would influence effectiveness. Dyadic studies in personal selling have operationalized the similarities in terms of physical characteristics, demographics, and irrelevant attitudes.

cific customer. The time spent collecting information about the customer is not directly related to the salesperson's effectiveness across customers. The salesperson's effectiveness might be higher if more time were spent selling the customer or calling on other customers.

Thus, one would hypothesize that adaptive sales behavior is positively related to sales performance when the benefits outweigh the costs of adapting. Such circumstances are likely to occur when the benefits of adapting are high (large potential orders, opportunity to use information in anticipated future interaction, high probability of securing an order because of a wide range of alternatives that can be offered) or the costs of adapting are low (low expected cost of collecting information due to good relationships with customers.) In contrast, one would hypothesize no relationship between adaptivity and performance when the costs typically equal or outweigh the benefits. This circumstance is likely to occur when the expected benefits are low (small orders with no potential for future orders) or the expected costs are high (a conflicting relationship that makes it difficult to collect information.) Some empirical support for this proposition is provided by Saxe (1979). He found that a salesperson's resources in terms of capabilities in satisfying customer needs moderated the relationship between effectiveness and the practice of customer-oriented, adaptive behaviors.

Support for these contingency hypotheses concerning adaptive behavior also can be found in the various sales approaches used in industry. Gwinner (1968) indicates that highly qualified and paid salespeople are needed to implement adaptive approaches like problem solution and need satisfaction. These approaches are typically used in industrial sales situations. The least adaptive approach, stimulus response, is limited to "very simple selling situations (low product complexity), to very low-priced products, or to buyer-seller relationships wherein time is an important factor" (Gwinner 1968, p. 39). Thus the stimulus-response approach has been used primarily in door-to-door selling of household products. The mental states approach, a more adaptive approach, is used "in those situations where the product or service is complicated and difficult to understand. In addition, this strategy may be employed when repeat calls on a long-run basis are required. A salesman representing a multiproduct line can effectively use this strategy since the method allows him to vary his sales presentation within the framework of an established plan" (Gwinner 1968, p. 40).

Propositions Concerning the Establishment of an Influence Base

Proposition 2: Attempting to establish an expertise base of influence is positively related to effectiveness in the following circumstances:

Salesperson resources—the salesperson has a high level of knowledge about the product and the customer's applications.

Customer buying tasks—the salesperson's customers typically are engaged in high risk, complex buying tasks.

Customer-salesperson relationship—the salesperson is typically an "out" supplier.

To establish an expertise base of influence or social power, salespeople need to create the impression that they possess superior skills or knowledge related to the purchase decision. It is reasonable to assume that salespeople who actually possess greater knowledge will be more effective in assuming the role of an expert.

The effectiveness of an expertise base of influence is related to the customer's need to make a correct decision. Thus, this base of influence will be more appropriate when customers are engaged in complex, high risk purchase decisions (new buy or modified rebuy tasks). In these purchase decisions, customers have a great need for information that will help in making a good decision. Salespeople who are perceived as experts or as possessing unique skills at reducing the risks associated with the customer's decision will be able to exert substantial influence on the customer's decision.

Wilson (1975) has suggested that the initial stage of customer encounters should be devoted to establishing "credibility and legitimation. Unless this basic acceptability is developed, further communication is likely to become quite ineffective if not impossible" (p. 394). Thus, establishing credibility by creating the impression of expertise would be most effective when an "out" salesperson makes initial contact with a customer.

Proposition 3: Attempting to establish similarities with a customer as a base of influence is positively related to effectiveness in the following circumstances:

Salesperson resources—the salesperson is actually similar to the customer in terms of characteristics related to the purchase decision.

Customer-buying task—the salesperson's customers typically are engaged in simple, low risk purchase decisions or in purchase decisions with high psychological or social risks.

Customer-salesperson relationship—the salesperson is typically an "in" supplier.

Wilson and Ghingold (1980) found that salespeople feel establishing rapport with customers is a critical aspect of effectiveness in sales interactions. One method for establishing rapport is for the salesperson to create a link with the customer by identifying similarities—characteristics they have in common. Establishing similarities may increase the trustworthiness of salespeople, facilitate the exchange of information about salespeople and customers, and lead customers to feel their needs and problems are well understood. Salespeople who actually are similar to their customer will be in a better position to establish this base of influence.

When customers are making simple purchase decisions, their information needs are not great. In these situations, an influence base associated with getting the customers to identify with the salesperson will more effective than an expertise base of influence. Capon and Swasy (1977) provides some support for this proposition. In a role playing situation, students felt that messages directed at establishing a similarity influence base would be more effective when selling to consumers as opposed to purchasing agents. Presumably consumers typically engage in simpler decision processes with higher psychological risks than purchasing agents.

It may be particularly important for the ''in'' salesperson to maintain good relations with a customer over a long time period by establishing a similarity base of influence. In support of this proposition, Bambic (1978) found that purchasing agents indicate the greatest preference for an attitudinally similar salesperson when the salesperson represents a qualified ''in'' supplier.

Proposition Concerning the Use of Influence Techniques

Proposition 4: The use of closed as opposed to open influence techniques is more effective under the following circumstances:

Customer-salesperson relationships—
a) The salesperson typically is more powerful than his/her customers.
b) The level of conflict between the customers and the salesperson is high.
c) The salesperson typically does not anticipate future interactions with the customer.

The use of closed influence techniques suggests that salespeople are willing to sacrifice a customer's long-term satisfaction so that they can make an immediate sale. This type of behavior would be most effective when customers do not have the opportunity to sanction the salesperson if they discover that they have been manipulated or deceived. If the customers will not be encountering the salesperson in the future, they will not have the opportunity to invoke sanctions such as not considering the salesperson's products in future applications. If the salespeople are more powerful than the customers, the customers will have to forego invoking sanctions because the salespeople control the degree to which the customers can satisfy their needs.

Salespeople might decide to sacrifice future sales to make an immediate sale. This would occur if the immedi-

ate sale is very large, larger than potential future sales. In this circumstance, salespeople would risk the long-term consequences associated with closed influence techniques to seek a short-term benefit.

Spiro and Perreault (1979) found that salespeople use closed influence techniques when engaging in difficult sales situations—situations characterized by poor customer-salesperson relationships, low customer interest, and routine purchase decisions involving undifferentiated products. Open influence tactics were used when there was a high level of buyer/seller involvement—situations characterized by good customer-salesperson relationships and purchase decisions that were important to both parties. Assuming that, on average, salespeople engage in appropriate sales behaviors, these findings indicate that closed influence tactics are most effective in sales situations with negotiating obstacles and open influence tactics are more effective in high involvement situations.

Proposition Concerning Control of the Sales Interactions

Proposition 5: Attempting to exert control over the sales interaction is related to effectiveness in the following circumstances:

Customer's buying task—customers are engaged in ambiguous purchase decisions.

Customer salesperson relationship—
a) future interactions between customers and the salesperson are not anticipated.
b) the salespeople typically are more powerful than the customers.

Salespeople who exert a high level of control in a sales interaction frequently direct the interaction toward an outcome that is more compatible with the needs of the salespeople than the needs of the customers. This behavior would be most effective when the customers are confronting an ambiguous problem and do not have adequate information to solve the problem. Since the exertion of control might sacrifice customer satisfaction, this behavior would be more effective when the salesperson has a goal of making an immediate sale. When future interactions with a customer are anticipated, the salesperson's long-term effectiveness will be more closely related to satisfying the customer's needs. Under these circumstances, salespeople might be less effective when they control the interaction towards an outcome desired by them. These conclusions are consistent with Bursk's (1947) description of situations in which low pressure selling is more effective than high pressure selling. Bursk suggests that low pressure selling (low control of the sales interaction) is most appropriate when the customer is knowledgeable and when continued goodwill is at stake.

The leadership research also provides support for this proposition. This research indicates that autocratic, "initiating structure" behaviors (high control behaviors) are most appropriate when the group is engaged in an ambiguous, stressful, and nonroutine task. In addition, the more the group members perceive that they possess the abilities to accomplish a task, the less willing they are to accept directive or coaching behavior from their leader (Filley et al. 1976, p. 255). Supportive, participative, consideration leader behaviors (low control behaviors) are most effective when group members possess information about the task and when the task is routine. Based on these research findings, salespeople will be more effective if they attempt to control sales situations when customers are engaged in routine buying decisions (straight rebuys).

Since little personal selling research has considered the effect of moderating variables, the previously stated propositions are quite speculative. Little empirical support can be provided at this time. A research program for developing and testing contingency hypotheses follows.

Developing and Testing Contingency Proposition

In this section, a research program is outlined for developing and testing contingency hypotheses. The three stages of this program are hypothesis generation, hypothesis testing in a laboratory environment, and hypothesis testing in a field setting. These stages parallel the general framework suggested by Ray (1978) for examining communication phenemona.[8] In discussing, the hypothesis testing stage, contingency research approaches are contrasted with the traditional research approach used in personal selling.

Generating Contingency Hypotheses

In the preceding section, a number of contingency propositions are presented. These propositions were developed by reviewing the limited amount of research in personal selling that has considered moderating variables and by translating relevant leadership research into a personal selling context. However, these propositions represent only a portion of the contingency "theories" used by salespeople in their customer interactions.

The everyday use of contingency influence strategies is illustrated in a recent study by Falbo and Peplau (1980). When asked to write open-ended essays on the topic "how I get my way," many subjects indicated that their power strategies varied depending on the target. Thus, the existence of contingency influence strategies arises naturally without prompting from researchers.

Methodologies for uncovering rules or "theories" em-

ployed by practitioners are reviewed in Zaltman, Lawther, and Heffring (1980). (See Wilson and Ghingold 1980 for an example of a "theories in use" approach used in a personal selling context.) These "theories in use" methodologies involve observing and questioning salespeople.

One approach for uncovering "theories in use" is to investigate how salespeople organize their knowledge and experience. A richer taxonomy of moderating variables can be developed by determining what characteristics salespeople use to classify customers and sales situations. (see Cantor and Mischel 1979 for a review of the research on social classification schemes used by people.)

Schank and Abelson (1977) proposed that part of knowledge is organized around hundreds of stereotypical situations and activities. The implications of these scripts (stereotypic-action sequences) have been empirically investigated by Bower, Black, and Turner (1979). Salespeople probably possess contingency selling scripts that guide their behavior in customer interactions. One might access these scripts by asking salespeople to describe their behavior in specific sales situations. The nature of the differences in scripts across sales situations should be useful in developing contingency propositions.

Theories in use also can be uncovered by using a cognitive response methodology. Salespeople can be asked to describe their thoughts during specific customer encounters. These thoughts can be collected directly after the encounter or during a replay of a recording of the encounter. A more structured format can be used to collect these cognitive responses by asking salespeople to indicate their thoughts when observing a standardized recording of a customer-sales encounter (Grikscheidt 1971).

In contrast to these open-ended methods for collecting information, salespeople can be asked to answer questions concerning the appropriate behavior when confronting a sales scenario (Capon and Swasy 1977) or questions concerning their behavior during a specific past sales encounter (Spiro and Perreault 1979). Vroom and Yetton (1973) have developed a method for soliciting contingency leader responses and describing relevant situational variables.

Experimental Testing of Contingency Propositions

Having developed contingency hypotheses, the next step is to test these hypotheses in a laboratory environment using an experimental design. Laboratory experiments are quick and effective ways for testing behavioral propositions. The control achieved in a laboratory allows the researcher to determine causal relationships between variables and eliminate potential alternative explanations.

The experimental approach has been used in several studies previously reviewed; however, these studies have not been designed to examine contingency hypotheses. Only main effect relationships between effectiveness and salesperson characteristics or behavior were considered in

---

8 The microtheoretical notions discussed by Ray (1978) are similar to the contingency propositions developed from the framework presented in this paper.

these studies. For example, Woodside and Davenport (1974) manipulated two sales behaviors (establishing an expertise base of influence, and establishing a similarity base of influence) and tested whether differences in these behaviors had an effect on purchasing behavior.

In contrast to these past studies, contingency propositions are tested in an experimental setting by examining the interaction between a sales behavior and a moderating variable. Thus, the second part of proposition 2 would be tested by manipulating the level of expertise expressed by the salesperson and the complexity of the buying decision confronting the subject (customer), and testing for a significant interaction between these two factors.

Levitt's (1965) classic study on industrial selling is the only study in which the effectiveness of a behavior-sales circumstance interaction was investigated. In this study, a behavior (quality of presentation) and a resource of the salesperson (company reputation) were manipulated. Unfortunately, there were methodological problems in examining the contingency (interaction) hypotheses (Capon et al 1972).

While laboratory experiments are an excellent method for testing theories and determining causality, there are two problems with laboratory experiments for testing hypotheses concerning personal selling. First, laboratory experiments typically sacrifice external validity to insure high internal validity. To insure homogeneous treatments, the salesperson frequently is removed from the experiment. In some experiments, the salesperson is replaced by a videotape (Busch and Wilson 1976), a film (Levitt 1965), or a paper and pencil description (Bambic 1978). In these experiments, the phenomenon under study is more closely related to impersonal, mass communication than interpersonal influence.

Second, laboratory experiments are most readily adapted to testing the effectiveness of sales behaviors in one-shot, selling situations. It is difficult to create laboratory situations that examine the effects of behaviors across sales interactions. This arises because some behaviors such as adaptation and the use of close influence techniques have "carry over" effects. Both adaptation and the close influence techniques can lead to increased effectiveness in one interaction but decreased effectiveness in subsequent interactions. These "carry over effects" are difficult to manipulate and measure in an experimental design. Due to this problem, some propositions can be tested only in field studies. In addition, field tests offer a method for assessing the impact of behavior across actual selling interactions.

Field Testing of Contingency Hypotheses

The steps in testing contingency hypotheses in the field are shown in Figure 3. When contingency hypotheses are tested in the field across interactions, the first step is to develop reliable and valid measures of typical sales behaviors and sales situations (moderator variables) in which sa-

lespeople engage.

Few measures of sales behaviors exist; however there are paper and pencil measures to determine influence techniques typically used (Arch 1979), the degree to which a customer-oriented behavior is employed (Saxe 1979), and behavioral predispositions such as self-monitoring. Although studies have postulated moderating variables in the sales situation, no measures of circumstances encountered in sales situations have been developed. Thus, research must be directed toward developing measures of sales behaviors and moderating variables before contingency hypotheses can be tested in field settings.

When behavior and situation measures have been developed, contingency hypotheses can be tested by getting measures of typical behavior patterns from salespeople, typical situation measures from independent sources such as sales managers or customers, and then relating these measures to salesperson effectiveness using techniques for examining moderator variable relationships (Allison 1973: Zedeck 1971). While traditional measures of sales performance such as sales or sales to quota can be used as measures of effectiveness, care must be taken to control for sources of variance unrelated to effectiveness in sales interactions (see Figure 1).

The difference between testing contingency hypotheses in the field and traditional correlational studies of salesperson effectiveness is illustrated by the shaded areas in Figure 3. Traditional correlational studies have considered only the shaded steps. In these studies, measures of salesperson behavioral predispositions and performance are collected. No measures are made of the typical sales situations encountered by the salesperson. Hypotheses are tested by correlating performance with behavioral predispositions.

Contingency studies necessitate the inclusion of the unshaded steps—the collection of situational measures. In addition, the test of contingency hypotheses requires the use of moderator variable regressions so that interactions can be examined.

Conclusion

Most empirical research on salesperson performance has been based on the implicit assumption that a universal set of characteristics or behaviors is associated with successful sales performance across all sales situations. It is reasonable to investigate such parsimonious propositions in the early stages of studying a problem, but more complex propositions are warranted if simple propositions fail to explain the phenomenon of interest. The review of the research of personal selling effectiveness at the beginning of this paper illustrates the lack of support for simple universal propositions. These universal propositions have been of some value, but few have consistently explained a significant proposition of the variance in performance. Thus, it is appropriate, at this time, to investigate the more com-

FIGURE 3
Steps in Correlational Test of Contingency Hypotheses

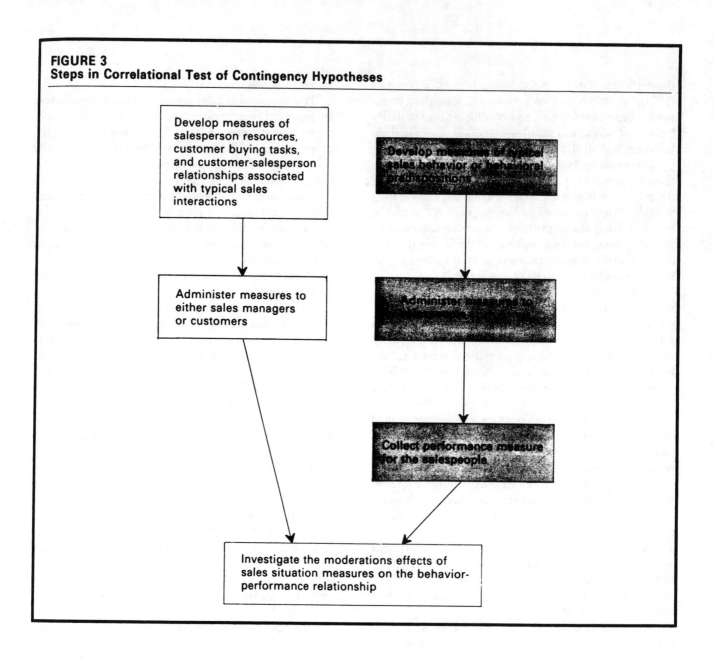

plex propositions in which circumstances of the sales situation moderate the relationship between the salesperson behavior and effectiveness.

To provide a direction for this research approach, some salesperson behaviors and moderating variables were defined and propositions suggested concerning the effectiveness of these behaviors in different sales interaction circumstances. The group of behaviors and moderating variables considered is intended to be suggestive rather than exhaustive. Little research has been directed toward developing a taxonomy of sales behaviors or characteristics of the salesperson-customer interaction. When descriptive research on classifying sales behaviors and interaction characteristics is more advanced, many additional and richer contingency propositions can be developed and tested.

Even though the propositions presented in this paper are limited, some new and potentially significant variables

for understanding personal selling effectiveness have been introduced. Sales behaviors related to adapting to the customer and controlling the sales interaction have not been investigated empirically, even though practitioners view these behaviors as critical to sales effectiveness. Dyadic research has focused on similarity, a dyadic characteristic which appears to have little relationship to effectiveness. Characteristics of the customer-salesperson relationship such as relative power, level of conflict, and the anticipation of future interactions have played an important role in interpersonal influence research in social psychology and organizational behavior, but have been ignored in personal selling research. While this new research direction suggests more complex propositions and research designs, it is anticipated that the effort expended on this new approach will lead to a substantial improvement in our understanding of personal selling effectiveness.

REFERENCES

Allison, P. D. (1973), "Testing for Interaction in Multiple Regression," *American Journal of Sociology*, 83 (July), 144-153.

Arch, David (1979), "The Development of Influence Strategy Scales in Buyer-Seller Interactions," in 1979 *Educators' Conference Proceedings*, N. Beckwith et al., eds., Chicago: American Marketing Association.

Baehr, Melany E. and G. Williams (1968), "Prediction of Sales Success from Factorially Determined Dimensions of Personal Background Data," *Journal of Applied Psychology*, 52 (April), 98-103.

Bagozzi, Richard P. (1978), "Salesforce Performance and Satisfaction as a Function of Individual Difference, Interpersonal and Situational Factors," *Journal of Marketing Research*, 15 (November), 517-531.

Baier, Donald and Robert D. Dugan (1957), "Factors in Sales Success," *Journal of Applied Psychology*, 41 (February), 37-40.

Bambic, Peter (1978), "An Interpersonal Influence Study of Source Acceptance in Industrial Buyer-Seller Exchange Process: An Experimental Approach," unpublished Ph.D. dissertation, Graduate School of Business, Pennsylvania State University.

Blake, Robert R. and J. S. Mouton (1970), *The Grid for Sales Excellence*, New York: McGraw-Hill Book Co.

Bower, Gordon H., John B. Black, and Terrence J.Turner (1979), "Scripts in Memory for Text," *Cognitive Psychology*, 11 (April), 177-220.

Boyd, Harper W., Michael L. Ray, and Edward C. Strong (1972), "An Attitudinal Framework for Advertising Strategy," *Journal of Marketing*, 36 (April), 27-33.

Brock, Timothy C. (1965), "Communicator-Recipient Similarity and Decision Change," *Journal of Personality and Social Psychology*, 1 (June), 650-654.

Bursk, Edward C. (1947), "Low Pressure Selling," *Harvard Business Review*, 25 (Winter), 227-242.

Busch, Paul and David T. Wilson (1976), "An Experimental Analysis of a Salesman's Expert and Referent Bases of Social Power in the Buyer-Seller Dyad," *Journal of Marketing Research*, 13 (February), 3-11.

Buzzotta, V. R., R. E. Lefton, and Manual Sherberg (1972), *Effective Selling Through Psychology*, New York: John Wiley & Sons.

Cantor, N. and W. Mischel (1979), "Prototypes in Person Perception," in *Advances in Experimental Social Psychology*, L. Berkowitz, ed., Vol. 12, New York: Academic Press, 3-52.

Capon, Noel (1975), "Persuasive Effects of Sales Messages Developed from Interaction Process Analysis," *Journal of Business Administration*, 60 (April), 238-244.

____, Morris Holbrook, and John Hulbert (1972), "Industrial Purchasing Behavior: A Reappraisal," *Journal of Business Administration*, 4, 69-77.

____, and John Swasy (1977), "An Exploratory Study of Compliance Gaining Techniques in Buyer Behavior," in *Contemporary Marketing Techniques*, B. Greenberg and D. Bellenger, eds., Chicago: American Marketing Association.

Chapple, Eliot and Gordon Donald, Jr. (1947), "An Evaluation of Department Store Salespeople by the Interaction Chronograph," *Journal of Marketing*, 112 (October), 173-185.

Churchill, Gilbert A., Jr., Robert H. Collins, and William A. Strang (1975), "Should Retail Salespersons be Similar to Their Customers," *Journal of Retailing*, 51 (Fall), 29-42+.

Cotham, James C., III (1969), "Using Personal History Information in Retail Salesman Selection," *Journal of Retailing*, 45 (Summer), 31-38+.

Davis, Harry L. and Alvin J. Silk (1972), "Interaction and Influ-

ence Processes in Personal Selling," *Sloan Management Review*, 13 (Winter), 56-76.

Doreen, Dale, Donald R. Emery, and Robert W. Sweitzer (1979), "Selling as a Dyadic Relationship Revisited." Paper presented at the 1979 AIDS Conference, New Orleans.

Dunnette, Marvin D. and Wayne K. Kirchner (1960), "Psychological Test Differences between Industrial Salesmen and Retail Salesmen," *Journal of Applied Psychology*, 44 (April), 121-125.

Emerson, Richard M. (1962), "Power-Dependence Relations," *American Sociological Review*, 27 (February), 31-41.

Evans, Franklin (1963), "Selling as a Dyadic Relationship_A New Approach," *American Behavioral Scientist*, 6 (May), 76.

Falbo, Toni (1977), "Multidimensional Scaling of Power Strategies," *Journal of Personality and Social Psychology*, 35 (August), 537-547.

____, and Letitia Peplau (1980), "Power Strategies in Intimate Relationships," *Journal of Personality and Social Psychology*, 38 (June), 618-628.

Farley, John and R. Swinth (1967), "Effects of Choice and Sales Message on Customer-Salesman Interaction," *Journal of Applied Psychology*, 51 (April), 107-110.

Fiedler, Fred E. and Martin M. Chemers (1974), *Leadership and Effective Management*, Glenview, Il: Scott, Foresman and Company.

Filley, Alan C., Robert J. House, and Steven Kerr (1976), *Managerial Process and Organizational Behavior*, 2nd ed., Glenview, Il.: Scott, Foresman and Company.

French, Cecil L. (1960), "Correlates of Success in Retail Selling," *American Journal of Sociology*, 66 (April), 128-134.

French, John R. P. and Bertram Raven (1959), "The Bases of Social Power," in *Studies in Social Power*, D. Cartright, ed., Ann Arbor: University of Michigan, Institute for Social Research, 150-167.

Gadel, M. S. (1964), "Concentration by Salesmen on Congenial Prospects," *Journal of Marketing*, 28 (April), 64-66.

Ghiselli, Edwin E. (1969), "Prediction of Success of Stockbrokers," *Personnel Psychology*, 22 (Summer), 125-130.

____ (1973), "The Validity of Aptitude Tests in Personnel Selection," *Personnel Psychology*, 26 (Winter), 461-477.

Greenberg, Herbert and David Mayer (1964), "A New Approach to the Scientific Selection of Successful Salesmen, *Journal of Psychology*, 57 (January), 113-123.

Grikscheit, Gary M. (1971), "An Investigation of the Ability of Salesmen to Monitor Feedback," Ph.D. dissertation, Michigan State University.

____, and William J. E. Crissy (1973), "Improving Interpersonal Communication Skill," MSU Business Topics, 21 (Autumn), 63-68.

Gwinner, Robert (1968), "Base Theory in the Formulation of Sales Strategy," *MSU Business Topics*, 16 (Autumn), 37-44.

Hakansson, Hakan, Jan Johanson, and Bjorn Wootz (1977), "Influence Tactics in Buyer-Seller Processes," *Industrial Marketing Management*, 5 (Fall), 319-332.

Harrell, Thomas W. (1960), "The Relation of Test Scores to Sales Criteria," *Personnel Psychology*, 13 (Spring), 65-69.

Howells, G. W. (1968), "The Successful Salesman: A Personality Analysis," *British Journal of Marketing*, 2, 13-23.

Jolson, Marvin A. (1975), "The Underestimated Potential of the Canned Sales Presentation," *Journal of Marketing*, 39 (January), 75-78.

Kahn, George N. and Abraham Shuchman (1961), "Specialize Your Salesmen!," *Harvard Business Review*, 39 (January/February), 90-98.

Kirchner, Wayne K., Carolyn S. McElwain, and Marvin D. Dunnette (1960), "A Note on the Relationship between Age and Sales Effectiveness," *Journal of Applied Psychology*, 44 (April), 92-93.

Lamont, Lawrence M. and William J. Lundstrom (1977), "Identifying Successful Industrial Salesmen by Personality and Personal Characteristics," *Journal of Marketing Research*, 14 (November), 517-529.

Levitt, Theodore (1965), *Industrial Purchasing Behavior: A Study in Communications Effects*, Boston, Ma: Division of Research, Harvard Business School.

McCall, Morgan, W., Jr. (1979), "Power, Authority, and Influence," in *Organizational Behavior*, S. Kerr, ed., Columbus, Oh: Grid Publishing Company, 185-206.

Mattheiss, T. H., Richard M. Durnad, Jan R. Muczyk, and Myron Gable (1977), "Personality and the Prediction of Salesmen's Success," in *Contemporary Marketing Thought*, B. Greenberg and D. Bellenger, eds., Chicago: American Marketing Association, pp. 499-502.

Merenda, Peter F., and Walter V. Clarke (1959), "Predictive Efficiency of Temperament Characteristics and Personal History Variables in Determining Success of Life in Insurance Agents," *Journal of Applied Psychology*, 43 (December), 360-366.

Miner, John B. (1962), "Personality and Ability Factors in Sales Performance," *Journal of Applied Psychology*, 46 (February), 6-13.

Mosel, James N. (1952), "Prediction of Department Store Sales Performance from Personnel Data," *Journal of Applied Psychology*, 36 (February), 8-10.

Newton, Derek A. (1967), "A Marketing Communication Model for Sales Management," in *Risk Taking and Information Handling in Consumer Behavior*, Donald F. Cox, ed., Boston: Division of Research, Graduate School of Business Administration, Harvard University.

Olshavsky, Richard W. (1973), "Customer-Salesmen Interaction in Appliance Retailing," *Journal of Marketing Research*, 10 (May), 208-212.

Pasold, Peter W. (1975), "The Effectiveness of Various Modes of Sales Behavior in Different Markets," *Journal of Marketing Research*, 12 (May), 171-176.

Pennington, Alan (1968), "Customer-Salesmen Bargaining Behavior in Retail Transactions," *Journal of Marketing Research*, 8 (November), 501-504.

Pondy, Louis R. (1967), "Organizational Conflict: Concepts and Models," *Administrative Science Quarterly*, 12 (September), 296-320.

Pruden, Henry O. and Robert A. Peterson (1971), "Personality and Performance-Satisfaction of Industrial Salesmen," *Journal of Marketing Research*, 8 (November), 501-504.

Raven, B. H. and J. Z. Rubin (1976), *Social Psychology: People in Groups*, New York: John Wiley & Sons.

Ray, Michael L. (1978), "The Present and Potential Linkages between the Microtheoretical Notions of Behavioral Science and the Problems of Advertising: A Proposal for a Research System," in *Behavioral and Management Science in Marketing*, Harry L. Davis and Alvin Silk, eds., New York: Ronald Press, 99-141.

Reed, Jim D. (1976), "Comments on 'The Underestimated Potential of the Canned Sales Presentation,'" *Journal of Marketing*, 40 (January), 67-68.

Reizenstein, Richard C. (1971), "A Dissonance Approach to Measuring the Effectiveness of Two Personal Selling Techniques through Decision Reversal," *Proceedings*, Fall Conference, Chicago: American Marketing Association, 176-180.

Reve, T. and L. Stern (1979), "Interorganizational Relations in Marketing Channels," *Academy of Management Review*, 4

(July), 80-91.

Riordan, Edward A., Richard L. Oliver, and James H. Donnelly, Jr. (1977), "The Unsold Prospect: Dyadic and Attitudinal Determinants," *Journal of Marketing Research*, 14 (November), 530-537.

Robinson, P. J., C. W. Farris, and Y. Wind (1967), *Industrial Buying and Creative Marketing*, Boston: Allyn and Bacon.

Rubin, Jeffrey Z. and Bert R. Brown (1975), *The Social Psychology of Bargaining and Negotiation*, New York: Academic Press. Sales and Marketing Management (1979), "1979 Survey of Selling Costs," 124 (February 26).

Saxe, Robert (1979), "The Customer Orientational Salespeople," unpublished Ph.D. dissertation, Graduate School of Management, University of California at Los Angeles.

Schank, R. C. and R. P. Abelson (1977), *Scripts, Plans, Goals and Understanding*, Hillsdale, NJ: Lawrence Erlbaum Associates.

Scheibelhut, John H. and Gerald Albaum (1973), "Self-Other Orientations Among Salesmen and Non-Salesmen," *Journal of Marketing Research*, 10 (February), 97-99.

Simons, Herbert W., Nancy N. Berkowitz, and R. John Moyer (1970), "Similarity, Credibility and Attitude Change: A Review and A Theory," *Psychological Bulletin*, 73 (January), 1-16.

Snyder, Mark (1974), "The Self-Monitoring of Expressive Behavior," *Journal of Personality and Social Psychology*," 30 (October), 526-537.

Spiro, Rosann L. and William D. Perreault, Jr. (1979), "Influence Used by Industrial Salesmen: Influence Strategy Mixes and Situational Determinants," *Journal of Business*, 52 (July), 435-455.

Tanofsy, Robert, R. Ronald Shepps, and Paul J. O'Neill (1969), "Pattern Analysis of Biographical Predictors of Success as an Insurance Salesman," *Journal of Applied Psychology*, 53 (April), 136-139.

Taylor, James L. and Arch G. Woodside (1968), "Exchange Behavior Among Life Insurance Selling and Buyer Centers in Field Settings," Working paper no. 72, Center for Marketing Studies, Research Division, College of Business Administration, University of South Carolina.

Thomas, Kenneth W. (1976), "Conflict and Conflict Management," in *Handbook of Industrial and Organizational Psychology*, M. Dunnette, ed., Chicago: Rand McNally.

Thompson, Joseph W. (1973), *Selling: A Managerial and Behavioral Science Analysis*, New York: McGraw-Hill Book Co.

Tobolski, Francis P. and Willard A. Kerr (1952), "Predictive Value of the Empathy Test in Automobile Salesmanship," *Journal of Applied Psychology*, 36 (October), 310-311.

Vroom, V. H. and P. W. Yetton (1973), *Leadership and Decision Making*, Pittsburgh: University of Pittsburgh Press.

Walker, O. C., Jr., G. A. Churchill, and W. M. Ford (1977), "Motivation and Performance in Industrial Selling: Existing Knowledge and Needed Research," *Journal of Marketing Research*, 14 (May), 156-168.

Weaver, Charles N. (1969), "An Empirical Study to Aid in the Selection of Retail Salesclerks," *Journal of Retailing*, 45 (Fall), 22-26.

Weitz, Barton A. (1978), "The Relationship Between Salesperson Performance and Understanding of Customer Decision Making," *Journal of Marketing Research*, 15 (November), 501-516.

____ (1979), "A Critical Review of Personal Selling Research: The Need for a Contingency Approach," in *Critical Issues in Sales Management: State-of-the-Art and Future Research Needs*, G. Albaum and G. Churchill, eds., Eugene,

OR: University of Oregon, College of Business Administration.

____ (1980), "Adaptive Selling Behavior for Effective Interpersonal Influence," Paper presented at AMA Conference on Theoretical and Empirical Research on Theoretical and Empirical Research on Buyer-Seller Interactions, Columbia, South Carolina.

Willett, Ronald P. and Alan L. Pennington (1966), "Customer and Salesman: The Anatomy of Choice and Influence in a Retail Setting," in *Science, Technology, and Marketing,* Raymond M. Hass, ed., Chicago: American Marketing Association, 598-616.

Wilson, David T. (1975), "Dyadic Interaction: An Exchange Process," in *Advances in Consumer Research*, B. Anderson, ed., Cincinnati, OH: Association for Consumer Research, 394-397.

____, and Ghingold, Morry (1980), "Building Theory from Practice: A Theory-in-Use Approach," in *Theoretical Developments in Marketing*, C. Lamb, Jr. and P. Dunne, eds., Chi-

cago: American Marketing Association, 236-239.

Woodside, Arch G. and William J. Davenport (1974), "The Effect of Salesman Similarity and Expertise on Consumer Purchasing Behavior," *Journal of Marketing Research*, 11 (May), 198-202.

Yalch, Richard F. (1979), "Closing Sales: Compliance-Gaining Strategies for Personal Selling," in *Sales Management: New Developments from Behavioral and Decision Model Research*, R. Bagozzi, ed., Cambridge, MA: Marketing Science Institute.

Zaltman, Gerald, Karen Lawther, and Michael Heffring (1980), *Theory Construction in Marketing*, New York: John Wiley & Sons.

Zdep, S. M. and H. B. Weaver (1967), "The Graphoanalytic Approach to Selecting Life Insurance Salesmen," *Journal of Applied Psychology*, 51 (June), 295-299.

Zedeck, Sheldon (1971), "Problems with the Use of 'Moderator' Variables," *Psychological Bulletin*, 76 (October), 295-310.

Theodore Levitt

Communications and Industrial Selling

This article reports on research that investigated the relative importance of company reputation, salesman effort, and sales-message quality in industrial selling. It distinguishes between the relative importance of "high risk" and "low risk" purchasing situations, between "high-competence" (well-informed) and "low-competence" purchasers, and between the immediate effects of a sales presentation and the abiding effects. And it evaluates differences in sales effectiveness between the "quality" of a salesman's presentation, his familiarity with the product, and how honest his prospects think he is.

—Does corporate or institutional advertising by industrial-product companies pay?

—Do the salesman of well-known industrial products companies have an automatic edge over the salesmen of little-known or unknown companies?

—Is it better for an industrial product company to spend its limited funds on aggressive advertising of its general competence or on more careful selection and training of its salesmen?

—Are the decisions of prospective buyers of new industrial products affected by the amount of personal risk these decisions expose them to?

—Are the buying decisions of practicing purchasing agents affected more by the reputation of a vendor-company than are the decisions of practicing engineers and scientists?

—Does the effect of a company's reputation on a customer's buying decision hold up over time, or does it erode as time passes?

THESE are some of the questions that have been investigated in a study recently completed at the Harvard Graduate School of Business Administration. Specifically, the questions focused on the extent to which an industrial-product company's generalized reputation af-

fects its ability to launch new products. The accelerating flood of new and often complex industrial products, coupled with the continuing shortage of capable salesmen and the rising costs of advertising make the above questions particularly timely.

'Source Effect'

This timeliness is further enhanced by studies by Harvard Business School Professor Raymond A. Bauer, which have suggested that business communicators have been inadequately aware of the extent to which their audiences influence the communicators, rather than the usual one-way preoccupation with how the communicators (or advertisers) influence their audiences.[1] To illustrate:

Research shows that a newspaper editorial identified to one group of Americans as emanating, say, from *The New York Times* and to a similar group of Americans as emanating, say, from Pravada would lead one to expect that a change in audience opinion in the direction advocated by the editorial would be greater for those who believed it was a *New York Times* editorial than those who believed it to be a *Pravda* editorial. In other words, the audience's feelings about the credibility of the message source help determine the persuasive effectiveness of the message itself. The greater the prestige or the more believable the message source, the more likely that it will influence the audience in the direction advocated by the message. The less prestigeful or believable the source, the less

About the author. Theodore Levitt is Professor of Business Administration at Harvard University. He is the author of three books published in the last five years and of numerous articles. His *Innovation in Marketing* (McGraw-Hill, 1962) won an award from the Academy of Management as one of the best management books of the year. Two of his articles, "Marketing Myopia" (1960) and "Innovative Imitation" (1966), won McKinsey Awards as one of the best articles of each year in the *Harvard Business Review*.

[1] Bauer, "The Obstinate Audience," *American Psychologist*, Vol. 19 (May 1964), pp. 319-328, and "Communication as a Transaction," *Public Opinion Quarterly*, Vol. 27 (Spring 1963), pp. 83-86.

The Journal of Marketing
Vol. 31 (April 1967), pp. 15-21

Communications and Industrial Selling / 173

likely that it will influence the audience in the direction advocated by the message.

This phenomenon is now generally referred to as "source effect." Obviously what source effect amounts to is some sort of independent judgment by the audience such that it is either more or less affected by the message. The audience takes a form of initiative, independent of the message, which affects its susceptibility to the message.[2]

If in their private lives people such as businessmen and scientists exhibit source effect and audience initiative in response to political communications and propaganda, there is the question of whether they do this same thing in their business lives in response to advertising and direct sales presentations. McGraw-Hill expresses its belief that source effect works powerfully in industrial selling in its famous advertisement of a stern-looking purchasing agent facing the reader (salesman) from behind his desk and saying:

> I don't know who you are.
> I don't know your company.
> I don't know your company's product.
> I don't know what your company stands for.
> I don't know your company's customers.
> I don't know your company's record.
> I don't know your company's reputation.
> Now—what was it you wanted to sell me?
> MORAL: Sales start before your salesman calls —
> with business publication advertising.

To test this and a variety of related hypotheses, an elaborate communications simulation was devised and administered. Participants included 113 practicing purchasing agents from a wide variety of companies, 130 engineers and scientists, and 131 business school graduate students. (For simplifying purposes, the engineers and scientists are in this article referred to as "chemist.") This article is a report on the results of this simulation. But while it is a "report," it is not a simple document. As will be seen, it is full of moderating qualifications and carefully-phrased conclusions. It cannot be read with easy speed or casual comfort. The more complex a subject, the more involuted its rhetoric. In the present case, the reader must be prepared to go slow along an agonizing path.

Methodology

Basically what was done in the research was to divide each audience group (purchasing agents, chemists, and students) into six separate subgroups and then to expose each subgroup to a ten-minute filmed sales presentation for a new, but fictitious, technical product for use as an ingredient in making paint. Each audience member was put into

the position of assuming he was listening to the presentation as it would be given by a salesman sitting across his desk. Some groups were asked to assume they were purchasing agents for a paint firm and some were asked to assume they were chemists. The film presentation technique and audience setup were created to make conditions as realistic as possible, with great care taken to prevent communications between subgroups and to create realistic and thoughtful responses by the subjects. All saw what was basically the same ten-minute film with the same actors. However, some subgroups saw a relatively good presentation and some a relatively poor one; for some the selling company was identified in the film as a relatively high-credibility company (the Monsanto Company), for other subgroups it was identified as a relatively lower credibility and less well-known company (the Denver Chemical Company), and for still others the company identity was kept anonymous. Immediately after the film was run, and then again in five weeks, each respondent filled out a detailed questionnaire.[3]

Results

Let us now take up each of the question areas posed at the outset of this article, and see how our findings respond to them.

1. Does Corporate or Institutional Advertising by Industrial-Product Companies Pay?

For complex industrial products or materials, a company's generalized reputation does indeed have an important bearing on how its sales prospects make buying decisions. While the research did not specifically investigate the influence of corporate or institutional advertising, the results show that to the extent that such advertising helps in building a company's reputation it clearly helps in making sales. Whether such advertising specifically helps build a reputation is, however, a separate question. But the presumption is that mere visibility of a company is in some way helpful and reassuring, provided that the impressions that are created are not negative.

Generally speaking, the better a company's reputation, the better are its chances (1) of getting a favorable *first hearing* for a new product among customer prospects, and (2) of getting early *adoption* of that product. Vendor reputation influences buyers, decision makers, and the decision-making process. But since industrial products, and particularly new products, generally require direct calls by salesmen, does the value of company reputation automatically give an edge to the salesman from a well-known company over the salesman from a less well-known or anony-

---

2 For the seminal research in this area, see Carl I. Hovland and Walter Weiss, "The Influence of Source Credibility on Communication Effectiveness," *Public Opinion Quarterly*, Vol. 15 (Winter 1951-1952), pp. 635-650, and Carl I. Hovland, A. A. Lumsdaine, and Fred D. Sheffield, *Experiments in Mass Communication* (Princeton: Princeton University Press, 1949).

3 The details of the research mechanism are spelled out in Theodore Levitt, *Industrial Purchasing Behavior: A Study in Communications Effects* (Boston, Massachusetts: Division of Research, Harvard Business School, 1965).

mous one?

2. Do Well-Known Company Salesmen Have an Edge Over the Salesmen of Other Companies?

The answer is "yes," but it is a more complex answer than one might offhand suspect. Just because his company is favorably well known and to this extent puts the customer in a more favorable frame of mind toward that company, does not give the salesman a simple and automatic leg up over the salesman of a less-known company. The fact seems to be that customers *expect* more, or at least a better sales-presentation job, from well-known company salesmen. Hence they judge their performance somewhat differently from the way they judge the performance of other salesmen. Indeed there is some indication that some types of customers (or "audiences" of sales presentations) almost unconsciously "help" the salesmen of lesser-known companies by lowering their expectations in order to encourage competition between vendors. Thus, when they eventually make buying decisions, while these customers tend clearly to favor the better known companies, they seem to give disproportionate encouragement to the salesmen of the less well-known companies.

Still, everyone knows from experience that a good sales presentation is always better than a poor one, regardless of company reputation. A vital question that therefore arises is whether it is generally better for an industrial products company to spend its limited funds on more aggressive or effective advertising of its general competence, or on more careful selection and training of its salesmen?

3. Is It Better to Advertise More or to Select and Train Salesmen Better?

As would be expected, the research found that the quality of a salesman's presentation in support of a technically-complex new product is an important variable in obtaining a favorable customer reaction. In other words, there is a "presentation effect" in favor of the product supported by a well-done sales presentation.

When the influences of source effect and presentation effect are combined, the research suggests that when a relatively unknown or anonymous company makes a good direct sales presentation, it may be just as effective in getting a favorable first hearing for a complex new industrial material as a well-known company making a poor presentation. Thus a well-known company loses the advantage of its reputation if its direct sales presentation is clearly inferior to that of an unknown or little-known company. Against a good sales presentation by a little-known company, a well-known one must also have a good presentation if the customer-getting value of its reputation is to be realized. Conversely, a little-known company, by concentrating strongly on training its salesmen to make good presentations, may be able to make considerable progress to-

ward overcoming the liability of its relative anonymity.

Combining this with the finding that certain buyers apparently want to favor less well-known companies and expect more of better-known companies, even though they are strongly attracted to the latter, the conclusion seems to be that the lesser-known company—particularly when its resources are limited—can do an unexpectedly effective job for itself through more careful salesman selection and training.

On the other hand, everyone knows that every buying decision for a new product, and some for an established product, involves a certain amount of risk for the buyer. Moreover, the buyer's personal risk (as opposed to the risk for his company) varies as between whether he has sole personal responsibility for the buying (or, indeed, the "rejection") decision or whether it is a shared or committee decision. To what extent does the degree of the decision-maker's personal risk affect the importance of vendor reputation and quality of a sales presentation in the buyer's decision process?

4. The Role of Personal Risk in Buying Decisions

The amount of personal risk to which the individual decision-maker is exposed in a buying or rejection decision proves to be a vital factor in his decisions. And it is vital in the extent to which source effect is influential. Company reputation clearly results in a higher proportion of high-risk decisions in favor of the well-known company. Presentation quality tends substantially to strengthen the position of the less well-known company in high-risk buying situations, but not as much in low-risk buying situations. While careful attention to salesman selection and training can be said to help equalize greatly the competitive position of lesser known firms, these help it more to get a foot in the door than help it get an immediate adoption for its product. When it comes to the most important and most risky of customer actions—actually deciding to buy or reject a new product—assuming the various suppliers' products to be equal in all respects, source credibility exerts a dominant influence over other considerations.

But this still leaves unanswered the question of whether and to what extent all of these influences are equal among customers with varying degrees of technical competencies. Do they apply equally, for example, to purchasing agents and technically-trained personnel such as chemists?

5. The Influence of Customer 'Competence'

The research found that the power of source effect (company reputation for credibility) varies by the character and "competence" of the recipient of a sales message. Thus, there is some indication that, in the case of complex industrial materials, purchasing agents, who are usually highly competent as professional buyers, may be less influenced by a company's generalized reputation than are technical personnel, who are presumably less competent as buyers but more competent as judges of a complex product's merits. In first appraising complex new materials on the basis of sales presentations made directly to them, technically-sophisticated personnel seem to be influenced by the seller's reputation to a point that is unexpectedly higher than the influence of that reputation on such technically less sophisticated personnel as purchasing agents. In short, technical personnel are probably influenced far more by company reputation than has been widely assumed, and certainly more than such technically less sophisticated people as purchasing agents.

While all audiences seem to be influenced by the quality of the sales presentation, important differences apparently exist between purchasing agents and technical personnel. In the lower-risk decision situation of whether to give a newly presented complex new product a further hearing, technical personnel are more powerfully influenced by the quality of a direct sales presentation than are purchasing agents. Put differently, on low-risk purchasing decisions, the technically less sophisticated purchasing agents seem to rely less heavily on the quality of the sales presentation than do the technically more sophisticated personnel in making their decisions. But on high-risk decisions (whether actually to buy the product) the reverse is true: that is, the greater the risk, the more favorably purchasing agents are influenced by good sales presentations, and the less favorably technical personnel are influenced by such presentations. The greater the risk, the more likely technical personnel are to rely on their technical judgments about a new product's virtues rather than on the quality of the sales presentation in favor of that product. But purchasing agents, being technically less sophisticated, seem forced, in high-risk situations, to rely more heavily on the seller's presentation.

6. The Durability of Vendor Reputation on Buying Decisions

Philip Wrigley, of the chewing gum empire, is alleged to have answered a query about why his company continues to spend so much on advertising now that it is successful with this observation: "Once you get a plane up in the air you don't turn off the engines." For industrial-product companies, a related question concerns the durability of buying inclinations (and even of buying decisions) that sales prospects exhibit immediately after hearing a sales presentation. Since few new industrial products are immediately purchased on the making of a sales presentation to a customer—since, for many reasons, there is generally a time lag before a decision is made, the question is: Does source effect hold up over time? For example, with the passage of time, does the prospect forget the source of a new product presentation, remembering only the facts and the claimed product performance, such that when the actual

buying decision is made at some later time the vendor's reputation plays little or no role? Similarly, does the importance of quality of the sales presentation hold up over time?

The present research indicates that there is in industrial purchasing a phenomenon which communications researchers call the "sleeper effect." The favorable influence of a company's generalized good reputation (source effect) does indeed erode with the passage of time. But the conditions under which this happens appear to be quite special. Based on what the present research was able to test, what can be said is that this erosion occurs specifically when there is no intervening reinforcement or reinstatement of the identity of the source. Put differently, in the absence of repeated sales callbacks or advertisements to reinstate the identity of the source, the seller tends, over time, to lose the favorable impact of his good reputation on the attitudes and actions of his sales prospects.

But the declining power of source effect over time on audience decision-making works *in opposite directions* for the well-known company than for the lesser-known company. Sleeper effect, in a manner of speaking, hurts the well-known company but helps the lesser-known company. In the case of the former, as the sales prospect forgets the well-known source his originally favorable attitude toward the product declines; and in the case of the latter, as he forgets the lesser-known source his originally less-favorable attitude toward the product also declines. That is, the likelihood of his buying from the high credibility company declines while the likelihood of his buying from the low-credibility company rises—even though the high-credibility company is still likely to get more customers in absolute terms.

Implications and Reservations

The implications of the present research for industrial products companies are numerous, but so also are the reservations and qualifications which must be attached to the research findings. While the research sought to simulate reality as carefully as possible, it still remains only a simulation. Moreover, individual competitive situations, product characteristics, and a vast variety of other conditions can greatly affect the value of these findings in specific cases. But in the absence of better information and research, the present findings may be viewed as at least a beginning toward unravelling some age-old mysteries.

Reputation and Presentation

From the point of view of a producer of industrial materials or components, it seems safe to conclude that the cultivation of a good reputation among potential customers will have some payoff in the sense that it will help his salesmen to get "a foot in the door" of a prospect. But the value of cultivating a good reputation seems to be considerably less when it comes to its effect on the likelihood of the prospect's *actually buying* a new product on being first exposed to it. A good reputation always helps, but it helps less as the riskiness of the customer's decision rises and as he has something else to rely on draw on.

Hence it seems safe also to suggest that a producer of technically-advanced products which are used as components or as ingredients by other manufacturers would be wise systematically to cultivate for himself a strongly favorable generalized reputation among technical personnel of prospective manufacturing customers. In other words, in trying to sell such products to technically-trained personnel it may not be wise to rely so extensively, as many such companies do, on the product's inherent virtues and on making strong technical product presentations. Technical personnel are not human computers whose purchasing and product-specification decisions are based on cold calculations and devoid of less rigorously rational influences. They do indeed seem to be influenced by the seller's general reputation.

However, as might have been expected, the quality of a salesman's presentation in support of a product is an important variable in obtaining favorable buyer reactions, regardless of the technical or purchasing competence of the audience. A good direct sales presentation is generally more effective than a poor one. There is a "presentation effect" in favor of the product supported by a well-done sales presentation. But, as in the case of source effect, the research indicates that a good sales presentation is generally more useful in getting a favorable first hearing for a new product (that is, in what is, for the prospect, a low-risk decision) than it is in getting a favorable buying decision (that is, a high-risk decision). A good sales presentation is definitely better than a poor one in getting product adoption, but it has even more leverage than a poor one in getting a favorable first hearing for a product.

All this indicates that both the reputation of a vendor company and the quality of its direct sales presentations are important elements in sales success, but that the way the importance of these elements varies as between audiences and between types of audience decision-situations greatly affects how a vendor might wish to shape his marketing tactics.

"Sleeper Effect"

The findings on "sleeper effect" are particularly interesting in that, contrary to the other findings, they suggest that some policies appropriate for the well-known company may not be appropriate for the lesser-known company. Thus, repeat advertising and sales callbacks reinstate the well-known company's identity and therefore influence the prospect in its favor. But since the sales prospect tends to forget the source over time and therefore makes a more "objective" decision, reinstating the identity of the lesser-known company could actually tend to hurt that company. All other things being equal, the lesser-known company may find it better to leave well enough

alone. But whether "all other things" are equal is highly doubtful, and in any case varies by the situation. The most that can be said here is that there can conceivably be circumstances in which sleeper effect can work to the advantage of the lesser-known company.

However, the research also found that the passage of time has different consequences for source effect than for presentation effect. A good sales presentation is more effective over time than a good reputation. Moreover, the better the original sales presentation, the greater the durability of its influence over the audience with the passage of time. That is, regardless of the presence of sleeper effect (the declining influences of source credibility with the passage of time), if the original sales presentation was relatively good, the prospects tend more strongly to favor the product in question at a later date than if that presentation had been poor. The originally favorable influence of the highly credible source declined less, and the originally unfavorable influence of the less credible source hurt less, as the original sales presentation was better. A good sales presentation has greater durability than a good company reputation. Company reputation, in order to work for that company, has to be more regularly reinforced (possibly through advertising repetition) than does the effect of a good sales presentation.

A related finding on the dynamics of sleeper effect involves the strength of a sales prospect's reaction to a sales presentation. Thus, there is some evidence that the more self-confidently a prospect refuses at the outset to permit a new product to be viewed and reviewed by others in his firm, the greater the likelihood later that he will change his mind and give such permission. That is, a strong outright refusal for a further hearing at the time of the first sales call may suggest greater probability of getting permission later than does a weak and vacillating original refusal. Hence the very vigor with which a new product is at first rejected by a prospect may, instead of signaling that it is a lost cause, actually signal that a later repeat call is likely to get a good hearing.

High Risk Situations

But this refers only to relatively low-risk decisions—decisions in which the prospect is asked merely to give the product serious consideration, not actually to buy it at that time. In high-risk decision situations the findings were different. The research confirms the common-sense expectation that the greater the personal risk to the responding sales prospect, the more persuasion it takes to get him to switch from a product he is currently using. Moreover, once a prospect has made a decision in a high-risk situation, the seller will generally have considerable difficulty both in getting the negative respondent subsequently to change his mind and in keeping the affirmative respondent from changing his mind. This means that, especially in high-risk situations, it pays to try to get a favorable customer decision at the outset. Once he has rejected a product, it appears to be extremely difficult to get the prospect to be willing to reopen the discussions. Similarly, once he has accepted a new product under high-risk conditions, the customer appears to suffer from considerable self-doubt about whether he has made the right decision. He is probably very susceptible to being ''unsold'' by a competitor. This suggests the need for continuous followup by the original seller to reassure the customer and thus keep him sold.

Salesman or Company?

It has already been pointed out that, generally speaking, the more credible the source the more likely it is that its message will get a favorable reception. But the question arises as to who ''the'' source is: Is it the salesman who makes the sales call, or is it the company he represents? Do customers perceive this ''source'' as being one and the same or different? The present research indicates that they think of them as being two different sources. The salesman is not automatically thought of as being the company. When asked to rank the trustworthiness of the salesman on the one hand and then the trustworthiness of the company he represented, respondents consistently scored the salesman lower than his company.

While this might reflect the relatively low esteem with which salesmen are generally held, paradoxically, in our highly sales-dependent society, a closer look at the results suggests a great deal more. It was found, for example, that respondents are more likely to favor the products of salesmen whom they rank low in trustworthiness when these salesmen represent well-known companies than they are to favor the products of salesmen whom they rank relatively high in trustworthiness but who represent unknown companies. A similar result occurred in connection with respondents' feelings about how well informed and competent the salesmen from high-vs.-low credibility companies are. Thus, offhand it would seem that favorably well-known companies operate at the distinct advantage of being able to afford to have less ''trustworthy'' and less ''competent'' salesmen, at least in the short run, than little-known anonymous companies. But close examination suggests something else. It suggests that source effect is such a uniquely powerful force that for respondents to favor well-known companies, their need to trust the salesmen of these companies and to think highly of their competence is much less urgent than it is in order for them to favor less-well-known and anonymous companies. In other words, the favorably well-known company does indeed have an advantage over its less well-known competitor in that its salesmen need to *seem* less trustworthy and competent in order to be effective. Well-known companies need not be as scrupulous in their hiring and training of salesmen. Source effect seems almost to conquer everything.

But not entirely everything. As noted above, presentation quality and quality of the message can overcome some of the disadvantages of being relatively anonymous.

So can, of course, trust in the salesman. What is it then that makes for an appearance of salesman trustworthiness? First of all, the results of the present research suggest that trustworthiness of the communicator (such as, for example, a salesman television announcer, etc.) is not as clearly related to the audience's feeling about his knowledge or understanding of the product he is selling as might be expected. While there is some relationship, trust is much more closely related to the overall quality or character of the salesman's sales presentation. Poor presentation in particular reduce trust in the message transmitter (salesman). They also reduce trust in the message source (the salesman's company). The better the presentation the more trustworthy both the company and the salesman are perceived to be. To say this, and what has been said before, is equivalent to saying that there is obvious merit in making sure that salesmen have quality sales presentations, and this holds true particularly for less well-known companies.

It is interesting to note from the research that there was only a very modest, certainly not a clear, connection between audience ratings of a salesman's trustworthiness and their judgments regarding the extent of his product competence. An audience's willingness either to recommend or adopt a product was not clearly related to its judgment about a salesman's product knowledge. Nor was it related, in the short run, to how much of the information which the salesman gave out was actually retained by the audience.

All this suggests that in making his adoption decisions the customer is influenced by more than what the salesman specifically says about the product or even how effectively he communicates product facts. It seems very probable that the communicator's personality and what he says about things other than the product in question play a vital role in influencing his audience. The effective transmission of product facts seems to be more important in the long run than in the short run. With the passage of time since the date of the original sales presentation, persons who retained more product information right after that presentation were more likely to make and hold decisions favorable to the source. Hence the importance of the effective transmission of product facts during the original presentation seems to increase as the product-adoption decision is delayed. But it is not clear that detailed recall of product facts ever becomes a paramount ingredient in obtaining favorable buying decisions.

Summary

It seems clear that company reputation is a powerful factor in the industrial purchasing process, but its importance varies with the technical competence and sophistication of the customer. The quality of a sales message and the way it is presented are capable of moderating the influence of this source effect, but again it varies by audience. Generally speaking, it pays for a company to be favorably well known, and perhaps especially among customers having some degree of technical sophistication, such as engineers and scientists. But superior sales messages and well-trained salesmen can help less well-known companies to overcome some of the disadvantages of their relative anonymity. A well-planned and well-executed direct sales presentation can be an especially strong competitive weapon for the less well-known company. Moreover, the greater the riskiness of the purchasing decision the customer is asked to make, the more likely it is that a good sales presentation will produce a customer decision in favor of the direction advocated by the source.

Frederick E. Webster, Jr.

Interpersonal Communication and Salesman Effectiveness

Behavioral science offers some important new insights into the determinants of a salesman's effectiveness. These insights can lead to the development of more productive sales presentations and sales training programs to maximize the contribution of personal selling in the marketing communications program.

"**W**HAT makes a successful salesman?" has been one of the most frequently asked and incompletely answered questions in marketing. The purpose of this paper is to trace briefly the evolution of answers to this question and to show how research findings from behavioral science suggest some new answers. An evaluation of historical explanations of salesman effectiveness suggests some more complex but more productive ways of looking at personal selling. A better understanding of the personal selling process can lead to more effective sales strategies and sales force development programs.

Historical Explanations of Salesman Effectiveness

The earliest, and the most persistent, answers to the question "What makes a successful salesman?" consisted of lists of the personal characteristics and traits of the salesman himself. Some of these lists generated criteria for evaluating application blanks: age, height, appearance, education, previous business experience, etc. Other lists formed the bases for, or were generated by, psychological tests: aggressiveness, dominance, extroversion, optimism, competitive spirit, etc. Despite some disenchantment with the efficacy of psychological tests, the search for the traits of successful salesmen has continued unabated, and more sophisticated and complex traits, such as "empathy" and

About the author. Frederick E. Webster is Associate Professor at The Amos Tuck School of Business Administration, Dartmouth College. He is the author of several recent articles on buyer behavior and sales force management and, with K. R. Davis, of *Sales Force Management* (Ronald Press Co., 1968). Dr. Webster is active as a consultant and as a lecturer in several management development programs for sales and marketing executives.

"ego drive," have recently been suggested.[1]

Another set of answers concentrated on the salesman's actions rather than his traits. Perhaps the simplest answers were those which described the steps in the successful sales call, for example, the AIDA formula: (1) get Attention; (2) arouse Interest; (3) stimulate Desire; (4) get buying Action. This "salesmanship" approach assumed that the outcome of the sales call depends on the specific actions of the salesman.

Recognizing that the buyer played a part in determining the outcome of the call, other answers suggested that the buyer's actions were also important.

The so-called "stimulus-response theory" of selling saw the salesman as being able to elicit the desired responses if he could provide the right stimuli, and treated the prospect in essentially mechanistic terms. Like the "salesman's traits" approach, the "salesman's action" approach credited the salesman with virtually complete responsibility for the outcome of the call.

With increasing emphasis on a consumer orientation in marketing, "need satisfaction theory" provided some slightly different answers to the question "What makes a successful salesman?" These answers showed that the successful salesman was the one who could identify the prospect's needs and turn them into buying motives. Guided by this theory, the salesman learns to ask questions designed to uncover the prospects's needs, to listen carefully to the answers, and then to show how his product meets those needs. Having built the groundwork, the salesman moves in with the presentation and close. Need satisfaction theory was really a variant of stimulus-response theory. Needs were seen as a determinant of response; to get

[1] David Mayer and Herbert M. Greenberg, "What Makes a Good Salesman," *Harvard Business Review*, Vol. 42 (July-August, 1964), pp. 119-125.

the desired response the salesman must choose the right stimuli (selling points) which show the prospect how buying will satisfy his needs. Authors of books that define selling as "helping prospects buy" have used this explanation. While these "salesmanship" theories recognized that the prospect has a role, he was still viewed in passive terms.[2]

These three kinds of "theory" identify three important determinants of selling effectiveness: the salesman's characteristics and traits, the salesman's actions, and the prospect's needs. These elements are plausible and valid, but incomplete for explaining and predicting the outcome of the sales interview. Why is it that the same salesman, using the same actions, is not always effective with prospects with the same kinds of needs? One logical and simple explanation is that there are attributes of prospects, other than their needs, which influence the outcome of the sales call. Or, there are some complex ways in which salesman characteristics and actions combine with prospect characteristics and actions to determine outcomes.

Interaction Theory

Evans was among the first to challenge seriously the traditional "salesmanship" explanations of selling effectiveness and to suggest that the prospect played an active role in determining the progress and outcome of the sales call. He observed that:

> "Very little is known about what takes place when the salesman and his prospect meet. The two parties meet in a highly structured situation, and the outcome of the meeting depends upon the resulting interaction. In this sense, the 'sale' is a social situation involving two persons. The interaction of the two persons, in turn, depends upon the economic, social, physical, and personality characteristics of each of them. To understand the process, however, it is necessary to look at both parties to the sale as a dyad, not individually."[3]

In his study of life insurance salesmen, Evans found evidence that the probability of a sale was influenced by the extent to which there was a *matching* of the prospect's and the salesman's characteristics. This was true for such factors as age, height, income, political opinions, religious beliefs, and smoking. *Perceived* similarity for religion and politics was more important than actual similarity. Evans concluded that the successful sale was situationally determined by the interaction between prospect and salesman, and not solely by the particular characteristics of one or the other party to the interaction.[4] Other researchers have

also reported evidence that successful salesmen tend to concentrate on particular kinds of prospects.[5] However, Evans' study did not consider the behavioral dynamics of the sales interaction itself.

Applying interaction theory to the study of selling recognized that selling is more than *individual* behavior. Rather, it is *social* behavior, behavior that is rewarded or punished, accepted or rejected, by another person. The essential feature of social behavior is that each of the persons in face-to-face interaction influences the behavior of the other.[6] Selling certainly fits this definition. Social behavior, or "interpersonal interaction," has also been characterized as behavior influenced by "How one person thinks and feels about another person, how he perceives him and what he expects him to do or think, how he reacts to the actions of the other...."[7]

Recognition that selling is, indeed, social behavior forces us to look beyond the salesman for factors determining his effectiveness. Specifically, we must take into account not only the characteristics and traits but also the actions, attitudes, perceptions, expectations, and reactions of both the prospect and the salesman. Analysis of the sales interaction along these lines suggests some important factors to consider in developing effective selling strategies. In this expanded view of the sales interaction, it can be seen that the salesman's effectiveness is determined by a complex set of factors surrounding both the prospect and the salesman. The outcome of the sales call depends upon how well the salesman and the prospect have communicated with each other—how well they have achieved a common understanding that will enable both to fill their needs and achieve their goals. Following is a consideration of the factors involved in interpersonal communication and their significance for the sales manager.

Perception

It is a well-known fact that human beings respond to their environment in terms of their perception of that environment, not necessarily the objective facts of the environment. Perception is a subjective process. How a person views the environment, including other persons, is a function of his psychological structure—his goals, values, attitudes, feelings, needs, and so on. An individual's perceptions of other people in the environment is complicated further by the fact that he makes inferences about the intentions, attitudes, emotions, ideas, abilities, etc., which

---

2 These theories are summarized in Harold C. Cash and W. J. E. Crissy, "Ways of Looking at Selling," in William Lazer and Eugene J. Kelley (eds.), *Managerial Marketing: Perspectives and Viewpoints*, 2nd ed. (Homewood, Ill.: Richard D. Irwin, Inc., 1962), pp. 554-559.

3 Franklin B. Evans, "Selling as a Dyadic Relationship—A New Approach," *The American Behavioral Scientist*, Vol. VI (May, 1963), pp. 76-79, at p. 76.

4 Same reference as footnote 3, at p. 79.

5 M. S. Gadel, "Concentration by Salesmen on Congenial Prospects," *Journal of Marketing*, Vol. 28 (April, 1964), pp. 64-66; and Lauren Edgar Crane, "The Salesman's Role in Household Decision-Making," in L. George Smith (ed.), *Reflections on Progress in Marketing* (Chicago: American Marketing Association, 1964), pp. 184-196.

6 George Caspar Homans, *Social Behavior: Its Elementary Forms* (New York: Harcourt, Brace & World, Inc., 1961), pp. 2-3.

7 Fritz Heider, *The Psychology of Interpersonal Relations* (New York: John Wiley & Sons, Inc., 1958), p. 1.

cause their behavior. Other human beings are described not only in terms of their actual behavior but in terms of the psychological attributes of their behavior. Most important of all, these attributes are looked upon as being directed toward us and having particular meaning for us. In other words, our reaction to others depends upon how we think they view their environment, including us.[8] One inference from this fact for the salesman is that just as he "sizes up" the prospect, so does the prospect "size up" the salesman. The prospect's perception of the salesman is an important determinant of the salesman's effectiveness.

Role Expectations

How each person perceives or "sizes up" the other is determined by his predispositions: the set of opinions, attitudes, and beliefs which determines the perceiver's cognitive structure. One of the most important sources of an individual's predispositions is the role that he is in. A role is the social position occupied by an individual, including the goals of that position, and the behavioral repertoire appropriate to that position and to the attainment of those goals. Social positions (like "father," "Protestant," "Republican," "salesman," and "purchasing agent") have associated with them a set of expectations as to how persons occupying that role should behave. These expectations are "bi-dimensional" in that they specify both how persons in that role should behave and how others should behave toward them.[9] Role expectations, therefore, provide important components of structure in the sales interaction in that they define the kinds of behavior that each of the actors expects both of himself and of the other person. To the extent that the prospect and the salesman have consistent role expectations (for both themselves and for each other) there will be more effective interaction and communication.

Sources of Role Expectations for the Salesman

There are two particularly important sources of prospects' role expectations for salesmen. The first is the stereotype of the salesman. A "stereotype" can be defined as a "consensus of role expectations shared by a large segment of the population." It is a well-known fact that there is a stereotype of the salesman that describes him as "talkative," "easy going," "competitive," "optimistic," and "excitable." Kirchner and Dunnette found that salesmen describe themselves in these terms.[10] This stereotype is one of the reasons why the salesman is not highly regarded by a large segment of the population.[11] Perception is subjec-

tive, and it is not important whether or not the stereotype is an objectively accurate one. The prospect who does not have previous experience with a particular salesman will respond to that salesman in terms of the stereotype which he has of salesmen in general. "Inaccurate" perception of the salesman by the prospect may lead to a lack of communication. On the other hand, by the virtue of their occupation, all salesmen are regarded as having manipulative intent—they want the prospect to behave in a particular way—and communications theory indicates that the perception of manipulative intent in the communicator leads to certain resistance.[12] This is one reason why some door-to-door salesmen deceptively pose as survey interviews; they know how housewives respond to door-to-door salesmen.

A second important source of "role expectations" held by a prospect for a salesman is the reputation of the selling company. This is a special case of the generalized concept of "source credibility" in communications theory. Several research studies have confirmed that the reputation of the source is an important determinant of response to persuasive communication.[13] In a recently published study, Levitt found that industrial purchasing agents' and chemists' responses to sales presentations were influenced strongly by the reputation of the company (source) which the salesman (communicator) represented. In general, the salesman for the company with the better reputation (created through advertising, for example) always obtained a more favorable response to his presentation.

On the other hand, Levitt also found that respondents tended to rank the salesman as lower in "trustworthiness" than they ranked the company that the salesman represented. While this finding probably reflects, in part, the low occupational prestige of the salesman, Levitt suggested that there was more involved. He concluded that the prospect's perception of the trustworthiness of the salesman was not as closely related to the salesman's product knowledge as it was to the overall quality of the sales presentation.[14] Furthermore, a poor presentation resulted in a reduction in the perceived trustworthiness of the company. Finally, Levitt's research suggested that for a company with an excellent reputation, the prospect has very high expectations for the kind of salesman that will represent that company—so high, in fact, that salesmen may

8 Renato Tagiuri and Luigi Petrullo (eds.), *Person Perception and Interpersonal Behavior* (Stanford, California: Stanford University Press, 1958), pp. x-xi.

9 Theodore Sarbin, "Role Theory," in Garner Lindzey (ed.), *Handbook of Social Psychology*, Vol. I (Cambridge, Mass.: Addison-Wesley, Inc., 1954), pp. 223-258.

10 Wayne K. Kirchner and Marvin D. Dunnette, "How Salesmen and Technical Men Differ in Describing Themselves," *Personnel Journal*, Vol. 37 (April, 1959), pp. 418-419.

11 John L. Mason, "The Low Prestige of Personal Selling," *Journal of Marketing*, Vol. 29 (October, 1965), pp. 7-10.

12 Carl I. Hovland, Irving L. Janis, and Harold H. Kelley, *Communication and Persuasion: Psychological Studies of Opinion Change* (New Haven: Yale University Press, 1953), p. 295.

13 Carl I. Hovland and Walter Weiss, "The Influence of Source Credibility on Communication Effectiveness," *Public Opinion Quarterly*, Vol. 15 (Winter, 1951-1952), pp. 635-650.

14 Theodore Levitt, *Industrial Purchasing Behavior: A Study of Communications Effects* (Boston: Division of Research, Graduate School of Business Administration, Harvard University, 1965), pp. 31-32.

not be able to meet these expectations. This finding emphasizes the importance of sales training.

To summarize briefly, the sales interaction is interpersonal communication in which the prospect's expectations about how the salesman will and should behave have an important influence on the outcome of the sales call. Further, we have said that the stereotype of the salesman and the reputation of the salesman's company are important determinants of the prospect's response. Next, consideration is given to how the prospect's and the salesman's perceptions of their own roles influence the direction of the sales interaction.

Determinants of How the Prospect "Plays His Role"

Interaction theory explains that the needs of the actors are important determinants of their predispositions and that these predispositions influence their perceptions of the situation. As Jones and Thibaut have stated:

> If we can successfully identify the goals for which an actor is striving in the interaction situation, we can begin to say something about the cues to which he will attend, and the meaning he is most likely to assign to them.[15]

The old "need satisfaction" theory of salesmanship recognized this basic fact, but said little about the true complexity of the prospect's needs.

Every prospective buyer has at least two kinds of needs: his *personal* needs which motivate his behavior and his *social* needs which define the kinds of need fulfillment activity which will be acceptable to relevant other persons in the social situation. While this is only a crude cut across the complex set of needs which determine behavior, it makes an important distinction. For example, the industrial buyer may be motivated by a personal need for recognition and advancement and by the social need to satisfy the using department. His need for the salesman's product will not exist unless he can see how a buying decision will allow him to satisfy both sets of needs. Those particular personal and social needs will determine: (1) whether the prospect grants an interview to the salesman, (2) which parts of the presentation he really listens to, (3) the information he will remember, and (4) the influence of the sales presentation on his decision to buy. In psychological terms, these are the processes of *selective exposure, selective attention, and selective retention,* and the final step of *conviction* or *attitude change.*

The prospect's social needs are defined by his social roles and relationships. Thus, the industrial buyer must consider how management expects him to perform his job, and the family buyer must remember his role of "father," for example, in buying an automobile. Role expectations define particular buying needs and appropriate buying behavior for the individual.

An important dimension of how the prospect behaves is his self-confidence in his ability to play the role. The prospect's self-confidence is a determinant of how much risk he perceives in the buying decision he is asked to make. Levitt's research, mentioned above, found that the influence of the salesman's presentation was in part determined by the riskiness of the decision (that is, actual purchase vs. recommend for further consideration) and by the self-confidence of the prospect. Cox found that women responded to a sales presentation for nylon hosiery according to their self-confidence. Women of medium self-confidence were *most* responsive. Those of low self-confidence tended to reject the salesgirl's advice because they didn't trust their ability to make a decision and because of the need to defend their egos. Those of high self-confidence rejected the advice because they didn't feel they needed it and rather preferred to trust their own judgment.[16]

Thus, the prospect's behavior in the sales interview is a function of his personal needs, his social needs, and his self-confidence, as well as the amount of risk he perceives in the buying decision. How the prospect perceives and plays his role as "buyer" determines the success of the sales call.

Another set of factors determining how the prospect plays his role in a specific sales interaction is other sources of information to which he has been exposed concerning the salesman's product. These can be grouped into two categories: impersonal, commercial sources of information such as media advertising and direct mail; and personal, noncommercial sources such as colleagues, friends, and neighbors. (The salesman can be characterized as a personal, commercial source of information.) Generally speaking, personal sources of information are known to be more effective in producing attitude change than impersonal sources.[17] On the other hand, commercial sources tend to be less effective than noncommercial sources. Therefore, salesmen tend to be more effective than advertising, but less effective than peers (such as colleagues and friends) in developing favorable attitudes toward products.

However, the importance of alternative sources of information varies with the stage of the buyer's decision and the product life cycle. As the buyer goes through the

15 Edward E. Jones and John W. Thibaut, "Interaction Goals as Bases of Inferences in Interpersonal Perception," in Taguiri and Petrullo, same reference as footnote 8, pp. 151-178, at p. 152.

16 Donald E. Cox, "Information and Uncertainty: Their Effects on Consumer Product Evaluations," unpublished doctoral dissertation, Graduate School of Business Administration, Harvard University, 1962.

17 Elihu Katz and Paul F. Lazarsfeld, *Personal Influence* (Glencoe, Ill.: The Free Press, 1955), pp. 183-184; and Paul F. Lazarsfeld, Bernard Berelson, and Hazel Gaudet, *The People's Choice* (New York: Duell, Sloan, and Pearce, 1944), pp. 49-50.

mental stages of deciding to buy a new product (or the "adoption process"—awareness, interest, evaluation, trial, and adoption), he relies on different sources of information. Furthermore, the people who buy a new product early in its life cycle (the innovators and early adopters) tend to rely upon different sources of information than later adopters.[18]

In reviewing the literature on the adoption of pharmaceuticals by physicians, Bauer and Wortzel found that doctors consistently ranked detailmen as the most important source of information.[19] Earlier studies found the detailman was more important as a source of first knowledge than as a source of influence, while colleagues and medical journal articles were more important as sources of influence than as sources of first knowledge.[20] Rogers and Beal found that dealers and salesmen served different functions (awareness, evaluation, etc.) for different adopter categories (early adopters vs. later adopters) in the acceptance of new farm products.[21] Thus, the salesman's influence and effectiveness are determined, in part, by the relative "innovativeness" of the prospect and the stage of the prospect's buying decision process. The prospect's innovativeness and his buying stages influence how he will use and respond to information provided by the salesman relative to the other commercial and noncommercial sources of information to which he is exposed.

To summarize, how the prospect "plays his role" in the sales interaction and how he responds to the salesman's effort is determined by his personal needs, his social needs, his self-confidence, the perceived risk in the buying decision, his innovativeness, and the stage of his buying decision process.

Determinants of How the Salesman "Plays His Role"

Many of the points developed above for the prospect apply to the salesman as well. The salesman's behavior is determined by his personal needs (for example, his desire to earn a commission on the sale) and his social needs. The salesman's behavior will be influenced by his desire to meet the expectations of relevant other persons including his manager, his salesman-peers, and the prospect himself. The salesman's confidence in his own ability to "play the role" of salesman is important in determining his behavior and is determined by his knowledge, training, personality, and previous experience.

Because of the importance of the prospect's behavior in determining the success of the sales call, the salesman's ability to infer the prospect's role expectations of him is a vitally important factor. This ability has been defined as "empathy" or "empathic ability"—the ability to put oneself into the position of another person, a feeling of oneness with the other person. There is an unresolved controversy about "empathy": whether it is an inborn personal-

ity trait or can be taught and learned; and whether persons who have empathic ability are always more effective or only more effective in interactions with specific types of persons. Nonetheless, the ability to sense how the prospect expects him to behave and how the prospect is reacting to what he says is an important determinant of how successfully the salesman plays his role.

The salesman's behavior will also reflect his perception of how his manager expects him to play the role of salesman. If these expectations have not been stated clearly by the manager, the salesman's behavior may not be consistent with management's expectations. Furthermore, management must be sure that its expectations about salesmen's behavior are consistent with buyer's expectations. Otherwise, the salesman is in the difficult position of having to resolve conflicting role expectations, which will lead to some frustration and anxiety, as well as reduction in his effectiveness.

The salesman's effectiveness also depends on his ability to determine the locus of responsibility for buying decisions within the buying organization. This is true for family buying decisions as well as industrial buying decisions. Where more than one person is involved in the buying decision (e.g., a purchasing agent and an engineer), the salesman may be faced with conflicting role expectations. Once again, the ability to sense and resolve conflicts in buyers' role expectations is an important determinant of his behavior.

To summarize, how the salesman plays his role is determined by his ability to infer the expectations of relevant others for how he should play his role. "Relevant others" include his manager and the buying decision influencers within the buying organization.

The Sales Presentation

Of course, a major determinant of the salesman's effectiveness is the quality of the sales presentation he delivers to the prospect. Viewing personal selling as interpersonal interaction suggests that the presentation should be tailored to fit the needs and expectations of the prospective customer. In addition, communications theory suggests several specific characteristics of effective sales presentations.

The quality of the sales presentation is an important fac-

---

18 Everett M. Rogers, *Diffusion of Innovations* (New York: The Free Press, 1962).

19 Raymond A. Bauer and Lawrence H. Wortzel, "Doctor's Choice: The Physician and His Sources of Information About Drugs," *Journal of Marketing* Research, Vol. 3 (February, 1966), pp. 40-47.

20 Elihu Katz, "The Social Itinerary of Technical Change: Two Studies on the Diffusion of Innovation," *Human Organization*, Vol. 20 (Summer, 1961), pp. 70-82.

21 Everett M. Rogers and George M. Beal, "The Importance of Personal Influence in the Adoption of Technical Changes," *Social Forces*, Vol. 36 (May, 1958), pp. 329-335.

tor both in getting a favorable first hearing for the salesman and in inducing buying action. In the sales presentation, the salesman should first arouse the interest and identify the needs of the prospect and *then* show how his product can fill those needs. He should present the prospect with the positive features and arguments first, saving negative features such as price for the last stages of the presentation. Wherever possible, he should attempt to get early commitment by taking the prospect through a series of minor decisions first and by encouraging the prospect to agree with a series of statements supporting the value of buying the product.

In a competitive situation, the salesman can "insulate" the prospect against competitors' claims by facing up to any limitations of his product and showing the prospect why his product has greater value. Communications theory suggests that a "two-sided" argument can be effective in anticipating and negating the effects of counterarguments. The salesman should explicitly point out the advantages of using his product and the need satisfactions to be derived. This conclusion-drawing can avoid the prospect's "missing the point," but must be used cautiously where the buyer is more "expert" than the salesman (such as when book salesmen call on college teachers).

Finally, emotional appeals are useful in heightening interest and attention, but only up to a point. Beyond that point, the prospect's increased anxiety and emotional involvement may actually decrease the effectiveness of the presentation by reducing attention, comprehension, and acceptance. All of these comments on sales presentations are drawn directly from the findings of communications research.[22]

Implications for Salesman Training

This analysis of the sales interaction suggests the value of viewing selling as a communication process. We have seen that the source (company), the communicator (salesmen), the message (presentation), and the receiver (prospect) all have an important influence on the outcome of the sales interaction. This expanded view of the determinants of salesman effectiveness has some clear implications for salesman training. Compared with the historical explanations of salesman effectiveness, this expanded view suggests more emphasis on training and less emphasis on selection criteria for sales force development.

First, the effective salesman needs sharply developed *listening skills.* He must listen carefully to the prospect's description of problems and to answers to his (the salesman's) questions designed to uncover the prospect's personal and social needs. He must understand how these motivate and legitimate buying behavior. He must be able to infer such needs as they are implied by the prospect's objections. Only when he knows the prospect's personal and social needs can he then develop the prospect's need for the product. Product needs do not exist *per se,* but only in the context of these broader and deeper personal and social needs. Thus, to aid his listening, the effective salesman needs a basic understanding of buyer behavior and the ability to analyze what he hears. Tape-recordings of actual sales calls can be a helpful aid to this kind of learning.

Second, the salesman needs the ability to sense the prospect's predispositions and, especially, how the prospect expects him to behave. He must be able to sense the impact of his comments on the prospect and to modify his comments in response to the feedback he receives on prospect reactions. These skills can be developed through well-designed role playing, but it is crucial that the salesman be exposed to many different kinds of "prospects" in the role playing session. To develop interaction skills through role playing limited to either a manager or a trainer as the "prospect" is a very narrow and unsatisfactory approach. The use of video-tape-recorders can help the salesman develop his ability to assess his impact on others.

Third, salesmen need some basic understanding of the nature of interpersonal interaction and the communication process. They need to know how the characteristics of receivers, messages, and communicators interact to determine selling effectiveness. They can also benefit from an awareness of how sales presentations can be tailored (in terms of order of arguments, types of appeals, for example) to meet a specific prospect's communication patterns. Some recent textbooks on salesmanship have incorporated communication theory in a way useful for this type of training.[23]

Other Guides to Effective Selling Strategy

This analysis has also suggested several other guidelines for the development of effective selling strategies. The reputation of the company (developed through advertising, research and publicity) is very important in determining how prospects respond to the salesman and his presentation. Salesmen for companies with good reputations will obtain better response to their efforts. But company reputation also creates expectations for that company's salesmen, and a high level of sales training must be maintained to assure that salesmen can fulfill these expectations.

A recognition that customers who buy early are different in many respects from those who buy later indicates the need to tailor selling strategy to fit the product life

---

22 Same reference as footnote 12. For a more thorough description of these research findings and their implications for selling strategy, see Kenneth R. Davis and Frederick E. Webster, Jr., *Sales Force Management: Text and Cases* (New York: Ronald Press Company, 1968), especially Chapter 3, "The Communications Process."

23 See, for example, Joseph W. Thompson: *Selling: A Behavioral Science Approach* (New York: McGraw-Hill Book Co., 1966).

cycle. Early buyers tend to rely upon different sources of information and to use these sources for different functions, than later buyers. The sales manager needs to explore and analyze systematically the particular nature of these differences in the markets served by his company. Studies of the adoption process suggest that the salesman is particularly important at the *trial* stage, to provide assistance and knowledge in product testing and the interpretation of trial results. Whether the product is an industrial chemical or a vacuum cleaner, successful demonstration and trial is a critical step in the prospect's buying decision. Once again, there are clear implications for salesman training.

Summary

The determinants of the salesman's effectiveness go considerably beyond the salesman himself. Thinking of selling as a form of communication leads to some new insights into the selling process and to some clear indications for salesman training and the development of selling strategies. The importance of personal selling in the marketing communications mix should be modified over the product life cycle to reflect differences in buyer characteristics. The company's reputation and the sales manager's expectations are also important determinants of salesman effectiveness. The sales manager who develops his understanding of buyer behavior and communications theory will be rewarded with significant clues for the development of more effective sales strategies.

Pricing

Stanley C. Hollander

The Wheel of Retailing

New types of retailing frequently start off with crude facilities, little prestige, and a reputation for cutting prices and margins. As they mature, they often acquire more expensive buildings, provide more elaborate services, impose higher margins, and become vulnerable to new competition.

The author examines the history of numerous retail institutions to determine if this process really constitutes a "natural law of retailing."

"T HE wheel of retailing" is the name Professor Malcolm P. McNair has suggested for a major hypothesis concerning patterns of retail development. This hypothesis holds that new types of retailers usually enter the market as low-status, low-margin, low-price operators. Gradually they acquire more elaborate establishments and facilities, with both increased investments and higher operating costs. Finally they mature as high-cost, high-price merchants, vulnerable to newer types who, in turn, go through the same pattern. Department-store merchants, who originally appeared as vigorous competitors to the smaller retailers and who have now become vulnerable to discount house and supermarket competition, are often cited as prime examples of the wheel pattern.[1]

Many examples of conformity to this pattern can be found. Nevertheless, we may ask: (1) Is this hypothesis valid for all retailing under all conditions? (2) How accurately does it describe total American retail development? (3) What factors cause wheel-pattern changes in retail institutions?

The following discussion assembles some of the slen-

der empirical evidence available that might shed some light on these three questions. In attempting to answer the third question, a number of hypotheses should be considered that marketing students have advanced concerning the forces that have shaped retail development.

Tentative Explanations of the Wheel

(A) *Retail* Personalities. New types of retail institutions are often established by highly aggressive, cost-conscious entrepreneurs who make every penny count and who have no interest in unprofitable frills. But, as P. D. Converse has suggested, these men may relax their vigilance and control over costs as they acquire age and wealth. Their successors may be less competent. Either the innovators or their successors may be unwilling, or unable, to adjust to changing conditions. Consequently, according to this view, deterioration in management causes movement along the wheel.[2]

(B) *Misguidance*. Hermann Levy has advanced the ingenious, if implausible, explanation that retail trade journals, seduced by profitable advertising from the store equipment and supply industry, coax merchants into superfluous "modernization" and into the installation of overly elaborate facilities.[3]

(C) *Imperfect Competition*. Although retail trade is often cited as the one type of business that approaches the Adam Smith concept of perfect competition, some econo-

About the author. Stanley C. Hollander (Ph.D., University of Pennsylvania) is Professor of Business Administration at Michigan State University. He is editor of a recent book of readings in retailing theory, "Explorations in Retailing" (Bureau of Business Research, Michigan State University, 1959), and was a panelist on retail pricing before the Joint Economic Committee, U. S. Congress, in 1958.

His previous work in marketing history has included several studies of discount retailing, one of which M.S.U. recently published as "The Rise and Fall of a Buying Club." He compiled the American Marketing Association's "Bibliography on Discount Selling" (1956) and has published articles and monographs on other aspects of retailing and marketing.

The author is indebted to the participants in the 1959 Marketing Theory Seminar at Boulder, Colorado, for many penetrating comments on an earlier draft of this paper.

1 M. P. McNair, "Significant Trends and Developments in the Postwar Period," in A. B. Smith (editor), *Competitive Distribution in a Free*, High-Level Economy and Its Implications for the University (Pittsburgh: University of Pittsburgh Press, 1958), pp. 1-25 at pp. 17-18.

2 P. D. Converse, "Mediocrity in Retailing," *Journal of Marketing*, Vol. 23 (April, 1959), pp. 419-420.

3 Hermann Levy, *The Shops of Britain* (London: Kegan Paul, Trench, Trubner & Co., 1947), pp. 210-211.

mists have argued that retailing actually is a good example of imperfect competition. These economists believe that most retailers avoid direct price competition because of several forces, including resale price maintenance, trade association rules in some countries, and, most important, the fear of immediate retaliation. Contrariwise, the same retailers feel that service improvements, including improvements in location, are not susceptible to direct retaliation by competitors. Hence, through a ratchet process, merchants in any established branch of trade tend to provide increasingly elaborate services at increasingly higher margins.[4]

(D) *Excess Capacity*. McNair attributes much of the wheel effect to the development of excess capacity, as more and more dealers enter any branch of retail trade.[5] This hypothesis rests upon an imperfect competition assumption, since, under perfect competition excess capacity would simply reduce margins until the excess vendors were eliminated.

(E) *Secular Trend*. J. B. Jefferys has pointed out that a general, but uneven, long-run increase in the British standard of living provided established merchants with profitable opportunities for trading up. Jefferys thus credits adjustments to changing and wealthier market segments as causing some movement along the wheel. At the same time, pockets of opportunity have remained for new, low-margin operations because of the uneven distribution of living-standard increase.[6]

(F) *Illusion*. Professor B. Holdren has suggested in a recent letter that present tendencies toward scrambled merchandising may create totally illusory impressions of the wheel phenomenon. Store-wide average margins may increase as new, high-markup lines are added to the product mix, even though the margins charged on the original components of that mix remain unchanged.

Difficulties of Analysis

An examination of the actual development of retail institutions here and abroad does shed some light on both the wheel hypothesis and its various explanations. However, a number of significant difficulties hinder the process.

(1) Statements concerning changes in retail margins and expenses are the central core of the wheel hypothesis. Yet valid information on historical retail expense rates is very scarce. Long-run changes in percentage margins probably do furnish fairly reliable clues to expense changes, but this is not true over short or intermediate periods. For example, 1957 furniture-store expense rates were about 5 percentage points higher than their 1949-1951 average, yet gross margins actually declined slightly over the same period.[7]

(2) Historical margin data are somewhat more plentiful, but these also have to be dredged up from fragmentary sources.[8]

(3) Available series on both expenses and margins merely note changes in retailers' outlays and receipts. They do not indicate what caused those changes and they do not report changes in the costs borne by suppliers, consumers, or the community at large.

(4) Margin data are usually published as averages that may, and frequently do, mask highly divergent tendencies.

(5) A conceptual difficulty presents an even more serious problem than the paucity of statistics. When we talk about "types" of retailers, we think of classifications based upon ways of doing business and upon differences in price policy. Yet census categories and other systems for reporting retail statistics are usually based upon major differences in commodity lines. For example, the "pineboard" druggists who appeared in the 1930s are a "type" of retailing for our purposes. Those dealers had cruder fixtures, charged lower prices, carried smaller assortments, gave more attention to turnover, and had less interest in prescriptions than did conventional druggists. Yet census reports for drugstores necessarily included all of the pineboards that maintained any sort of prescription department.

Discount houses provide another example of an important, but amorphous, category not reflected in census classifications. The label "discount House" covers a variety of retailers. Some carry stocks, others do not. Some have conventional store facilities, whereas others operate in office buildings, lofts, and warehouses. Some feature electrical appliances and hard goods, while others emphasize soft goods. Some pose as wholesalers, and others are practically indistinguishable from all other popular priced retailers in their fields. Consequently discount dealers' operating figures are likely to be merged into the statistics reported for other appliance, hardware, or apparel merchants.

Examples of Conformity

British

British retailing provides several examples of conformity to the wheel pattern. The grocery trade has gone through several wheel-like evolutions, according to a detailed anal-

4 D. L. Shawver, *The Development of Theories of Retail Price Determination*, (Urbana; University of Illinois Press, 1956), p. 92.

5 Same reference as footnote 1.

6 J. B. Jefferys, *Retail Trading in Great Britain*, 1850-1950 (Cambridge: Cambridge University Press, 1954), various pages, especially p. 96.

7 Cited in Fabian Linden, "Department Store Operations," *Conference Board Business Record*, Vol. 14 (October, 1958), pp. 410-414, at p. 411.

8 See Harold Barger, *Distribution's Place in the American Economy Since 1869* (Princeton: Princeton University Press, 1955).

ysis made by F. G. Pennance and B. S. Yamey.[9] Established firms did initiate some changes and some margin reductions, so that the pattern is obscured by many cross currents. But the major changes seem to have been due to the appearance and then the maturation, first, of department-store food counters; then, of chain stores; and finally, of cut-price cash-and-carry stores. Now supermarkets seem to be carrying the pattern through another evolution.[10]

Jefferys also has noted a general long-run upgrading in both British department stores and chains.[11] Vague complaints in the co-operative press and a decline in consumer dividend rates suggest that wheel-like changes may have occurred in the British co-operative movement.[12]

American

Very little is known about retail margins in this country before the Civil War. Our early retail history seems to have involved the appearance, first, of hawkers, walkers, and peddlers; then, of general stores; next, of speciality stores; and finally, of department stores. Each of these types apparently came in as a lower-margin, lower-price competitor to the established outlets, and thus was consistent with the wheel pattern. We do not know, however, whether there was simply a long-run decline in retail margins through successive improvements in retail efficiency from one type to another (contrary to the wheel pattern), or whether each of the early types was started on a low-margin basis, gradually "up-graded," and so provided room for the next entrant (in accordance with the pattern).

The trends toward increasing margins can be more easily discerned in many branches of retailing after the Civil War. Barger has described increases over the years 1869-1947 among important retail segments, including department stores, mail-order firms, variety stores, and jewelry dealers. He attributes much of the pre-World War I rise in department-store margins to the absorption of wholesaling functions. Changes in merchandise mix, such as the addition of soda fountains and cafeterias to variety stores and the upgrading of mail-order merchandise, seem to have caused some of the other increases. Finally, he believes changes in customer services have been a major force in raising margins.[13] Fabian Linden has extended Barger's ob-

servations to note similar 1949-1957 margin increases for department stores, variety chains, and appliance dealers.[14]

Some other examples of at least partial conformity to the wheel pattern may be cited. Many observers feel that both discount-house services and margins have increased substantially in recent years.[15] One major discount-house operator has stated that he has been able to keep his average markup below 12%, in spite of considerable expansion in his facilities and commodity mix.[16] However, the concensus seems to be that this probably is an exception to the general rule.

A study of gasoline pricing has pointed out how many of the so-called "off-brand" outlets have changed from the "trackside" stations of pre-war days. The trackside dealers typically maintained unattractive and poorly equipped installations, at out-of-the-way locations where unbranded gasoline was sold on a price basis. Today many of them sell well-promoted regional and local brands, maintain attractive, efficient stations, and provide prompt and courteous service. Some still offer cut prices, but may have raised their prices and margins up to or above national brand levels.[17] Over time, many of the pineboard druggists also seem to have become converted to fairly conventional operations.[18]

Non-conforming Examples

Foreign

In underdeveloped countries, the relatively small middle- and upper-income groups have formed the major markets for "modern" types of retailing. Supermarkets and other modern stores have been introduced in those countries largely at the top of the social and price scales, contrary to the wheel pattern.[19] Some non-conforming examples may also be found in somewhat more industrialized environments. The vigorous price competition that developed among Japanese department stores during the first three decades of this century seems directly contrary to the wheel hypothesis.[20] B. S. Yamey's history of resale price maintenance also reports some price-cutting by tradi-

9 F. G. Pennance and B. S. Yamey, "Competition in the Retail Grocery Trade, 1850-1939," *Economica*, Vol. 22 (March, 1955), pp. 303-317.

10 "La Methode Americaine," *Time*, Vol. 74 (November 16, 1959), pp. 105-106.

11 Same reference as footnote 6.

12 "Battle of the Dividend," *Co-operative Review*, Vol. 36 (August, 1956), p. 183; "Independent Commission's Report," *Co-operative Review*, Vol. 38 (April, 1958), pp. 84-489; "£52 Million Dividend in 1957," *Co-operative Review* (August, 1958), pp. 171-172.

13 Same reference as footnote 8, p. 82.

14 See footnote 7.

15 D. A. Loehwing, "Resourceful Merchants," *Barron's*, Vol. 38 (November 17, 1958), p. 3.

16 S. Masters, quoted in "Three Concepts of Retail Service," *Stores*, Vol. 41 (July-August, 1959), pp. 18-21.

17 S. M. Livingston and T. Levitt, "Competition and Retail Gasoline Prices," *The Review of Economics and Statistics*, Vol. 41 (May, 1959), pp. 119-132 at p. 132.

18 Paul C. Olsen, *The Marketing of Drug Products* (New Brunswick: Rutgers University Press, 1948, pp. 130-132.

19 H. S. Hettinger, "Marketing in Persia," *Journal of Marketing*, Vol. 15 (January, 1951), pp. 289-297; H. W. Boyd, Jr., R. M. Clewett, & R. L. Westfall, "The Marketing Structure of Venezuela," *Journal of Marketing*, Vol. 22 (April, 1958), pp. 391-297; D. A. Taylor, "Retailing in Brazil," *Journal of Marketing*, Vol. 24 (July, 1959), pp. 54-58; J. K. Galbraith and R. Holton, *Marketing Efficiency in Puerto Rico* (Cambridge: Harvard University Press, 1955), p. 35.

20 G. Fukami, "Japanese Department Stores," *Journal of Marketing*, Vol. 18 (July, 1953), pp. 41-49 at p. 42.

tional, well-established British merchants who departed from the wheel pattern in the 1880s and 1890s.[21] Unfortunately, our ignorance of foreign retail history hinders any judgment of the representativeness of these examples.

American

Automatic merchandising, perhaps the most "modern" of all American retail institutions, departed from the wheel pattern by starting as a high-cost, high-margin, high-convenience type of retailing.[22] The department-store branch movement and the concomitant rise of planned shopping centers also has progressed directly contrary to the wheel pattern. The early department-store branches consisted of a few stores in exclusive suburbs and some equally high-fashion college and resort shops.

Only in relatively recent years have the branches been adjusted to the changing and more democratic characteristics of the contemporary dormitory suburbs. Suburban shopping centers, too, seem to have appeared first as "Manhasset Miracle Miles" and "Ardmores" before reaching out to the popular price customers. In fact, complaints are still heard that the regional shopping centers have displayed excessive resistance to the entry of really aggressive, low-margin outlets.[23] E. R. A. Seligman and R. A. Love's study of retail pricing in the 1930s suggests that pressures on prices and margins were generated by all types of retailers. The mass retailing institutions, such as the department and chain stores, that had existed as types for many decades were responsible for a goodly portion of the price cutting.[24] As McNair has pointed out, the wheel operated very slowly in the case of department stores.

Finally, Harold Barger has described the remarkable stability of over-all distributive margins during the years 1919-1947.[25] Some shifting of distributive work from wholesalers to retailers apparently affected their relative shares of the total margins during this period, but this is not the type of change contemplated by the wheel pattern. Of course, the stability Barger notes conceivably could have been the result of a perfectly smooth functioning of the pattern, with the entrance of low-margin innovators providing exactly the right balance for the upcreep of margins in the longer established types. But economic changes do not come in smooth and synchronized fashion, and Barger's data probably should indicate considerably wider oscillations if the wheel really set the mold for all retailing in the post-war period.

Conclusions

The number of non-conforming examples suggests that the wheel hypothesis is not valid for all retailing. The hypothesis, however, does seem to describe a fairly common pattern in industrialized, expanding economies. Moreover, the wheel is not simply an illusion created by scrambled merchandising, as Holdren suggests. Undoubtedly some of the recent "upcreep" in supermarket average margins is due to the addition of nonfood and other high margin lines. But in recent years the wheel pattern has also been characteristic of department-store retailing, a field that has been relatively unreceptive to new commodity groups.[26]

In some ways, Jefferys' secular trend explanation appears most reasonable. The tendency of many established retailers to reduce prices and margins during depressions suggests also that increases may be a result of generally prospering environments. This explanation helps to resolve an apparent paradox inherent in the wheel concept. Why should reasonably skilled businessmen make decisions that consistently lead their firms along seemingly profitable routes to positions of vulnerability? Jefferys sees movement along the wheel as the result of sensible, businesslike decisions to change with prospering market segments and to leave the poorer customers to low-margin innovators. His explanation is supported by the fact that the vulnerability contemplated by the wheel hypothesis usually means only a loss of market share, not a loss of absolute volume. At least in the United States, though, this explanation is partially contradicted by studies showing that prosperous consumers are especially prone to patronize discount houses. Also they are equally as likely to shop in supermarkets as are poorer consumers.[27]

The imperfect competition and excess capacity hypotheses also appear highly plausible. Considerably more investigation is needed before their validity can be appraised properly. The wheel pattern developed very slowly, and very recently in the department-store field. Yet market imperfections in that field probably were greater before the automobile gave the consumer shopping mobility. Major portions of the supermarket growth in food retailing and discount-house growth in appliance distribution occurred during periods of vastly expanding consumption, when excess capacity probably was at relatively low levels. At the moment there is little evidence to suggest any clear-cut correlation between the degree of market imperfection and

21 "The Origins of Resale Price Maintenance," *The Economic Journal*, Vol. 62 (September, 1952), pp. 522-545.

22 W. S. Fishman, "Sense Makes Dollars," 1959 *Directory of Automatic Merchandising* (Chicago: National Automatic Merchandising Association, 1959), p. 52; M. V. Marshall, Automatic Merchandising (Boston: Graduate School of Business Administration, Harvard University, 1954), pp. 108-109, 122.

23 P. E. Smith, *Shopping Centers* (New York: National Retail Merchants Association, 1956), pp. 11-12; M. L. Sweet, "Tenant-Selection Policies of Regional Shopping Centers," *Journal of Marketing*, Vol. 23 (April, 1959), pp. 399-404.

24 E. R. A. Seligman and R. A. Love, *Price Cutting and Price Maintenance* ,(New York: Harper & Brothers, 1932).

25 Same reference as footnote 8, pp. ix, x.

26 R. D. Entenberg, *The Changing Competitive Position of Department Stores in the United States by Merchandise Lines* (Pittsburgh: University of Pittsburgh Press, 1957), p. 52.

27 R. Holton, *The Supply and Demand Structure of Food Retailing Services, A Case Study* (Cambridge: Harvard University Press, 1954).

the appearance of the wheel pattern. However, this lack may well be the result of the scarcity of empirical studies of retail competition.

Managerial deterioration certainly must explain some manifestations of the wheel, but not all. Empires rise and fall with changes in the quality of their leadership, and the same thing seems true in business. But the wheel hypothesis is a hypothesis concerning types of retailing and not merely individual firms. Consequently, the managerial-deterioration explanation holds true only if it is assumed that new people entering any established type of retailing as the heads of both old and new companies are consistently less competent than the first generation. Again, the fact that the wheel has operated very slowly in some fields suggests that several successive managerial generations can avoid wheel-like maturation and decay.

Reavis Cox

Non-price Competition and the Measurement of Prices

I

UNTIL quite recently most economists probably would have accepted without serious question the dictum that the economic concepts of value and price are easily defined. As one of them wrote some thirty-five years ago:

> Ever since the publication of *The Wealth of Nations* the notion of exchange value has remained the most fundamental and possibly the most consistently defined concept of economic science. Bickerings as to whether "power in exchange," "quantity received in exchange," or "ratio of exchange" best expresses the concept, as to whether exchange value is a variable attribute of a commodity or merely a disembodied ratio, have not been taken as seriously affecting its precision. Possibly these differences, if consistently followed out, might have led to various differences in doctrine. But historically, if not logically, the differences alluded to have been verbal. I do not propose to suggest any revision of an elementary concept which has worn well in actual service.[1]

In most textbooks on economics this attitude persists. A few authors make no attempt to define the term. The others almost unanimously restrict themselves to variants of the familiar statements that, for purposes of economic analysis, value is the command of one good over others in exchange and that price is value expressed in money. Some of them object to the elimination of all ethical connotations from the term value; but the brevity of their discussion once they have climbed this hurdle indicates their belief that from here on the going is easy. Tacitly, if not explicitly, they agree that "the definition of exchange value or price offers no great difficulty and gives rise to no special ambiguity."[2]

With the development of theories of monopolistic and imperfect competition, the application of statistical methods to ever-widening areas of economic behavior, and the extension of theoretical analysis to new fields, such as that of marketing, the assurance that price as an economic concept offers no particularly important difficulties has lost much of its power to comfort.

Spreading out into new and exciting areas of investigation, students have stumbled onto large and ill-defined but evidently important areas that seem to fall within the field of exchange but do not fit into the traditional concept of price. It is to these that the phrase non-price competition

---

[1] Allyn A. Young, "Some Limitations of the Value Concept" in *Economic Problems New and Old* (Boston: Houghton Mifflin Co., 1927), p. 198. (Reprinted from the Quarterly Journal of Economics, May, 1911) Cf. also his article on "Price" in the *Encyclopaedia Britannica*, 14th Edition, Vol.18, p.468.

[2] Knut Wicksell, *Lectures on Political Economy* (N.Y.: Macmillan, 1934, Vol. 1), p. 16. The opinion expressed above as to how economists view the concept of price is based upon consultation of the following publications. C.E. Ayres, *The Theory of Economic Progress*, (Chapel Hill: Univ. of North Carolina, 1944), pp. 79, 209, 226; O. Fred Boucke, *Principles of Economics* (N.Y.: Macmillan Company, 1925, Vol. 1), p. 419; Kenneth Boulding, Economic Analysis (N.Y.: Harper & Bros., 1941), pp. 6, 256; H. G. Brown, Economic Science and the Common Welfare, 6th ed. (Columbia, Mo.: Lucas Bros., 1936), passim; C. K. Brown, Introduction to Economics (N.Y.: American Book Co., 1941), passim. Raymond T. Bye, Principles of Economics: A Restatement, (N.Y.: F.S. Crofts & Co., 1941), pp. 289-290; Gustav Cassel, The Theory of Social Economy, (N.Y.: Harcourt, Brace & Co., 1932), p. 47; Clyde G. Chenoweth, An Introduction to Economics, (N.Y.: H. Holt & Co., 1941), p. 491.; H. J. Davenport, The Economics of Enterprise, 4th ed. (N.Y.: Macmillan Co., 1919), p. 23; Fairchild Furniss and Buck, Elementary Economics (N.Y.: Macmillan Co., 1937, Vol. 1), p. 74; Frank A. Fetter, Principles of Economics, rev. ed. (N.Y.: Century Co., 1922), pp. 45, 51; Irving Fisher, Elementary Principles of Economics, (N.Y.: Macmillan Co., 1912), pp. 14, 15, 17; Gemmill & Blodgett, Economics: Principles and Problems (N.Y.: Harper & Bros., 1942), pp. 193-194; B. W. Knight, Economic Principles in Practice, rev. ed. (N.Y.: Farrar & Rinehart, 1942), p. 10; Alfred Marshall, Principles of Economics, 8th ed. (London: Macmillan & Co., Ltd., 1920), p. 60-61; Sumner H. Slichter, Modern Economic Society (N.Y.: H. Holt & Co., 1931), pp. 263, 264; F. W. Taussig, Principles of Economics, 4th ed. (N.Y.: Macmillan Co., 1939, Vol. 1), pp. 101-103; F. M. Taylor, Principles of Economics, 9th ed. (N.Y.: Ronald Press Co., 1925), pp. 242-244; Myron W. Watkins, "The Price System," in Encyclopaedia of the Social Sciences, Vol. XII, p. 373.

The Journal of Marketing
Vol. 10 (April 1946), pp. 370-383

has been applied.

Taken in its widest sense, this term is used to denominate an enormous range and variety of market phenomena. Wilcox, it is true, sums them up in a few words as comprising "competition in quality, in service, in style, and in advertising and salesmanship";[3] but Nelson requires nearly forty pages to describe what the term means to him.[4] He includes in his list competition in physical quality or content, extending all the way from measurable factors such as tensile strength to imponderable elements such as style or exclusiveness; many sorts of guarantees; the use of "price lines"; advertising and sales promotion; and all the ingenious devices by means of which business men evaded the restrictions on price cutting set up in the N.R.A. codes.

Although the phrase non-price is awkward at best and becomes unmanageable when loaded with so much meaning, it is useful in that it forces reconsideration of a concept accepted uncritically for so long as to become more an impediment than an aide to effective analysis. This is true particularly in the statistical measurement of prices, where one's first impulse is to treat non-price elements as outside or disturbing factors that must be eliminated in order to obtain unambiguous data.

As the area assigned to non-price aspects expands and that assigned to price aspects shrinks, the point is reached at which price seems to be left with very little substance that can be measured. A rethinking of the whole concept becomes necessary. It truly "has worn well in actual service"; but it needs to be refurbished if it is to wear equally well in the analysis of a more complicated society by more refined statistical methods.[5]

II

For abstract reasoning from purely hypothetical assumptions of fact where the purpose is to deduce laws of price determination rather than to measure observed prices, perhaps the problem can be handled adequately by some such procedure as that of Chamberlin. He, in effect, avoids the issue by drawing a distinction between what he calls costs of selling and costs of production. The terminology probably could be improved; but the distinction seems clear enough.

Cost of production includes all expenses which must be met in order to provide the commodity or service, transport it to the buyer, and put it into his hands ready to satisfy his wants. Cost of selling includes all outlays made in order to secure a demand, or a market, for a product. The former costs create utilities in order that demands may be satisfied, the latter create and shift the demands themselves. A simple criterion is this: of all the costs incurred in the manufacture and sale of a given product, those which alter the demand curve for it are selling costs, and those which do not are costs of production.[6]

The commodity or service exchanged in this view, is an objective entity embodying the results of someone's incurring a series of "costs of production." The deductive analyst need not determine very closely what elements of so-called non-price competition enter into the "given product" and what elements represent attempts by the seller to influence the buyer's subjective response to the "given product."

He can simply assume that any given market does in fact define the product with which it is concerned. In so doing, it differentiates between price factors that enter directly as quantities or terms into the objective ratio of exchange and non-price factors that affect the ratio of exchange only indirectly through their influence upon the subjective responses of buyers to given products. Against this background special analysis can be confined to those non-price factors assumed to be identifiable as such in the market.[7]

This solution is satisfactory, even for abstract deductive analysis, only in a superficial sense. Clark has stated the underlying problem clearly:

> In formulating economic laws, the student has the choice of two policies. He may make the statement in the simplest terms, leaving out most of the disturbing elements, which must then appear as forces causing variations from the standard, or he may so state his law as to include as many of the disturbing elements as possible, thus sacrificing simplicity, but gaining in completeness, and cutting down the number of necessary exceptions.[8]

As knowledge grows of the difficulties involved in drawing a sharp line between price and non-price, one comes to feel that Chamberlin's treatment includes so many undefined and unanalyzed elements in the concept of price

3 Clair Wilcox, Competition and Monopoly in American Industry, T.N.E.C. Monograph No. 21, 1940, p. 3.

4 Saul Nelson in Nelson, Keim and others, Price Behavior and Business Policy, T.N.E.C. Monograph, No. 1, 1940, pp. 63-101.

5 In justice to such price collecting agencies as the Bureau of Labor Statistics it should be said that they have given much thought in recent years to the problems here raised and have made much progress in allowing for the non-price factors here discussed. However, their interest is limited by the fact that they are concerned more with price trends then with price levels and differentials. It is for these last that the refinements here proposed are particularly important, as we shall see.

6 Edward Chamberlin, The Theory of Monopolistic Competition, 3rd ed. (Cambridge, Mass.: Harvard University Press, 1938), p. 123. The terminology is unfortunate because selling is an ambiguous term often taken to cover many marketing activities that are not aggressively promotional.

7 Chamberlin himself apparently is not certain as to where to draw the line between what others call price and non-price in working with actual market data as distinct from assumed ones. (Op. cit., pp. 73, 124-125). Although he does not use the term non-price, his influence has no doubt been in part responsible for associating "non-price" with "monopolistic" in the minds of economists. Nelson is well advised when he says (op. cit., p. 70), "It is important to emphasize that the presence or absence of price competition is not of itself a criterion of monopoly or collusion."

8 J. M. Clark, "A Contribution to the Theory of Competitive Price," in Preface to Social Economics (N. Y.: Farrar & Rinehart, 1935), p. 273.

as to render it almost meaningless and submerges from view many important problems. So much of completeness is sacrificed to the achievement of simplicity as to move the discussion almost entirely out of the field of human affairs and into the area of pure logic.

III

For empirical economic research involving price measurement, this way of settling the matter is no solution at all. Here, the most important consideration is precisely that in practice one can separate market behavior properly denominated price competition from market behavior properly considered non-price competition only with very great difficulty.[9]

A host of investigators looking into economic behavior in a wide range of industries, trades, places, and times find a bewildering multiplicity of ways by which ratios of exchange are stated, computed, and changed. Most of these have been included at one time or another in somebody's illustration of non-price competition. The true facts of the matter are not easily determined.

Furthermore, even when these practices are successfully classified according to whether they change what the buyer is offered or change his valuation of what is offered, there remains the formidable problem of reducing those accepted as constituting changes in what the buyer is offered to forms capable of measurement and comparison. Economic analysis is not made easier when (to take a single example out of many possible ones) a survey of pricing practices in the steel industry leads to the conclusion that on the basis of available information one cannot determine "the actual prices paid for the nation's basic durable good" and quotes the president of a large steel company as saying:

> "Our established prices were not prevailing nor obtainable nor controlling....They didn't tie into the published prices which you call official prices in any sense of the word."[10]

Highly important and controversial problems such as price discrimination and price flexibility defy effective isolation and analysis in the absence of ways to allow for these devices by means of which the ratio of exchange is altered without changing the formal quotation.

Until a great deal was learned about the pervasiveness of so-called non-price ways of changing prices and the quantitative importance of their effects upon what is actually paid and received for goods, they could be considered disturbances and abnormalities, even for purposes of price measurement. Without thinking too much about it explicitly, students of price problems seem to have felt that back of the confusing surface of things there lay some specific datum properly to be denominated "price."

Their problem was somewhat like that of the topographer who sets out to find a "sea level" he can use as the surface from which to measure the contour of the earth's land surfaces. He finds no great difficulty in working out a concept of sea level as the level to which the waters of the oceans would settle if they were freed from the influence of such transient and variable disturbances as winds, tides, barometric pressure, degree of salinity, and temperature. Subjecting his concept to measurement with a high degree of mathematical precision is another matter. Here he encounters very great difficulties. So when it comes to practical surveying, he is likely to forget his underlying concept and settle for an arbitrary sea level determined by selecting some point on the seashore and computing the mean of a long series of observations of high and low tide.

For the statistical measurement of prices, this solution fails to work, partly because it is not easy to find a generally acceptable economic Sandy Hook whose mean prices can serve as the datum level from which to measure all other price levels, partly because the departures from any assumed level (i.e., the so-called abnormalities and disturbances) often are as important as the level itself.[11] Many of the most important problems of price have to do precisely with these abnormalities or differentials.[12]

Examples could be multiplied almost indefinitely, but a few will serve to make the point clear. The problem of dividing price differentials into those that are and those that are not discriminatory and monopolistic is an obvious example.[13] Differentials are of primary importance in using price data to measure the absolute and relative wellbeing of particular groups of the population; to make an effective comparison of the bargains offered buyers by different sellers; to compare the cost of alternative methods of

9 Cf., for example, the discussion in Arthur R. Burns, The Decline of Competition (N. Y.: McGraw Hill, 1936), pp. 373-375. Burns himself does not offer a simple, straightforward statement of what the term non-price means to him.

10 Blair and Reeside, Price Discrimination in Steel, T.N.E.C. Monograph No. 41, 1941, p. 29

11 The liking of economists and statisticians for future prices on commodity exchanges as an illustration of the nearest approach in practice to the perfect market in which there is only one price at any time for any one commodity, probably grows out of acceptance of the traditional way of thinking about prices. It is true that something one may call "the price" for, say, cotton or wheat can be found in these exchange quotations; but one should not overlook the significant fact that practically no cotton or wheat changes hands at these specific prices.

12 Cf. the discussion of this point in F. C. Mills. "Price Statistics," Encyclopaedia of the Social Sciences, Vol. XII. especially P. 385. An exceptionally interesting description of the complexities of price in practice may be found in Erdman and Alcorn, "The Price-Making Process in The Los Angeles Egg Market," The Journal of Marketing, April, 1942, pp. 349-357.

13 For an interesting discussion of some economic issues involved in differential pricing, see four articles in The Journal of Marketing, April, 1942, Part 2: Corwin D. Edwards, "Types of Differential Pricing," pp. 156-167; Burton N. Behling, "Differential Pricing of Public Utility Services," pp. 168-170; E. E. Vial, "Some Examples of Differential Pricing of Milk," pp. 171-173; and A. C. Hoffman, "Agricultural Surplus Programs," pp. 174-176.

distribution and production; to measure the cost elements in a price or group of prices; to measure income and its distribution; and so on through a long list.

The costs and prices of some important types of enterprises appear only in non-price form. For example, if non-price is taken literally in its broadest sense to include all competition in service, retailing and wholesaling will be virtually eliminated from the area of price. In a very real sense merchants have little to sell except the service of differentiating the location, ownership, and possession of their wares in such ways to make them fit the needs of individual customers as precisely as possible.[14]

IV

Insofar, then, as mathematicians and statisticians undertake to work with measurements of objective data rather than with abstract formulas illustrated by application to assumed data, they must reexamine their concept of price. For their comparisons and computations they need unambiguous prices; but, looked at with fresh eyes, price as customarily viewed is seen to be neither so obvious nor so free from ambiguity as it has been conventional to think.

The larger the element of non-price is permitted to become, and the more blurred the boundary between price and non-price, the more difficult it is to attach exact meaning to the central tendencies, correlations, dispersions, trends, and models one can compute from prices published in private or governmental journals or made available from the files of private business. Furthermore, the greater the degree of ambiguity and uncertainty in the raw data, the greater the danger of misleading the reader by an appearance of precision that is largely spurious. One may well be discouraged by the difficulties of achieving precision; but the effort needs to be made.[15]

The Committee on Price Determination, in its study of the relations between costs and prices, struggles with this same problem and summarizes its views in the most comprehensive recent analysis of the concept of price the present writer has found.[16] Its discussion is not entirely appli-

cable to the present problem, since the purpose for which it wants to identify and measure price is quite specialized. The ideas it presents are nevertheless significant here.

It offers a number of different definitions of price. Thus price may be "equivalent to average revenue per unit of product at the point at which transfer of ownership takes place." It also may be "net realization per unit of product at the point at which transfer of ownership takes place." It also may be "net realization per unit of product in a single transaction" or "revenue net of any services or discounts rendered or granted by the buyer," and it may be regarded as "comprising a whole series of terms of sale."

The Committee makes some suggestions for the improvement of terminology, as by the use of "price," "price structure," and "price system" to designate different aspects of what ordinarily is called "price" alone. It develops the concept of treating terms of sale as "dimensions" of price "used to set different prices (in the sense of average revenue) in different markets and yet maintain an equal list price in all markets." Finally, it lays great stress on the idea that "reference to a 'price' must always rigorously designate the corresponding 'product' if clarity is to be maintained."[17]

To the present writer, the most promising opportunities for developing more exact price measurement seem to lie in directions suggested by the terms *product* and *dimensions* in the Committee's analysis. This can be put another way and expanded to include the money as well as the product aspect of any transaction by saying that economists and statisticians should take a more careful look than they have at what lies behind the terms quantity of goods or services and quantity of money lying on either side of the ratio of exchange.

If goods or services and money are taken as given in every detail, establishment of a price becomes by definition establishment of a simple numerical ratio between them. If goods, services, and money are themselves taken as variables, however, price becomes not a simple ratio but an attempt to measure quantitatively in a multiple ratio a complex of human behavior. The measurement is more or less accurate as the factors involved are measurable and are in fact measured.

Price, then, must be considered a summary of an agreement between buyer and seller whose full meaning depends not only upon the numbers given but also upon a complicated group of understandings lying outside of the formal ratio. Most of the so-called non-price factors (taking the term in its broadest sense) appear among these understandings.

They may be stated explicitly and in very great detail as terms of shipment, or conditions of sale, or terms of sale, or descriptions of quality, or a procedure for making

14 Henry Smith, Retail Distribution: A Critical Analysis (London: Oxford Univ. Press, 1937), Chapter I, gives a stimulating discussion of the economic functions of retailing that is useful for present purposes.

15 Nelson, Keim, and others, op. cit., p. 63, come to the conclusion that "no strict line of demarcation between price competition and non-price competition is practicable." Earl J. Hamilton, in "Use and Misuse of Price History," The Tasks of Economic History, Supplement IV to The Journal of Economic History, Dec., 1944, p. 60, does not comment on the possibility of improving price data in the future but does warn against the "specious accuracy" that comes from attempting greater exactitude in the statistical manipulation of historical price series than the data will permit.

16 Cost Behavior and Price Policy: A Study Prepared by The Committee on Price Determination for the Conference on Price Research (N. Y.: National Bureau of Economic Research, 1943), pp. 33-42.

17 The importance of the product is also emphasized by Chamberlin, op. cit., p. 113.

specified allowances for deviation from an assumed standard of quality. They may not appear as such in the contract but be stated on the sales slip or invoice or in a catalogue. Sometimes they are written in by simple reference to an elaborate and detailed set of trade rules drawn up by some association or exchange; sometimes they are not stated formally at all but are merely implicit in the customs of buyers or sellers in a particular community or trade or in the laws of the jurisdictions governing particular transactions.

Whether formal or informal, explicit or implicit, they are vital parts of the price and must be taken into account in any attempt to explain price as an economic phenomenon or to measure price as an economic record. Indeed, Edwards goes so far as to maintain that price differentials seldom appear in forms other than discounts, charges, and formulas of the sort here visualized.[18]

V

At first glance, the multiplicity of variation in detail may seem to preclude effective handling by statistical techniques. Here, as elsewhere, however, it should be possible to make a workable compromise between simplicity and completeness by classifying the non-price factors into a small number of groups. The precise number and character of the groups can be determined only after a good deal of experimentation, but, as a starter, four would seem to be sufficient.

That is, price can be defined for this purpose as an agreement between seller and buyer concerning what each is to receive, embodied in a formal ratio between quantities of money and quantities of goods or services modified by formal and explicit or informal and implicit understandings as to:

1. The quality of the goods or services to be provided, or, alternatively, the premiums and discounts to be applied to deliveries whose quality varies from a specified standard.

2. The times and places at which the privileges and responsibilities of (a) possession and (b) ownership are to pass from seller to buyer.

3. The particular form of money to be tendered in payment.

4. The times and places at which payments are to be made and accepted.[19]

Thus a price of, say, iron ore becomes not merely $4.60 a ton but $4.60 per gross long ton of 2,240 pounds of Mesaba Bessemer ore containing exactly 51.5 per cent of iron and 0.045 per cent of phosphorus, with specified premiums for ore with a higher iron content or a lower phosphorous content and with specified discounts[20] for ore with a lower iron content or a higher phosphorous content; samples to be drawn and analyzed on a dry basis by a specified chemist at Cleveland, the cost being divided equally between seller and buyer; 48,000 tons to be delivered at the rate of approximately 8,000 tons per month during April-September, inclusive, on board freight cars of the New York Central Railroad at Cleveland, Ohio; the purchaser to pay all charges involved in moving ore from the rail of the lake steamer to the freight car and other port charges, such as unloading, dockage, storage, reloading, switching and handling; ore to be weighed on railroad scale weights at Cleveland; payment to be made in legal tender or bank checks of the buyer to the Cleveland agent of the mining company on the 15th of each month for all ore received during the preceding month.

The precise form in which the ratio of money to goods is stated will vary considerably from trade to trade. In the illustration just given, the ratio is a simple statement of so many units of money per unit of goods. Alternatively, it can be stated as a price described by some such name as list, base, catalogue, or cash subject to one or more discounts or extras whose number and variety are limited only by the ingenuity of buyer and seller.

As a general rule, prices in sales to ultimate consumers tend to be simpler in form and to leave more to the buyer's own judgment of quality and to local custom than do prices in exchanges among business enterprises; but there are important exceptions. In any event, for purposes of price measurement, the substance of the price is the important thing, the form being of decidedly secondary consequence.

VI

A price under this concept is changed not only when the number of monetary units or the number of commodity units changes, but also when any of the underlying understandings change.

The price of iron ore could be raised by changing the formal quotation from $4.60 to $5.00 per ton; or by, in effect, changing the formal quotation from $4.60 per ton to $4.60 per 7/8 of a ton through the device of the buyer's accepting short weight; or by requiring the buyer to accept ownership and possession at Duluth, to pay cash with the order, and to make his payments in United States currency at the office of the mining company in Hibbing.

Correspondingly, the price could be lowered either by changing the formal quotation or by changing the premiums and discounts for divergencies in quality, making the transfer of possession and ownership at the buyer's blast furnaces in Pittsburgh, and granting credit for six months.

The effect of this analysis is to arrive by a different route at a concept of price much like that implicit in Cham-

18 Corwin D. Edwards, op. city., pp. 156-157.

19 For consumers' goods, it has been suggested to the author, a fifth group of factors might include a variety of services furnished by the seller without extra charge, such as advertising, servicing the product, and return privileges.

20 Premiums and discounts in practice are calculated by the use of formulas and tables too complicated to include here.

berlin's reasoning, but also to put the concept in terms more adaptable to statistical measurement.

This concept of price brings into the definition all (or all that is practicable) of the expenditures made, or the revenues sacrificed, that directly alter the objective ratio of exchange. It increases the degree of accuracy in the quotation by curtailing the area of uncertainty embraced under conventional assumptions of other things equal. It eliminates most of the ambiguities in the common concept of non-price competition by restricting the term to expenditures that affect the ratio of exchange only indirectly through altering the subjective valuations consumers put upon given products. Finally, it shows some of the directions in which empirical research must move if it is to provide the unambiguous data required for effective use of refined statistical and mathematical procedures.

This is not the same as saying that it simplifies the problem of the statistician or econometrist. On the contrary, although it holds out possibilities of making the use of statistical methods in economic analysis more fruitful and more meaningful, it does so only at the cost of making the problems and procedures more complicated and more difficult.

This is true because it substitutes for the tidy traditional concept of a ratio between two precise quantities of precisely defined commodities the more realistic but rather untidy concept of a multiple ratio between ill-defined and continually changing "bundles" of commodities and services—a ratio that changes not only with variations in the formal quantum of money and quantum of goods or services involved, but also with variations in the internal composition of the two quanta.

The statistical problem becomes one, not of finding devices for eliminating from consideration all variations in the composition of the bundles, but of finding devices for reducing the bundles to meaningful quantitative measurements that can be subjected to effective comparison and analysis.

Presumably this means two things: (1) effective sampling so as to make any price data assembled adequately representative of the assortment of bundles bought and sold in the particular markets being subjected to analysis; (2) the devising of techniques of measurement whereby variations in different parts of the bundles can be reduced to comparable quantities.

The second is by far the more difficult of the two tasks. It is particularly difficult in the areas of consumer marketing, where variations in the "bundles" from the consumer's point of view may be thought to take the form of satisfactions received or sacrifices borne that have not as yet been reduced to precise quantitative measurement. Here, presumably, recourse must be had to qualities that are measurable as physical entities or in terms of costs required to produce them.

VII

Two directions may be pointed out in which experiments with quantitative measurement of prices can well be pushed. The first of these is to devise techniques whereby individual markets can be dissected out for investigation, measurement, and evaluation. Much of the discussion of so-called non-price factors in competition represents efforts to explain differences between prices of seemingly similar goods in what is apparently the same market.

Edwards, for example, finds one of the two respects in which all price differentials are alike to be "conditions in the market that permit a rough division of buyers or sellers into non-competing groups."[21] In other words, what ought to be a single market is divided into several markets by circumstances or stratagems. Where by definition there should be only one price for any one commodity at any one time, there are in fact several prices. It is easy to explain matters by saying that some form of non-price competition has been used to split one market into several.

Since all this is significant only if there really is one market artificially divided into segments rather than the several apparent ones, statistical methods by which markets can be delimited more precisely are needed. For this purpose the conventional definition of a market as a point at which the forces of supply and demand come to a focus in price has little immediate utility. It is better to think of a market as a group of people tied more or less closely together in a nexus of buying and selling and to view the task of empirical research as being to isolate and subject to quantitative analysis this group of people and their interrelations.

The principal technical difficulty is that the sources from which prices must be obtained (usually the sellers of goods and services) are not in practice very reliable as sources from which to draw data that make it possible to identify, count, measure, and evaluate the buyers and sellers whose behavior is summarized neatly but abstractly in the phrase "forces that come to a focus in price."

The problem ordinarily has been attacked (although not usually in these specific terms) by relying upon a number of supposedly valid assumptions. Prices are obtained from the sellers in some specified geographic area (say, a shopping center, a city, a trading area, or a country). The sellers are selected from specified trades, being classified by the kinds of goods or services constituting the greater part of their sales volume. They are asked to quote prices (net after discounts, allowances, returns, and so on) at

---

21 Corwin D. Edwards, op. cit., p. 157. The other respect in which all price differentials are alike is the presence of "some similarity in the nature of the product, the conditions of the supply, or its destination and use which creates an expectation that the price will be more nearly uniform than it actually is." As with the first characteristic common to all price differentials discussed above in the main text, this one is significant only insofar as the factor involved (the "product" in this instance) can be clearly defined and identified.

which they make the bulk of their sales of goods or more or less well specified types and qualities.

It is assumed that from knowledge of the location of the sellers, the trades represented and the qualities of goods handled, a separable group of buyers and sellers can be identified precisely enough to give meaning for purposes of economic analysis to the price quotations obtained.

Very little has been done with the reverse procedure of isolating the group of people to be studied and determining their behavior as buyers or sellers of goods in order, first, to divide them into clearly differentiable markets and, second, to find out where the prices they establish in the course of their buying and selling can best be obtained as statistical data.

As an example, one may take an effort to make meaningful analyses of prices obtained in retail stores scattered over a metropolitan area. The wants and needs of consumers for retail service are provided by a large and complex group of retail establishments that distribute themselves spatially and by types of store according to principles that are little understood.

If the territory to be analyzed is large enough, as when an entire metropolitan area embracing a central city and its surrounding suburbs and hinterland is studied, representative and meaningful data for the area probably can be obtained (with careful selection and weighing) by seeing to it that quotations are obtained from stores representing each important type within each class of location, i.e., downtown, outlying shopping center, string shopping street, neighborhood store cluster, isolated neighborhood store, roadside stand, and so on.

The difficulties arise when more refined analysis is desired such that the prices paid by a particular group of consumers who make up what can be considered a market are identified, measured, and compared among themselves, over time, and with prices paid by other groups. Corresponding difficulties arise when matters are approached from the other end, an effort being made to identify the particular people whose behavior as sellers and producers lies behind the prices established in particular stores.

In these days of extreme mobility among people both as earners and as spenders it is not safe to assume, as is often done, that the prices paid by the people living in some neighborhood or trading area are sampled adequately by going into the stores in the same neighborhood or into these plus other stores in some nearby shopping center. Similarly the prices obtained from some group of stores cannot adequately be explained by looking to the people who live nearby.

Investigations are badly needed that will permit the drawing of lines connecting people as exactly as possible into carefully defined points of purchase. For this purpose, markets presumably will have to be defined as groups of people clustered in an economic but not necessarily in a geographic sense about groups of more or less closely competing stores. The groups of people separated out for analysis may be people living in a particular area, employed in a particular area or in a particular industry, falling into a particular income class, belonging to a particular race, earning their living in a particular occupation, and so on.

Once a group has been isolated, the problem will be to find out where they buy the commodities and services to be studied. This investigation may disclose that they purchase predominantly in one or two stores in one shopping center or in several widely scattered stores. When the distribution of their trade among the stores in which they do their buying is known, however, it becomes possible to find the price quotations that are significant for them.

The problem can be approached, of course, the other way round. That is, groups of stores can be taken as the starting point and their trade traced back to the consumers from whom it comes. In some instances the results probably will not be very different from those obtained by mapping out residential areas and assuming, first, that the stores within each area receive practically all of their trade from people living within its boundaries and, second, that the people living in an area do all of their buying within it. The exceptions are so numerous and so great, however, that the approach here proposed would unquestionably improve the accuracy of the picture of marketing habits and procedures obtained.

In order to pull together the various strands that constitute the market clustered about the prices being studied, it will, of course, be necessary to obtain many supplemental data concerning the consumers affected. Significant data about consumers are collected on various overlapping but different geographic bases. Population data, for example, are available chiefly according to place of residence; but the other significant data necessary for an effective analysis are available chiefly according to place of employment or place of purchase. To permit very significant conclusions, the people making up a market must be located geographically for all three purposes.

The end product of all this would be the isolation of markets that really mean something for economic research. The theoretical concept of a market as a point at which supply and demand forces come to a focus in a price is conceptually sound but extraordinarily difficult to apply in practice with the kinds of data and procedures thus far used. Success in efforts to tie groups of consumers and suppliers to specific points of purchase or sale at which price quotations can be obtained would almost certainly make for a considerable advance in our use of this basic concept to enlarge our understanding of prices and pricing procedures.

VIII

The second direction in which statistical experimentation can well be pushed leads toward an explanation of seeming differences among prices within a particular market.

The most promising way of achieving progress here seems to be to work toward reducing the concept of "bundles" discussed above to quantitative measurement.

Differences among prices for a single commodity in a given market at any one time are ordinarily taken to indicate the presence of friction and imperfection in the market. The conclusion is justified, however only if there really is a single commodity. To be sure of his ground, one must make certain that there are no substantial differences in the bundles offered the buyer.

Correspondingly, an apparent equality of prices cannot be assumed to indicate true equality unless the bundles for which outwardly equal prices are set also are equal. If, then, meaningful comparisons are to be made of prices at any time or over a period of time, some system must be worked out for separating differences due to variations in the bundle from those that represent variations in the value attached to a given bundle.

Although the discussion is not customarily stated in these terms, the statistical methods already in use have made some progress in this direction. These methods fall into two major classes.

1. Division of production and distribution into successive stages for which different prices are obtained. It is on this basis that prices are obtained separately for, say, raw materials and processed materials, or producer's goods and consumer's goods, or wholesale transactions and retail transactions.

Unfortunately the concepts upon which these stages are based are far from precise and invariable. Furthermore, the stages are themselves broad enough to permit a considerable variation within them. To take the most extreme example, the term wholesale can cover so wide an expanse of business that a wholesale price not otherwise defined more precisely virtually defies useful analysis. Even the term retail is far from specific and stable in meaning.[22]

An excellent example of the difficulties that arise in economic research from uncertainties as to the bundle offered the consumer by the retailer may be found in Rolph and Carroll, *Retail Operating Costs Within a Community*.[23] It is concerned with differences in the expense ratios of retail stores rather than with prices but illustrates the point at hand. Using data from the 1929 census, the authors compute for stores classified into 9 groups and subclassified into 70 trades, figures on important items of expense covering stores in the downtown shopping district of St. Louis and those in the rest of the city.

The differences are substantial but cannot be interpreted very effectively in the absence of a clear statement of the differences among the various groups and trades as regards what they offer their customers under the term "retailing."

2. Allowance for differences in the services provided with goods where the cost is readily separable and measurable in money. This allowance is what the collectors of prices have in mind when they differentiate between say, f.o.b. and delivered prices, or between cash and credit prices. Here too, the terminology and the procedures are far from precise, leaving large areas of uncertainty concerning the prices obtained.

In order to improve price quotations from this point of view, the most promising procedure would seem to be to refine the familiar metaphor of a channel down which goods move on their way through the successive processes of production and distribution into consumption. The ideas of movement down a channel (which is borrowed by analogy from other sciences) and of using position in the channel to put meaning into the price obtained, are doubtless sound enough.

However, it is doubtful whether the usual attempt to limit this concept to a single channel is equally sound. A more precise approach would look upon goods as moving simultaneously through a group of related but different channels, each representing a succession of enterprises that perform some part of the complex of activities necessary to move goods into consumption

The traditional channel of distribution is the succession of owners through whose hands the goods pass. It is on this basis that goods are said to move from producer to wholesaler, to retailer, to consumer. Quite different patterns would result if the channel were thought of as being the succession of agencies that handle goods physically. In that event the goods might move from factory to railroad, to trucking company, to public warehouse, to trucking company, to wholesale warehouse, to express company, to railroad, to retail stores, to parcel delivery service to consumer.

Similarly, channels can be set up representing the succession of agencies through which information concerning the offerings of producers and distributors and information concerning the demands of consumers is passed back and forth; or the succession of agencies through which impulses to buy or actual orders for goods are passed; or the succession of agencies through which consumers' payments for goods work their way back through various distributors and processors, each taking out its share of the total.

The precise number and nature of channels to be set up for purposes of effective price measurement is a matter upon which very careful experimentation is needed. This is, in any event, the easier part of the problem. Whatever the final pattern of channels may be, it will be necessary to work out measurements of position within a channel

22 F. C. Mills, op. cit., pp. 382-383, discusses at some length the difficulties of specifying the stage of the marketing process at which prices are taken. He is apparently somewhat better satisfied than the present writer with the utility of retail as a term of specific and stable meaning but has the same feeling about the general problem faced by anyone who wants to work with the available price data.

23 Bureau of Foreign and Domestic Commerce, Domestic Commerce Series No. 8, Washington, 1934.

much more precise than those which simply differentiate, for example, retail from wholesale. What is needed, obviously, is some system of measurement analogous to those used in the physical sciences to indicate distance traveled or work done.

It may never be possible to devise units of measurement as precise or as universally accepted as are, say, meters, ergs, and dynes. It should be possible, however, to come much closer than anyone has as yet, to establishing units by which economic distance and economic work can be determined with a fair degree of precision. It also should be possible to set up points of reference by which to determine position in any channel.

The most obvious of such points are the beginnings of production, in the broadest sense of the term, and the completion of consumption, also in the broadest sense of the term. Fixing the position of a purchase or sale in terms of economic work done or to be done, or of economic distance traveled or to be traveled, would introduce a much higher degree of precision into price measurement than is possible through the use of vaguely defined stages or steps of marketing.[24]

The measurements themselves and the procedures for using them will not be worked out too easily, but some suggestions as to how to go about the matter can be derived from the work done to facilitate the analysis of distribution costs from the point of view of individual firms seeking to maximize their profits.

The types of work started two decades ago by the United States Department of Commerce in its Louisville Grocery Survey and St. Louis Drug Survey, and by the Comptroller's Congress of the National Retail Dry Goods Association in its system for analyzing department store expenses, offer germs of ideas that probably can be applied to social, as distinct from individual, costs and work done.

These procedures, which have been copied, expanded, and refined by a great many other investigators, proceed on the basis of breaking down the work done by distributive agencies into a limited number of functions. The best feasible measure of cost incurred in performing any given function is then worked out in order to permit an allocation of costs among particular lots of goods, particular departments of the business, and so on.

Although arbitrary in some degree, and subject to sharp limitations in practice, these methods of analysis have proved extremely useful to business management where applied with imagination and discrimination. If they can be as fruitful in social research as they have been in individual research, they should contribute substantially to the measurement of market position in specific cases.

By their aid, apparently similar prices can be tested to see whether the similarity is only apparent or real. Likewise seemingly different prices may turn out to be virtually equivalent. In either event, a situation will be set up that makes much easier than at present analysis and understanding of the so-called non-price elements in competition.

---

24 Precision in the comparison of bundles or, more narrowly, of position in a group of marketing channels would be helpful in many kinds of research other than that concerned directly with prices. An interesting example will be found in Ralph F. Breyer, Bulk and Package Handling Costs (N. Y.: American Management Association, 1944). Breyer, in trying to determine the cost to the consumer of putting rice up in packages as compared with selling it in bulk to be weighed out in the store, found himself compelled to make an intricate series of comparisons extending through alternative lines of movement of rice all the way from the mill to the consumer's homes.

Bill R. Darden

An Operational Approach To Product Pricing

This article presents a new approach to product pricing which provides a formal vehicle to harness the judgment, experience, and intuition of businessmen. It provides an operational approach for quantifying the hypotheses of market pricers. Thus, this approach does not require the average product pricer to be a combination statistician, economist, and quantitative methods expert.

THE best brains in the business and academic worlds labor to provide the product pricer with a repertoire of sophisticated techniques and approaches, and he continues pricing products in his usual manner. While the economist expounds use of concepts of demand and marginal analysis, the pricer uses experience, intuition, and cost-plus. While the statistician calls for probability and payoff tables, the pricer uses experience, intuition, and cost-plus. While the professional expounds the use of price elasticity and cross-elasticity concepts, the pricer again uses experience, intuition, and cost-plus.

Obstacles to Optimal Product Pricing

Why does the pricer persist in this "irrational" behavior? This question seems to evoke answers from academicians and professionals that are as "irrational" as the pricer's behavior. Actually, the answers are simpler than presupposed and are all in the form of obstacles to "optimal" pricing. Some of these obstacles are:

1. The pricer does not have the time, nor the interest, to read and digest the latest literature on pricing, even if it

About the author. Bill R. Darden is Assistant Professor of Marketing and Management in the Department of Marketing and Management at the College of Business Administration of Louisiana State University at Baton Rouge. A graduate of the Industrial Management School at Georgia Institute of Technology, he also received the Master of Science at the institution and the Ph.D. in Marketing from the University of North Carolina at Chapel Hill in 1966. He taught at both Georgia Institute of Technology and the University of North Carolina, before going to Louisiana State University.

Dr. Darden is a lecturer for the Mid-South Executive Development Program in the area of quantitative methods in business. He is also a lecturer for the Great Books in Marketing and Management Series at Louisiana State University.

were directly applicable in practice, which it is not.

2. In many cases the objectives of the pricer may be quite different from the objectives assumed in the literature for arriving at optimal guides to action.

3. The typical pricer usually has many product lines, and in each product line he may have many products. Thus, the time that he may allot to pricing each product may be very small.

4. Also, while the pricer recognizes that many products are substitutes or complementary to each other, he has no way to quantify or measure these effects properly.

5. The product pricer also has problems in determining competitor reactions to price strategies. The direction and degree of price reactions is a prime trouble area.

6. Again, the pricer does not have the methods, time, or money to measure demand curves or other consumer response curves properly. From experience, intuition, and judgment he must make hypotheses about future decision relationships. Future positive feedback increases the belief in these hypotheses, while negative feedback decreases the belief in these hypotheses. With negative feedback, the pricer begins to investigate his "key" hypotheses, sequentially, and these may be revised.

The above "obstacles" do not begin to show the difficulties of the "complete" pricer. The "complete" pricer must deal with all the myriad combinations of price, advertising, sales promotion, personal selling, place, and product. Heuristically, he must hypothesize about the degree to which competitors will react to his price change and in what form this reaction will occur. The product pricer must "guess"—on the basis of his present hypotheses— what blend of marketing decisions will go best with a given price, and he must in turn determine what effect the given price will have on the sales of other products in the

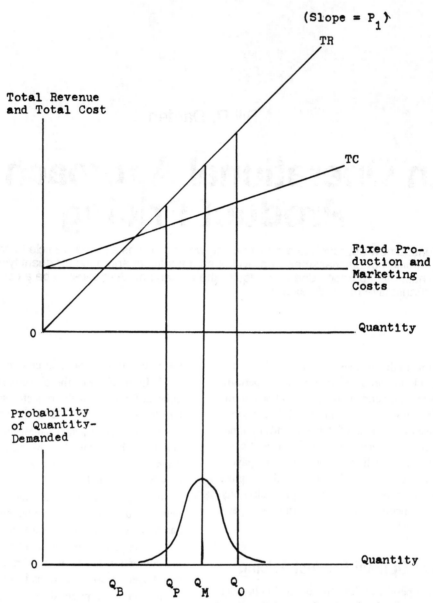

FIGURE 1. At a given price (P_1), the use of three volume estimates to fit a beta probability distribution.

product line (both in the short run and in the long run). To continue with the latter thought, the product pricer must coordinate pricing policy with channel decisions, product decisions, and promotion decisions. *This coordination must take place through time,* not only at a point in time (as economic analysis often assumes).

It is not surprising, then, that the product pricer cannot predict the quantity demanded for a given price during a given period. However, it is probable that the product pricer does use an implicit, informal method of determining a sales volume range for a given price. Thus, it is believed that most product pricers *do* consider more than cost and turnover in pricing. It is hypothesized in this paper that many pricers use experience and intuition to arrive operationally at hypotheses which serve as a basis for price making. The purpose of this paper, then, is to formal-

ize, heuristically, an operational approach to pricing, given the beliefs of the pricer.

Profit Variance and Price Limits

The central concept of the proposed pricing approach is exemplified in Figure 1. Assuming some given price, P_1, the breakeven chart in Figure 1 can be easily produced. The typical marketing executive will determine the most likely quantity demanded at P_1—in this case, Q_M. Now the marketing student determines the most likely profit at Q_M, as well as the breakeven quantity, Q_B. This approach is likely to be repeated for several prices, yielding respective profit and breakeven quantities of each price. Actually, the marketer is using repetitive breakeven analysis to feel out demand.

In addition, the marketer may determine optimal advertising and sales promotion for each price, which in turn also affects the profit and breakeven quantities received for each price. It is also recognized that the final most likely price is that which reflects judgments about competitive reactions.

Now the price investigator can estimate for a given price a pessimistic quantity demanded and an optimistic quantity demanded. These estimates are Q_P and Q_O, respectively, for price P_1 in Figure 1. Thus the pricing specialist has three sales volume estimates at a given price, P_1: a most likely estimate (Q_M), a pessimistic estimate (Q_P), and an optimistic estimate (Q_O).

Rationale and Uses of Quantity Estimates

In the Program Evaluation and Review Technique, commonly called PERT, the planner is faced with the problem of estimating times required for accomplishing particular activities. In order to draw upon the judgment and experience of the superintendent or foreman in charge of completing the activity, and at the same time eliminate bias, the planner asks for three time estimates. These time estimates include an optimistic estimate, a pessimistic estimate, and a most likely estimate. In the cases of optimistic and pessimistic estimations, the planner counsels the estimator to choose times that have a chance of 1 in 100 of occurring. The rational behind this counsel is that such estimates can be used to approximately fit a beta probability density function to the time occurrence of the given activity.

The same rational lies behind the estimations of Q_P, Q_M, and Q_O at P_1 in Figure 1. The marketer is unsure what future volume will be generated by the projected marketing mix (including, of course, the price, P_1). For example, the degrees to which competitors may react, the change in marketing environment, and changes in company implementation effectiveness are all subject to varying degrees of change. However, using the three quantity estimates and assuming a beta probability distribution, the price-maker can determine a sales volume which stands a 50-50 chance of occurring. This volume will be called "largest expected volume" and is denoted by QE. Borrowing from PERT network analysis, the following yields an approximation of QE, using the three quantity estimates:

$$1. \quad Q_E = \frac{Q_P + 4Q_M + Q_O}{6}$$

An important characteristic of this approach is the flexibility of the beta distribution. It allows the volume estimator to make the extreme volume estimates asymmetrical around the most likely volume, if he so chooses. Thus, the probability distribution fitted to the volume estimates may be positively skewed, negatively skewed, or symetrically distributed.

Variance of the Sales Volume

In addition to yielding the "largest expected volume" for a given price, this "operational approach" produces a good estimate of the volume variance. Using again the volume estimates at P_1, the marketer can compute this approximate variance with Equation 2 shown below:

$$2. \quad \sigma^2 = \frac{(Q_O - Q_P)^2}{36}$$

Price Range and the "Operational Approach"

The major strength of the "operational approach" lies in its ability to draw on the experience and judgment of marketing specialists in the firm. The knowledge in regard to competitor reactions, market changes, consumer behavior, and company implementation effectiveness should to a great degree be reflected in the estimates of volume at a given price. Using a repetitive approach, the same analysis can be made for several prices.

Specifically, the pricer wishes to determine some upper and lower limits for prices that must be investigated. Figure 2 shows a special type of demand curve (or curves). This demand curve actually represents three demand curves: the first (D_O) indicates optimistic quantity estimates at various prices; the second (D_M) shows most likely sales volume at all prices; and the third (D_P) shows pessimistic estimates. These three curves generate three total revenue curves in Figure 2: the optimistic revenue curve, the most likely revenue curve, and the pessimistic revenue curve.

The marketer begins at a high price level, decreasing the price until at a given price (in this case P_1) the pessimistic quantity estimate generates only enough revenue to just break even (BEP_1). At a higher price P_{1+}, the volume Q_{P1-} will not cover costs and at a lower price P_{1-}, the volume Q_{P1+} will generate profits. The price (P_1) which accompanies Q_{P1} becomes the upper price limit, ensuring the firm that it will do better than break even over 99% of the time at this price.

In order to establish a lower price limit, in Figure 2, the marketer lowers the price past P_1 until a price is reached which allows the pessimistic revenue curve to break even again (BEP_2). At P_2, such a situation occurs and this price, again, will generate profits 99% of the time.

The marketer has now "bracketed" the feasible prices available to him. This price range may be so small that the respective quantity estimates of the two extreme prices may overlap; however, this seems unlikely in most cases.

The price range determined above provides a very conservative price zone for analysis. Actually, there are other criteria which provide a wider range of prices for investigation. For example, the product pricer could determine the upper and lower price limits on the basis of the largest expected quantity estimates. The probability of breaking

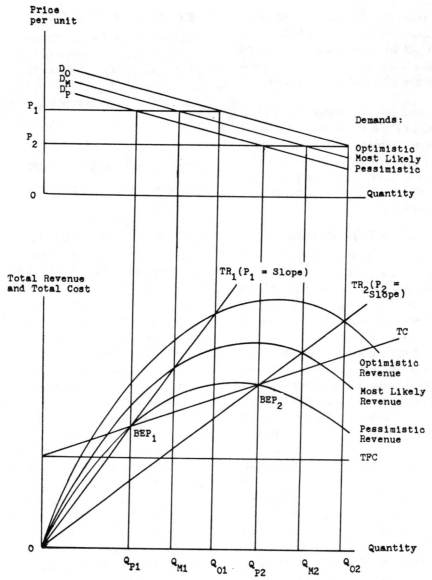

FIGURE 2. Determination of feasible price range through the interaction of pessimistic, most likely, and optimistic demands with cost curves.

even using this criterion (at either price limit) drops from .99 to .50. Another criterion, the most likely quantity estimate, provides a compromise, most likely guide, and, depending upon the individual industry and market, may prove the most feasible criterion for most firms.

After the upper price limit ($P_1 = P_U$) and the lower price limit ($P_2 = P_1$) have been determined, the firm may wish to find the largest expected quantities and the quantity variances at each price limit. From this information, the largest expected profit can be determined at both P_U and P_L as shown below.

$$Q_{E1} = \frac{Q_{P1} + 4Q_{M1} + Q_{O1}}{6}$$

Expected Profit = $PR_E = Q_{E1} (P_U) - TFC - (V) Q_{E1}$
Where V = Average Variable Cost

TFC = Total Fixed Cost

Now the same information can be determined at the lower end of the price bracket.

Implications for Pricing Strategy

The "operational approach" provides the product pricer with a formal vehicle to summarize and integrate his various hypotheses into a clear picture of economical alternatives. Some considerations for the pricer are:

1. The quantity estimates for the upper price limit and the lower price limit may overlap. For example, the upper limit may have an optimistic quantity estimate of 500,000 units, while the lower price limit may have a pessimistic quantity estimate of 499,000.

2. While Figure 2 assumes that costs remain constant in determining the upper and lower price limits, this as-

sumption is not necessary. Thus, the pricer can change marketing blends to optimize some given objective at each price without changing the usefulness of the operational approach.

3. The use of three quantity estimates for a given price *does not* require that pricing specialists within a firm reach complete agreement as to forecasted sales. Thus, the difficult problem of "consensus" in pricing is largely overcome.

4. Once the product pricer has "bracketed in" the upper and lower price limits, he can use a sequential approach to test the expected profitability of intermediate prices.

5. The product pricer can not only compute and compare expected largest profits, but he can also compute and compare quantity and profit variances at various prices. There is no guarantee that quantity variances will be similar at different prices; therefore, a product pricer may be willing to accept a lower expected largest profit at some price in exchange for a much smaller variance (in other words, the pricer may be willing to trade off expected profit for a greater degree of certainty).

Conclusion

In general, the product pricer must use experience, intuition, and cost to price products. The pricer cannot wholly rely on sophisticated techniques and theory for optimal pricing of products. If it can be accepted that product pricers must rely on "operational" techniques for pricing then it would appear that one of the principal tasks of the marketing academician is the exploration of these approaches. Thus, major contributions can be made to marketing by providing marketing management with operational approaches which allow the executive to efficiently use his hypotheses about the decision situation. Bayesian decision theory is one move in this direction; however, the complexity of its methodology, as well as the problem of determining subjective probabilities for the various alternative outcomes of a given price strategy, prohibit its use by most product pricers.

This paper presents an operational approach to pricing that takes into consideration the above complexities and provides a formal vehicle to quantify the pricing hypotheses of businessmen. The approach involves no change in thinking. However, the methodology does allow use of a sequential approach and probability theory.

Products & Services

George S. Day

The Product Life Cycle: Analysis and Applications Issues

Each of the articles in this special section makes a distinctive contribution to the long-standing controversy over the managerial value of the product life cycle concept. This overview is designed to put these articles into a broader perspective by analyzing the major issues of identification, forecasting, and strategy formulation encountered in any meaningful application of the product life cycle.

THERE is a tremendous ambivalence toward the product life cycle concept within marketing. On one hand, the concept has an enduring appeal because of the intuitive logic of the product birth → growth → maturity → decline sequence based on a biological analogy. As such, it has considerable descriptive value when used as a systematic framework for explaining market dynamics.

However, the simplicity of the product life cycle concept makes it vulnerable to criticism, especially when it is used as a predictive model for anticipating when changes will occur and one stage will succeed another, or as a normative model which attempts to prescribe what alternative strategies should be considered at each stage. Underlying these criticisms are five basic issues that must be faced in any meaningful application of the concept:

- How should the product-market be defined for the purpose of life cycle analysis?
- What are the factors that determine the progress of the product through the stages of the life cycle?
- Can the present life cycle position of the product be unambiguously established?
- What is the potential for forecasting the key parameters, including the magnitude of sales, the duration of the stages, and the shape of the curve?
- What role should the product life cycle concept play in the formulation of competitive strategy?

Each of the articles in this special section provides useful insights into one or more of these application issues. In addition, each article adds support to the emerging consensus that the product life cycle represents the outcome or summary of numerous forces for change present in the

relevant product-market, each force acting in concert with others to facilitate or inhibit the rate of product sales growth or decline. This perspective on the nature of the product life cycle will also guide the analysis of the application issues in this overview article.

What Is A Product-Market for the Purpose of Life Cycle Analysis?

A problem that confronts all strategy analysis is the variety of levels of aggregation that characterize hierarchical product structures, ranging from the generic product class and industry, to the product type or form, and down to variants and brands. The extreme positions on the question of appropriate level of aggregation for life cycle analysis are: look at all levels, on the grounds that they each yield different insights, or forget the whole concept because generic product classes serve such enduring needs that meaningful trends are not usually apparent, while product forms are so volatile that it is difficult to judge with accuracy in which stage of the life cycle the form is or when it will proceed to the next stage (Dhalla and Yuspeh 1976). Intermediate positions include those who argue that since managers cannot control product forms or classes, the analysis must be confined to the brand level (Enis, LaGarce, and Prell 1977).

The relevant question is which level best captures the consequences of the underlying forces for change. However, there are many dimensions along which a product can change. When is a change sufficiently distinct to justify a separate life cycle analysis? One useful answer is proposed by Abell (1980), who defines a product as the application of a distinct technology to the provision of a particular function for a specific customer group. Only when there is a change along one or more of these dimensions

About the author. George S. Day is Professor of Marketing, University of Toronto.

that involves a sharp departure from the present strategies of the participating competitors is a separate life cycle necessary. The advantage of this heuristic can be seen from its application to problem situations that in the past have fueled enduring doubts about the life cycle:

- The timeless consumer product. Was the chairman of Procter and Gamble justified in saying they don't believe in the product life cycle by citing the case of Tide synthetic laundry detergent which was introduced in 1947 and was still growing in 1976? During the 29-year lifetime, it had undergone 55 significant modifications in response to changes in consumer preferences, laundry habits, washing machines, and fabrics (Hopkins 1977). Clearly they have successfully adapted this product to extended maturity without significantly changing either function, technology, or customer.
- The multiple function material. Is there a meaningful life cycle for a material such as nylon, which is subsequently processed further to be suitable for different applications such as carpeting, tire cord, and hosiery? (Levitt 1965) The answer is certainly no, for each application requires an entirely different strategy. Indeed, it would be more meaningful to construct a life cycle for synthetic carpet fibers, for example.
- Technological substitution processes. Until the mid-sixties, beverage cans were almost exclusively three-piece steel/tin combinations, until two-piece aluminum cans began to replace them. Then in the mid-seventies two-piece steel cans were developed to recapture the position of steel (Machnic 1980). But during this period, neither the functions nor the customers of metal cans were changed. Thus a new product life cycle was not necessary.
- Sequentially unfolding segments. Some life cycles are a composite of the sequential introduction and development of a basic function/technology within a series of related customer segments. Cardozo (1979) describes how a specialized communications system was first accepted for process control applications and then extended to security applications within the same adopting firms. After two years a new segment for combined security and process applications was identified.

As each of these examples demonstrates, product life cycles summarize the effects of many concurrent changes. While these influences must be understood, they may not dictate an entirely new product life cycle.

What Are The Underlying Factors That Determine The Parameters of the Life Cycle?

Numerous forces have been hypothesized to influence the sequence and duration of the stages, the shape of the curve, and the magnitude of sales at each transition to a new stage. Past attempts to validate the existence of the life cycle have uncovered many shapes, durations, and sequences (Buzzell 1966, Cox 1967, Polli and Cook 1969, Rink and Swan 1979). These efforts have not been matched by systematic research into the reasons for the difference between shapes. Yet, this knowledge is critical to informed forecasting and strategy development. The limited evidence, however, suggests that while most of the underlying forces are operating during several stages, their relative importance changes during the transition from one stage to another.

Initial Trajectory Stage

Some new products, such as industrial robots, diffuse very slowly into their potential market, while other products virtually bypass this stage. The determinants of the rate of diffusion (Zaltman and Stiff 1973) include:

- The perceived comparative advantage of the new product relative to the best available alternative.
- The perceived risk, or the subjective estimate by a prospective buyer of the probability of a negative outcome (Webster 1969). This risk is a joint function of the financial exposure in the event of failure coupled with uncertainty as to the outcome. This uncertainty has many origins, including an unpredictable rate of technical obsolescence, the uneven quality of early production runs, or a lack of product standardization. Thus, potential videodisc buyers may wait to see whether grooved or grooveless capacitance systems will dominate solid-state laser systems, since the discs are incompatible.
- Barriers to adoption (such as commitment to existing facilities or incompatibility with existing values) will slow acceptance even when other factors are supportive.
- Information and availability. Not only must the product be readily available (for purchase and servicing), but the buyer must be aware of the product and informed of the benefits.

Influencing the rate of diffusion. Much of the research on diffusion of innovations has dealt with information variables and the capacity of formal and informal sources to reduce perceived risk. The value of this work for the purposes of life cycle analysis is compromised by taking the comparative advantages of the product as fixed. In reality these are conditional variables that can be influenced by the strategic decisions of both the pioneer firm and the followers. Thus, manufacturers can invest in promotion and distribution coverage to increase awareness, expand sales activity to induce trial, reduce risk by providing technical service, warranties and after-sales service support, and enhance the relative advantage by reducing the delivered price or adding new features.

Experience effects. The only systematic consideration of the relationship of strategic decisions and life cycle consequences has come from analyses of the effect of cumulative industry experience on average industry costs. This experience effect is reliably present in high technology industries, where real cost declines of 15-30% with each doubling of industry output are consistently encountered (Abell and Hammond 1979, Boston Consulting Group 1972, Yelle 1979). Reduced costs should eventually lead to lowered prices, which in turn will improve the comparative advantage of the new product. It is a highly interactive effect, for an increased comparative advantage should accelerate the rate of acceptance and hence the rate of accumulation of experience. Whether this acceleration of demand will materialize depends on the initial pricing strategies and the persistence of the remaining barriers to diffusion.

Other exogenous factors. The early history of many new products is shaped by factors beyond the immediate industry and the potential substitutes. Included in this category are changes in the position of complementary products and changes in government regulations and policies. For example, the demand for electronic home entertainment products such as television and videodiscs was or is dependent on the growth of broadcast capabilities and programming. Similarly, the growth of new computer-based office services is contingent on the availability of software. The impact of government policies can be especially dramatic, for they frequently are abrupt events. Consider the impact on demand for automatic teller machines of a ruling that these machines are not considered branches in states where branch banking is not permitted.

The Transition to Rapid Growth

A number of factors, which were latent during the period when the initial uncertainties were being resolved, assume importance as growth accelerates.

Changes in the relationships with substitute products. These changes reflect improvements in the price-performance ratio as experience accumulates, designs are improved, new features are added, and the real price declines. This will determine how quickly the new product will replace the substitute, and how much of the volume will be replaced. Substitution will also be triggered by large jumps in the price of the substitute, as happened in 1974-1975 when powdered soft drink mixes grew rapidly at the expense of canned fruit juices, which had to absorb large sugar price increases.

Competitive entry strategies. In many product-markets the strategic window seems to open at roughly the same time for most potential entrants. First, the initial acceptance of the product helps reduce the uncertainties that clouded the early prospects. This uncertainty may have also encouraged experimentation with alternative process technologies, designs, and marketing strategies. The results of these experiments and ongoing marketing research reduce the uncertainty to a level that is tolerable for larger firms with lower risk profiles—witness recreational vehicles, video games, and solar heating (Porter 1980). A second incentive is the widespread belief that it is "easier" to gain share in high growth markets. The combined impact of many competitors, each investment spending to gain a sustainable market position, may create significant acceleration in the rate of growth.

The influence of repeat buying. Sooner or later a significant proportion of sales in a product category will be repeat or replacement purchases. As Midgeley (1981) shows, the shape of the life cycle curve can be explained by the ratio of mean adoption time (which depends on the duration of the diffusion process) to mean interpurchase time. This analysis helps explain why the life cycles for many of the durable products described by Harrell and Taylor (1981) in this issue exhibit a primary sales cycle followed by one or more recycles at a lower level of sales. In markets with shorter repurchase intervals, the repeat buying combines with initial purchases as a further source of growth.

Does growth induce growth? As the market expands, there are new opportunities for segmentation, and the adaptation of the product or service to better fit the needs of customer groups whose requirements were previously too modest to be served with a tailored offering. These niches, of course, make the rapidly growing market even more attractive to prospective entrants.

Evolution to Maturity

As the cumulative sales penetration approaches the ultimate market capacity and the growth rate slows, the dominating factor becomes the replacement rate. However, this is not a period of stability, for the ultimate potential is frequently an elusive target and new forces come into play.

Expanding market potential. While the market capacity for use or consumption may be stable on a per capita basis, there still could be expansion from demographic changes that cause the target market to expand or shrink. At the same time, changes in social or economic trends influencing underlying needs—such as protection against property theft, or energy conservation—will affect consumers' demands for end products such as security devices and energy saving products, which filters back to component suppliers.

Buyer learning. This becomes an increasingly significant factor with repeat buying and the accumulation of usage experience. The most general consequences are systematic shifts in the elasticities or response coefficients. Over the long run, as products approach a familiar commodity status, buyers become more price sensitive and less responsive to advertising and promotion efforts either by the industry or by individual competitors. While these hypotheses have almost become conventional wisdom, there is growing evidence of their validity (Erickson and Montgomery 1980).

Competitive turbulence. One version of the product life cycle incorporates a distinct competitive turbulence stage (Wasson 1978), preceding the maturity stage. According to this analysis, the slowdown in the growth rate that signals impending maturity reveals excess capacity and triggers a competitive battle for market share. This pattern has been partially corroborated by Boston Consulting Group (Conley 1970) analyses of rapid declines in real prices, triggered by an unexpected economic slowdown, the desire of the pioneer to minimize further share erosion, or a major thrust by a new entrant. Despite the importance of these hypothesized relationships of changes in price, competitive structure, and life cycle stage, there is virtually no direct empirical evidence. Some indirect support comes from the analyses of the PIMS data base reported by Thorelli and Burnett (1981) in this issue. There is, however, no support for a further hypothesis that market shares will stabilize after the period of competitive stability. Indeed, Buzzell (1981) has found that mature markets tend to become less concentrated as the larger firms lose share because they cannot maintain their initial cost advantage.

The Onset of Decline

One recent analysis of declining industries (Harrigan 1980) observed that there had been virtually no attempt to sort out the factors that influence the strategic choices managers face during a decline. This study found that some declining environments were much more favorable than others in terms of long run sales, profitability, and price stability. Generally, the least favorable environments were the result of fashion or demographic changes because they were much less predictable than declines created by technological change. An important conclusion was that some declining markets were more favorable than others if there were pockets of enduring demand, which could be protected from incursions by displaced competitors. It may also prove useful to distinguish a stage of petrification following decline if sales stabilize at some lower level (Michael 1971).

Can The Present Life Cycle Position Be Unambiguously Identified?

The notion of distinct stages, which reflect different opportunities and threats with respect to marketing strategy and profit potential (Kotler 1980), is an integral part of the product life cycle concept. The usefulness of such analyses is frequently compromised by the elusive nature of the boundaries between the stages.

Some of the boundary identification problems stem from the sensitivity of life cycle analyses to the choice of measures (Wind 1981). Should one use unit volume, current or constant dollar total revenue, or per capita consumption to measure sales? What adjustments should be made to eliminate the effects of economic conditions? Consumer durables and industrial materials are especially susceptible to changes in economic activity that can cloud the interpretation of the prospects for the product.

Further complicating the identification of boundaries is the variety of possible life cycle patterns. This makes it unlikely that a product's position in its life cycle can be established simply by observing changes in the past sales pattern. The implications of the difference between a temporary or even an extended pause in sales growth versus a true topping out of growth are profound. Thus, one cannot avoid forecasting the future sales path of the product if sensible judgments about the present life cycle position are to be made.

What Is The Potential For Forecasting The Key Parameters of the Life Cycle?

The ability of a forecasting model to account for the driving forces during the various stages of the life cycle generally determines the accuracy of the predictions. As support for this assertion we can contrast the promising track record of diffusion models that are suited to the rapid growth stage with the relative absence of successful forecasting models for the maturity and decline stages.

First Purchase Diffusion Models

The most popular models such as the Bass (1969) model, share four distinguishing features (Wind 1981):
• a constraint on long run growth within a level of saturation
• an S-shaped diffusion curve
• an assumption about the homogeneity of consumers
• no explicit consideration of marketing decision variables

When these assumptions are not unduly limiting, and there is sufficient prior sales data to obtain stable parameter estimates (Heeler and Hustad 1980), then reasonable forecasts can be achieved. However, the experience of Tigert and Farivar (1981) with optical scanning equipment for supermarkets, reported in this issue, suggests this frequently is not the case.

Improvements to the forecasting accuracy of these models have been sought mainly through the addition of decision variables (Bass 1980, Dolan and Jeuland 1981, Lillien 1980, Robinson and Lakhani 1975). However, as Mahajan and Muller (1979) point out in their review of these efforts, progress has been piecemeal as the extensions have usually incorporated only one decision variable at a time. This is partly a consequence of attempts to make the model as generally applicable as possible. Judging by the success of the proprietary model developed for analyzing the housewares market, described by Harrell and Taylor (1981) in this issue, there may be a greater payoff from the development of models that incorporate a rich array of marketing variables but are only applicable to a narrow set of products.

Forecasting Repeat and Replacement Sales

The relationship of the initial purchase rate with the timing of repurchases dictates both the duration of the rapid growth stage and the eventual shape of the life cycle curve. Yet, other than work on consumer nondurables (Ehrenberg 1972), little is known of the factors that influence the timing of repeat or replacement sales. Even this work is of limited value for it only applies within established markets where there is no sales trend. However, work by Midgeley (1981) and Harrell and Taylor (1981) provides a promising basis for further progress in this area.

Forecasting the Maturity and Decline Stages

A recent review of the state of strategic planning concluded that "probably the area in which strategic planning has performed the poorest is with the well established product line that has only average growth . . . what has created disaster for the planners is the difficulty in accurately determining the maturity of a product, particularly when outside forces can change that designation almost overnight" (*Business Week* 1978, p. 68). No single reason for the poor forecasting performance has been osilated, other than the general inability of sales forecasting models to incorporate forecasts of important underlying forces that determine whether a product will stagnate, decline, or revive. While many of these factors are undoubtedly industry-specific, there are numerous variables that have been hypothesized to behave as leading indicators of the top-out point when product sales growth slows to the GNP rate (Patel and Younger 1978, Porter 1980, Wilson 1969). Unfortunately, there has been no systematic study of the predictive validity of these variables.

The essence of forecasting during the decline stage is the recognition that while products provide specific functions, the customers seek the benefits delivered by the product. Thus, the rate of decline will depend on changes in the demand for the benefits, or the ability of emerging substitute products to do a superior job of delivering the benefits. Where the latter threat is dominant the issue is the rate of penetration by the new product, and the forecasting problem has come full circle.

The Role of the Product Life Cycle in the Formulation of Strategy

The derivation of generalized strategic prescriptions for each stage of the life cycle has been widely criticized—and for good reason. Such prescriptions are bound to be misleading for they assume a single role for the life cycle as a determinant of strategy, structure, and performance. Unfortunately this role is implicitly endorsed by a majority of marketing textbooks through an emphasis on strategic guidelines appropriate to the various stages. A more realistic view is that life cycle analysis serves several different roles in the formulation of strategy, such as an enabling condition, a moderating variable, or a consequence of strategic decisions.

The life cycle serves as an enabling condition in the sense that the underlying forces that inhibit or facilitate growth create opportunities and threats having strategic implications. Market growth—or the expectation of growth—enables competitors to enter the market and creates opportunities for offerings directed to segments previously uneconomic to serve.

The stage of the life cycle also acts as a moderating variable through its influence on the value of market share position and the profitability consequences of strategic decisions. This role is recognized through the inclusion of product growth rates or life cycle stages as a major dimension in virtually all portfolio classification models. Finally, a product life cycle forecast is not a fait accompli, which can only be reacted to, but instead is only one of several scenarios that are conditional on competitive actions.

A Summary Perspective on Strategic Relevance

The product life cycle is a versatile framework for organizing contingent hypotheses about appropriate strategy alternatives (Hofer 1975) and directing management attention toward anticipation of the consequences of the underlying dynamics of the served market. To enhance both the descriptive and explanatory value of the concept, much more attention needs to be directed toward understanding recurring patterns of successful strategies organized according to the stages of the life cycle models that are adapted to differences in the important underlying forces.

Overview of Papers in the Special Section

This special section was motivated by the continuing controversy over whether or how marketing decision makers actually adapt the product life cycle concept to their needs. Consequently, the emphasis is on empirical papers that address the realities of identifying, forecasting, and applying the concept in a wide variety of contexts.

The first set of four papers is devoted to specific applications. Harrell and Taylor discuss the validity and strategic value of a model used for assessing new houseware products. This model supports decision makers effectively because it is built on an intimate understanding of recurring patterns in the housewares market. The second paper by Qualls, Olshavsky, and Michaels complements this by documenting the rate at which life cycles have been shortening in the overall appliance industry. Tigert and Farivar next show that life cycle models can be effectively adapted to high technology industrial markets. Their evaluation of the ability of a modified Bass model to forecast initial installations of supermarket optical scanning equipment clearly shows that these models can play a significant supportive role so long as the limitations are recognized. The final paper in the first section by Ayal examines the ability of a well-known extension of the life cycle to explain international trade patterns and finds that astute strategies by exporters can often defeat the predictions.

The second set of papers deals with the soundness of the theoretical framework for product life cycle analysis. Thorelli and Burnett set the scene by analyzing characteristic patterns of strategy, structure, and performance over time, using the PIMS data base for industrial products. Their results cast into doubt any interpretation of the product life cycle as a fundamental dependent variable guiding strategic decisions. Midgley then addresses a major gap in life cycle theory by examining the underlying processes that influence the shape of the life cycle. The ratio of mean interpurchase time to mean adoption time is found to be a very useful forecasting variable.

An important theme linking all the papers in this spe-cial section is the need to incorporate the underlying factors and processes within the particular market situation into the life cycle model. Sproles demonstrates the value of this perspective by proposing an integrated theory of short and long run fashion acceptance. Finally, Tellis and Crawford show that this adaptive view of the life cycle is indeed consistent with comprehensive theories of biological evolution and that the deterministic life-death analogy so often used in marketing is wrong.

While each paper in this special section makes a distinctive contribution, the cumulative impact of all these papers on the quality of thinking about a fundamental element of marketing theory should be much greater than the sum of the parts.

REFERENCES

Abell, Derek F. (1980), *Defining the Business: The Starting Point of Strategic Planning*, Englewood Cliffs NJ: Prentice-Hall.

_____, and John S. Hammond (1979), *Strategic Market Planning: Problems and Analytical Approaches*, Englewood Cliffs NJ: Prentice-Hall.

Ayal, Igal (1981), "International Product Life Cycle: A Re-Assessment and Product Policy Implications," *Journal of Marketing*, 45 (Fall).

Bass, Frank M. (1969), "A New Product Growth Model for Consumer Durables," *Management Science*, 15 (January), 215-227.

_____(1980), "The Relationship Between Diffusion Rates, Experience Curves, and Demand Elasticities for Consumer Durable Technological Innovations," *Journal of Marketing*, 53, 551-567.

Boston Consulting Group (1972), *Perspectives on Experience*, Boston: Boston Consulting Group.

Business Week (1978), "The New Planning," (December 18), 62-68.

Buzzell, Robert D. (1966), "Competitive Behavior and Product Life Cycles," in *New Ideas for Successful Marketing*, John Wright and Jac Goldstucker, eds., Chicago: American Marketing Association.

_____ (1981), "Are There 'Natural' Market Structures?" *Journal of Marketing*, 45 (Winter), 42-51.

Cardozo, Richard N. (1979), *Product Policy: Cases and Concepts*, Reading, MA: Addison-Wesley.

Conley, Patrick (1970), "Experience Curves as a Planning Tool," *IEEE Spectrum*, 7 (June), 63-68.

Cox, William Jr. (1967), "Product Life Cycles as Marketing Models," *Journal of Business*, 40 (October), 375-384.

Dhalla, Nariman and Sonya Yuspeh (1976), "Forget the Product Life Cycle Concept," *Harvard Business Review*, 54 (January/February), 102-112.

Dolan, Robert J. and Abel P. Jeuland (1981), "Experience Curves and Dynamic Demand Models: Implications for Optimal Pricing Strategies," *Journal of Marketing*, 45 (Winter), 52-73.

Ehrenberg, A. S. C. (1972), *Repeat Buying*, London: North-Holland.

Enis, Ben M., Raymond LaGarce, and Arthur E. Prell (1977), "Extending the Product Life Cycle," *Business Horizons*, 20 (June), 46-56.

Erickson, Gary and David B. Montgomery (1980), "Measuring the Time-Varying Response to Market Communication Instruments," in David B. Montgomery and Dick R. Wittink, *Market Measurement and Analysis*, Cambridge: Marketing Science Institute.

Harrell, Stephen G. and Elmer D. Taylor (1981), "Modeling the Product Life Cycle for Consumer Durables," *Journal of Marketing*, 45 (Fall).

Harrigan, Kathryn Rudie (1980), "Strategies for Declining Industries," *Journal of Business Strategy*, 1 (Fall), 20-34.

Heeler, Roger M. and Thomas P. Hustad (1980), "Problems in Predicting New Product Growth for Consumer Durables," *Management Science*, 26 (October), 1007-1020.

Hofer, Charles W. (1975), "Toward a Contingency Theory of Business Strategy," *Academy of Management Journal*, 18 (December), 784-810.

Hopkins, David S. (1977), *Business Strategies for Problem Products*, New York: Conference Board.

Kotler, Philip (1980), *Marketing Management: Analysis, Planning and Control*, 4th edition, Englewood Cliffs, NJ: Prentice-Hall.

Levitt, Theodore (1965), "Exploit the Product Life Cycle," *Harvard Business Review*, 43 (November-December), 81-94.

Lillien, Gary L. (1980), "The Implications of Diffusion Models for Accelerating the Diffusion of Innovation," *Technological Forecasting and Social Change*, 17, 339-351.

Machnic, John A. (1980), "Multi-Level Versus Single-Level Substitution: The Case of the Beverage Can Market," *Technological Forecasting and Social Change*, 18, 141-149.

Mahajan, Vijay and Eitan Muller (1979), "Innovation Diffusion and New Product Growth Models in Marketing," *Journal of Marketing*, 43 (Fall), 55-68.

Michael, George C. (1971), "Product Petrification: A New Stage in the Life Cycle Theory," *California Management Review*, 9 (Fall), 88-91.

Midgley, David F. (1981), "Toward a Theory of the Product Life Cycle: Some Testable Propositions," *Journal of Marketing*, 45 (Fall).

Patel, Peter and Michael Younger (1978), "A Frame of Reference for Strategy Development," *Long Range Planning*, 11 (April), 6-12.

Polli, Rolando and Victor Cook (1969), "Validity of the Product Life Cycle," *Journal of Business*, 42 (October), 385-400.

Porter, Michael E. (1980), *Competitive Strategy: Techniques for Analyzing Industries and Competitors*, New York: The Free Press.

Qualls, William, Richard Olshavsky, and Ronald E. Michaels (1981), "Shortening of the PLC_An Empirical Test," *Journal of Marketing*, 45 (Fall).

Rink, David R. and John E. Swan (1979), "Product Life Cycle Research: A Literature Review," *Journal of Business Research*, 78 (September), 219-242.

Robinson, B. and C. Lakhani (1975), "Dynamic Price Models for New Product Planning," *Management Science*, 21 (June), 1113-22.

Sproles, George B. (1981), "Analyzing Fashion Life Cycles: Principles and Perspectives," *Journal of Marketing*, 45 (Fall).

Tellis, Gerard J. and C. Merle Crawford (1981), "An Evolutionary Approach to Product Growth Theory," *Journal of Marketing*, 45 (Fall).

Thorelli, Hans B. and Stephen C. Burnett (1981), "The Nature of Product Life Cycles for Industrial Goods Businesses," *Journal of Marketing*, 45 (Fall).

Tigert, Douglas and Behrooz Farivar (1981), "The Bass New Product Growth Model: A Sensitivity Analysis for a High Technology Product," *Journal of Marketing*, 45 (Fall).

Wasson, Chester R. (1978), *Dynamic Competitive Strategy and Product Life Cycles*, St. Charles, IL: Challenge Books.

Webster, Frederick E., Jr. (1969), "New Product Adoption in Industrial Markets: A Framework for Analysis," *Journal of Marketing*, 33 (July), 35-39.

Wilson, Aubrey (1969), "Industrial Marketing Research in Britain," *Journal of Marketing* Research, 6 (February), 15-28.

Wind, Yoram (1981), *Product Policy: Concepts, Methods, and Strategy,* Reading, MA: Addison-Wesley.

Yelle, Louis E. (1979), "The Learning Curve: Historical Review and Comprehensive Survey," *Decision Sciences*, 10, 302-328.

Zaltman, Gerald and Ronald Stiff (1972), "Theories of Diffusion," in *Consumer Behavior: Theoretical Sources*, Scott Ward and Thomas S. Robertson, eds. Englewood Cliffs, NJ: Prentice-Hall.

George S. Day

Diagnosing the Product Portfolio

How to use scarce cash and managerial resources for maximum long-run gains

THE product portfolio approach to marketing strategy formulation has gained wide acceptance among managers of diversified companies. They are first attracted by the intuitively appealing concept that long-run corporate performance is more than the sum of the contributions of individual profit centers or product strategies. Secondly a product portfolio analysis suggests specific marketing strategies to achieve a balanced mix of products that will produce the maximum long-run effects from scarce cash and managerial resources. Lastly the concept employs a simple matrix representation which is easy to communicate and comprehend. Thus it is a useful tool in a headquarters campaign to demonstrate that the strategic issues facing the firm justify more centralized control over the planning and resource allocation process.

With the growing acceptance of the basic approach has come an increasing sensitivity to the limitations of the present methods of portraying the product portfolio, and a recognition that the approach is not equally useful in all corporate circumstances. Indeed, the implications can sometimes be grossly misleading. Inappropriate and misleading applications will result when:

- The basic **assumptions** (especially those concerned with the value of market share dominance and the product life cycle) are violated.

- The **measurements** are wrong, or

- The **strategies** are not feasible.

This article identifies the critical assumptions and the measurement and application issues that may distort the strategic insights. A series of questions are posed that will aid planners and decision-makers to better understand this aid to strategic thinking, and thereby make better decisions.

What Is the Product Portfolio?

Common to all portrayals of the product portfolio is the recognition that the competitive value of market share depends on the structure of competition and the stage of the product life cycle. Two examples of this approach have recently appeared in this journal.[1] However, the earliest, and most widely implemented is the cash quadrant or share/growth matrix developed by the Boston Consulting Group.[2] Each product is classified jointly by rate of present or forecast **market growth** (a proxy for stage in the product life cycle) and a measure of **market share dominance.**

The arguments for the use of market share are familiar and well documented.[3] Their basis is the cumulation of evidence that market share is strongly and positively correlated with product profitability. This theme is varied somewhat in the BCG approach by the emphasis on relative share—measured by the ratio of the company's share of the market to the share of the largest competitor. This is reasonable since the strategic implications of a 20% share are quite different if the largest competitor's is 40% or if it is 5%. Profitability will also vary, since according to the experience curve concept the largest competitor will be the most profitable at the prevailing price level.[4]

The product life cycle is employed because it highlights the desirability of a variety of products or services with different present and prospective growth rates. More important, the concept has some direct implications for the cost of gaining and/or holding market share:

- During the **rapid growth stage,** purchase patterns and distribution channels are fluid. Market shares can be increased at "relatively" low cost by capturing a disproportionate share of incremental sales (especially where these sales come from new users of applications rather than heavier usage by existing users).

- By contrast, the key-note during the **maturity stage** **swings** to stability and inertia in distribution and purchasing relationships. A substantial growth in share by one competitor will come at the expense of another competi-

About the author. George S. Day is Professor of Marketing, University of Toronto.

EXHIBIT 1
The Cash Quadrant Approach to Describing the Product Portfolio•

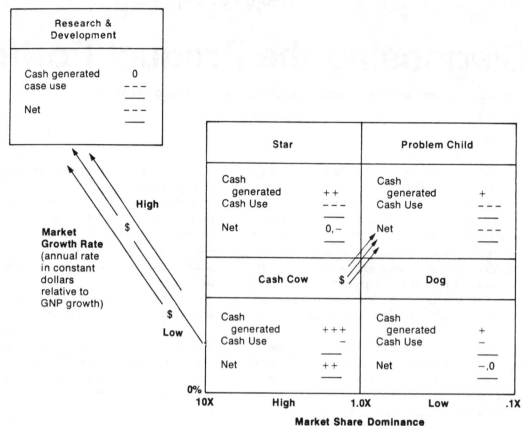

Market Share Dominance
(Ratio of company share to share of largest competitor)

tor's capacity utilization, and will be resisted vigorously. As a result, gains in share are both time-consuming and costly (unless accompanied by a breakthrough in product value or performance that cannot be easily matched by competition).

Product Portfolio Strategies

When the share and growth rate of each of the products sold by a firm are jointly considered, a new basis for strategy evaluation emerges. While there are many possible combinations, an arbitrary classification of products into four share/growth categories (as shown in Exhibit 1) is sufficient to illustrate the strategy implications.

Low Growth/Dominant Share
(Cash Cows)

These profitable products usually generate more cash than is required to maintain share. All strategies should be directed toward maintaining market dominance—including

investments in technological leadership. Pricing decisions should be made cautiously with an eye to maintaining price leadership. Pressure to over-invest through product proliferation and market expansion should be resisted unless prospects for expanding primary demand are unusually attractive. Instead, excess cash should be used to support research activities and growth areas elsewhere in the company.

High Growth/Dominant Share
(Stars)

Products that are market leaders, but also growing fast, will have substantial reported profits but need a lot of cash to finance the rate of growth. The appropriate strategies are designed primarily to protect the existing share level by reinvesting earnings in the form of price reductions, product improvement, better market coverage, production efficiency increases, etc. Particular attention must be given to obtaining a large share of the new users or new applications that are the source of growth in the market.

Low Growth/Subordinate Share (Dogs)

Since there usually can be only one market leader and because most markets are mature, the greatest number of products fall in this category. Such products are usually at a cost disadvantage and have few opportunities for growth at a reasonable cost. Their markets are not growing, so there is little new business to compete for, and market share gains will be resisted strenuously by the dominant competition.

The slower the growth (present or prospective) and the smaller the relative share, the greater the need for positive action. The possibilities include:

1. Focusing on a specialized segment of the market that can be dominated, and protected from competitive inroads.
2. Harvesting, which is a conscious cutback of all support costs to some minimum level which will maximize the cash flow over a foreseeable lifetime—which is usually short.
3. Divestment, usually involving a sale as a going concern.
4. Abandonment or deletion from the product line.

High Growth/Subordinate Share (Problem Children)

The combination of rapid growth and poor profit margins creates an enormous demand for cash. If the cash is not forthcoming, the product will become a "Dog" as growth inevitably slows. The basic strategy options are fairly clear-cut; either invest heavily to get a disproportionate share of the new sales or buy existing shares by acquiring competitors and thus move the product toward the "Star" category or get out of the business using some of the methods just described.

Consideration also should be given to a market segmentation strategy, but only if a defensible niche can be identified and resources are available to gain dominance. This strategy is even more attractive if the segment can provide an entree and experience based from which to push for dominance of the whole market.

Overall Strategy

The long-run health of the corporation depends on having some products that *generate* cash (and provide acceptable reported profits), and others that *use* cash to support growth. Among the indicators of overall health are the size and vulnerability of the "Cash Cows" (and the prospects for the "Stars," if any), and the number of "Problem Children" and "Dogs." Particular attention must be paid to those products with large cash appetites. Unless the company has abundant cash flow, it cannot afford to sponsor many such products at one time. If resources (including debt capacity) are spread too thin, the company simply will wind up with too many marginal products and suffer a reduced capacity to finance promising new product entries or acquisitions in the future.

The share/growth matrix displayed in Exhibit 2, shows how one company (actually a composite of a number of situations) might follow the strategic implications of the product portfolio to achieve a better balance of sources and uses of cash. The *present* position of each product is defined by the relative share and market growth rate during a representative time *period*. Since business results normally fluctuate, it is important to use a time period that is not distorted by rare events. The *future* position may be either (a) a momentum forecast of the results of continuing the present strategy, or (b) a forecast of the consequences of a change in strategy. It is desirable to do both, and compare the results. The specific display of Exhibit 2 is a summary of the following strategic decisions.

- Aggressively **support** the newly introduced product A, to ensure dominance (but anticipate share declines due to new competitive entries).
- Continue present strategies of products B and C to ensure **maintenance** of market share.
- Gain share of market for product D by investing in **acquisitions.**
- Narrow and modify the range of models of product E to **focus** on one segment.
- **Divest** products F and G.

Pitfalls in the Assumptions

The starting point in the decision to follow the implications of a product portfolio analysis is to ask whether the underlying assumptions make sense. The most fundamental assumptions relate to the role of market share in the businesses being portrayed in the portfolio. Even if the answers here are affirmative one may choose to not follow the implications if other objectives than balancing cash flows take priority, or there are barriers to implementing the indicated strategies.

What Is the Role of Market Share?

All the competitors are assumed to have the same overhead structures and experience curves, with their position on the experience curve corresponding to their market share position. Hence market share dominance is a proxy for the *relative* profit performance (e.g., GM vs. Chrysler). Other factors beyond market share may be influential in dictating absolute, *profit performance (e.g., calculators versus cosmetics).*

The influence of market share is most apparent with high value-added products, where there are significant barriers to entry and the competition consists of a few, large, diversified corporations with the attendant large overheads (e.g., plastics, major appliances, automobiles, and semi-conductors). But even in these industrial environments there are distortions under conditions such as:

EXHIBIT 2
Balancing the Product Portfolio

(Diameter of circle is proportional to products contribution to total company sales volume)

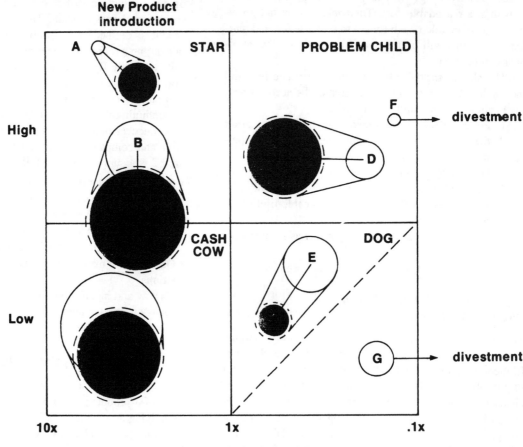

Forecast position of product — **Present position**

• One competitor has a significant technological advantage which can be protected and used to establish a steeper cost reduction/experience curve.

• The principal component of the product is produced by a supplier who has an inherent cost advantage because of an integrated process. Thus Dupont was at a cost disadvantage with Cyclohexane vis-a-vis the oil companies because the manufacture of the product was so highly integrated with the operations of an oil refinery.[5]

• Competitors can economically gain large amounts of experience through acquisitions or licensing, or shift to a

lower (but parallel) cost curve by resorting to off-shore production or component sourcing.

• Profitability is highly sensitive to the rate of capacity utilization, regardless of size of plant.

There are many situations where the positive profitability and share relationship becomes very tenuous, and perhaps unattainable. A recent illustration is the building industry where large corporations—CNA with Larwin and ITT with Levitt—have suffered because of their inability to adequately offset their high overhead charges with a corresponding reduction in total costs.[6] Similar problems are also encountered in the service sector, and contribute to the many reasons why services which are highly labor-intensive and involve personal relationships must be approached with extreme caution in a product portfolio analysis.[7]

There is specific evidence from the Profit Impact of Market Strategies (PIMS) study[8] that the value of market share is not as significant for consumer goods as for industrial products. The reasons are not well understood, but probably reflect differences in buying behavior, the importance of product differentiation and the tendency for proliferation of marginally different brands in these categories. The strategy of protecting a market position by introducing line extensions, flankers, and spin-offs from a successful core brand means that product class boundaries are very unclear. Hence shares are harder to estimate. The individual brand in a category like deodorants or powdered drinks may not be the proper basis for evaluation. A related consequence is that joint costing problems multiply. For example, Unilever in the U.K. has 20 detergent brands all sharing production facilities and marketing resources to some degree.

When Do Market Shares Stabilize?

The operating assumption is that shares tend toward stability during the maturity stage, as the dominant competitors concentrate on defending their existing position. An important corollary is that gains in share are easier and cheaper to achieve during the growth stage.

There is scattered empirical evidence, including the results of the PIMS project, which supports these assumptions. Several qualifications must be made before the implications can be pursued in depth:

- While market share *gains* may be costly, it is possible to mismanage a dominant position. The examples of A&P in food retailing, and British Leyland in the U.K. automobile market provide new benchmarks on the extent to which strong positions can erode unless vigorously defended.

- When the two largest competitors are of roughly equal size, the share positions may continue to be fluid until one is finally dominant.

- There are certain product categories, frequently high technology oriented, where a dominant full line/full service competitor is vulnerable if there are customer segments which do not require all the services, technical assistance, etc., that are provided. As markets mature this "sophisticated" segment usually grows. Thus, Digital Equipment Corp. has prospered in competition with IBM by simply selling basic hardware and depending on others to do the applications programming.[9] By contrast, IBM provides, for a price, a great deal of service backup and software for customers who are not self-sufficient. The dilemma for the dominant producer lies in the difficulty of serving both segments simultaneously.[10]

What Is the Objective of a Product Portfolio Strategy?

The strategies emerging from a product portfolio analysis emphasize the balance of cash flows, by ensuring that there are products that use cash to sustain growth and others that supply cash.

Yet corporate objectives have many more dimensions that require considerations. This point was recognized by Seymour Tilles in one of the earliest discussions of the portfolio approach.[11] It is worth repeating to avoid a possible myopic focus on cash flow considerations. Tilles' point was that an investor pursues a balanced combination of risk, income, and growth when acquiring a portfolio of securities. He further argued that "the same basic concepts apply equally well to product planning." The problem with concentrating on cash flow to maximize income and growth is that strategies to balance risks are not explicitly considered.

What must be avoided is excessive exposure to a specific threat from one of the following areas of vulnerability:

- The economy (e.g., business downturns).

- Social, political, environmental pressures.

- Supply continuity.

- Technological change.

- Unions and related human factors.

It also follows that a firm should direct its new product search activities into several different opportunity areas, to avoid intensifying the degree of vulnerability. Thus, many companies in the power equipment market, such as Brown Boveri, are in a quandry over whether to meet the enormous resource demands of the nuclear power equipment market, because of the degree of vulnerability of this business compared to other possibilities such as household appliances.

The desire to reduce vulnerability is a possible reason for keeping, or even acquiring, a "Dog." Thus, firms may integrate backward to assure supply of highly leveraged materials.[12] If a "Dog" has a high percentage of captive business, it may not even belong as a separate entity in a portfolio analysis.

A similar argument could be used for products which have been acquired for intelligence reasons. For example, a large Italian knitwear manufacturer owns a high-fashion dress company selling only to boutiques to help follow and interpret fashion trends. Similarly, because of the complex nature of the distribution of lumber products, some suppliers have acquired lumber retailers to help learn about patterns of demand and changing end-user requirements. In both these cases the products/businesses were acquired for reasons outside the logic of the product portfolio, and should properly be excluded from the analysis.

Can the Strategies Be Implemented?

Not only does a product portfolio analysis provide insights into the long-run health of a company; it also implies the basic strategies that will strengthen the portfolio. Unfortunately, there are many situations where the risks of failure of these strategies are unacceptably high. Several of these risks were identified in a recent analysis of the dangers in the pursuit of market share.[13]

One danger is that the company's financial resources will not be adequate. The resulting problems are enormously compounded should the company find itself in a vulnerable financial position if the fight were stopped short for some reason. The fundamental question underlying such dangers is the likelihood that competitors will pursue the same strategy, because they follow the same logic in identifying and pursuing opportunities. As a result, there is a growing premium on the understanding of competitive responses, and especially the degree to which they will be discouraged by aggressive action.

An increasingly important question is whether government regulations will permit the corporation to follow the strategy it has chosen. Antitrust regulations—especially in the U.S.—now virtually preclude acquisitions undertaken by large companies in related areas. Thus the effort by ITT to acquire a "Cash Cow" in Hartford Fire and Indemnity Insurance was nearly aborted by a consent decree, and other moves by ITT into Avis, Canteen Corp., and Levitt have been divested by court order at enormous cost. Recent governmental actions—notably the *ReaLemon* case—may even make it desirable for companies with very large absolute market share to consider reducing that share.[14]

There is less recognition as yet that government involvement can cut both ways; making it difficult to get *in or out of a business.* Thus, because of national security considerations large defense contractors would have a difficult time exiting from the aerospace or defense businesses. The problems are most acute in countries like Britain and Italy where intervention policies include price controls, regional development directives and employment maintenance which may prevent the replacement of out-moded plants. Unions in these two countries are sometimes so dedicated to protecting the employment status quo that a manager may not even move employees from one product line to another without risking strike activity.

The last implementation question concerns the viability of a niche strategy, which appears at the outset to be an attractive way of coping with both "Dogs" and "Problem Children." The fundamental problem, of course, is whether a product or market niche can be isolated and protected against competitive inroads. But even if this can be achieved in the long-run, the strategy may not be attractive. The difficulties are most often encountered when a full or extensive product line is needed to support sales, service and distribution facilities. One specialized product may simply not generate sufficient volume and gross mar-

gin to cover the minimum costs of participation in the market. This is very clearly an issue in the construction equipment business because of the importance of assured service.

Pitfalls in the Measures

The "Achilles' Heel" of a product portfolio analysis is the units of measure; for if the share of market and growth estimates are dubious, so are the interpretations. Skeptics recognize this quickly, and can rapidly confuse the analysis by attacking the meaningfulness and accuracy of these measures and offering alternative definitions. With the present state of the measurements there is often no adequate defense.

What Share of What Market?

This is not one, but several questions. Each is controversial because they influence the bases for resource allocation and evaluation within the firm:

- Should the definition of the product-market be broad (reflecting the generic need) or narrow?
- How much market segmentation?
- Should the focus be on the total product-market or a portion served by the company?
- Which level of geography: local versus national versus regio-centric markets?

The answers to these questions are complicated by the lack of defensible procedures for identifying product-market boundaries. For example, four-digit SIC categories are convenient and geographically available but may have little relevance to consumer perceptions of substitutability which will influence the long-run performance of the product. Furthermore, there is the pace of product development activity which is dedicated to combining, extending, or otherwise obscuring the boundaries.

Breadth of Product-Market Definition? This is a pivotal question. Consider the following extremes in definitions:

- Intermediate builder chemicals for the detergent industry *or* Sodium Tri-polyphosphate.
- Time/information display devices *or* medium-priced digital-display alarm clocks.
- Main meal accompaniments *or* jellied cranberry.

Narrow definitions satisfy the short-run, tactical concerns of sales and product managers. Broader views, reflecting longer-run, strategic planning concerns, invariably reveal a larger market to account for (a) sales to untapped but potential markets, (b) changes in technology, price relationships, and supply which broaden the array of potential substitute products, and (c) the time required by present and prospective buyers to react to these changes.

Extent of Segmentation? In other words, when does it become meaningful to divide the total market into subgroups for the purpose of estimating shares? In the tire industry it is evident that the OEM and replacement markets are so dissimilar in behavior as to dictate totally different marketing mixes. But how much further should segmentation be pushed? The fact that a company has a large share of the high-income buyers of replacement tires is probably not strategically relevant.

In general the degree of segmentation for a portfolio analysis should be limited to grouping those buyers that share situational or behavioral characteristics that are strategically relevant. This means that different marketing mixes must be used to serve the segments that have been identified, which will be reflected in different cost and price structures. Other manifestations of a strategically important segment boundary would be a discontinuity in growth rates, share patterns, distribution patterns and so forth when going from one segment to another.

These judgments are particularly hard to make for geographic boundaries. For example, what is meaningful for a manufacturer of industrial equipment facing dominant local competition in each of the national markets in the European Economic Community? Because the company is in each market, it has a 5% share of the total EEC market, while the largest regional competitor has 9%. In this case the choice of a regional rather than national market definition was dictated by the *trend* to similarity of product requirements throughout the EEC and the consequent feasibility of a single manufacturing facility to serve several countries.

The tendency for trade barriers to decline for countries within significant economic groupings will increasingly dictate regio-centric rather than nationally oriented boundaries. This, of course, will not happen where transportation costs or government efforts to protect sensitive industry categories (such as electric power generation equipment), by requiring local vendors, creates other kinds of barriers.

Market Served versus Total Market?

Firms may elect to serve only just a part of the available market; such as retailers with central buying offices or utilities of a certain size. The share of the market served is an appropriate basis for tactical decisions. This share estimate may also be relevant for strategic decisions, especially if the market served corresponds to a distinct segment boundary. There is a risk that focusing only on the market served may mean overlooking a significant opportunity or competitive threat emerging from the unserved portion of the market. For example, a company serving the blank cassette tape market only through speciality audio outlets is vulnerable if buyers perceive that similar quality cassettes can be bought in general merchandise and discount outlets.

Another facet of the served market issue is the treatment of customers who have integrated backward and now satisfy their own needs from their own resources.

Whether or not the captive volume is included in the estimate of total market size depends on how readily this captive volume can be displaced by outside suppliers. Recent analysis suggests that captive production—or infeeding—is "remarkably resilient to attack by outside suppliers."[15]

What Can Be Done?

The value of a strategically relevant product-market definition lies in "stretching" the company's perceptions appropriately—far enough so that significant threats and opportunities are not missed, but not so far as to dissipate information gathering and analysis efforts on "long shots." This is a difficult balance to achieve, given the myriads of possibilities. The best procedure for coping is to employ several alternative definitions, varying specificity of product and market segments. There will inevitably be both points of contradiction and consistency in the insights gained from portfolios constructed at one level versus another. The process of resolution can be very revealing, both in terms of understanding the competitive position and suggesting strategy alternatives.[16]

Market Growth Rate

The product life cycle is justifiably regarded as one of the most difficult marketing concepts to measure—or forecast.

There is a strong tendency in a portfolio analysis to judge that a product is maturing when there is a forecast of a decline in growth rate below some specified cut-off. One difficulty is that the same cut-off level does not apply equally to all products or economic climates. As slow growth or level GNP becomes the reality, high absolute growth rates become harder to achieve for all products, mature or otherwise. Products with lengthy introductory periods, facing substantial barriers to adoption, may never exhibit high growth rates, but may have an extended maturity stage. Other products may exhibit precisely the opposite life cycle pattern.

The focus in the product portfolio analysis should be on the long-run growth rate forecast. This becomes especially important with products which are sensitive to the business cycle, such as machine tools, or have potential substitutes with fluctuating prices. Thus the future growth of engineered plastics is entwined with the price of zinc, aluminum, copper and steel; the sales of powdered breakfast beverages depends on the relative price of frozen orange juice concentrate.

These two examples also illustrate the problem of the self-fulfilling prophecy. A premature classification as a mature product may lead to the reduction of marketing resources to the level necessary to defend the share in order to maximize net cash flow. But if the product class sales are sensitive to market development activity (as in the case of engineered plastics) or advertising expenditures (as is the case with powdered breakfast drinks) and these budgets are reduced by the dominant firms then, indeed, the product growth rate will slow down.

The growth rate is strongly influenced by the choice of product-market boundaries. A broad product type (cigarettes) will usually have a longer maturity stage than a more specific product form (plain filter cigarettes). In theory, the growth of the individual brand is irrelevant. Yet, it cannot be ignored that the attractiveness of a growth market, however defined, will be diminished by the entry of new competitors with the typical depressing effect on the sales, prices and profits of the established firms. The extent of the reappraisal of the market will depend on the number, resources, and commitment of the new entrants. Are they likely to become what is known in the audio electronics industry as ''rabbits,'' which come racing into the market, litter it up, and die off quickly?

Pitfalls from Unanticipated Consequences

Managers are very effective at tailoring their behavior to the evaluation system, *as they perceive it.* Whenever market share is used to evaluate performance, there is a tendency for managers to manipulate the product-market boundaries to show a static or increasing share. The greater the degree of ambiguity or compromise in the definition of the boundaries the more tempting these adjustments become. The risk is that the resulting narrow view of the market may mean overlooking threats from substitutes or the opportunities within emerging market segments.

These problems are compounded when share dominance is also perceived to be an important determinant of the allocation of resources and top management interest. The manager who doesn't like the implications of being associated with a ''Dog,'' may try to redefine the market so he can point to a larger market share or a higher than average growth rate. Regardless of his success with the attempted redefinition, his awareness of how the business is regarded in the overall portfolio will ultimately affect his morale. Then his energies may turn to seeking a transfer or looking for another job, and perhaps another prophecy has been fulfilled.

The forecast of market growth rate is also likely to be manipulated, especially if the preferred route to advancement and needed additional resources is perceived to depend on association with a product that is classified as ''Star.'' This may lead to wishful thinking about the future growth prospects of the product. Unfortunately the quality of the review procedures in most planning processes is not robust enough to challenge such distortions. Further dysfunctional consequences will result if ambitious managers of ''Cash Cows'' actually attempt to expand their products through unnecessary product proliferation and market segmentation without regard to the

impact on profits.

The potential for dysfunctional consequences does not mean that profit center managers and their employees should not be aware of the basis for resource allocation decisions within the firm. A strong argument can be made to the effect that it is worse for managers to observe those decisions and suspect the worst. What will surely create problems is to have an inappropriate reward system. A formula-based system, relying on achievement of a target for return on investment or an index of profit measures, that does not recognize the differences in potential among business, will lead to short-run actions that conflict with the basic strategies that should be pursued.

Alternative Views of the Portfolio

This analysis of the share/growth matrix portrayal of the product portfolio supports Bowman's contention that much of what now exists in the field of corporate or marketing strategy can be thought of as contingency theories. ''The ideas, recommendations, or generalizations are rather dependent (contingent) for their truth and their relevance on the specific situational factors.''[17] This means that in any specific analysis of the product portfolio there may be a number of factors beyond share and market growth with a much greater bearing on the attractiveness of a product-market or business; including:
• The contribution rate.
• Barriers to entry.
• Cyclicality of sales.
• The rate of capacity utilization.
• Sensitivity of sales to change in prices, promotional activities, service levels, etc.
• The extent of ''captive'' business.
• The nature of technology (maturity, volatility, and complexity).
• Availability of production and process opportunities.
• Social, legal, governmental, and union pressures and opportunities.

Since these factors are situational, each company (or division) must develop its own ranking of their importance in determining attractiveness.[18] In practice these factors tend to be qualitatively combined into overall judgments of the attractiveness of the industry or market, and the company's position in that market. The resulting matrix for displaying the positions of each product is called a ''nine-block'' diagram or decision matrix[19]

Although the implications of this version of the product portfolio are not as clear-cut, it does overcome many of the shortcomings of the share/growth matrix approach. Indeed the two approaches will likely yield different insights. But as the main purpose of the product portfolio analysis is to help guide—but not substitute for—strategic thinking, the process of reconciliation is useful in itself. Thus it is desirable to employ both approaches and compare results.

Summary

The product portfolio concept provides a useful synthesis of the analyses and judgments during the preliminary steps of the planning process, and is a provocative source of strategy alternatives. If nothing else, it demonstrates the fallacy of treating all businesses or profit centers as alike, and all capital investment decisions as independent and additive events.

There are a number of pitfalls to be avoided to ensure the implications are not misleading. This is especially true for the cash quadrant or share/growth matrix approach to portraying the portfolio. In many situations the basic assumptions are not satisfied. Further complications stem from uncertainties in the definitions of product-markets and the extent and timing of competitive actions. One final pitfall is the unanticipated consequences of adopting a portfolio approach. These may or may not be undesirable depending on whether they are recognized at the outset.

Despite the potential pitfalls it is important to not lose sight of the concept; that is, to base strategies on the perception of a company as an interdependent group of products and services, each playing a distinctive and supportive role.

REFERENCES

1. Bernard Catry and Michel Chevalier, "Market Share Strategy and the Product Life Cycle," *Journal of Marketing*, Vol. 38 No. 4 (October 1974), pp. 29-34; and Yoram Wind and Henry J. Claycamp, "Planning Product Line Strategy: A Matrix Approach," *Journal of Marketing*, Vol. 40 No. 1 (January 1976), pp. 2-9.

2. Described in the following pamphlets in the *Perspective* series, authored by Bruce D. Henderson, "The Product Portfolio" (1970), "Cash Traps" (1972) and "The Experience Curve Reviewed: The Growth-Share Matrix or the Product Portfolio." (Boston Consulting Group 1973). By 1972 the approach had been employed in more than 100 companies. See "Mead's Technique to Sort Out the Losers," *Business Week* (March 11, 1972), pp. 124-30.

3. Sidney Schoeffler, Robert D. Buzzell and Donald F. Heany, "Impact of Strategic Planning on Profit Performance," *Harvard Business Review* Vol. 52 (March-April 1974),pp. 137-45; and Robert D. Buzzell, Bradley T. Gale and Ralph G. M. Sultan, "Market Share—A Key to Profitability," *Harvard Business Review*, Vol. 53 (January-February 1975), pp. 97-106.

4. Boston Consulting Group, *Perspectives on Experience* (Boston: 1968 and 1970), and "Selling Business a Theory of Economics," *Business Week*, September 8,1974, pg. 43-44.

5. Robert B. Stobaugh and Philip L. Towsend, "Price Forecasting and Strategic Planning: The Case of Petrochemicals," *Journal of Marketing Research*, Vol. XII (February 1975), pp. 19-29.

6. Carol J. Loomis, "The Further Misadventures of Harold Geneen," *Fortune*, June 1975.

7. There is incomplete but provocative evidence of significant share-profit relationships in the markets for auto rental, consumer finance, and retail securities brokerage.

8. Same as reference 3 above.

9. "A Minicomputer Tempest," *Business Week*, January 27, 1975, pp. 79-80.

10. Some argue that the dilemma is very general, confronting all pioneering companies in mature markets. See Seymour Tilles, "Segmentation and Strategy," *Perspectives* (Boston: Boston Consulting Group, 1974).

11. Seymour Tilles, "Strategies for Allocating Funds," *Harvard Business Review*, Vol. 44 (January-February 1966), pp. 72-80.

12. This argument is compelling when $20,000 of Styrene Monomer can affect the production of $10,000,000 worth of formed polyester fiberglass parts.

13. William E. Fruhan, "Pyrrhic Victories in Fights for Market Share," *Harvard Business Review*, Vol. 50 (September-October 1972), pp. 100-107.

14. See Paul N. Bloom and Philip Kotler, "Strategies for High Market-Share Companies," *Harvard Business Review*, Vol. 53 (November-December 1975), pp. 63-72.

15. Aubrey Wilson and Bryan Atkin, "Exorcising the Ghosts in Marketing," *Harvard Business Review*, Vol. 54 (September-October 1976), pp. 117-27. See also, Ralph D. Kerkendall, "Customers as Competitors," *Perspectives* (Boston: Boston Consulting Group, 1975).

16. George S. Day and Allan D. Shocker, *Identifying Competitive Product-Market Boundaries: Strategic and Analytical Issues* (Boston: Marketing Science Institute, 1976).

17. Edward H. Bowman, "Epistemology, Corporate Strategy, and Academe," *Sloan Management Review* (Winter 1974), pp. 35-50.

18. The choice of factors and assessment of ranks is an important aspect of the design of a planning system. These issues are described in Peter Lorange, "Divisional Planning: Setting Effective Direction," *Sloan Management Review* (Fall 1975), pp. 77-91.

19. William E. Rothschild, *Putting It All Together: A Guide to Strategic Thinking* (New York: AMACOM, 1976).

James H. Myers

Benefit Structure Analysis: A New Tool for Product Planning

THE 1960's saw the introduction of several technologies/models/processes for providing *structure* for consumer markets. Most of these involved the application of multivariate statistical techniques to problems of product positioning, market segmentation, the new product development process, and determining the order and structure underlying sets of marketing variables. A recent article by Green reviews and critiques many of these efforts.[1]

This article presents another approach to structuring consumer markets: Benefit Structure Analysis. It differs from other methods in several important respects:

1. It was developed especially for finding new product opportunities in very broad product/service categories, such as entirely new types of food or beverages, new forms of banking services (e.g., the bank credit card), or new multi-purpose tools for home repair or redecoration.
2. It determines consumer reactions to a large number (75-100) of relatively specific *benefits* desired from a type of product/service and to many (50-75) *features* or *physical characteristics* of the product/service.
3. These reactions are in terms of both desire for and perceived *deficiencies* in each benefit and characteristic.
4. The technique also provides relatively complete information as to ambient conditions surrounding the use of the product (time of day, other persons present, use or task, etc.).

A benefit structure study also provides a complete cross-sectional view of current usage patterns (i.e., what products/services are now used for each purpose or objective) within the broad product/service category selected.

About the author. James H. Myers is DeBell professor of business administration in the School of Business Administration of UCLA.

For most products/services this information is not available elsewhere, yet it can be obtained easily from data collected for a Benefit Structure Analysis study.

To illustrate this technique a study of household cleaning products is presented. This study is hypothetical, but the data shown are actual results from a composite of three separate commercial studies conducted by the author in broad product areas involving foods, beverages, and recreational vehicles.

Benefit Structure Study for Household Cleaning Products

Household cleaning products were defined as any product used to clean surfaces within the home other than rugs, drapes, furniture, or to be used for dusting. Examples of products used for these purposes are *Ajax, Lysol, 409, Ammonia, Glo Coat, Windex, etc.*

Qualitative Phase

The study began with 25-50 in-depth interviews (for some studies focus groups would work as well). The interviewer asks the respondent to recall all occasions when she cleaned any interior surfaces during the day prior to the interview. For each of these occasions she is asked:

1. *What was the cleaning chore?* (e.g., sink, floor, walls, bathtub, toilet bowl, shower stall, appliances; cabinet facings)
2. *What product(s) were used in this operation?* (type and brand)
3. *What benefits were sought, or what were the objectives of this cleaning?* (see Exhibit 1 for examples of benefits)
4. *What were the physical characteristics or attributes of the product(s) used?* (see Exhibit 1 for examples of product characteristics)
5. *What applicator (if any) was used?* (e.g., mop, brush, sponge, rag)

EXHIBIT 1

EXAMPLES OF BENEFITS

Bleaches	Chrome Sparkles
Removes stains	Doesn't dull
Removes grease	Doesn't hurt hands
Removes built-up dirt	Dissolves grease
Cleans tub ring	Doesn't remove gloss from paint
Less elbow grease	Boosts detergents
Can see it work	Strips wax
Cleans cracks (grout) better	Less build-up
Doesn't leave residue	Lets color come through
No rinsing necessary	Stands up to damp mopping
Doesn't damage surfaces	Seals porous floors
Kills mildew	Doesn't yellow
Disinfects	No streaking
Removes discoloration	Does two jobs at once
Removes soap scum	Leaves it "squeaky clean"

EXAMPLES OF PRODUCT CHARACTERISTICS

Strong smell	Biodegradable
Abrasive/scratchy	Concentrated
Thin liquid	Self-polishing
Low suds	Can spray on
Quick drying	Attractive color
Can wipe on	Contains deodorant
Dark color	Economical
Caustic	Pine smell
Contains wax	Perfumed smell
Contains ammonia	Lemon smell
Thick liquid	Stains
Light color	Little odor
Contains antiseptic	No deterioration when stored

---

6. *What time of day was the work done; were other family members involved, etc.?*

In this study it was also necessary to ask about other cleaning tasks done during the past week. Since many items are cleaned only on an infrequent basis by housekeepers (e.g., windows, appliances, broiler pans, etc.), they might be missed in a discussion of cleaning chores undertaken only the day before. In studies of food or beverage products consumed frequently, it is usually not necessary to go back beyond the previous day.

It may even be possible to omit the qualitative phase of the study entirely if a company already has extensive information about the product/service area from previous research.

The various cleaning occasions, products, benefits, attributes, etc. derived from the interviews were used to design a large scale study to determine the structural relationships among these elements in quantitative terms.

Quantitative Phase—Methodology

The quantitative phase of the study determined the degree to which each benefit and each product characteristic was *desired* by the consumer for each usage (cleaning occasion) and *the extent to which they were or were not being received.*

A nation-wide survey of 500 housekeepers was conducted in 12 metropolitan areas. The home interview began by questioning the woman about all the cleaning occasions she encountered during the previous day. Going through the entire day, she told what cleaning chores she did and what products were used for each occasion.

The interviewer then selected a single cleaning occasion from all that were mentioned by the respondent, using a rotational sampling pattern. This one occasion became the focus of a much more intensive probe about product(s) used, benefits/characteristics desired and received, etc. Note that this random cross-section of one cleaning oc-

EXHIBIT 2
MOST USEFUL LINKAGE ANALYSES

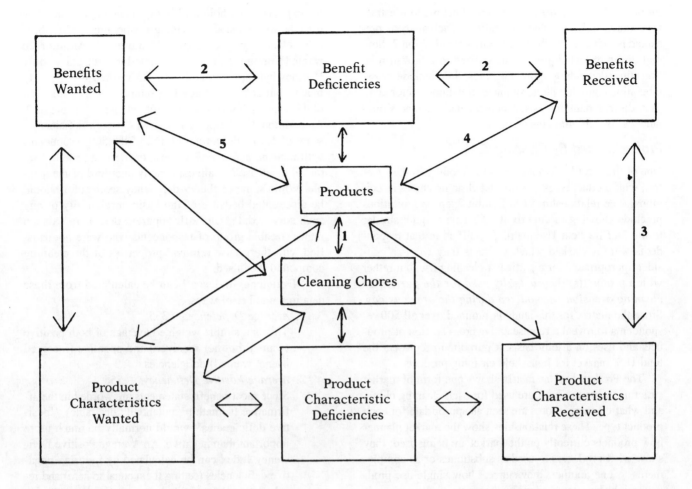

casion should represent all U.S. household cleaning occasions (within usual survey limitations) *in proportion to the frequency with which they occur.* (Care must be taken in survey timing, since patterns may differ over different days of the week and for the time of year —e.g. Spring cleaning.)

For this one occasion respondents were asked the degree to which each of the 75-100 benefits was received; then she was asked whether she *wanted* that benefit any more or any less than she actually got it. For these measurements a four-point scale was used: 4 = a whole lot, 3 = pretty much, 2 = somewhat, 1 = not at all. The verbal descriptors for this scale were selected based on a pre-test using the Thurstone Equal-Interval technique. For example, a respondent might report that when cleaning her linoleum floor yesterday, she wanted the benefit, "cleans without scrubbing," "a whole lot" (scale value = 4), but that she received it only "somewhat" (scale value = 2), resulting in a *benefit deficiency* of 4 minus 2, or 2.

Similarly, respondents were asked how much they wanted and how much they got of each of the 50-75 product characteristics. Finally, various types of supporting information were collected, such as: (1) what cleaning product(s) were used (if any) and brand; (2) applicator used; (3) at what time of day; (4) other persons present; (5) activities both before and after the cleaning process; (6) how often this item is normally cleaned.

The resulting data comprised a multi-dimensional matrix: *Benefits Wanted × Benefits Received × Product Characteristics Wanted × Product Characteristics Received × Cleaning Chores × Product(s) Used × Brands × Applicators Used × Various Supporting Data.* Each dimension had from perhaps five to as many as 100 categories. This n-dimensional matrix is called the *Complete Benefit Matrix.* It comprises the data bank for several simple and cross-tabulations, as well as for a wide variety of multivariate analyses. Only a few of the more useful types of analysis can be shown below; space limitations preclude showing the full spectrum of possible analytic approaches.

Primary Analytic Paradigm

All analyses were done on an aggregate basis, with responses pooled across all survey respondents or across some selected sub-group of respondents. Exhibit 2 shows schematically the principal types of analyses and relationships that are normally most useful for product planning purposes. Some of these are presented below, to illustrate procedures and suggested applications. Each analysis presented is indicated by the small numbers in Exhibit 2. Several different techniques can be utilized to establish relationships, depending upon objectives; they include cross-tabulations, graphic plots, simple correlations, factor analysis, discriminant analysis, canonical analysis, and simultaneous row-column clustering.

Products Used By Cleaning Task

One of the most basic analyses is the Product-by-Use matrix, with product types as rows and cleaning chores as columns. (See relationship #1 in Exhibit 2; space limitations preclude showing the matrix itself.) This is quite similar to the Stefflre Item-Use matrix;[2] it differs in that respondents were not asked which products they would "consider appropriate" for a particular cleaning use, but rather which product(s) they *actually used for the particular cleaning occasion encountered during the previous day.* Since the matrix for this study is summed over all 500 respondents to reveal a representative cross-section of products and uses on a joint basis, it purports to represent the total U.S. market for household cleaning products.

The Product-by-Use matrix shows one form of market structure: what products are used for each cleaning chore, and what cleaning chores are seen as appropriate for each product type. These relationships show the market planner how products currently on the market are being used; they show what products are used as substitutes or as complements to one another; they suggest how single-use products might be altered to make them into multi-use products; they reveal cleaning tasks where now only a single product is considered appropriate, so that competitive entries might be considered. Perhaps most important, they show the relative frequency of the various cleaning tasks; if "amount used" is requested, then volumetric analysis is also possible.

Benefits Wanted vs. Benefits Received

At the heart of a Benefit Structure Analysis study is an examination of how much each of the 75-100 benefits is *wanted* and *received.* This is done by summing the ratings across all respondents and across all cleaning occasions. Exhibit 3 shows a Benefit Deficiency matrix for one specific benefit: "Removes Grease." Marginal totals show the extent to which removing grease was both wanted and received by housewives, on the four-point scale (see relationship #2 in Exhibit 2).

Exhibit 3 shows that 196 of the 500 respondents said they wanted to remove grease "a whole lot"; 143 said "not at all"; frequencies for benefits received are similar (147 reported being able to remove grease "a whole lot" while 187 said "not at all"). However, simple comparisons of marginal frequencies obscure *the extent to which specific benefits are wanted but not received.*

For example, 34 respondents said they wanted to remove grease "a whole lot" but the cleaning product they used did so "not al all," yielding a rather impressive "benefit deficiency" score of 3 (4 minus 1). Another 26 wanted to remove grease "a whole lot" but did so only "somewhat" (4 minus 2 = 2); 23 wanted this "pretty much" but got it "not at all" (3 minus 1 = 2), for a total of 49 respondents with a "benefit deficiency" score of 2. An additional 79 respondents had a "benefit deficiency" score of 1, making a total of 162 of the 500 respondents with *some perceived deficiency* in the desired benefit, "removal of grease" —almost exactly one-third of the sample. While some of the 79 deficiency scores of 1 should be discounted because of the basic unreliability of any such survey data, it is still apparent that there exists a rather sizeable group of respondents who were not satisfied with the grease removal properties of the cleaning compound they used.

"Deficiency Indexes" can be calculated from these data in a number of ways:

1. *Average Deficiency:* .355
   This is a simple weighted average of both positive (wanted but not received) and negative (received by not wanted) deficiencies.

2. *Average Positive Deficiency:* .566
   Since most benefit statements are worded in the affirmative (something potentially desirable), "positive deficiencies" would normally be much more important than negative. An Average Positive Deficiency Index can be calculated by ignoring negative deficiencies (setting them equal to zero) and recalculating the weighted average deficiency, which more accurately reflects the extent to which housewives wanted a particular benefit but did not get it.

3. *Proportion With Deficiency:* .329
   The above weighted averages are useful in later plots but they do not communicate very meaningful information to management. The proportion of the sample with some specified deficiency (1 or more, 2 or more, etc.) is much clearer and is calculated easily.

4. *Average Negative Deficiency:* .231
   Setting all positive deficiencies equal to zero and calculating a weighted average negative deficiency yields the Average Negative Deficiency.

5. *Proportion With Negative Deficiency:* .150
   Proportion of all respondents having a negative deficiency of 1 or more (or 2 or more, if desired), indicating they got the benefit more than they wanted it.

Similar deficiencies can be calculated for each of the product characteristics; however, the situation here is quite different than for benefits. Since product characteristics are *neutral* (i.e., purely descriptive), whereas most benefits are *positive,* negative deficiency indexes for the former should be more important than the negatives in the case of benefits, since they reflect the extent to which a par-

EXHIBIT 3

BENEFIT DEFICIENCY MATRIX

Benefit #49: "Removes grease"

Received:	"Not at all"	"Somewhat"	"Pretty Much"	"A Whole Lot"	Marginal Sums	
					Wanted	Got
Wanted						
"A whole lot"	34	26	27	109	196	147
"Pretty much"	23	30	25	20	98	75
"Somewhat"	22	15	13	6	56	84
"Not at all"	108	13	10	12	143	187
TOTAL:	187	84	75	147		

Averages: Wanted: 2.70   Received 2.36

Want minus Received =	-3	-2	-1	0	1	2	3
No. of Respondents:	12	16	46	257	79	49	34

(Please note that these totals include different combinations of "Want minus Got").

---

ticular characteristic was received although not wanted (e.g., strong aroma, grittiness). A Product Characteristic Deficiency matrix may be prepared for each of the 50-75 characteristics using the same format as for benefits.

Plots of Benefits Wanted vs. Deficiencies

While the above information provides useful diagnostics for each benefit and product characteristic, it needs to be organized and summarized for the market planner. Plotting the *Average Wanted Benefit scores* (as columns) vs. *Average Deficiency scores* (as rows) for *each* benefit/ characteristic is a simple and very useful first step. Using benefits to illustrate several possible plots would be meaningful: Average Wanted Benefit score vs. Average Positive Deficiency score for each benefit; Average Wanted Benefit score vs. Proportion of Sample with Some Deficiency; Average Wanted Benefit score vs. Proportion Wanting the Benefit "pretty much" or "a whole lot" that felt some deficiency.

The plots enable rapid identification of "opportunity points" as a basis for focusing further diagnostic and planning efforts. Opportunity points are benefits/characteristics that are wanted but not received, or product characteristics that are received although not wanted. In the case of characteristics, the planner can instruct the development labs to add or remove certain product features (e.g., color, odor, antiseptic), assuming this is possible.

A single plot can portray the entire cleaning products market. But even more useful information may be gained from plots for *each* of the major product types as well as plots for *each* of the major cleaning uses. Such plots often show two or three products types (or uses) which are particularly vulnerable because they are not adequately meeting some needs that are highly desired or even moderately

desired. Carefully designed new product entries could be expected to compete effectively in these product areas *because they are specifically targeted at benefits which people say they want a great deal but are not getting now.*

This type of analysis was used for two clients in the food and beverage industry and clearly revealed the existence of such gaps for several major product types; for example, a "pick-me-up" beverage that failed to "pick up"; a type of sauce that was considered far too fattening and that stained clothing and table coverings.

Major Benefit and Deficiency Structure

The next analytic step is to construct a Benefit and Deficiency Structure graph for the household cleaning products market *on an aggregate basis.* This analysis shows that the primary benefits which people want from cleaning products can be grouped into seven major categories, labeled A through G, as shown in Exhibit 4. For example, Benefit Group A includes benefits that are similar in terms of removal of surface dust, dirt, film; Segment D includes the removal of heavy grease, wax, or stains; Segment F involves odor and aroma.

These benefit segments are produced by grouping together specific benefits that are perceived as similar across all respondents and all cleaning occasions. What is needed is a technique that simultaneously *groups* benefits and *weights* them in rank-order of frequency desired. If one or more benefits that are wanted "a great deal," are, in fact, "isolates" (i.e., are not perceived as similar to any other benefits) then the technique used must identify "isolates" as well as groupings. Presumably the desired technique would be sequential: extracting first the benefit or benefit cluster desired most, then the one desired next, and so on until all of the most important benefits are accounted for.

BENEFIT GROUPING		% of Sample Wanting Benefit Pretty Much or More	% of Sample Having Deficiency
A. Removes dust/ dirt/film		76%	32%
B. Removes porcelain stains		63	28%
C. Leaves no film/ residue/scratches		61	26%
D. Removes grease/ wax/stains		59	41%
E. Convenient to use/ store		58	34%
F. No unpleasant odor during/after use		54	62%
G. Gentle on hands/skin		35	56%

Unfortunately, no such technique appears to have been developed. The best that can be done is to judgmentally combine the information from a factor analysis of all 75-100 benefits (from "benefits wanted" ratings) plus the average "benefit wanted" *scores* for key "marker" benefits which most clearly define a cluster (i.e., have the highest factor loadings). These groupings can then be displayed in bar graph form, in rank-order of desired intensity. Deficiencies for each of these benefit structure dimensions may be developed and juxtaposed on the same graph.

Exhibit 4 shows at a glance the "benefit and deficiency structure" of the household cleaning products market. Note that it shows each benefit grouping separately; combinations of two or more desired benefit groupings that are wanted can be developed also. The exact same analysis should be done for product characteristics, to develop a market structure in comparable terms. Large desired benefit linkages with large deficiencies can be quickly spotted, as well as smaller desired benefit linkages with large deficiencies. The latter often signal *market segments* that offer real promise for some new product, or for the repositioning of some existing product. For example, analysis of these linkages showed that not many respondents wanted to remove grease/wax/stains with a product that had no unpleasant odor, but among those who

did, a sizeable proportion perceived that the products they were using were not delivering this combination of benefits.

Relationships of Benefits and Characteristics

Once it is determined what benefits and combinations of benefits are wanted, how are these benefits achieved? A Benefit Structure Analysis study shows *what types of product characteristics are seen by respondents as being most closely associated with any single benefit or any group of related benefits*. This provides a linkage between benefits and those product characteristics which produce the desired benefits (see relationship #3 in Exhibit 2).

While this can be done in several ways, the simplest is to correlate benefit received scores with product characteristics received scores, across all respondents and cleaning occasions. Since both are measured on the same four-point interval scale, the size of the correlation should be quite meaningful.

The sizes of the correlations are important. Seldom are any correlations in excess of .40 found. Most benefits show highest correlations in the .30 range. This makes the job of the new product planner more difficult, in that relationships are not high enough to clearly indicate which product characteristics should be used to produce a given benefit. Still, comparisons of those relating highest with those relating lowest usually indicate rather clear differences in the *general types* of product characteristics that are and are not perceived to be related to a particular benefit. If none of the relationships is high (perhaps .30 or more), it would suggest that the planner is free to use any product characteristics he chooses, since no specific characteristic is related strongly to the particular benefit under study, when viewed across *all* products and respondents.

Relationships of Benefits and Products

In a manner parallel to linking benefits with *product characteristics,* benefits can be linked to products to show what types of products are considered best at delivering each of the benefits. One useful approach is to rank-order all product categories in terms of their *average benefit received* scores for each benefit, with summation across all respondents who reported on a particular product. The resultant rankings have been found to be quite useful in indicating the general types of products that are most (and least) likely to produce a specific benefit (see relationship #4 in Exhibit 2).

Simultaneous Row/Column Linkages

Up to this point, all benefit linkages have been done one-at-a-time, and the resultant data are more diagnostic than structural. The same general types of information can be presented in a form that provides more over-all structure to the market at the same time that it allows specific diagnostic information although presented in a different format. This is done using a process that groups and displays two variables simultaneously.

The simultaneous row/column clustering algorithm used in Benefit Structure Analysis was developed by Dr. Edward W. Forgy[3] and named "LARC" (large row/column simultaneous clustering). Exhibit 5 shows the LARC analysis of cleaning tasks (columns) vs. benefits wanted (rows). Cleaning tasks that are seen as similar in terms of benefits desired are grouped together, and benefits that are seen as similar in terms of cleaning tasks are grouped. Heavy lines have been drawn arbitrarily around blocks of the largest numbers; these blocks show the most clearly-defined linkages between benefit groupings and cleaning task groupings. That is, lines show what groups of similar benefits are desired by housewives for a particular grouping of *similar* cleaning tasks, and vice versa.

It is important to note that LARC or any other similar process will not define *clusters* of rows or columns as clearly and accurately as will the various algorithms that have been designed solely for clustering, such as optimal partition clustering, heirarchical clustering, and even factor analysis. However, this weakness is compensated for by the ability of a LARC-type analysis to both group and display simultaneously the linkages between the two variables under study (see relationship #5 in Exhibit 2).

Several types of row/column analysis are useful:

1. Products by cleaning task
2. Products by benefits wanted, received, and the var-

ious benefit deficiencies
3. Cleaning tasks by benefits wanted, received, and the various benefit deficiencies
4. Products by characteristics desired, received, and their deficiencies
5. Cleaning tasks by characteristics desired, received and their deficiencies
6. Benefits/characteristics wanted, received, and their deficiencies vs. such other questionnaire information as demographics, psychographics, brand, usage volume, etc., as available

Row/column clustering provides a highly useful form of structure for the market planner. By looking at the linkages of cleaning tasks and benefits (indicated by the larger numbers that have been enclosed within the heavy lines on Exhibit 5), he can see at a glance which *general types* of cleaning tasks require which *general types* of benefits (or product characteristics). For example, the first four columns of Exhibit 5 show that cleaning tasks involving furniture (nos. 19, 4, 14, 20) require products that remove dust, dirt, and film (benefit nos. 12, 38, 42, 14), and that leaves no residue or scratches (benefit nos. 17, 36, 43). The market planner can check the array of existing products to see if they deliver each of the specific benefits wanted in each grouping. And the groupings themselves may suggest other similar or related benefits that were not covered specifically in the study that should be considered.

With this information the planner can:

- See how many general types of products should be on the market.
- Consider possible additional uses for existing products (i.e., a product designed for one task in a particular cluster should also be suitable for other tasks in that cluster —or could be modified to do so).
- Conceive new products that deliver the exact combinations of benefits wanted for a single cleaning task (or for a group of related tasks).
- Reposition existing products by stressing additional benefits within a benefit cluster that are already offered by a company's own products, etc.

Additional Analyses

There are many additional analyses that might be useful for the market planner. For example, those respondents who most wanted a particular cleaning benefit or characteristic can be sorted out and compared to the total sample of respondents in terms of demographics, at what time of day, and other questionnaire data not included in previous analyses. One firm asked for mental and physical "feeling tone," plus limited psychographics.

Another useful analysis consists of isolating those respondents who most wanted a particular benefit (or benefit cluster, obtained from factor scores) and determining the following averages for each product characteristic: (1) average wanted score; (2) average received score; (3) av-

Exhibit 5
Benefits Wanted by Cleaning Occasion

Cleaning Tasks
Data ordered by row/column similarities

Benefit #	Freq.	1 (18/19)	2 (3/4)	3 (13/14)	4 (19/20)	5 (2/3)	6 (6/7)	7 (12/13)	8 (21/22)	9 (1/2)	10 (7/8)	11 (9/10)	12 (17/18)	13 (10/11)	14 (20/21)	15 (16/17)	16 (8/9)	17 (4/5)	18 (11/12)	19 (5/6)	20 (15/16)	21 (14/15)
2	12	716	127	104	74	76	11	19	9	20	37	34	12	9	6	4	4	5	3	2	77	44	39
28	38	540	95	68	49	49	18	12	7	15	22	21	7	8	5	5	8	4	5	4	61	35	42
32	42	416	79	66	41	45	9	10	6	8	18	12	7	9	4	6	4	7	3	3	40	20	19
4	14	852	39	44	47	41	40	41	43	43	37	37	39	36	36	33	34	34	32	33	44	53	66
12	22	108	5	8	8	7	4	4	3	4	6	8	3	6	4	4	8	6	4	5	2	3	6
50	60	140	6	4	7	7	11	10	9	8	7	7	8	10	5	6	7	6	5	4	5	3	5
22	32	197	7	8	7	11	6	4	9	11	14	14	6	13	11	9	12	12	16	16	1	3	7
8	18	190	6	8	11	10	9	9	5	9	12	16	6	8	7	7	12	11	11	7	4	10	12
47	57	211	11	13	10	12	9	7	13	13	12	11	8	11	7	12	9	8	11	6	11	8	9
37	47	230	13	18	14	11	11	14	12	16	12	14	8	13	9	13	8	7	11	7	9	4	6
49	59	257	11	12	11	12	10	19	17	21	14	17	11	12	10	14	12	14	11	8	5	6	10
30	40	282	12	10	12	15	9	14	15	18	19	16	14	16	14	13	11	12	15	15	10	12	10
19	29	286	10	14	18	11	11	12	19	16	17	12	11	18	16	20	13	16	16	13	6	9	8
51	61	333	10	10	16	24	41	19	18	16	12	14	15	14	13	17	20	20	17	13	6	7	11
39	49	352	10	5	16	22	46	21	20	18	16	18	15	18	17	17	19	15	18	14	8	8	11
21	31	369	14	21	21	15	33	22	25	26	26	17	18	17	10	11	12	13	8	5	22	17	16
13	23	353	19	24	20	15	19	23	27	24	29	18	14	22	12	13	6	7	9	8	19	14	11
36	46	284	10	22	18	11	5	21	22	26	25	17	21	17	10	11	5	5	8	7	10	8	5
41	51	332	13	18	10	11	10	39	33	33	21	22	30	24	19	6	5	9	10	12	4	3	3
44	54	460	14	10	17	18	20	44	40	38	30	35	47	33	29	13	12	16	15	18	3	3	5
10	20	512	11	17	17	19	18	52	48	46	38	42	45	39	29	15	15	14	19	16	5	4	5
7	17	594	24	28	36	34	16	43	45	47	38	40	40	37	30	19	20	17	20	23	6	11	15
26	36	520	23	30	33	36	18	34	42	45	34	38	31	33	24	16	10	15	14	21	6	7	10
33	43	506	31	36	32	32	15	33	38	37	34	30	35	31	27	17	12	14	19	18	5	5	5
34	44	508	30	30	31	27	27	28	27	28	29	25	25	21	21	20	16	17	21	23	15	19	32
48	58	518	21	24	23	25	29	40	28	32	29	31	30	25	25	23	24	21	23	20	13	15	15
20	30	560	16	12	20	34	66	35	31	24	31	33	27	27	27	21	29	33	30	27	9	11	17
17	27	562	11	12	20	38	75	31	29	24	29	28	25	27	26	26	31	36	28	47	12	14	19
9	19	515	13	18	22	19	20	24	24	21	22	25	27	25	31	30	40	30	32	36	10	26	20
40	50	544	20	23	31	21	14	13	25	24	31	24	23	28	32	32	31	34	35	37	11	36	19
42	52	494	21	23	24	20	14	20	24	26	26	25	21	25	24	28	27	27	29	20	20	20	24
29	39	454	17	17	23	15	16	14	14	15	18	20	20	20	32	34	31	31	30	31	23	17	16
43	53	424	12	16	15	16	15	14	15	19	23	16	22	24	33	29	34	34	33	36	2	8	6
5	15	408	18	21	14	15	13	22	20	17	14	17	22	22	30	31	28	27	28	47	5	6	6
45	55	373	21	19	15	16	15	12	11	12	17	16	16	14	21	24	29	31	25	28	10	11	10
23	33	357	13	17	14	19	11	14	9	8	10	13	17	13	19	18	20	26	20	21	31	22	22
6	16	295	6	6	3	7	12	11	7	5	5	8	15	13	18	21	22	29	22	23	25	18	19
31	41	250	10	8	8	9	12	6	6	5	7	6	10	11	10	19	22	22	21	22	11	14	11
15	25	233	8	8	8	9	18	5	8	7	8	7	6	11	10	24	22	17	18	15	5	6	13
14	24	235	12	12	16	10	16	6	6	7	8	10	8	11	8	11	19	12	13	10	14	13	13
35	45	236	13	5	10	10	9	8	10	10	8	11	12	12	10	14	14	15	12	14	12	14	13
25	35	372	10	10	11	11	12	8	15	10	13	12	17	20	25	30	25	23	28	30	20	25	17
3	13	395	15	16	20	14	12	5	15	16	19	15	11	17	18	27	29	24	24	30	6	37	25
24	34	458	16	19	17	16	27	14	19	18	23	17	13	19	21	27	24	29	28	17	38	30	26
38	48	439	8	10	11	13	23	10	15	12	12	10	16	20	21	31	27	29	28	26			
16	26	632	18	15	21	27	34	46			31	21	39	43	31	30	27	27	29				
46	56	570	24	29	27	27	38	16			17	23	25	19	17								
18	28	592	23	15	14	13	24	20	13		14	15	22	25	28	29	30			27			
27	37	583	16	12	15	13					17	14	14	30	34								
11	21	668	17	15	19	13	24	27			19	19	27	36	30								
1	11	824	19	17	27	17	28				30	24	21	40									

erage positive deficiency score; (4) average negative deficiency score. Comparisons among these average scores show which characteristics are particularly crucial for a given benefit or benefit cluster. (This also can be done by correlation analysis, as reported earlier.)

The limit of possible useful analyses is based largely upon the imagination of the research analyst or market planner.

Summary

Benefit Structure Analysis (BSA) was developed out of a confluence of ideas from several earlier new product development models. Its greatest legacy is from the Market Structure Study process proposed in the early 1960's by

Stefflre.[4] In particular, his Item-Use matrix showed how an array of existing products could be systematically related to the various uses for which each product *was seen as being suitable*. This provided "structure" for a particular type of consumer product or service market. The household cleaning products study utilizes this basic idea in relating products to uses, benefits wanted/received and deficiencies to products and to uses (see Exhibit 5), product characteristics desired/received and deficiencies to products and uses, plus many additional relationships within the complete benefit matrix.

BSA also draws on the work of Haley, who was not the first to be concerned with the benefits which people wanted from products/services but who best showed how markets could *and should* be segmented on the basis of benefits, since "the benefits which people are seeking in consuming a given product are the basic reasons for the existence of true market segmentation."[5]

Finally, BSA is related to the various product positioning models proposed by Green,[6] Johnson,[7] and others. These efforts utilize quantitative techniques to identify the principal types of product characteristics/benefits that are used by consumers in *perceiving* or *evaluating* competing products within a specified product type. This is similar to the Benefit and Deficiency Structure graph shown in Exhibit 4. (In the household cleaning products study products were plotted on the first three benefit segment dimensions; this 3-dimensional configuration was not shown due to space limitations).

Managerial Considerations

Benefit Structure Analysis does not directly compete with any of the above models. It was developed especially for locating new product opportunities in very *broad* product or service categories, such as an entirely new type of food (e.g., *Instant Breakfast*) or banking service (e.g., bank credit card) or alcoholic beverage (e.g., *Malcolm Hereford's 30-proof Cows*). In such cases the market planner cannot be at all sure where his best opportunities might lie and needs a technique to analyze many different types of loosely related products/services in a single study. BSA enables him to spot weaknesses and opportunities in each general type of product or type of use, opportunities that might well be overlooked on an *a priori* basis.

For example, it was pointed out earlier that one BSA study identified a type of beverage product that was used primarily for a "pick-up" but that failed to deliver this benefit sufficiently. In this particular case the client company: (1) decided it would not develop and introduce a product *of this same type* that provided more pick-up; (2) spent many hours of discussion with planning, laboratory, and management personnel considering new types of pick-up beverages that would be entirely different from anything on the market; (3) decided to abandon the project entirely as being incompatible with the basic product technology

the company had had its primary experience with. In the case of the sauce product that was considered too fattening and staining, that particular company also decided not to develop and introduce a product of this type since it did not have resources to take on the existing well-established brands; however, it did utilize this information in reviewing its own sauce products and in planning entirely new types of sauces.

On the other hand, if the market planner is asked to work within a rather specific product category, such as white liquor beverages, soft drinks, small cars, or beer, he is probably better advised to utilize one or more of the models or research processes proposed by Green, Johnson, and others discussed above. In such cases the range of benefits and/or product characteristics that have primary relevance is much narrower. Most investigators, including the present author, have found that the two or three major benefits (i.e., groupings of similar individual benefits/characteristics) will often account for upwards of 70% of the variance in overall evaluations of products or frequency of use for a specific type of product.

The rather simple principal line of questioning that is at the heart of Benefit Structure Analysis (benefits/characteristics wanted/received and their deficiencies) can easily be included as part of many consumer surveys that have some other primary objective. This is especially appropriate when a firm has conducted previous research on a particular product line and feels confident that it understands the benefits/characteristics that are important for its product. Sometimes only ten to twenty benefits or characteristics need to be covered.

No single study can provide all types of market information needed by the planner. The technique presented here provides direction as to general areas of greatest opportunity for new product/service development plus specific diagnostic information useful for either modifying or repositioning existing products. Through broad application it may prove to be a useful tool for market analysis and planning.

REFERENCES

1. Paul E. Green, "Marketing Applications of MDS: Assessment and Outlook," *Journal of Marketing*, Vol. 39, No. 1 (January 1975), pp. 24-31.
2. Volney Stefflre, "New Products and New Enterprises," Market Structure Studies, Inc., 1968.
3. Dr. Edward W. Forgy is a statistical consultant in Los Angeles, CA. His program is proprietary, but a somewhat similar procedure is described in "Some Eliciting and Computational Procedures for Descriptive Semantics," V. Stefflre, P. Reich, and M. Wendell, in *Explorations in Mathematical Anthropology*, P. Kay, ed. (Cambridge: M.I.T. Press, 1971).
4. Stefflre, same as reference 2 above.
5. Russell I. Haley, "Benefit Segmentation: A Decision Oriented Research Tool," *Journal of Marketing*, Vol. 32 No. 3 (July 1968), pg. 30.
6. Paul E. Green and Yoram Wind, *Multiattribute Decisions in Marketing: A Measurement Approach* (Hinsdale, Illinois: The Dryden Press, 1973).
7. Richard Johnson, "Market Segmentation: A Strategic Management Tool," *Journal of Marketing Research*, Vol. VIII (February 1971), pp. 13-18
8. Benefit Structure Analysis was not actually used for any of these products, however.

A. Parasuraman, Valarie A. Zeithaml, & Leonard L. Berry

A Conceptual Model of Service Quality and Its Implications for Future Research

The attainment of quality in products and services has become a pivotal concern of the 1980s. While quality in tangible goods has been described and measured by marketers, quality in services is largely undefined and unresearched. The authors attempt to rectify this situation by reporting the insights obtained in an extensive exploratory investigation of quality in four service businesses and by developing a model of service quality. Propositions and recommendations to stimulate future research about service quality are offered.

"People want some wise and perceptive statement like, 'Quality is ballet, not hockey.'" — Philip Crosby (1979)

Q UALITY is an elusive and indistinct construct. Often mistaken for imprecise adjectives like "goodness, or luxury, or shininess, or weight" (Crosby 1979), quality and its requirements are not easily articulated by consumers (Takeuchi and Quelch 1983). Explication and measurement of quality also present problems for researchers (Monroe and Krishnan 1983), who often bypass definitions and use unidimensional self-report measures to capture the concept (Jacoby, Olson, and Haddock 1973; McConnell 1968; Shapiro 1972).

While the substance and determinants of quality may be undefined, its importance to firms and consumers is unequivocal. Research has demonstrated the strategic benefits of quality in contributing to market share and return on investment (e.g., Anderson and Zeithaml 1984; Phillips, Chang, and Buzzell 1983) as well as in lowering manufacturing costs and improving productivity (Garvin 1983). The search for quality is arguably the most important consumer trend of the 1980s (Rabin 1983) as consumers are now demanding higher quality in products than ever before (Leonard and Sasser 1982, Takeuchi and

Quelch 1983).

Few academic researchers have attempted to define and model quality because of the difficulties involved in delimiting and measuring the construct. Moreover, despite the phenomenal growth of the service sector, only a handful of these researchers have focused on service quality. We attempt to rectify this situation by (1) reviewing the small number of studies that have investigated service quality, (2) reporting the insights obtained in an extensive exploratory investigation of quality in four service businesses, (3) developing a model of service quality, and (4) offering propositions to stimulate future research about quality.

Existing Knowledge about Service Quality

Efforts in defining and measuring quality have come largely from the goods sector. According to the prevailing Japanese philosophy, quality is "zero defects—doing it right the first time." Crosby (1979) defines quality as "conformance to requirements." Garvin (1983) measures quality by counting the incidence of "internal" failures (those observed before a product leaves the factory) and "external" failures (those incurred in the field after a unit has been installed.)

Knowledge about goods quality, however, is insufficient to understand service quality. Three well-documented characteristics of services—*intangibility, heterogeneity*, and *inseparability*—must be acknowledged for a full understanding of service quality.

First, most services are intangible (Bateson 1977,

About the authors. A. Parasuraman and Valarie A. Zeithaml are Associate Professors of Marketing, and Leonard L. Berry is Foley's/Federated Professor of Retailing and Marketing Studies, Texas A&M University. The research reported in this article was made possible by a grant from the Marketing Science Institute, Cambridge, MA.

Berry 1980, Lovelock 1981, Shostak 1977). Because they are performances rather than objects, precise manufacturing specifications concerning uniform quality can rarely be set. Most services cannot be counted, measured, inventoried, tested, and verified in advance of sale to assure quality. Because of intangibility, the firm may find it difficult to understand how consumers perceive their services and evaluate service quality (Zeithaml 1981).

Second, services, especially those with a high labor content, are heterogeneous: their performance often varies from producer to producer, from customer to customer, and from day to day. Consistency of behavior from service personnel (i.e., uniform quality) is difficult to assure (Booms and Bitner 1981) because what the firm intends to deliver may be entirely different from what the consumer receives.

Third, production and consumption of many services are inseparable (Carmen and Langeard 1980, Gronroos 1978, Regan 1963, Upah 1980). As a consequence, quality in services is not engineered at the manufacturing plant, then delivered intact to the consumer. In labor intensive services, for example, quality occurs during service delivery, usually in an interaction between the client and the contact person from the service firm (Lehtinen and Lehtinen 1982). The service firm may also have less managerial control over quality in services where consumer participation is intense (e.g., haircuts, doctor's visits) because the client affects the process. In these situations, the consumer's input (description of how the haircut should look, description of symptoms) becomes critical to the quality of service performance.

Service quality has been discussed in only a handful of writings (Gronroos 1982; Lehtinen and Lehtinen 1982; lewis and Booms 1983; Sasser, Olsen, and Wyckoff 1978). Examination of these writings and other literature on services suggests three underlying themes:

- Service quality is more difficult for the consumer to evaluate than goods quality.

- Service quality perceptions result from a comparison of consumer expectations with actual service performance.

- Quality evaluations are not made solely on the outcome of a service; they also involve evaluations of the *process* of service delivery.

Service Quality More Difficult to Evaluate

When purchasing goods, the consumer employs many tangible cues to judge quality: style, hardness, color, label, feel, package, fit. When purchasing services, fewer tangible cues exist. In most cases, tangible evidence is limited to the service provider's physical facilities, equipment, and personnel.

In the absence of tangible evidence on which to evaluate quality, consumers must depend on other cues. The nature of these other cues has not been investigated by researchers, although some authors have suggested that

price becomes a pivotal quality indicator in situations where other information is not available (McConnell 1968, Olander 1970, Zeithaml 1981). Because of service intangibility, a firm may find it more difficult to understand how consumers perceive services and service quality. "When a service provider knows how [the service] will be evaluated by the consumer, we will be able to suggest how to influence these evaluations in a desired direction" (Gronroos 1982).

Quality Is a Comparison between Expectations and Performance

Researchers and managers of service firms concur that service quality involves a comparison of expectations with performance:

> Service quality is a measure of how well the service level delivered matches customer expectations. Delivering quality service means conforming to customer expectations on a consistent basis. (Lewis and Booms 1983)

In line with this thinking, Gronroos (1982) developed a model in which he contends that consumers compare the service they expect with perceptions of the service they receive in evaluating service quality.

Smith and Houston (1982) claimed that satisfaction with services is related to confirmation or disconfirmation of expectations. They based their research on the disconfirmation paradigm, which maintains that satisfaction is related to the size and direction of the disconfirmation experience where disconfirmation is related to the person's initial expectations (Churchill and Surprenant 1982).

Quality Evaluations Involve Outcomes and Processes

Sasser, Olsen and Wyckoff (1978) discussed three different dimensions of service performance: levels of material, facilities, and personnel. Implied in this trichotomy is the notion that service quality involves more than outcome; it also includes the manner in which the service is delivered. This notion surfaces in other research on service quality as well.

Gronroos, for example, postulated that two types of service quality exist: *technical quality,* which involves what the customer is actually receiving from the service, and *functional quality,* which involves the manner in which the service is delivered (Gronroos 1982).

Lehtinen and Lehtinen's (1982) basic premise is that service quality is produced in the interaction between a customer and elements in the service organization. They use three quality dimensions: *physical quality,* which includes the physical aspects of the service (e.g., equipment or building); *corporate quality,* which involves the company's image or profile; and *interactive quality,* which derives from the interaction between contact personnel and customers as well as between some customers and other customers. They further differentiate between the quality associated with the process of service delivery and the quality associated with the outcome of the service.

Exploratory Investigation

Because the literature on service quality is not yet rich enough to provide a sound conceptual foundation for investigating service quality, an exploratory qualitative study was undertaken to investigate the concept of service quality. Specifically, focus group interviews with consumers and in-depth interviews with executives were conducted to develop a conceptual model of service quality. The approach used is consistent with procedures recommended for marketing theory development by several scholars (Deshpande 1983; Peter and Olson 1983; Zaltman, LeMasters, and Heffring 1982).

In-depth interviews of executives in four nationally recognized service firms and a set of focus group interviews of consumers were conducted to gain insights about the following questions:

- What do managers of service firms perceive to be the key attributes of service quality? What problems and tasks are involved in providing high quality service?
- What do consumers perceive to be the key attributes of quality in services?
- Do discrepancies exist between the perceptions of consumers and service marketers?
- Can consumer and marketer perceptions be combined in a general model that explains service quality from the consumer's standpoint?

Service Categories Investigated

Four service categories were chosen for investigation: retail banking, credit card, securities brokerage, and product repair and maintenance. While this set of service businesses is not exhaustive, it represents a cross-section of industries which vary along key dimensions used to categorize services (Lovelock 1980, 1983). For example, retail banking and securities brokerage services are more "high contact services" than the other two types. The nature and results of the service act are more tangible for product repair and maintenance services than for the other three types. In terms of service delivery, discrete transactions characterize credit card services and product repair and maintenance services to a greater extent than the other two types of services.

Executive Interviews

A nationally recognized company from each of the four service businesses participated in the study. In-depth personal interviews comprised of open-ended questions were conducted with three or four executives in each firm. The executives were selected from marketing, operations, senior management, and customer relations because each of these areas could have an impact on quality in service

firms. The respondents held titles such as president, senior vice president, director of customer relations, and manager of consumer market research. Fourteen executives were interviewed about a broad range of service quality issues (e.g., what they perceived to be service quality from the consumer's perspective, what steps they took to control or improve service quality, and what problems they faced in delivering high quality services).

Focus Group Interviews

A total of 12 focus group interviews was conducted, three for each of the four selected services. Eight of the focus groups were held in a metropolitan area in the southwest. The remaining four were conducted in the vicinity of the participating companies' headquarters and were therefore spread across the country: one on the West Coast, one in the Midwest, and two in the East.

The focus groups were formed in accordance with guidelines traditionally followed in the marketing research field (Bellenger, Berhardt, and Goldstucker 1976). Respondents were screened to ensure that they were current or recent users of the service in question. To maintain homogeneity and assure maximum participation, respondents were assigned to groups based on age and sex. Six of the twelve groups included only males and six included only females. At least one male group and one female group were interviewed for each of the four services. Consistency in age was maintained within groups; however, age diversity across groups for each service category was established to ascertain the viewpoints of a broad cross section of consumers.

Identities of participating firms were not revealed to focus group participants. Discussion about quality of a given service centered on consumer experiences and perceptions relating to that service in general, as opposed to the specific service of the participating firm in that service category. Questions asked by the moderator covered topics such as instances of and reasons for satisfaction and dissatisfaction with the service; descriptions of an ideal service (e.g., ideal bank or ideal credit card); the meaning of service quality; factors important in evaluating service quality; performance expectations concerning the service; and the role of price in service quality.

Insights from Exploratory Investigation

Executive Interviews

Remarkably consistent patterns emerged from the four sets of executive interviews. While some perceptions about service quality were specific to the industries selected, commonalities among the industries prevailed. The commonalities are encouraging for they suggest that a general model of service quality can be developed.

Perhaps the most important insight obtained from analyzing the executive responses is the following:

FIGURE 1
Service Quality Model

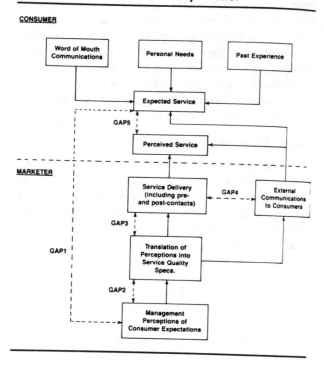

A set of key discrepancies or gaps exists regarding executive perceptions of service quality and the tasks associated with service delivery to consumers. These gaps can be major hurdles in attempting to deliver a service which consumers would perceive as being of high quality.

The gaps revealed by the executive interviews are shown in the lower portion (i.e., the MARKETER side) of Figure 1. This figure summarizes the key insights gained (through the focus group as well as executive interviews) about the concept of service quality and factors affecting it. The remainder of this section discusses the gaps on the service marketer's side (GAP1, GAP2, GAP3, and GAP4) and presents propositions implied by those gaps. The consumer's side of the service quality model in Figure 1 is discussed in the next section.

Consumer expectation–management perception gap (GAP1): Many of the executive perceptions about what consumers expect in a quality service were congruent with the consumer expectations revealed in the focus groups. However, discrepancies between executive perceptions and consumer expectations existed, as illustrated by the following examples:

- Privacy or confidentiality during transactions emerged as a pivotal quality attribute in every banking and securities brokerage focus group. Rarely was this consideration mentioned in the executive interviews.
- The physical and security features of credit cards (e.g., the likelihood that unauthorized people could use the cards) generated substantial discussion in the focus group interviews but did not emerge as critical in the ex-

ecutive interviews.

- The product repair and maintenance focus groups indicated that a large repair service firm was unlikely to be viewed as a high quality firm. Small independent repair firms were consistently associated with high quality. In contrast, most executive comments indicated that a firm's size would signal strength in a quality context.

In essence, service firm executives may not always understand what features connote high quality to consumers in advance, what features a service must have in order to meet consumer needs, and what levels of performance on those features are needed to deliver high quality service. This insight is consistent with previous research in services, which suggests that service marketers may not always understand what consumers expect in a service (Langeard et al. 1981, Parasuraman and Zeithaml 1982). This lack of understanding may affect quality perceptions of consumers:

> Proposition 1: The gap between consumer expectations and management perceptions of those expectations will have an impact on the consumer's evaluation of service quality.

Management perception–service quality specification gap (GAP2): A recurring theme in the executive interviews in all four service firms was the difficulty experienced in attempting to match or exceed consumer expectations. Executives cited constraints which prevent them from delivering what the consumer expects. As an example, executives in the repair service firm were fully aware that consumers view quick response to appliance breakdowns as a vital ingredient of high quality service. However, they find it difficult to establish specifications to deliver quick response consistently because of a lack of trained service personnel and wide fluctuations in demand. As one executive observed, peak demand for repairing air conditioners and lawnmowers occurs during the summer months, precisely when most service personnel want to go on vacation. In this and numerous other situations, knowledge of consumer expectations exists but the perceived means to deliver to expectations apparently do not.

Apart from resource and market constraints, another reason for the gap between expectations and the actual set of specifications established for a service is the absence of total management commitment to service quality. Although the executive interviews indicated a genuine concern for quality on the part of managers interviewed, this concern may not be generalizable to all service firms. In discussing product quality, Garvin (1983) stated: ''...the seriousness that management attached to quality problems [varies]. It's one thing to say you believe in defect-free products, but quite another to take time from a busy schedule to act on that belief and stay informed'' (p. 68). Garvin's observations are likely to apply to service businesses as well.

In short, a variety of factors—resource constraints, market conditions, and/or management indifference—may result in a discrepancy between management perceptions of consumer expectations and the actual specifications established for a service. This discrepancy is predicted to affect quality perceptions of consumers:

> Proposition 2: The gap between management perceptions of consumer expectations and the firm's service quality specifications will affect service quality from the consumer's viewpoint.

Service quality specifications–service delivery gap (GAP3): Even when guidelines exist for performing services well and treating consumers correctly, high quality service performance may not be a certainty. Executives recognize that a service firm's employees exert a strong influence on the service quality perceived by consumers and that employee performance cannot always be standardized. When asked what causes service quality problems, executives consistently mentioned the pivotal role of contact personnel. In the repair and maintenance firm, for example, one executive's immediate response to the source of service quality problems was, "Everything involves a person—a repair person. It's so hard to maintain standardized quality."

Each of the four firms had formal standards or specifications for maintaining service quality (e.g. answer at least 90% of phone calls from consumers within 10 seconds; keep error rates in statements below 1%). However, each firm reported difficulty in adhering to these standards because of variability in employee performance. This problem leads to a third proposition:

> Proposition 3: The gap between service quality specifications and actual service delivery will affect service quality from the consumer's standpoint.

Service delivery–external communications gap (GAP4): Media advertising and other communications by a firm can affect consumer expectations. If expectations play a major role in consumer perceptions of service quality (as the services literature contends), the firm must be certain not to promise more in communications than it can deliver in reality. Promising more than can be delivered will raise initial expectations but lower perceptions of quality when the promises are not fulfilled.

The executive interviews suggest another perhaps more intriguing way in which external communications could influence service quality perceptions by consumers. This occurs when companies neglect to inform consumers of special efforts to assure quality that are not visible to consumers. Comments of several executives implied that consumers are not always aware of everything done behind the scenes to serve them well.

For instance, a securities brokerage executive mentioned a "48-hour rule" prohibiting employees from buying or selling securities for their personal accounts for the first 48 hours after information is supplied by the firm. The firm did not communicate this information to its customers, perhaps contributing to a perception that "all the good deals are probably made by the brokers for themselves" (a perception which surfaced in the securities brokerage focus groups). One bank executive indicated that consumers were unaware of the bank's behind the counter, on-line teller terminals which would "translate into visible effects on customer service." Making consumers aware of not readily apparent service related standards such as these could improve service quality perceptions. Consumers who are aware that a firm is taking concrete steps to serve their best interests are likely *to perceive* a delivered service in a more favorable way.

In short, external communications can affect not only consumer expectations about a service but also consumer *perceptions* of the delivered service. Alternatively, discrepancies between service delivery and external communications—in the form of exaggerated promises and/or the absence of information about service delivery aspects intended to serve consumers well—can affect consumer perceptions of service quality.

> Proposition 4: The gap between actual service delivery and external communications about the service will effect service quality from a consumer's standpoint.

Focus Group Interviews

As was true of the executive interviews, the responses of focus group participants about service quality were remarkably consistent across groups and across service businesses. While some service-specific differences were revealed, common themes emerged—themes which offer valuable insights about service quality perceptions of consumers.

Expected service–perceived service gap (GAP5): The focus groups unambiguously supported the notion that the key to ensuring good service quality is meeting or exceeding what consumers expect from the service. One female participant described a situation when a repairman not only fixed her broken appliance but also explained what had gone wrong and how she could fix it herself if a similar problem occurred in the future. She rated the quality of this service excellent because it exceeded her expectations. A male respondent in a banking services focus group described the frustration he felt when his bank would not cash his payroll check from a nationally known employer because it was postdated by one day. When someone else in the group pointed out legal constraints preventing the bank from cashing his check, he responded, "Well, nobody *in the bank* explained that to me!" Not receiving an explanation in the bank, this respondent perceived that the bank was *unwilling* rather than *unable* to cash the check. This in turn resulted in a perception of poor service quality.

Similar experiences, both positive and negative, were described by consumers in every focus group. It appears that judgments of high and low service quality depend on how consumers perceive the actual service performance in the context of what they expected.

> Proposition 5: The quality that a consumer perceives in a service is a function of the magnitude and direction of the gap between expected service and perceived service.

A Service Quality Model

Insights obtained from the executive interviews and the focus groups form the basis of a model summarizing the nature and determinants of service quality as perceived by consumers. The foundation of this model is the set of gaps discussed earlier and shown in Figure 1. Service quality as perceived by a consumer depends on the size and direction of GAP5 which, in turn, depends on the nature of the gaps associated with the design, marketing, and delivery of services:

> Proposition 6: GAP5 = f(GAP1, GAP2, GAP3, GAP4)

It is important to note that the gaps on the marketer side of the equation can be favorable or unfavorable from a service quality perspective. That is, the magnitude *and direction* of each gap will have an impact on service quality. For instance, GAP3 will be favorable when actual service delivery exceeds specifications; it will be unfavorable when service specifications are not met. While proposition 6 suggests a relationship between service quality as perceived by consumers and the gaps occurring on the marketer's side, the functional form of the relationship needs to be investigated. This point is discussed further in the last section dealing with future research directions.

The Perceived Service Quality Component

The focus groups revealed that, regardless of the type of service, consumers used basically similar criteria in evaluating service quality. These criteria seem to fall into 10 key categories which are labeled ''service quality determinants'' and described in Table 1. For each determinant, Table 1 provides examples of service specific criteria that emerged in the focus groups. Table 1 is not meant to suggest that the 10 determinants are non-overlapping. Because the research was exploratory, measurement of possible overlap across the 10 criteria (as well as determination of whether some can be combined) must await future empirical investigation.

The consumer's view of service quality is shown in the upper part of Figure 1 and further elaborated in Figure 2. Figure 2 indicates that perceived service quality is the result of the consumer's comparison of expected service

with perceived service. It is quite possible that the relative importance of the 10 determinants in molding consumer expectations (prior to service delivery) may differ from their relative importance vis-à-vis consumer perceptions of the delivered service. However, the general comparison of expectations with perceptions was suggested in past research on service quality (Gronroos 1982, Lehtinen and Lehtinen 1982) and supported in the focus group interviews with consumers. The comparison of expected and perceived service is not unlike that performed by consumers when evaluating goods. What differs with services is the *nature* of the characteristics upon which they are evaluated.

One framework for isolating differences in evaluation of quality for goods and services is the classification of properties of goods proposed by Nelson (1974) and Darby and Karni (1973). Nelson distinguished between two categories of properties of consumer goods: *search properties,* attributes which a consumer can determine prior to purchasing a product, and *experience properties,* attributes which can only be discerned after purchase or during consumption. Search properties include attributes such as color, style, price, fit, feel, hardness, and smell, while experience properties include characteristics such as taste, wearability, and dependability.

Darby and Karni (1973) added to Nelson's two-way classification system a third category, *credence properties*—characteristics which the consumer may find impossible to evaluate even after purchase and consumption. Examples of offerings high in credence properties include appendectomies and brake relinings on automobiles. Few consumers possess medical or mechanical skills sufficient to evaluate whether these services are necessary or are performed properly, even after they have been prescribed and produced by the seller.

Consumers in the focus groups mentioned search, experience, and credence properties when asked to describe

FIGURE 2
Determinants of Perceived Service Quality

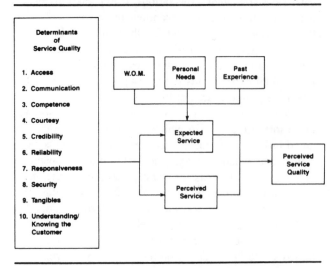

TABLE 1
Determinants of Service Quality

RELIABILITY involves consistency of performance and dependability.
It means that the firm performs the service right the first time.
It also means that the firm honors its promises. Specifically,it involves:
 —accuracy in billing;
 —keeping records correctly;
 —performing the service at the designated time.

RESPONSIVENESS concerns the willingness or readiness of employees to provide service. It involves timeliness of service:
 —mailing a transaction slip immediately;
 —calling the customer back quickly;
 —giving prompt service (e.g., setting up appointments quickly).

COMPETENCE means possession of the required skills and knowledge to perform the service. It involves:
 —knowledge and skill of the contact personnel;
 —knowledge and skill of operational support personnel;
 —research capability of the organization (e.g., securities brokerage firm).

ACCESS involves approachability and ease of contact. It means:
 —the service is easily accessible by telephone (lines are not busy and they don't put you on hold);
 —waiting time to receive service (e.g., at a bank) is not extensive;
 —convenient hours of operation;
 —convenient location of service facility.

COURTESY involves politeness, respect, consideration, and friendliness of contact personnel (including receptionists, telephone operators, etc.). It includes:
 —consideration for the consumer's property (e.g., no muddy shoes on the carpet);
 —clean and neat appearance of public contact personnel.

COMMUNICATION means keeping customers informed in language they can understand and listening to them. It may mean
that the company has to adjust its language for different consumers—increasing the level of sophistication with a well-
educated customer and speaking simply and plainly with a novice. It involves:
 —explaining the service itself;
 —explaining how much the service will cost;
 —explaining the trade-offs between service and cost;
 —assuring the consumer that a problem will be handled.

CREDIBILITY involves trustworthiness, believability, honesty. It involves having the customer's best interests at heart. Contributing to credibility are:
 —company name;
 —company reputation;
 —personal characteristics of the contact personnel;
 —the degree of hard sell involved in interactions with the customer.

SECURITY is the freedom from danger, risk, or doubt. It involves:
 —physical safety (Will I get mugged at the automatic teller machine?);
 —financial security (Does the company know where my stock certificate is?);
 —confidentiality (Are my dealings with the company private?).

UNDERSTANDING/KNOWING THE CUSTOMER involves making the effort to understand the customer's needs. It involves:
 —learning the customer's specific requirements;
 —providing individualized attention;
 —recognizing the regular customer.

TANGIBLES include the physical evidence of the service:
 —physical facilities;
 —appearance of personnel;
 —tools or equipment used to provide the service;
 —physical representations of the service, such as a plastic credit card or a bank statement;
 —other customers in the service facility.

and define service quality. These aspects of service quality can be categorized into the 10 service quality determinants shown in Table 1 and can be arrayed along a continuum ranging from *easy to evaluate to difficult to evaluate.*

In general, offerings high in search properties are easiest to evaluate, those high in experience properties more difficult to evaluate, and those high in credence properties hardest to evaluate. Most services contain few search properties and are high in experience and credence properties, making their quality more difficult to evaluate than quality of goods (Zeithaml 1981).

Only two of the ten determinants—tangibles and credibility—can be known in advance of purchase, thereby making the number of search properties few. Most of the dimensions of service quality mentioned by the focus group participants were experience properties: access, courtesy, reliability, responsiveness, understanding/knowing the customer, and communication. Each of these determinants can only be known as the customer is purchasing or consuming the service. While customers may possess some information based on their experience or on other customers' evaluations, they are likely to reevaluate these determinants each time a purchase is made because of the heterogeneity of services.

Two of the determinants that surfaced in the focus group interviews probably fall into the category of credence properties, those which consumers cannot evaluate even after purchase and consumption. These include competence (the possession of the required skills and knowledge to perform the service) and security (freedom from danger, risk, or doubt). Consumers are probably never certain of these attributes, even after consumption of service.

Because few search properties exist with services and because credence properties are too difficult to evaluate, the following is proposed:

Proposition 7: Consumers typically rely on experience properties when evaluating service quality.

Based on insights from the present study, perceived service quality is further posited to exist along a continuum ranging from ideal quality to totally unacceptable quality, with some point along the continuun representing satisfactory quality. The position of a consumer's perception of service quality on the continuum depends on the nature of the discrepancy between the expected service (ES) and perceived service (PS):

Proposition 8: (a) When ES > PS, perceived quality is less than satisfactory and will tend toward totally unacceptable quality, with increased discrepancy between ES and PS; (b) when ES = PS, perceived quality is satisfactory; (c) when ES < PS, perceived quality is more than satisfactory and will tend toward ideal quality, with increased discrepancy between ES and PS.

Directions for Future Research

The proposed service quality model (Figure 1) provides a conceptual framework in an area where little prior research has been done. It is based on an interpretation of qualitative data generated through a number of in-depth executive interviews and consumer focus groups—an approach consistent with procedures recommended for marketing theory development. The conceptual model and the propositions emerging from it imply a rich agenda for further research.

First, there is a need and an opportunity to develop a standard instrument to measure consumers' service quality perceptions. The authors' exploratory research revealed 10 evaluative dimensions or criteria which transcend a variety of services (Table 1). Research is now needed to generate items or statements to flesh out the 10 dimensions, to devise appropriate rating scales to measure consumers' perceptions with respect to each statement, and to condense the set of statements to produce a reliable and comprehensive but concise instrument. Further, the statements generated should be such that with appropriate changes in wording, the same instrument can be used to measure perceived quality for a variety of services.

Second, the main thesis of the service quality model is that consumers' quality perceptions are influenced by a series of distinct gaps occurring on the marketers' side. A key challenge for researchers is to devise methods to measure these gaps accurately. Reliable and valid measures of these gaps will be necessary for empirical testing the propositions implied by the model.

Third, research is needed to examine the *nature* of the association between service quality as perceived by consumers and its determinants (GAPS 1-4). Specifically, are one or more of these gaps more critical than the others in affecting quality? Can creating one ''favorable'' gap—e.g., making GAP4 favorable by employing effective external communications to create realistic consumer expectations and to enhance consumer perceptions—offset service quality problems stemming from other gaps? Are there differences across service industries regarding the relative seriousness of service quality problems and their impact on quality as perceived by consumers? In addition to offering valuable managerial insights, answers to questions like these may suggest refinements to the proposed model.

Fourth, the usefulness of segmenting consumers on the basis of their service quality expectations is worth exploring. Although the focus groups consistently revealed similar criteria for judging service quality, the group participants differed on the *relative importance* of those criteria to them, and their *expectations* along the various quality dimensions. Empirical research aimed at determining whether distinct, identifiable service quality segments exist will be valuable from a service marketer's viewpoint. In this regard, it will be useful to build into the service quality measurement instrument certain statements for ascertaining whether, and in what ways, consumer expectations differ.

Fifth, as shown by Figure 1, expected service—a critical component of perceived service quality—in addition to being influenced by a marketer's communications, is shaped by word-of-mouth communications, personal needs, and past experience. Research focusing on the relative impact of these factors on consumers' service expectations, within as well as across service categories, will have useful managerial implications.

Summary

The exploratory research (focus group and in-depth executive interviews) reported in this article offers several insights and propositions concerning consumers' perceptions of service quality. Specifically, the research revealed 10 dimensions that consumers use in forming expectations about and perceptions of services, dimensions that transcend different types of services. The research also pinpointed four key discrepancies or gaps on the service provider's side that are likely to affect service quality as perceived by consumers. The major insights gained through the research suggest a conceptual service quality model that will hopefully spawn both academic and practitioner interest in service quality and serve as a framework for further empirical research in this important area.

REFERENCES

Anderson, Carl and Carl P. Zeithaml (1984), "Stage of the Product Life Cycle, Business Strategy, and Business Performance," *Academy of Management Journal*, 27 (March), 5-24.

Bateson, John E. G. (1977), "Do We Need Service Marketing?," in *Marketing Consumer Services: New Insights*, Cambridge, MA: Marketing Science Institute, Report #77-115.

Bellenger, Danny N., Kenneth L. Berhardt, and Jac L. Goldstucker (1976), *Qualitative Research in Marketing*, Chicago: American Marketing.

Berry, Leonard L. (1980), "Services Marketing is Different," *Business*, 30 (May-June), 24-28.

Booms, Bernard H. and Mary J. Bitner (1981), "Marketing Strategies and Organizations Structures for Services Firms," in *Marketing of Services*, J. Donnelly and W. George, eds., Chicago: American Marketing, 47-51.

Carmen, James M. and Eric Langeard (1980), "Growth Strategies of Service Firms," *Strategic Management Journal*, 1 (January-March), 7-22.

Churchill, G. A., Jr., and C. Surprenant (1982), "An Investigation into the Determinants of Customer Satisfaction," *Journal of Marketing Research*, 19 (November), 491-504.

Crosby, Philip B. (1979), *Quality Is Free: The Art of Making Quality Certain*, New York: New American Library.

Darby, M. R. and E. Karni (1973), "Free Competition and the Optimal Amount of Fraud," *Journal of Law and Economics*, 16 (April), 67-86.

Deshpande, Rohit (1983)," 'Paradigms Lost': On Theory and Method Research in Marketing," *Journal of Marketing*, 47 (Fall), 101-110.

Garvin, David A. (1983), "Quality on the Line," *Harvard Business Review*, 61 (September-October), 65-73.

Gronroos, Christian (1978), "A Service-Oriented Approach to Marketing of Services," *European Journal of Marketing*, 12 (no. 8), 588-601.

____ (1982), *Strategic Management and Marketing in the Service Sector*, Helsingfors: Swedish School of Economics and Business Administration.

Jacoby, Jacob, Jerry C. Olson and Rafael A. Haddock (1973), "Price, Brand Name and Product Composition Characteristics as Determinants of Perceived Quality," *Journal of Applied Psychology*, 55 (no. 6), 570-579.

Langeard, Eric, John E. G. Bateson, Christopher H. Lovelock, and Pierre Eiglier (1981), *Service Marketing: New Insights from Consumers and Managers*, Cambridge, MA: Marketing Science Institute.

Lehtinen, Uolevi and Jarmo R. Lehtinen (1982), "Service Quality: A Study of Quality Dimensions," unpublished working paper, Helsinki: Service Management Institute, Finland OY.

Leonard, Frank S. and W. Earl Sasser (1982), "The Incline of Quality," *Harvard Business Review*, 60 (September-October), 163-171.

Lewis, Robert C. and Bernard H. Booms (1983), "The Marketing Aspects of Service Quality," in *Emerging Perspectives on Services Marketing*, L. Berry, G. Shostack and G. Upah, eds., Chicago: American Marketing, 99-107.

Lovelock, Christopher H. (1980), "Towards a Classification of Services," in *Theoretical Developments in Marketing*, C. Lamb and P. Dunne, eds., Chicago: American Marketing, 72-76.

____ (1981), "Why Marketing Management Needs to be Different for Services," in *Marketing of Services*, J. Donnelly and W. George, eds. Chicago: American Marketing, 5-9.

____ (1983), "Classifying Services to Gain Strategic Marketing Insights," *Journal of Marketing*, 47 (Summer), 9-20.

McConnell, J. D. (1968), "Effect of Pricing on Perception of Product Quality," *Journal of Applied Psychology*, 52 (August), 300-303.

Monroe, Kent B. and R. Krishnan (1983), "The Effect of Price on Subjective Product Evaluations," Blacksburg: Virginia Polytechnic Institute, working paper.

Nelson, P. (1974), "Advertising as Information," *Journal of Political Economy*, 81 (July/August), 729-754.

Olander, F. (1970), "The Influence of Price on the Consumer's Evaluation of Products," in *Pricing Strategy*, B. Taylor and G. Wills, eds. Princeton, NJ: Brandon/Systems Press.

Parasuraman, A. and Valarie A. Zethaml (1982), "Differential Perceptions of Suppliers and Clients of Industrial Services," in *Emerging Perspectives on Services Marketing*, L. Berry, G. Shostack, and G. Upah, eds., Chicago: American Marketing, 35-39.

Peter, J. Paul and Jerry C. Olson (1983), "Is Science Marketing?," *Journal of Marketing*, 47 (Fall), 111-125.

Phillips, Lynn W., Dae R. Chang, and Robert D. Buzzell (1983), "Product Quality, Cost Position, and Business Performance: A Test of Some Key Hypotheses," *Journal of Marketing*, 47 (Spring), 26-43.

Rabin, Joseph H. (1983), "Accent is on Quality in Consumer Services This Decade," *Marketing News*, 17 (March 4), 12.

Regan, William J. (1963), "The Service Revolution," *Journal of Marketing*, 27 (July), 57-62.

Sasser, W. Earl, Jr., R. Paul Olsen, and D. Daryl Wyckoff (1978), *Management of Service Operations: Text and Cases*, Boston: Allyn & Bacon.

Shapiro, Benson (1972), "The Price of Consumer Goods: Theory and Practice," Cambridge, MA: Marketing Science Institute, working paper.

Shostack, G. Lynn (1977), "Breaking Free from Product Marketing," *Journal of Marketing*, 41 (April), 73-80.

Smith, Ruth A. and Michael J. Houston (1982), "Script-Based Evaluations of Satisfaction with Services," in *Emerging Perspectives on Services Marketing*, L. Berry, G. Shostack, and G. Upah, eds., Chicago: American Marketing, 59-62.

Takeuchi, Hirotaka and John A. Quelch (1983), "Quality Is More Than Making a Good Product," *Harvard Business Review*, 61 (July-August), 139-145.

Upah, Gregory D. (1980), "Mass Marketing in Service Retailing: A Review and Synthesis of Major Methods," *Journal of Retailing*, 56 (Fall), 59-76.

Zaltman, Gerald, Karen LeMasters, and Michael Heffring (1982), *Theory Construction in Marketing: Some Thought on Thinking*, New York: Wiley.

Zeithaml, Valarie A. (1981), "How Consumer Evaluation Processes Differ between Goods and Services," in *Marketing of Services*, J. Donnelly and W. George, eds., Chicago: American Marketing, 186-190.

Understanding the Consumer

Steuart Henderson Britt

The Strategy of Consumer Motivation*

AN analysis of the strategy of consumer motivation does not imply one easy lesson in "how to win consumers and influence customers." But it does imply a more thorough understanding of the basic *motives* of man when he behaves like a consumer.

You might argue, of course, that there really is no great problem of consumer motivation. Just look around us, you might say, at the greatest period of economic prosperity that the United States has ever known. In the light of the present prosperous state of the nation's business, why do we need to worry about consumers and consumption?

After all, total consumer dollar income in the United States is 190 per cent higher than in 1939. And real personal income is over 70 per cent more than ten years ago.

Marketing Facts and Psychological Information

But if our prosperity is to continue, we must recognize that the much touted "buyer's market" is no empty phrase. Our problem is that we have available all kinds of facts and figures about *markets,* but that we sometimes forget that these markets, after all, are made up of *human beings.* And we simply do not have enough information about the why's and wherefore's of their buying behavior.

It is true that we have access to all kinds of market data books, and handbooks of facts and figures. After proper probing in our libraries and files, we can find all kinds of authoritative and complete indexes of buying power on all consumer markets—national, farm, state county, and city. We can obtain excellent estimates of present "market sizes," and of "distribution channels"—but still fail to learn very much about *people.*

You and I undoubtedly have seen and read dozens of studies on automobiles, asparagus, atomizers, appetizers,

*Speech presented at the National Convention of the American Marketing Association, New York City, December 27, 1949.

or whatnot, that never came to grips with the fundamental problem of *why* people buy. For example, there are detailed reports on the soft-drink market which tell us the seasonal fluctuation in the consumption of soft drinks, the types of beverages purchased, the percentage of families purchasing, and the average monthly family purchases, and so on—but we still do not know much about the very complicated motives that result in the sipping, swallowing, and guzzling by Americans of almost one billion *cases* of carbonated beverages annually. The factors that will cause millions of men, women, and children to take into their intestinal tracts various kinds of sweetened or bubbling liquids in a variety of different colors are not easy to explain.

The point is that, if we would devote only one-tenth as much time and money to as rigorous a study of this problem as we have to a mere *counting* of people and bottles, the sales problems of the carbonated beverage industry would be simpler. The same reasoning holds for automobiles, refrigerators, canned goods, household furnishings, and other major industries of America. These industries have poured hundreds of thousands of dollars into market research—in the sense of fact gathering—but have not devoted much money to learning about the fundamental motives of consumers.

The record of market research during the past decade is an impressive one. There are better sampling methods than ever before. There is more careful phrasing of questions. There is more accurate cross-checking of data. There is better interpretation of the significance of the facts secured. But we still do not know very much about the underlying motives that cause most consumers to dress as we do, eat as we do, and engage in a hundred other acts of our everyday existence.

The Problem of Classifying Motives

"Men learn to be plumbers, drug addicts, psychologists, golfers, pinochle players, diet cranks, theosophists, fly fishermen, head-hunters, yachtsmen, camera enthusiasts. The variety of things that men learn to do appears a hopeless confusion. But there have always been efforts to classify the behavior that men are prone to learn. Such classifications have been in terms of urges or motives, passions, desires, interests."[1]

However, when we try to classify motives, we run into all sorts of difficulties. Actually, every social situation is different from every other and requires a separate analysis. This means that there is no such thing as a universal set of explanatory motives. Any list of motives can be classified under a number of different headings; and then someone else can rearrange that same list and assign them to different headings.

"The trouble with lists of motives lies not in their length but in their sharp separation of one drive from another, their sharp separation of innate from acquired need, and their sharp demarcation of focus points in the body which are supposed to underly motion toward a goal. Nevertheless, if these limitations are kept in mind, there seems to be a distinct value in listing four groups of human motives.[2]"

Visceral Drives	Activity Drives	Aesthetic Drives	Emotions
Hunger	Exercise	Color	Fear
Thirst	Rest	Tone	Rage
Air-getting	Perseveration	Specific qualities	Disgust
Temperature	Rhythm	of taste, smell,	Shame
regulation	Novelty	and touch	etc.
Sexual	Exploration	Rhythm	
etc.	etc.	etc.	

The names for the drives, of course, simply indicate convenient *abstractions* from our complex life activities. In other words, the visceral drives, activity drives, aesthetic drives, and emotions (grouped in the table) represent a useful classification of drives or motives which are important in human behavior. These are not, however, the only possible lists; and they occur in conjunction with each other in almost infinitely complex patterns.

Thorstein Veblen did not need to have a list of motives before him when he made the sage observation that a "fancy bonnet of this year's model appeals to our sensibilities to-day much more forcibly than an equally fancy bonnet of the model of last year; although. . . it would be a matter of the utmost difficulty to award the palm for intrinsic beauty to the one rather than to the other of these structures."[3] Nor did Veblen have a long list of motives in mind when he remarked that, "the high gloss of a gentleman's hat or of a patent-leather shoe has no more of intrinsic beauty than a similarly high gloss on a thread-bare sleeve."[4] And he gave numerous examples of how a thing which is basically beautiful, but which is not expensive, is not thought of as beautiful by most consumers. Some intrinsically beautiful flowers, for instance, pass for nothing more than offensive weeds, whereas in the florist shop those flowers which are the most expensive are usually considered the most beautiful.

After all, man is a complicated animal. Because of his (at times) superior intelligence, he succeeds in making life even more complicated for himself than it already is.

But man is more than an animal or a *physiological* being. In addition to his basic visceral, activity, and aesthetic drives, he is also a *social* being. He belongs to all sorts of clubs, and institutions, and organizations.

Man the Consumer belongs to a particular nationality group—he is a member of a certain community—more often than not, he is affiliated with a church—he shows allegiance to a political party—he pays dues and maintains a membership in his labor union or professional organization—he pays additional dues to belong to a lodge or fraternal association—and he may belong to a club of some kind. Each and every one of these and other social institutions has an "emotional pull" for him. Here is where we find out about his basic loyalties, his beliefs, his prejudices. Consider his nationality, his labor union, his club—it is areas like these that need investigation if we are to obtain an adequate picture of Man the Consumer.

And then we need to find out about his special likes and dislikes, and how he got them. It is not enough to know that a green package is more effective than a red package (or vice versa) in getting attention for a certain product. It is not enough to know that most men prefer cigarettes to other forms of smoking. It is not enough to know that young women use more hand lotions than older women. The point is to find out *why* people have these preferences.

As Kornhauser has said: "Why does a man purchase the clothes he does? Is it enough to learn that he looks for a suit that fits well or that has style and quality? Certainly these attitudes tell something beyond even more specific explanations pertaining to store location, brand name, window display, etc., although these, too, are significant. But 'fit' may, in terms of more general desires, mean primarily bodily comfort to one man, social distinction to another, security from disapprobation to a third, or the increased affection of his lady-love, or a feeling of effectiveness and proper workmanship."[5]

I think you will agree that no *list* or classification of motives—even the one given earlier—is sufficient to answer questions of this kind. All that such lists can accomplish is to provide us with suitable check lists. We can then use these lists as guides in attempting to understand *homo sapiens.*

[1] Edwin R. Guthrie, *The Psychology of Human Conflict* (New York: Harper & Brothers, 1938) page 89.

[2] Gardner Murphy, Lois Barclay Murphy, and Theodore M. Newcomb, *Experimental Social Psychology* (New York: Harper & Brothers, 1937) revised edition, pages 98-99.

[3] Thorstein Veblen, *The Theory of the Leisure Class* (New York: Modern Library 1934) page 131.

[4] Veblen, same citation as footnote 3, pages 132-133.

[5] Arthur W. Kornhauser, "The Role of Psychological Interpretation in Market Research," *Journal of Consulting Psychology,* 1941, volume 5, pages 187-193, page 192.

Principles of Motivation

The problem of developing some suitable *principles of motivation* is equally difficult. All of us who have been serious students of advertising and selling have considered all kinds of different ways for obtaining effective emphasis. As you know, a great many alternate types of appeal have been studied in detail. Consider the following, for instance:

Positive appeals *versus Negative* appeals
Emotional appeals *versus Rational* appeals
Suggestive appeals *versus Argumentative* appeals
Consumer appeals *versus Product* appeals

Like our lists of motives, however, there is no ready-made answer to the question of which appeals should be used. This depends entirely upon the *specific* sales problem involved. Sometimes positive appeals are useful, and sometimes negative appeals are better. The same holds true for emotional versus rational appeals, suggestive versus argumentative appeals, and consumer versus product appeals.

The one eventual aim of advertisers and salesmen must be to see that consumers develop an *intensified desire to buy*. But, in stimulating consumer buying, have the best approaches always been used? Some critics of advertising have not thought so. Thus, Peter Odegard has said:

> "Have we held up to the American people a romantic dream world that can be had for the asking?....No one, we are told, can be happy, or successful without this new gadget or that, without two cars in every garage, a beautiful woman on each arm, a streamlined home on a high hill with a summer place in New England and a winter one in California or Miami. All this is fine and dandy as a goal. But how do you get all this? By the ancient methods of hard work, intelligence, thrift? Ah, no! Beauty and good health, success in business, in courtships and marriage can be had by going to your local dealer for a box of this or a bottle of that—and be sure to get the large economy size!"[6]

Now, this is not to suggest that advertising copy should begin to read like a treatise on physiology or physics; it is to question whether such appeals to consumers can be continued indefinitely, with effective results. Remember that consumers are human beings with deep-seated emotions. They hunger for security, for recognition, for health and beauty, for a successful marriage, for a happy home—such desires are deep and abiding. "But is it necessary. . . in seeking to win the consumer's allegiance for a product to appeal to his lust or his avarice or his superstitious and synthetic fears?"[7]

Is it not possible and more propitious to appeal to his *real* motives? We should then be in the proud position of selling goods and services in such a way that people have more confidence in them than ever before. Consumers must not be regarded as people who can be fooled.

A further problem is that so many attempts to influence the consumer sound or read pretty much alike. If we examine the basic advertising campaigns for some leading

products, it is difficult to find many real differences in the underlying advertising themes. One investigator has reported the following experimental evidence: "We may take current issues of any five national magazines and cut out all the advertisements for whiskey, soap, cosmetics, tires, refrigerators, etc., and group them together. Although every manufacturer will disclaim any similarity of quality and service between his and other products, we find that three out of four of the advertisements for each type of product read almost alike.

"There is no toilet soap that will not give the user lovelier skin, no face cream that will not secure romance and eternal love for the purchaser, and no whiskey that is not milder, smoother, and longer aged than all others on the market."[8]

What has all this got to do with principles of motivation? The answer is simply this. We need to develop some basic *principles* that will help us to understand consumer buying. The present kinds of strategy are not the whole answer.

Need for Qualitative Research

What do we really know about such things as the following: Why do people brush their teeth? Why do people drink orange juice? Why do some men smoke pipes? Why do some women read the *Ladies' Home Journal?* One thing is certain—we do not know much about the *real* reasons.

But if we take an area of behavior, like that of teeth brushing, we are beginning to find out the reasons. This is not due to our great acumen as marketing men or sales-

---

6 Peter Odegard, "Advertising in a Consumer Economy," address at Pacific Council Convention of American Association of Advertising Agencies, Santa Barbara, California, November 6, 1946.

7 Odegard, same citation as footnote 6.

8 Ernest Dichter, "A Psychological View of Advertising Effectiveness," *The Journal of Marketing*, 1949, volume 14, pages 61-66, page 63.

men or advertisers. It is due, instead, to a new discovery—*ammoniated* toothpaste. Practically all toothpaste over the years has been advertised and sold on the basis that you would have a beautiful smile, gleaming teeth, and get your man! Yet, some of us with psychological training knew that these were not the real reasons why most people brushed their teeth.

William A. Yoell, for example, knew that the reasons were to get little pieces of food unlodged from the teeth, and to prevent decay. How did he know? Because he had taken the trouble to conduct intensive *qualitative* or *depth interviews* with enough people to find out the why's of their teeth-brushing. But almost no one would listen. Yoell's was a voice crying in the wilderness. But suddenly, in the last few months, a lot of people have now "discovered"—in terms of the sales of ammoniated toothpaste—that people really brush their teeth to prevent decay.

As marketing people, some of us have been so busy *quantifying* that we have forgotten about *qualitative* research. We have added up numbers of people, and of pantries, and of products, until we have amassed figures without any *human* side.

Too many market researchers have mistakenly thought that mere counting of noses was a substitute for thinking. Too few people have turned to psychologists to find out what they could find out about specific motives.

An enormous number of well intentioned marketing people have been so content with the grinding out of questionnaires, which ask people to put little check marks after this, that, and the other thing, that they have forgotten what kind of a *human* animal they are studying.

They have forgotten all about the following psychological facts—and we certainly cannot turn them up on questionnaires. First of all, almost all people have terrific feelings of *insecurity*. With this goes fear and hate and prejudice, and sometimes desperate feelings of helplessness. Second, and closely related to insecurity, is the enormous amount of *aggression* and *hostility* which is in the unconscious thinking of most people. Third, almost all people seem to require *symbols of prestige*, in order to bolster up their own ego-deflated selves.

These three psychological facts do not represent a short course in psychology. Instead, they are just some basic examples of the kinds of factors that we have to keep constantly in mind if we are to understand consumers—in other words, *people*.

It is my contention that the great majority of market research questionnaires do not come reasonably close to finding out *why* and *how* people think and act as they do. It is too easy for the respondent just to check one of the answers listed by the interviewer, or to give socially desirable responses. This tendency to say the socially acceptable thing is with all of us most of the time, and as researchers we do not get "underneath" it very much.

If we are observant, however, we can get interesting

glimpses as to what people really think. For example, in paying my respects to a luncheon speaker recently, following his talk, the man with me also thanked him for his "wonderful speech"; but then, as the two of us turned away, said to me, "I think he is a stinker, and that was one of the most terrible speeches I have ever heard."

All of us have had similar experiences, and know that the words people utter do not necessarily represent truth. Even the reasons people give in all sincerity for their behavior are not necessarily the real reasons. But some of us are still content to hand out mimeographed questionnaires, in a debonair manner, which are not always very meaningful in results.

This is definitely *not* an attack on questionnaires. They have an important place in almost every market research program. I simply want to caution all of us against the wholesale acceptance of figures or statistics whenever the questions could not really produce accurate information. I have seen questionnaires so badly designed that, no matter how many people are interviewed, the results are worthless. And so have you.

Take the problem of learning *why* people do not buy a certain product, or *why* they do. Whether the product is a stick of chewing gum or an automobile, it is possible to interview as few as 50 people with the *right* questions, and to come up with more useful answers than by asking 500 or even 50,000 people the *wrong* questions.

Yoell reports "looking for information to help a leading soap manufacturer produce a new soap powder. Housewives told us that a certain powder they were using was 'excellent. . . the best ever. . . and so efficient.' Yet, when they described in detail, step by step, exactly how they washed dishes, we found they were. . . using another soap product to make the first one work."[9]

What, then, is the approach? The method of finding out is that of the *qualitative interview,* which I mentioned earlier. This is basically the *clinical* approach to interviewing. "The qualitative interview is variously called the intensive interview, detailed interview, non-directive interview, depth interview, conversational interview, and informal interview."[10] The psychologist undertaking this type of interview must establish sufficient *rapport* that he can have a protracted one-,two-,or three-hour session with a respondent in a pleasant, relaxed, and "easy" interviewing session.

To carry out qualitative or depth interviews does not mean that your present interviewers can put their hats on the other way round and suddenly become depth interviewers. The mere ability to ring doorbells and check answers

9 William A. Yoell, "Depth Interviewing Measures Belief in Advertising—and Reaction to It," *Printers' Ink,* March 18, 1949, volume 226, pages 48, 50, 55, page 48.

10 "Questionnaire Preparation and Interviewer Technique," report by a subcommittee of the Marketing Research Techniques Committee, *The Journal of Marketing,* 1949, volume 14, pages 399-413, page 425.

to "like. . . dislike. . . don't know," or to "more. . . same . . . less," does not by any means qualify one to deal with a lengthy clinical discussion with strangers. This is a serious problem, for those trained in clinical and social psychology.

In this connection, we should remember the tremendous importance of *unconscious* motivation. Even our supposedly forgotten experiences may have far-reaching effects on our lives. Certainly we need to take into account the unconscious habits, purposes, needs, and motives that influence our buying behavior.

Many of our daily acts are based on factors of which we are not consciously aware. Here is a significant example. It concerns the effect of wrapper design upon soap sales in a grocery store. "The same bar of soap was placed on the shelves in two different types of wrappers. The soap in one wrapper outsold the soap in the other wrapper nearly two to one. Now it is self-evident that the average housewife does not consciously go to the grocery store to buy package designs; she goes to buy ham, vegetables, soap, canned fruit, and so on. Only rarely does she consciously consider the container in which these items are sold."[211]

This means that unconscious factors affected buying behavior. They always do. Our problem is to discover what these factors are and how they work.

Information from Psychology and Sociology

We may say, then, that social scientists and their methods are having a real effect on modern marketing practices. In fact, a large part of the effectiveness of advertising has come about in recent years as people in the advertising profession have learned to use *research* and *fact-finding* techniques. These research methods have been developed, by and large, by psychologists and sociologists. These two groups have produced techniques which are now employed as a matter of course in everyday advertising and market research. I only need to mention the developments in copy testing. . . controlled opinion tests. . . inquiry and coupon tests. . . recall tests. . . recognition and identification tests. . . sales tests.

But what may not be so well known are the areas of research being opened up by psychologists and sociologists,

which have a definite bearing on consumer problems. There are all sorts of studies, which, as marketing people, we should know about if we are adequately to perform our function as advisers on business problems.

One of the more important studies, for example, is that contained in a recent issue of the *Journal of Marketing*, where a special subcommittee, composed of Blankenship, Crossley, Heidingsfield, Herzog, and Kornhauser, issued a special report on questionnaire preparation and interviewer technique.[212] I recommend this report for careful study and use, especially if we are to overcome some of the objections I have raised to certain kinds of questionnaire research.

But there are other investigations as well which we should know about. They may not give us precise answers as to why people use toothpaste or tobacco; but, if we will take the trouble to become familiar with these studies, we shall find that our own grasp of consumer problems is much greater. Here are just a few examples from the considerable literature of social psychology and allied fields:

> Paul Lazarsfeld's ingenious study on how voters make up their minds in a presidential campaign is a joy to any market researcher.[213] This analysis of voters choosing candidates provides some real clues as to how we might study individuals when they are behaving as consumers choosing products.
>
> Lloyd Warner's studies on social classes represent, in my opinion, the most important step forward in market research in many years, if we will take the trouble to follow his lead. Although his book, *Social Class in America*, gives not the slightest hint on marketing methods, it occurs to me that his methodology in measuring social classes could be taken over and used effectively in many a marketing study.[214]
>
> Careful reading of various volumes on communities will also help us to be better market researchers. I think of Warner's studies of "Yankee City," the Lynds' famous books on "Middletown," and James West''s (Carl Withers') analysis of "Plainville."[215]
>
> In this same connection, we should note the important studies of regionalism, carried out by Odum and Moore, and others.[216] Then, there are the inquiries into semantics, or language in action, by Ogden and Richards, Stuart Chase, and Hayakawa.[217]
>
> We should be aware, too, of the important work on readability done by Rudolf Flesch, and also of the signifi-

211 Louis Cheskin and Lewis B. Ward, "Indirect Approach to Market Reactions," *Harvard Business Review*, 1948, volume 26, pages 572-580, page 573.

212 Same citation as footnote 10.

213 Paul F. Lazarsfeld, Bernard Berelson, and Hazel Gaudet, *The People Choice: How the Voter Makes Up His Mind in a Presidential Campaign* (New York: Columbia University Press, 1948).

214 W. Lloyd Warner, Marchia Meeker, and Kenneth Eells, *Social Class in America: A Manual of Procedure for the Measurement of Social Status* (Chicago: Science Research Associates, 1949).

215 W. Lloyd Warner and Paul S. Lunt, *The Social Life of a Modern Community* (Volume I of "Yankee City Series") (New Haven: Yale University Press, 1941). Robert S. Lynd and Helen Merrell Lynd, Middletown: *A Study in Contemporary American Culture* (New York: Harcourt, Brace and Company 1929) Robert S.Lynd and Helen Merrell Lynd, *Middletown in Transition: A Study in Cultural Conflicts* (New York: Harcourt, Brace and Company, 1937). James West, Plainville, U.S.A. (New York: Columbia University Press, 1945).

216 Howard W. Odum and Harry E. Moore, *American Regionalism: A Cultural Historical Approach to National Integration* (New York: Henry Holt and Company, Inc., 1938).

217 Charles K. Ogden and Ivor A. Richards, *The Meaning of Meaning: A Study of the Influence of Language Upon Thought and of the Science of Symbolism* (New York: Harcourt, Brace and Company, 1930) revised edition. Stuart Chase, *The Tyranny of Words* (New York: Harcourt, Brace and Company, 1938). S. I. Hayakawa, Language in Action (New York: Harcourt, Brace and Company, 1939).

cant studies on legibility of printed matter, by Paterson and Tinker.[18]

There are the significant studies of social movements by Cantril, which give real insight into various kinds of group behavior.[19]

We ought to know about the problems of minority groups, and the ways in which prejudice acts in relation to important segments of our population. Consider, for example, the work of Dollard, of Myrdal, and of Arnold and Caroline Rose.[20]

Personality analysis should also be taken into account—and I think of such an important contribution as *Assessment of Men*, written by the O.S.S. Assessment Staff, which gives important insights into human behavior.[21]

And we should certainly not overlook the famous Kinsey studies on sex behavior.[22]

At this point you will probably say—"What on earth do sex, and semantics, and social movements, and social class have to do with each other?" Granted that they are not related in any apparent sense, I am simply suggesting to you that there are many broad and important areas which social scientists have investigated which will give marketing experts a clearer concept of how human beings act, and why they act that way.

We have seen the difficulty of making up adequate lists of motives, or of classifying motives in any abstract way. If we will take the trouble, however, to find out about some of these areas of behavior—including person-

ality and prejudice and participation—we will know a lot more about our basic problem—Man the Consumer.

Need for Knowledge About People

The history of the United States is one of great physical, economic, and social growth. We have developed unusual skills and unique techniques of production. We are able to turn out more goods and services in every hour we work than any other people in the entire world.

But along with our tremendous technical knowledge of *production,* we need to develop even greater knowledge about *people.* Over 100 million dollars have been allotted by the Federal Government this year for research purposes, and an additional 25 million dollars have been made available to the colleges by business and industry for research.[23] However, about 97 percent of these total funds are allotted for the engineering, physical, biological, and agricultural sciences—only 3 per cent is left for the humanities, the social studies, and the liberal arts.

If ever there were a need for significant studies of social behavior, now is the time. In the long run, this is the only way we shall obtain really effective answers to questions about people as consumers. So far, we have only scratched the surface in learning about the strategy of consumer motivation.

As marketing men, it is good business for us to start *now* to learn more about the *real* motives that stimulate Man the Consumer to buy.

18 Rudolf Flesch, *The Art of Plain Talk* (New York: Harper & Brothers, 1946). Donald G. Paterson and Miles A. Tinker, *How to Make Type Readable* (New York: Harper & Brothers, 1940).

19 Hadley Cantril, *The Psychology of Social Movements* (New York: John Wiley & Sons, 1941).

20 John Dollard, *Caste and Class in a Southern Town* (New Haven: Yale University Press, 1937). Gunner Myrdal and others, *An American Dilemma: The Negro Problem and Modern Democracy* (New York: Harper & Brothers, 1944). Arnold and Caroline Rose, *America Divided: Minority Group Relations in the United States*, (New York: Alfred A. Knopf, 1948).

21 O.S.S. Assessment Staff, *Assessment of Men* (New York: Rinehart & Company, Inc., 1948).

22 Alfred C. Kinsey, Wardell B. Pomeroy, and Clyde E. Martin, *Sexual Behavior in the Human Male* (Philadelphia: W.B. Saunders Company, 1948).

23 Benjamine Fine, "Education in Review," *The New York Times*, December 11, 1949, Section 4, page E9.

Seymour Banks

The Relationships Between Preference and Purchase of Brands

Purpose and General Summary

THE purpose of the research discussed below was the investigation of the relationships between preference and purchases by housewives of brands of seven classes of household products. Two bodies of data were collected and analyzed for correspondence: existing levels of preference for the brands of these products on the Chicago market, and purchases of these products by a panel of Chicago housewives during a three-week period.

A brief summary of the results is as follows:

(1) It was found that brand preference was almost identical with purchase intention; about 96 percent of the panel included their most preferred brands in their purchase intentions.

(2) Preference for brands was a good predictor of purchase; the average coefficient of correlation between preference for a brand and the relative share of purchases obtained by that brand was .918 for the seven product classes. Last purchase made and statements of purchase intentions were even better predictors of relative brand purchase by the panel.

(3) Preference was a fairly good predictor of purchase for the individual panel member as well as for the entire group. Only 15 per cent of the group who stated brand purchase intentions bought brands entirely different from those mentioned. However, another 15 per cent performed only partially on their brand purchase intentions. There was much greater variance quantitatively between predicted and actual purchases.

(4) Preference ratings on product attributes of brands of scouring cleanser and coffee were related to brand purchase by means of linear discriminant functions. The most important attributes for scouring cleanser were found to be cleansing ability and knowledge of price; for coffee the most important attributes were flavor and knowledge of price.

Collection of Data

The basic data were collected from a panel of 465 housewives in the city of Chicago during April-June, 1948. Each respondent was interviewed twice, the second interview coming three weeks after the first. During this three-week period, respondents reported purchases weekly by mail. The first interview was used to obtain information upon brands on hand, preference statements for brands, and a statement of purchase intentions for seven classes of household products. The products used were scouring cleanser, coffee, ice cream, peanut butter, potato chips, mayonnaise and salad dressing, and catsup.[1]

During the second interview, preference statements were collected again for brands of scouring cleanser and coffee. In addition, the respondents were asked to give preference scores on the product attributes of these brands. If comparison of mailed-in diaries and the original questionnaire showed that a housewife had failed to buy according to her stated intentions she was asked why. And if on the first interview the respondent had expressed an intention of purchasing a lower-rated brand, she was asked the reason during the second interview.

A numerical rating scale for preferences was developed for the research. It was thought that its use would avoid difficulties arising from differences of verbalization among respondents. It meant also that the respondent, not the interviewer, coded the respondent's answer. The scale used was read vertically and was portrayed in the shape of a thermometer. Numerals (0-8) were placed on the left

---

[1] The criteria used in selecting these products were: (a) wide use; (b) high rate of purchase; (c) equal availability to housewives; (d) absence of a brand completely dominating the market.

side of the tube and phrases descriptive of the even numbered ratings were on the right. The highest rating was 8—very satisfactory; the lowest was 0—very unsatisfactory. Satisfactory was used as the basic word in the descriptions because this word conveyed the desired meaning—the ability of a product to produce utility for the housewife. The neutral point of the scale was placed at 2. The asymmetry was used because few pre-test respondents had unfavorable impressions of brands that had been on the market for some time. In the rating procedure, the respondent held the preference scale and gave the numerical rating that best matched her feeling about a brand when that brand name was read to her by the interviewer. The respondents rated only the brands they had used.

The sample of housewives used in this study was drawn from the city of Chicago by an area sampling technique. Comparison of sample and population data showed the sample to be representative as checked by the following statistics: number of dwellings per block; percentage Negro; age of housewife; and years of school completed by housewife. It was recognized early in the planning of this study that the procedure used to collect the data might seriously bias the results. The housewife who had bought something she had previously given a low rating might feel ashamed to admit it and so would report purchasing her most preferred brand to avoid "losing face." Doubt on this point could be reduced substantially by obtaining objective measures of brand purchase by pantry audits, collection of labels or packages, etc. However this would increase cost considerably and would do nothing to keep a resolute respondent from cheating—she could always hide the bargain brand. To cope with this very real problem of procedural bias, the following precautions were taken: preference and purchase data were obtained for many brands of seven different product classes; the interviewer was instructed to set a non-committal tone with the respondent, "Just write down what you buy; a report of no purchase is a good report if that's what you did"; the diaries were to be mailed to the director of the study so the respondent would report her purchases to some one other than the person to whom she reported her preferences and purchase intentions; the diaries were mailed in weekly to reduce the amount of evidence available to the respondent to remind her of her statements or previous purchases. Still, the question of procedural bias is not completely settled; work remains to be done.[2]

---

2 It is felt that the findings were not seriously affected by a procedural bias, if one remained. There was great variation in performance on purchase intentions by the respondents from product class to product class and by different individuals within the various product classes. Conversations with other researchers showed substantial agreement of the purchase data with reported sales of the brands of coffee and ice cream in Chicago at the time of study.

Discussion of the Relations Between Brand Preference and Purchase

The basic data which were analyzed to determine the relations between preference and purchase were as follows, for each brand of each of the seven product classes: number of respondents who had used it and could remember it well enough to give it a preference rating, the number of those who had used it but could not remember much about it, and the number of those who had heard of the brand but had not used it—these numbers add up to yield the total knowledge level for the brand; the proportion of 8's among raters; the brand's share of the panel's inventory of the corresponding product class at the first interview; the brand's share of the panel's inventory of the corresponding product class at the first interview; the brand's share of the panel's purchase intentions for the product class; and the brand's share of the actual purchases of the product class. The distribution of actual purchases of brands by product classes was the datum plane for the analysis. All other data were compared in turn to the actual purchases to determine the degree of relationship between them.

The major interest of the study was in establishing the value of brand preference as a predictor of purchase. The basic hypothesis was that preference would show itself to be a good predictor of purchase. If this were upheld the basic purpose of the work was accomplished. Two other possible predictors of purchase (past purchases as represented by brands on hand at the first interview, and future purchase intentions) were included in the data to serve as standards against which the predictive performance of preference might be compared. The information on the relative merits of these three as predictors of purchase was to be a byproduct, not a main finding of the study.

The number of 8's among raters was chosen as the measure of preference for brands. This was chosen over several other possible indications of preference, proportion of 8's, a scale value, or an average rating. Almost all of the respondents intended buying only the brands rated 8. This meant lower ratings did not affect purchase decisions. Both scale values and average ratings include low ratings as well as high ratings. The proportion of 8's among raters is a measure of satisfaction with a brand; it could be used as a predictor of relative purchase of brands only when the numbers of raters for all brands were equal. This was not the case within the data. Nor can it be the case in the usual situation in which brands are on the market for varying amounts of time and with varying amounts of advertising and promotional effort.[3]

Table 1 summarizes the performance of the various predictors of purchase tested. The simplest predictor, the num-

---

3 Correlation of proportion of 8's per brand with purchases gave a weighted mean coefficient of .434 for the seven classes. This is much lower than any entry in Table 1.

| Product Class | No. of Brands | Predictors of Relative Purchase | | | |
| | | No. of Raters per Brand | No. of 8's per Brand | Brand's Share of Panel Inventory, 1st Interview | Brand's Share of Purchase Intentions |
(1)	(2)	(3)	(4)	(5)	(6)
Scouring cleanser	11	.828	.932	.985	.991
Coffee	20	.644	.670	.985	.898
Ice cream	15	.628	.750	.869	.912
Peanut butter	11	.945	.985	.997	.995
Potato chips	10	.853	.962	.987	.981
Mayonnaise and salad dressing	16	.859	.954	.995	.991
Catsup	13	.895	.974	.990	.992
Weighted average		.812	.918	.986	.977

ber of people rating each brand, was fairly good as a predictor of the relative purchase of brands. But the number of 8's per brand, which takes into consideration the distribution of preferences for each brand as well as the number rating the brands, was significantly better in predicting relative purchase than the simple number of raters per brand. The number of raters per brand could equal the predictive performance of the number of 8's per brand only if the distributions of preference were the same for all brands. And the basic data showed this not to be the case; there was great variation in the proportion of 8's from brand to brand in each of the product classes.

One might raise the question of the relation between the number of raters of a brand and the proportion of 8's given to that brand by its raters. Correlation of these two series gives a coefficient not significantly different from zero. Therefore, the better known brands were not more or less liked by their raters than the less well known brands.

The weighted average of column 4 of Table 1 is .918. This figure establishes the fact that there was a close relationship between preference (in terms of number of 8's per brand) and relative purchase of brands—84 per cent of the variation in relative purchase of brands is concomitant with variations in preference for those brands. The fluctuation of product-class coefficients of correlation in column 4 of Table I about their weighted mean is greater than might be expected from sampling fluctuation alone. The low r's are for coffee and ice cream. Those products are characterized by large numbers of brands on the market and great variation in knowledge and use of those brands by panel members.

Two other items of data were tried as predictors of sales. These are last purchase made and future purchase intentions. Future purchase intentions were weighted by amount to be bought within the coming three weeks' period. This was the only weighted predictor used. The difference between the weighted averages of columns 5 and 6 is not significant. These last predictors of purchase were better than was number of 8's per brand. This is understandable. Preference measurements leave out important factors like price, accessibility of brands, etc., which affect purchase behavior. Last purchase made and future purchase intentions reflect the impact of these other market factors, as well as preference, upon the housewife's actions.[4]

Individual Performances

So far the discussion has been in terms of aggregates, and the question of how well the panel predicted the purchases

---

[4] The basic purchase data used in the research discussed below were collected only for a three week-period. An obvious question of the findings is: over how long a period will a single statement of preference serve as an adequate predictor of purchase? To attempt an answer to this, preference data were collected from the families of the writer's market research classes for brands of scouring cleanser and coffee, and weekly reports of purchase were made for fifteen weeks afterwards, from October, 1949, to January, 1950. The correlation coefficients of preference ratings in terms of number of 8's with combined purchase date for the fifteen week period was .817 for the scouring cleanser and .841 for the coffee. These are at about the same levels as the early data which only covered three weeks. As in the earlier data, purchase intentions and past purchase data gave better predictive performances than number of 8's. The levels of predictive performance for these predictors were about the same height for each of the five three-week periods for both products except for that of past purchase with coffee. The distribution of brands of coffee found on the panel's shelves in October declined rather consistently in predictive ability throughout the study. It is not unexpected that in the fluctuating market that did obtain the distribution of brands on hand in October gave a poorer prediction of purchase in January than it did in November. The surprise is that the correlation was as good as it was: .79 in January compared to .96 in November.

These findings have test-tube value only, because of the small size of the sample and its atypicalness. But the results do indicate the basic procedures described above may have ability to predict brand purchases over a much longer period of time than the three weeks of the major work discussed above.

of the entire group. The excellent performance obtained might have come about through every one doing exactly as forecast or by everyone doing the exact opposite, with the mistakes and errors offsetting one another. To investigate this, it was necessary to study individual performances, not group relationships.

There are two steps between preference and purchase—from preference to intention to buy and from intention to actual purchase. When one tabulates the purchase intentions of the members of the panel, a very close relation appears between preference, as measured by the highest rating used, and intention to purchase. Over the seven product classes, 96.4 per cent of the brands included in purchase intentions received a preference rating that was the highest or was tied with the highest the respondent used for that product class. The most common situation was for a housewife to give her highest preference rating to a single brand and name that brand in her purchase intentions; 65.8 per cent of the brands named in purchase situations were so rated. There was some variation in this from product class to class, with potato chips having the highest number of unitary preference-choice situations and catsup the least.

Relation of Purchase Intention to Actual Purchase

If there is a very close relation between the individual housewife's preference for brands and her purchase intentions, what is the relation between her purchase intentions and actual purchases? Considering all purchase intention statements, positive and negative, 52.4 per cent of the housewives' purchase intentions were carried out exactly: if they named a specific brand, they bought it; if they were going to buy from a group of named brands, not specifying which one, they bought from that group; if they said they were not going to buy anything during the time of the study, they reported no purchase.[5] Apparently the housewives who did not intend to buy anything during the three weeks of the study were better prophets of their behavior than those who stated intentions to buy, 72.4 per cent of the former and 47.7 per cent of the latter type of purchase intention being sustained exactly. However, the performance, brandwise, on individual purchase intentions was really better than the last figure indicates, for there were many degrees of performance on brand purchase intentions (Table 2). Some of the housewives carried out their purchase intentions partially either by buying only part of the brands mentioned or by buying their intended brands plus some others—14.9 per cent of those with brand purchase intentions fell into this class. Those who failed completely to fulfill their purchase intentions

can be divided into two groups, those who failed to forecast correctly the time of purchase and those whose intentions and purchases do not agree at all, brandwise. It is only this last subgroup that might be considered as being really indifferent to brands or completely unable to predict their purchases. These people represent 15.3 per cent of those who gave brand purchase intentions and 12.4 per cent of the entire panel.

The impulsive nature of the purchase of ice cream is clearly illustrated; the smallest percentage of complete success on prediction of purchase and the highest amount of brand switching was reported for this product class. Coffee seems to be the product for which housewives did the best job of predicting brand purchases.

Preference Ratings of Brands Purchased

One can make a further study of the directness of the relationship between preference and purchase. This can be done by determining the preference ratings given to the brands actually purchased by the respondents. For the seven product classes over-all, the panel members bought four or five times as many 8-rated brands as they bought of lower-rated brands. Again ice cream showed up as a product in which there was less insistence upon preferred brands. This is only by contrast with the other product classes, for even in respect to ice cream the ratio of 8-rated brands purchased to lower-rated brands was three to one.

Purchases of previously non-rated brands bulked fairly high in the cases of ice cream and potato chips—the two chief examples of impulse goods in the study. It may be that the housewife was quite willing to buy unfamiliar brands of these products or that the interviewing procedure failed to elicit the full knowledge of the respondents. This latter is quite possible for respondents were not asked to give preference ratings to brands they had never used. If information on preferences of this group were obtained by the method DuBois uses,[6] it is very likely that these figures of purchase of non-rated brands would be reduced.

Another way of determining the effect of preference upon purchase is to inquire into the motivation of those who intended purchases of less-preferred brands. This gives a look into those cases in which preference is not operative. Some of the respondents had stated intentions of buying brands of scouring cleanser and coffee they had given low ratings during the first interview. On the second interview, three weeks later, they were asked the reason for this intention. The reason for the intention was asked after the purchases, and not before, to avoid self-conscious action on the part of respondents.

Only a small number of housewives gave reasons for their previous intentions to buy lower rated brands of scour-

---

5 The following is a breakdown of the types of purchase intention found in the data: named specific brand(s) 71.8 per cent; named group without further specification, 10.2 per cent; and intended to buy nothing, 19.0 per cent.

---

6 Cornelius DuBois, *The Mind is Bigger than the Pocketbook* (New York: Cornelius DuBois and Co., 1949), Pamphlet.

(Data in percentage of respondents)

Product Class	Type of Purchase Intention								
	Intended to Buy Some Brand(s)					Intended Not to Buy			
	Number	Degree of Performance				Number	Degree of Performance		
		Complete	Partial	Switched Completely	Bought Nothing		Complete	Failure	
Scouring cleanser	452	56.7	14.8	11.7	16.8	5	20.0	80.0	
Coffee	442	60.2	22.9	11.5	5.4	18	55.6	44.4	
Ice cream	337	32.3	19.6	29.7	18.4	101	61.4	38.6	
Peanut butter	276	45.3	6.5	8.7	39.5	181	80.7	19.3	
Potato chips	272	47.0	10.7	9.6	32.7	182	73.2	26.8	
Mayonnaise and Salad dressing	409	43.0	16.1	16.7	24.2	53	68.0	32.0	
Catsup	399	43.5	9.8	18.9	27.8	62	71.0	29.0	
Weighted average		47.7	14.9	15.3	22.1		72.4	27.6	

ing cleanser and coffee. The predominant reason was lower price on the lower-rated brand for both products. Other reasons such as coupon offers, desire for change, and convenience got one or two mentions. The effect of price upon intention shows up quite strongly here. A question not answered by the preference measurement technique used is, how important is price in determining preference? These data gave evidence that in some cases price and preference are independent.

Failure to Make Intended Purchases

Preference affects purchase only through its effect upon purchase intentions. Failures of housewives to carry out their purchase intentions distorts the relation between preference and purchase. The second interview was used to ask those respondents whose mailed-in diaries showed failure to perform on their purchase intentions of brands of scouring cleanser and coffee why this had happened.

Leaving out those who had failed to buy because they had overestimated their needs, three main reasons were given for failure to buy brands of scouring cleanser and coffee as intended. They are price reduction on other brands, desire for change, and out of stock. The order is reversed for the two products. Of the three main reasons, price reductions on other brands was the most important reason for not buying scouring cleanser as intended and least important for coffee. "Out of stock" is the most important reason for buying other brands of coffee, and least important for scouring cleanser. Apparently the difference in housewives' minds between brands of cleanser is so small that small price changes will cause them to switch from one brand to another. The difference among coffees is

greater; housewives switch brands only when the desired one is not available. The preference for a specified brand is probably not great enough for them to go to another store if the desired brand is not on hand at the first store. Coffee is still a convenience good.

The presence of desire for change is a limitation upon direct extrapolation of preference to predicted purchase. Because of its presence, the apparent and real choice situations of individuals are different. It is likely that satiation is a randomly occurring event and its effect will be cancelled out in a group purchase situation.

Analysis of Quantities Bought

As predictors of the number of units to be purchased, the panel fared poorly. Over-all, they bought 61.4 per cent more units of the seven product classes than they expected. The biggest error was for ice cream; the panels' members bought 2.6 times the predicted amount; the best job of quantitative prediction was for peanut butter, in which they exceeded their predictions by only 12.4 per cent. The errors by the respondents were not uniform in either direction or amount; 35.4 per cent of the predictions were correct, 38.8 per cent of the purchases were underestimated, and 22.3 per cent overestimated. The average error of underestimation was larger than the average error of overestimation.

The Effect of Preference for Attributes of Brands

The preceding discussion has related brand preference to purchase as if brands were indivisible objects. However, brands are made up of many product attributes, some of which affect overall preference and purchase strongly and others weakly or not at all. If a manufacturer wishes to increase sales by improving his product, he needs to know the most crucial attributes of his brand. The discussion which follows is based upon an exploratory effort to develop a technique for determining the relative importance of the various product attributes of a brand upon buyers' purchase decisions. The basic technique was multiple regression analysis of data for brands of scouring cleanser and coffee. Two types of studies were made, one on the relation between product attribute preference scores of brands and the over-all brand preference scores, and the other on the relation between brand attribute preference scores and brand purchase by the respondents. The major portion of the following discussion will be devoted to the latter type of study. Some comment upon the regression analysis of brand attribute ratings upon over-all brand preference scores can be found in an article by George H. Brown.[7]

In this discussion in the first of this paper, the relation between brand preference scores and purchase was investigated by means of simple correlation. The obvious parallel for the study of the relationship between brand attribute preference scores and brand purchase is multiple regression with quantity of purchase as the dependent variable and the attribute scores as the independent variables. However, the quantity of a brand purchased by a housewife is affected by many things other than preference on product attributes—size of family, income, shopping habits, etc. for which no data were available. It was feared that omission of these variables would give regression functions that would do a poor job of fitting the data since most of the relevant variables were not included. To overcome this difficulty, it was decided to classify respondents into buyers and non-buyers of brands, and find out how important these product attributes were in this separation. A technique known as linear discriminant function analysis has been developed to sort objects into two classes on the basis of their measurements on several variables.[8]

The usual method of separating individuals into two groups on the basis of quantitative variables is to use a measurement on one variable at a time. The variable which gives the widest difference between means of the two groups is used for further work. This method is inefficient in that it cannot make use of several variables simultaneously. The linear discriminant function analysis allows the use of several variables at once to effect a separation into two classes and permits evaluation of each of the variables in this differentiation process.

The principal difference between a linear discriminant function and a linear regression function lies in the nature of the dependent variable. A linear regression function uses values of the dependent variable to determine a linear function that will estimate the values of the dependent variable. The discriminant function uses a two-way classifica-

tion of the data to determine the linear function.[9] Thus the dependent variable for regression is quantitative, the dependent variable for the discriminant is qualitative. The solution techniques of linear regression and linear discriminant functions are quite similar since they are both problems of variate analysis using linear functions. In both cases, equations are set up using variance and covariances of the independent variable scores and solved simultaneously.

The linear discriminant function is used to create an index number that determines which of two classifications an individual is to receive. The index number for each individual is calculated by summing the products of the scores of that individual on each of the independent variables multiplied by the coefficient determined for the strength of that variable in the function. The procedure for discrimination consists of finding some critical score such that index scores above this would result in the individual being classified with one group, and below this with the other. The weight given to each variable is a measure of its importance in this process of separation. These weights are what we are interested in for this study. They give the relative importance of each product attribute in separating the members of the panel into potential buyers and non-buyers of brands of scouring cleanser and coffee.

Collection of Data

In the second interview, the respondent was asked to rate brands of scouring cleanser and coffee as she had done before. Then, ratings on attributes were obtained. All rated brands were scored on one attribute before going on to the next. This procedure was used to avoid a halo effect which would have obtained if all attributes of a brand were rated before going on to the next brand.[10]

The product attributes used for scouring cleanser and coffee were developed from free response questioning of a group of housewives. They were asked what interested them most when shopping for brands of scouring cleanser and coffee. The most frequently given responses were used as the product attributes of the study, as follows (these are not the order of frequency of mentions): *Scour-*

7 George H. Brown, "Measuring Consumer Attitudes Toward Products," *Journal of Marketing*, Vol. XIV (April, 1950), pp. 691-698.

8 R. A. Fisher, "The Use of Multiple Measurements in Taxonomic Problems," *Annals of Eugenics*, VIII (1938), pp. 179-188.

David Durand, *Risk Elements in Consumer Installment Financing: Technical Edition* (New York: National Bureau of Economic Research, 1941), Appendixes A and B.

9 Paul Hoel, *Introduction to Mathematical Statistics* (New York: John Wiley & Sons, Inc., 1947), pp. 121-126.

10 Examination of the data leads one to the belief that a halo effect was avoided. The first order correlations within the scouring cleanser data between brand ratings and the product attribute ratings were tested for homogeneity. These coefficients are heterogeneous from product attribute to product attribute within brands and between brands. There is fairly high intercorrelation among the independent variables however.

TABLE 3. RELATIVE VALUES OF BETA PARTIAL REGRESSION COEFFICIENTS AND DISCRIMINANT COEFFICIENTS OF SIX PRODUCT ATTRIBUTES ON PREFERENCE AND PURCHASE OF BRANDS OF SCOURING CLEANSER
(Pooled Data on 8 Leading Brands)

Case	Package Appearance	Cleansing Ability	Grittiness in Use	Harshness on Hands	Odor	Knowledge of Price
Preference	.10*	1.00*	.25*	.02	—	.10*
Purchase	.03	1.00*	.02	.27*	.14	.41*

* Original coefficients significantly different from 0 at the 1 per cent level of confidence.
Note: Entries converted from original coefficients, largest in each series given the value of 1.0 and others in relative terms.

ing cleanser, package appearance, cleansing ability, grittiness or scratchiness in use, harshness on hands, odor, and price; Coffee, package appearance, flavor, ability to make many cups per pound, and price.

In the regression analysis which follows, price was coded as 3 if the housewife knew the brand and 0 if she did not.[11]

The attributes listed above are not unidimensional, nor are they independent. One housewife may give a brand of scouring cleanser 8 on grittiness because she likes the speedy way its coarse particles cut through dried food crusts. Another would give this brand 0 because she fears scratches on her porcelain sink from the coarse particles. The size of the partial regression coefficients were of more interest in this study than their sign. If flavor has a negative partial regression coefficient with brand preference or purchase for coffee, what should the manufacturer do, make the flavor stronger or weaker? The present data cannot tell. This work on fragmentation of brand preference is frankly exploratory. If it establishes certain attributes as critical for preference and purchase, it well have accomplished its purpose.

Before the preference data could be used for regression analysis, it had to be normalized. The original data were piled up around 8's, 6's and 0's. The data were coded by transforming the original values into values of 1, 0, -1, -2, -3. The zero corresponds to the original value of 7. The coded data are grouped within three standard deviations of their mean whereas the raw data were very much skewed toward the low values.

Discussion of Results

Linear discriminant functions were computed, one relating the preference ratings on attributes of the major brands of scouring cleanser to purchase or lack of purchase of the eight leading brands of scouring cleanser, and the other doing the same with the eight major brands of coffee.[12] The coefficients of these functions were converted to units of the standard deviation of the corresponding variable—a process analogous to the computation of beta partial coefficients in multiple regression. In this form, the relative sizes of the coefficients come closest to stating the

relative importance of the various product attributes in the discrimination process.[13]

Only three of the six product attributes of scouring cleanser were found to have partial discriminant coefficients significantly greater than zero. In order of relative size (and importance), they are cleansing ability, knowledge of price, and harshness on hands. Apparently preference scores on package appearance, grittiness in use, and odor had no effect upon housewives purchase of brands of scouring cleanser. The bottom row of Table 3 shows the relative importance of the six product attributes for brand purchase. The top row of Table 3 summarizes the results of the regression analysis of attribute preference scores of over-all brand preference ratings.[14] Cleansing ability is the most important product attribute for both purchase and over-all brand preference rating; however its dominance is different in the two cases. For preference, knowledge of price is only one-tenth as important as cleansing ability, but for purchase decisions knowledge of price is forty per cent as important as cleansing ability.

For coffee, only two of the four product attributes had partial discriminant coefficients significantly different from zero—flavor and knowledge of price. Table 4 summarizes for coffee the relative sizes of the attribute coefficients for purchase and contrasts them with the relative sizes of the partial regression coefficients for the attributes upon brand preference. As with cleansers, knowledge of price is several times more important in discriminating between buyers and non-buyers of brands of coffee than it

---

11 Actually this procedure transforms a brand attribute into an attribute of the housewife. It was felt that she would be aware of the price if it was far out of line with other brands. The above process tests the ability of price to affect housewives' memory.

12 See Palmer O. Johnson, *Statistical Methods in Research*, (New York: Prentice-Hall, Inc., 1949), pp. 347-53 for a discussion and demonstration of a solution procedure. However he does not calculate the standard errors of the coefficients but this can be done by means of the Fisher multiplers—Johnson, pp. 330-338.

13 Durand, op. cit., p. 129.

14 S. Banks, *Some Application of Psychological Measurement and Attitude to Market Research*, Unpublished Ph.D. Thesis, University of Chicago, P. 113 for the scouring cleanser and p. 115 for coffee data.

TABLE 4. RELATIVE VALUES OF BETA PARTIAL REGRESSION COEFFICIENTS AND DISCRIMINANT COEFFICIENTS OF FOUR PRODUCT ATTRIBUTES ON PREFERENCE AND PURCHASE OF BRANDS OF COFFEE
(Pooled Data on 8 Leading Brands)

Case	Package Appearance	Flavor	Ability to Make Many Cups per Pound	Knowledge of Price
Preference	.03	1.00*	.10*	.05*
Purchase	.09	1.00*	.08	.43*

* Original coefficients significantly different from 0 at the 1 per cent level of confidence.
Note: Entries converted from original coefficients; largest in each series given the value of 1.0 and others in relative terms.

was in explaining variations in over-all brand preference scores. This finding is not surprising. However it is comforting to have intuition supported by evidence. This statistical confirmation of intuition underlines two statements: in considerable measure, preference and price are independent factors; and, preference and purchase situations are different.[15]

The findings on critical attributes cannot be exploited too far. Apparently, package appearance had no significant effect upon purchases of brands of scouring cleanser and coffee. This finding might have been an artifact of the research procedure. But even if it were not, a manufacturer should not feel free to package his coffee in torn, dirty bags. The results merely suggest that with present packages there is no apparent relation between preferences on this product attribute and purchase. This situation might have come about because all packages now in use are acceptable. Package appearances could come to have an effect upon purchase if some of the present packages were either improved or allowed to deteriorate.

Concluding Comments

On Methodology

All the information on brand and product attribute preferences used in this paper was based upon unaided recall. The results might well have been different if the respondents were confronted with actual packages, used the cleansers, drank the various brands of coffee, etc. Much research work needs to be done on the correct procedure for obtaining valid measurements of brand and product attrib-

ute preferences. Home tests with code-marked samples followed by preference tests and probing questions may be found to yield more valid data.

Possibly the product attributes used in this study need more refining than the method of measuring satisfaction upon them. They are chiefly verbal symbolizations of the product, and not single, unidimensional attributes. Attention must be given to the definition of attributes so they are equally meaningful to respondents and to the production departments of manufacturers. Cleansing ability of scouring cleanser is based upon two factors, detergent action and abrasive action; the preference test should treat them separately and find which of these two factors is more important

On Applications of the Research

The direct findings of this research are given in the opening paragraphs. They may be summarized briefly as follows: there is a direct and close relationship between existing levels of preference for brands of seven classes and household products and their relative purchase by housewives. The first or highest choice is the most important factor in the preference-purchase relationship.[16] By regression analysis, it was possible to point out crucial attributes of scouring cleanser and coffee. It was found that different factors affect preference and purchase of brands. The factors which operate in both situations have different relative importance in the two situations.

The indirect findings of the study are the suggestions it offers for the application of the techniques and results to future research. In the views of the writer, preference measurement can come to have a wider application than the prediction of the relative purchase of a series of competing alternatives. It can offer basic information as a guide to the formation of marketing policy. Market by market, the mar-

---

15 The evidence for the last statement comes partially from Tables 3 and 4 which show the differing effects of the variables in the two situations and partially from the multiple correlation coefficients of the two sets of equations. The multiple correlation coefficients of product attribute ratings with brand preference ratings are .836 for scouring cleanser and .882 for coffee; the multiple correlation coefficients for the discriminant analyses are .471 for the scouring cleanser and .537 for coffee. Thus a given set of variables does a much poorer job of explaining variation of brand purchase than it did in explaining variations of brand preference.

16 The statement that only the first choice is important in choice is made by L. L. Thurstone, "The Prediction of Choice," *Psychometrika*, X (1945), pp. 237-253. The work in this paper supports this statement. If this finding is carried over into psychometric tests, it will simplify procedures now used to select the best or most preferred of a series of objects, such as illustrations, package designs, etc.

keting manager can determine how well his product or brand is known, what people who have used it think of it, and the purchase intentions of users and non-users. These findings will serve to point directly to basic marketing weaknesses. Remedies can be proposed for the weaknesses revealed by these diagnostic tests—advertising and sampling to increase knowledge level, product or package improvement to raise preferences for the product, and the use of price reductions or special promotional deals to increase purchase intentions if preference is high and purchase is low. If product improvement is suggested, overall brand preference can be fragmented in terms of individual product attributes to determine the relative importance of these individual attributes in preference and purchase. These findings will permit the improvement in product to be directed more precisely than if it were guided by hunch or custom alone.[17]

Preference measurement can do more than serve as a means of discovering the basic marketing information mentioned above. It can also measure the response to marketing experiments designed to correct the deficiencies revealed by the first investigation. Thus, advertising campaigns can be evaluated in terms of their effect upon knowledge level and intentions to purchase. Product attribute

---

[17] See Brown, *op. cit.*, for an extended comment on the use of preference measurement in diagnosis of a brand's market position.

changes can be evaluated in terms of product preference. Finally, change in knowledge level might be evaluated against change in preference as a means of increasing the purchase intentions for the brand in question.

A final consideration in this discussion on the use of preference measurement as a guide to marketing policy is the matter of costs to produce the desired change. If it becomes possible to evaluate the relative importance of knowledge level, product preference, merchandising factors, and price differentials in an equation, as it was possible to use product attribute preferences to predict over-all brand preferences, the problem is not ended when the relative importance of these factors is determined. For both the problem of market strategy and the problem of product improvement, the size of the coefficient in a regression equation is only part of the solution. It may be that some factors will respond much more easily to a given amount of effort and money than others. Thus it may work out that a change of knowledge level is more important in affecting relative sales of a brand than changes in the preference level but the return in sales for a given investment is greater when a given sum of money is spent in increasing the preference for the brand through product improvement. For either change in factors outside the product or for changes of the product, the important consideration is the increase in sales per dollar expenditure. Preference measurement can serve to point out need changes and to evaluate the performance of test solutions.

W. Edwards Deming

Statistical Techniques and International Trade*

WE are in a new industrial age. Almost every type of activity in production and distribution has been remade several times over, during the past 10 or 12 years, by new uses of statistical theory. The same statistical techniques that have remade marketing research have helped industry to achieve great increases in output without capital expenditure for new machines or for additional floor space. They have saved scarce materials, and have brought forth quality and uniformity not dreamed of a few years ago.

Everyone knows the impact of new statistical techniques on marketing research, and on production, quality, and uniformity of product, but few people have seen the day ahead when marketing research must be considered an important part of the statistical control of quality. The reason is that good quality and the right uniformity have no meaning *except with reference to the consumer's demands.*

International trade is an essential component of prosperity, political stability, and peace. But international trade depends not only on a competitive price, but also on dependable quality and uniformity, which in turn depend to a large extent on intelligent marketing research.

As most of you know, the simple statistical techniques of the control chart have brought forth in recent Japanese experience increases in production that range from 5 per cent to 230 per cent, *without expansion of plant.* Some firms are saving 10 per cent of their raw material, compared with their performance of a year ago. In some cases, the savings are much greater. The Fuji Steel Company reported they were able to cut their fuel bill by 29 per cent over their performance a year ago. All these achievements, and more, were reported at the convention held in Osaka the 22d September 1951 at the occasion of the Dem-

ing Award. In the mill of the Toyo Cotton Spinning Company that I visited during my work here during the summer of 1951, three quarters of the girls who had been engaged in re-work and repair a year before had been moved into production, because of the improved quality of the product. Result: increased production, better quality, greater uniformity.

The gain in production and profit, although considerable from such achievements, are the least of the gains. The gains from a better competitive position through improved quality and ability to lower the price are much greater, though more difficult to measure.

In these ways, and in many other ways, statistical techniques help greatly to meet the requirements for increased international trade.

Moreover, I cannot emphasize too strongly that increased use of statistical techniques can contribute vitally toward the maintenance of private enterprise, which must depend more and more on the continual improvement of the efficiency of production and of distribution, and on the continual improvement of the design of product, in respect to both quality and uniformity, to meet the changing needs and the demands of the consumer, wherever he may be.

In any manufacturing plant, raw materials come in, and product flows out. The raw materials may indeed by raw, or they may be sub-assemblies or piece-parts from another manufacturer. Eventually, the product goes to people who will judge it. The finished product may indeed be finished, and go to thousands or millions of consumers, or it may be raw material for a relatively small number of other manufacturers.

Anyway, there will be a chain of production, as illustrated crudely by Figure 1. By the statistical control of quality I mean statistical work applied in all stages of production, from raw material to consumer, and back again (see Figure 3). *The statistical control of quality is the application of statistical principles and techniques in all stages of production, directed toward the most economic manufac-*

*Excerpts from an address delivered in Tokyo the 14th January 1952 at a meeting of industrial executives sponsored by the Nihon Kezai and the Union of Japanese Scientists and Engineers.

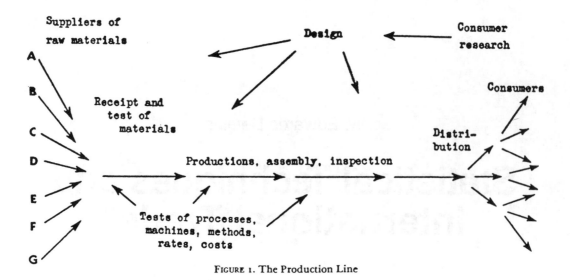

Suppliers of raw materials

Design

Consumer research

A
B
C
D
E
F
G

Receipt and test of materials

Productions, assembly, inspection

Tests of processes, machines, methods, rates, costs

Distribution

Consumers

FIGURE 1. The Production Line

ture of a product that is maximally useful and has a market.

Benefits of Quality Control

Through the full use of the statistical control of quality, from raw material to the consumer, a manufacturer may expect to achieve in some measure the following advantages:

1. Increased production, without investment in capital equipment or expansion of plant.
2. Better quality at lower cost, and better suited to the market.
3. Better uniformity at lower cost, and better suited to the market.
4. Savings on raw materials and fuel (a particularly vital advantage when scarcity of materials threatens production).
5. Better operating efficiency: (a) idle time of machines decreased; fewer rejections; less scrap and re-work; (b) better prediction of the market, through consumer research, by which the purchase of materials, and the expansion and contraction of the plant are carried out rationally, resulting in better economy than would be possible otherwise.
6. Decreased inspection, but with increased assurance of dependable quality.
7. Greater precision of dimensions when required (as when parts are to be interchangeable).
8. Design, better suited to the market, through consumer research carried out by modern methods of sampling and design of experiment.
9. Stronger competitive position, through ability to meet world requirements in price, quality and uniformity.
10. Use of an international language by which to furnish statistical proof of quality and uniformity.

I must now ask you to think with me in broad terms just what good quality and economic production really mean. Some people think in terms of price alone. Others think in terms of quality alone. Some people think of economic production as saving 10 per cent in the cost of some operation. All these ideas are important, but we must go deeper.

In the first place, *price has no meaning except in terms of the quality of the product.* But that is not enough. *"Good quality" and "uniform quality" have no meaning except with reference to the consumer's needs.* This is why I must speak to you in terms of the entire production line, which begins with the producers of your raw materials, and ends with the consumer—the man who uses your product.

Incidentally, the consumer is more important than raw material. It is usually easier to replace a supplier of raw material with another one than it is to find a new consumer. And a non-consumer, one who has not yet tried your product, is still more important to you, because he represents *a possible additional user of your product.* For this reason I shall speak to you of *consumer research,* because I believe in the importance of consumer research to Japanese industry, particularly for its export trade.

Importance of Consumer Research

Some manufacturers think of consumer research as analysis of complaints from purchasers and users. Certainly, no one can deny the great importance of the analysis of consumers' complaints. No matter how silly and unjust a complaint may be, it is still important to a manufacturer, because it shows him *where he has failed in public relations*—that is, failed to make clear to the public just what quality they have a right to expect when they buy his product. A legitimate complaint helps the manufacturer to improve his quality, provided he has real quality control, and can be used by the manufacturer in tracing the cause of trouble all the way back to production and raw material.

But complaints are only a part of the problem of public relations. Complaints come from a very biased sample of consumers. Complaints do not provide communication with the other consumers nor with the non-consumer.

For reliable and economical communication with the consumers and non-consumers of a product, it is necessary to communicate with all users and non-users, through the medium of statistical tests and surveys. The aim of this particular aspect of quality control is *re-design* of the quality of your product (Figure 3); also *adjustment* of your plant, and *contraction or expansion* of the output of particular products to *meet rationally predicted changes in demand.*

As the consumer has been left out of the chain of production in many parts of the world where industry needs expansion, I shall go into more detail on the subject.

The main use of consumer research should be to feed consumer reactions back into the design of the product, so that management can anticipate changing demands and requirements and set economical production levels. Consumer research takes the pulse of the consumer's reactions and demands, and seeks explanations for the findings.

Consumer research is not merely selling. Real consumer research, geared to design and production, is an indispensable modern tool for modern problems.

Consumer research is *communication* between the manufacturer and the users and potential users of his product, like this:

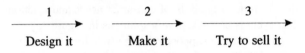

This communication may be carried out reliably and economically today only by sampling procedures and tests designed according to modern statistical procedures. Through this communication the manufacturer discovers how his product performs *in service,* what people think of his product, why some people will buy it, why others will not, or will not buy it again, and he is able to redesign his product, to make it better as measured by the quality and uniformity that are best suited to the end-uses of the product and to the price that the consumer can pay.

Consumer research acts as a governor or servo-mechanism which by probing into the future market regulates both the design of the product and the amount of production.

In the olden days, before the industrial era, the tailor, the carpenter, the shoemaker, the milkman, the blacksmith knew his customers by name. He knew whether they were satisfied, and what he should do to improve appreciation for his product. With the expansion of industry, this personal touch was lost. The wholesaler, the jobber, and the retailer have now stepped in, and in effect have set up a barrier between the manufacturer and the ultimate consumer. But sampling, a new science, steps in and pierces that barrier. The manufacturer of today, but for sampling, would be out of touch with the people who use his product, or those who might use it.

Manufacturers used to think of manufacturing in three steps, as shown in Figure 2. Success depended on guesswork—guessing what type and design of product would sell, how much of it to make. In the old way, the three steps of Figure 2 are completely independent.

1	2	3
Design it	Make it	Try to sell it

FIGURE 2: The Old Way

In the new way, management introduces, through consumer research, a 4th step, and runs through the four steps in a *cycle,* over and over as in Figure 3, and not in the line of Figure 2.

1. Design the product (with appropriate tests);
2. Make it; test it in the production line and in the laboratory;
3. Put it on the market;
4. Test it in service; through market research, find out what the user thinks of it, and why the non-user has not bought it;
5. *Re*-design the product, in the light of consumer reactions to quality and price;

Continue around and around the cycle.

This 4th step in Figure 3 was impossible until recently—i.e., it could not be carried out economically or reliably. Intelligent manufacturers have always been interested in discovering the needs and the reactions of the user and of the potential user, but until recently they had no economical or reliable way of investigating them.

The 4th step, communication between the manufacturer and the user and the potential user, gives the public

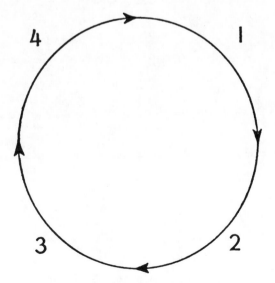

FIGURE 3. The New Way

a chance. It gives the user a better product, better suited to his needs, and cheaper. *Democracy in industry,* one might say.

A still better way is to begin the manufacturing and marketing of a product on a pilot scale, and to build up its production on a sound economic basis, only as fast as market conditions indicate, re-designing the product from time to time in the light of consumer needs and reactions. The cycle is best taken on a spiral, as in Figure 4.

It is not to be supposed that the first three steps are the same in the figures that display the old and new ways. Consider, for example, design in step 1. Proper design today means not only attention to color, shape, size, hardness, strength, and finish, but attention also to a suitable degree of uniformity. Paradoxically, through the statistical control of quality, great uniformity often costs less than nonuniformity without statistical methods. However, with some products, extreme uniformity may be costly, and the manufacturer must be careful and not price his product out of the market. In consumer research, the 4th step, the manufacturer studies the requirements of uniformity, as well as of color, shape, size, hardness, etc. Then, through statistical procedures he achieves the required uniformity with economy, and his *control charts furnish proof of the uniformity achieved* in an international language, known and studied now the world over.

Consumer research is a continuous process, by which the product is improved continually and modified to meet changing abilities of the manufacturer and changing requirements of the consumer. Consumer research, used in-

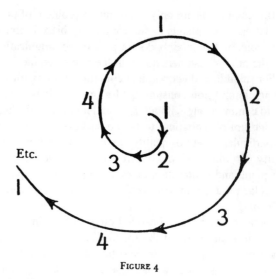

FIGURE 4

telligently, enables the manufacturer to run his factory on an even keel, neither greatly over-producing nor under-producing. He is not likely to let out 300 men one month and then try to recover them the next. Consumer research used to smooth out production is a powerful factor in economical production. Again, it is only one of the indispensable statistical tools of production.

W. Edwards Deming

*Bureau of the Budget and
New York University*